# Cold Climbs

'And what joy, think ye, did they feel after the exceeding long and troublous ascent? – after

Scrambling, slipping
Pulling, pushing
Lifting, gasping
Looking, hoping
Despairing, climbing
Holding on, falling off
Trying, puffing
Loosing, gathering
Talking, stepping
Grumbling, anathematising
Scraping, hacking
Bumping, jogging
Overturning, hunting
Straddling, –

for know you that by these methods alone are the most divine mysteries of the Quest reached.

Divine Mysteries of the Oromaniacal Quest by Norman Collie
*Scottish Mountaineering Club Journal 1894*

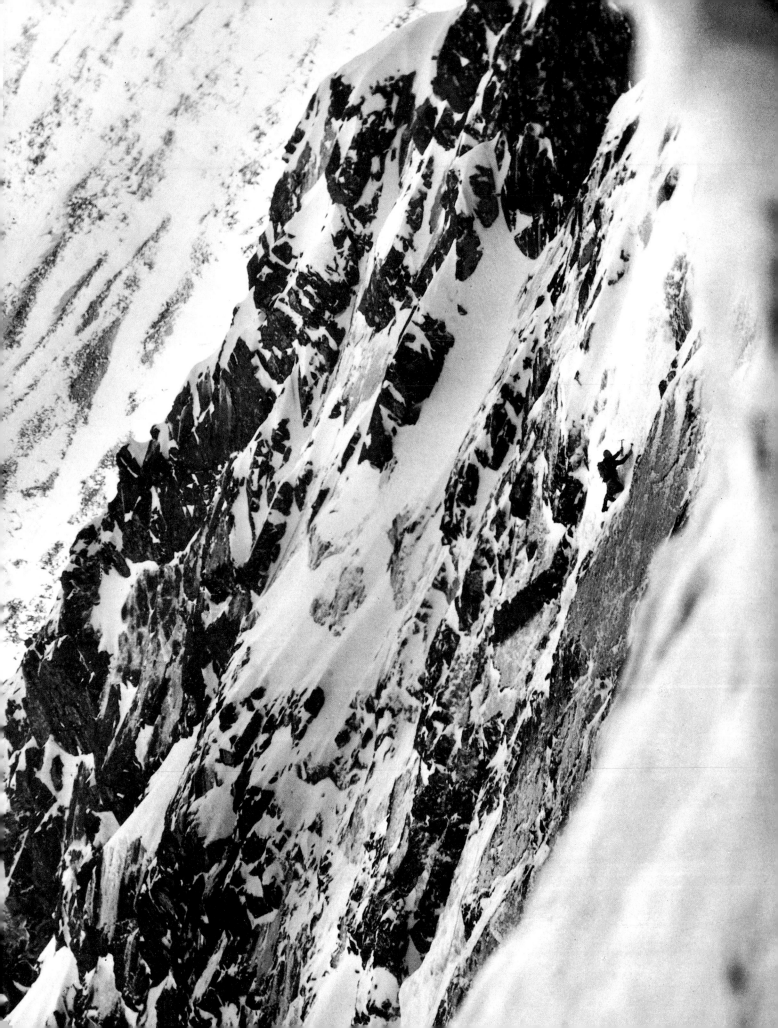

THE GREAT SNOW AND ICE CLIMBS
OF THE BRITISH ISLES

# COLD CLIMBS

## COMPILED BY KEN WILSON
## DAVE ALCOCK AND JOHN BARRY

with editorial assistance
from Jim Perrin

diagrams by Tim Pavey

Diadem Books · London

Other books in this series:

Hard Rock

Classic Rock

Extreme Rock

The Big Walks

Classic Walks

Wild Walks

Published in 1983 by Diadem Books, London
Reprinted 1991

All trade enquiries to:
Hodder and Stoughton, Mill Road
Dunton Green, Sevenoaks TN13 2YA

Copyright © by Dave Alcock

*British Library Cataloguing and Publication Data:*
Cold climbs
   1. Mountaineering–Great Britain–Description and
travel
   I. Wilson, Ken  II. Alcock, Dave
   III. Barry, John
   796.5'22    DA650
   ISBN 0-906371-16-3

Colour separations by
Fleet Litho, Tunbridge Wells, Kent

Printed in Great Britain by
Butler and Tanner, Frome, Somerset

Frontispiece: A view across Hadrian's Wall
on Ben Nevis, from Point Five Gully.
*Photo: Ian Sykes*

# Contents

# Preface

The series of books recording different aspects of British mountaineering continues with *Cold Climbs* – a compendium of snow and ice climbs. Each title in the series has acquired its own particular character. *Hard Rock* and *Classic Rock* dealt with predictable objectives: routes with precise, well-known and sometimes notorious difficulties, the contemplation of which, before, during and after an ascent, is a key element in the satisfaction felt by the rock climber. *The Big Walks* and *Classic Walks* portrayed the world of the mountain walkers: fine mountain ranges with the promise of prolonged strenuous exercise, challenging route-finding problems and all the marvels of seasonal variations.

*Cold Climbs* deals with climbing of a less tangible nature, rarely predictable, often dangerous and uncomfortable, and set in an impressively hostile environment. Snow and ice climbs vary greatly in condition and difficulty. This unpredictability brings its own special appeal. A winter climb done quickly in perfect conditions will leave a pleasurable, yet rarely profound impression; conversely, a storm-lashed epic struggle, followed by a fight across some summit plateau in a white-out is an altogether headier experience. It is climbs of this kind – titanic struggles, relying not so much on technique but more on character, determination based on experience, and a degree of humility for the mountain scene – that form the grist for this book.

Happily, climbers still feel an urge to write about their most trying climbs and, as a fair proportion of those (for most British climbers at least) take place in winter, a collection of such writings was likely to include plenty of stirring material. So it has proved, and thus *Cold Climbs* is, in literary terms, perhaps the most exciting of the five books in the series to date.

Sadly the factors that make for such gripping ascents often scheme against good photography. There is a strong degree of visual similarity between ice gullies, one ice bulge can look like another and there is rarely sufficient permanent detail to lend a picture any enduring technical value. The winter light in the bed of a gully is usually poor, the view frequently enclosed or clouded. Good action photos then, particularly ones that offer useful information about the climb, are rare. The equipment revolution which has brought climbers out from gullies onto open and exposed ice sheets, has helped in this respect but the problem will never be entirely solved.

Mountain architecture is the standby for the winter-climbing photographer. From a distance, a gully, buttress or mountain face looks infinitely more interesting when cloaked in snow and ice. The depressing features of dripping, gloomy north-facing cliffs can be transformed by winter into crag scenery of unexpected magnificence. Accordingly, in this book, cliff panoramas have been given more emphasis than close-up action shots.

## A Brief Historical Summary

Despite early activity in the Lakes and Wales, in terms of history winter climbing in Britain has meant winter climbing in Scotland. Only in Scotland has it been consistently recorded, and Scottish practice, grades and styles have come to dominate the sport nationally.

Important events have occurred elsewhere but they have been poorly recorded. The Lakes and Wales have much to offer, but the sport there is perforce sporadic – at the mercy of fickle and short winters. In Scotland, true winter conditions can usually be found somewhere between December and April, and there has therefore been steady development with activity recorded yearly in the SMC Journal.

The sport had an eventful start in the 20 years that preceded the First World War. At that time, British alpine activity was at its zenith and some of the finest alpinists (e.g. Collie, Naismith, Slingsby, O. G. Jones and Raeburn) took time off to investigate the alpine potential of the home mountains. Some classic climbs resulted, still numbered amongst the finest in the country. The First World War ended all this and a period of relative inactivity followed until the sport was regenerated in the late thirties by men like MacPhee, Bell, Mackenzie and Murray. The fifties saw intense activity with a number of ambitious and able climbers vying for the great lines. The names of MacInnes, Patey, Marshall and Smith stand out, but there were others and together they injected a degree of inspiration from which the sport still benefits.

Up to the end of the sixties winter climbing had an intrinsically heroic character, due to the rudimentary nature of the equipment and the consequent time taken on climbs, and a high degree of risk. With the seventies came a sea-change following small but crucial improvements in equipment design. The harder climbs, hitherto considered the preserve of a few well-trained experts, became available to many. The sport was transformed becoming less esoteric, less challenging and more popular. It is fair to say, however, that enough mystery and challenge remained to preserve its intrinsic character for most climbers. With their newly acquired skills, the experts transferred the bulk of their efforts to the greater ranges but for the majority, despite better equipment and knowledge, winter climbing is still a chancy business. For most the pay-off in satisfaction after a major ascent remains immense. It is both as a pointer to, and a celebration of such satisfaction that gives this book its purpose.

## Some Explanatory Notes on the Book

As in the other volumes the aim has been to commission new writing from climbers recording their experiences on repeat ascents. There are several first ascent accounts however, two of which have been previously published. Four climbs have merited two articles because historical and literary claims gave rise to difficult choices we were reluctant to make. Although the selection of climbs has a wide geographical spread, emphasis has been given to Ben Nevis, Creag Meagaidh and Lochnagar. In addition there are a number of climbs from the fascinating Northern Highlands area, sections on the Lakes and Wales and one chapter dealing with Irish climbing. Two fictional items have been included. The final selection represents scores of climbs of equal quality. There will be unforgivable omissions in the eyes of some, but we are confident that a good cross-section of the best climbs has been chosen.

Grading has also provided problems. Rather than impose a uniform system of our own we have opted for the most commonly used grades. In the case of Ben Nevis, certain climbs have been given Grade 6, reflecting the recent Grindley/Cicerone attempt to divide the overloaded Grade 5 sector. On this basis, there are several other climbs in the book that would also merit Grade 6, but which still retain their traditional Grade 5. To resolve this anomaly we have assembled a graded list of difficulty by taking a consensus of opinion from a group of experienced climbers. The nature of winter climbing makes this a rather imprecise exercise but, given all the obvious provisos about conditions, the table provides a rough correlation between the climbs mentioned in the book. It should be remembered that all the climbs in this book are potentially lethal. Avalanche conditions or poor belays render winter climbs objectively dangerous in a manner unknown to most rock climbs. Whatever the difficulty of the route, a prudent approach to one's objective is essential. There are fatal accidents every winter, many occurring on easy routes or during descents. It is well to maintain a healthy respect for any mountains in snow and ice conditions.

An attempt to produce a satisfactory historical introduction in narrative form proved curiously inadequate and we eventually concluded that the task was too complex. Instead we have opted for a detailed historical table of events, the study of which might assist future commentators to make some sense of the sport's development. There are many gaps, notably in the recording of activities in Wales and the Lakes, and the production of a really authoritative history may

be impossible while so much uncertainty remains. Filling these gaps is a task that guidebook writers and journal editors might undertake.

It may be said that recording such detail is unimportant or that it is an exercise in self-aggrandisement, but this is to devalue one of the mainsprings of climbing interest which feeds avidly on historical information. In this respect we have been struck by the consistently high standard of factual reporting in the SMC Journal and, until recently, in SMC guidebooks. The SMC's practice from its earliest days of recording mountaineering activity has been a major factor in the development of winter mountaineering. The policy has been imperiously maintained over the years by the club's editors and fully supported by key figures, free from petty regional jealousies and oblivious to the demands of narrow-minded elitism. One might select as examples, MacPhee, Murray, Lovat, MacInnes, Mac Smith and Patey; and the open attitude that they championed perhaps reached its highest expression in Smith's outstanding two-volume guidebook to the Cairngorms with its innovative grading system and stirring descriptions. Although others have since striven to maintain this policy, there have been signs of late that it is threatened with subversion. Recent attempts by the SMC to bottle up information, as typified by its new guidebook policies (favouring a selected approach) and its no-guidebook policy for the Northern Highlands, go directly against the early principles of the club prosecuted so vigorously over the years. One can only hope that the traditional views, and confidence will soon re-emerge.

## Acknowledgements

The three compilers have contributed to the book in diverse ways. We have been helped by Jim Perrin, who worked on the manuscript, Tim Pavey, who produced the diagrams, and Bert Jenkins, who helped with the photography. We have also been assisted by the contributions of others whose keenness for the project was a tonic. For technical and factual advice we have relied heavily on a team comprising Hamish MacInnes, Bill Brooker, Robin Campbell, Jimmy Marshall, Allen Fyffe, Greg Strange, John Mackenzie and Paul Nunn. Others who have given technical advice include Andrew Nisbet, Alan Rouse, Mike Geddes, Pete Macdonald, Tom Weir, W. H. Murray, Ed Grindley, Mick Fowler, Martin Boysen and Rick Newcombe. The photographic effort was buttressed by Hamish MacInnes, John Cleare, Alex Gillespie and Malcolm Griffith. Trevor Jones gave us valuable assistance at the proof-reading stage. We are indebted to all those who have made photographic and literary contributions to the book; each item being duly credited. Others have offered photographs and articles which we were unable to use, and they are thanked for their forbearance. There is also a group of people who have had their privacy interrupted by strident demands (often by telephone and late at night) to dredge their memories for long-dormant historical facts; to them we offer both apologies and thanks. The book therefore represents the creative efforts of a large number of climbers, which may give it some extra degree of historical relevance as a statement of the sport. A full list of contributors follows, we salute them all.

Toddy Alcock, John Allen, Rab Anderson, Sheridan Anderson, Mo Anthoine, Rob Archbold, Steve Ashton, Rusty Baillie, Pete Baines, Nick Banks, Kathy Barry, John Beatty, Colin Beechey, Rob Bennett, Donald Bennet, Bill Birkett, Geoff Birtles, Jean Marc Boivin, Chris Bonington, Martin Boysen, Hamish Brown, Joe Brown, Martin Burrows-Smith, Robin Campbell, Rab Carrington, John Cheesmond, John Cleare, Ed Cleasby, Geoff Cohen, Rob Collister, A. D. M. Cox, Malcolm Creasey, Ken Crocket, Sid Cross, Sam Crymble, Ivan Cumberpatch, Frank Davies, James Divall, Harold Drasdo, G. J. F. Dutton, Rowland Edwards, Rob Ferguson, Pete Fleming, Colin Foord, Mick Fowler, Calum Fraser, Allen Fyffe, Mike Geddes, Richard Gibbens, Richard Gilbert, Alex Gillespie, Colin Goodey, Ken Grassick, Van Greaves, Dennis Grey, Malcolm Griffith, M. A. Griffiths, Chris Griffiths, Ed Grindley, Chris Hall, Edwin Hammond, Fred Harper, Herbert Hartley, Steve Howe, Kevin Howe, David Howard Jones, Wil Hurford, Mark Hutchinson, Andy Hyslop, Tim Jepson, Bert Jenkins, Trevor Jones, Dave Kay, Ally Kellas, Dave King, Derek Laird, Gareth Lambe, Doug Lang, G. H. Leslie, Adrian Liddell, Pat Littlejohn, Sir Jack Longland, L. S. Lovat, Vincent Lowe, Jim Loxham, Mike Lynch, Joss Lynam, Pete Macdonald, Hamish MacInnes, John Mackenzie, Alister McQuiod, Philip Mangham, Bill March, Jimmy Marshall, Rob Matheson, Derek Mayes, Allan Moist, Paul Moores, Al Morgan, Neil Morrison, Dick Morsley, Tony Moulam, Rick Newcombe, Hamish Nicol, Andrew Nisbet, Paul Nunn, Tim Pavey, Dick Peart, Bill Peascod, Jim Perrin, Derek Peterson, Al Phizacklea, Tom Price, Neil Quinn, Dick Renshaw, Phil Rigby, Tony Riley, Mungo Ross, Alan Rouse, Des Rubens, Bill Ryan, Tony Saunders, Klaus Schwartz, Doug Scott, Nigel Shepherd, Ray Simpson, Dave Siviter, Malcolm Slesser, Bill Skidmore, Norman Smith, Stuart Smith, Colin Stead, Dawson Stelfox, Rhod Stewart, Terry Storry, Greg Strange, John Sumner, Ian Sykes, Phill Thomas, Mick Tighe, Graham Tiso, G. Townsend, Walt Unsworth, Dave Walsh, Tom Weir, Andrew Wielochowski, Dave Wilkinson, Taf Williams, Colin Wornham, Blyth Wright and anyone else that we may inadvertently have overlooked.

KEN WILSON, DAVE ALCOCK & JOHN BARRY
November 1982

# The Development of Snow and Ice Climbing in Britain

This table lists the main winter ascents that have been recorded in journals, magazines and guidebooks. Some previously unrecorded ascents have also been included, their sources noted in brackets at the end of the entry. In order to save space, climbers have been given single initials, except where a climber is usually identified by more (e.g. W. H. Murray, J. H. B. Bell). Current guidebook grades are used, those in italics indicating a climb that has been re-graded since its original ascent. Grade 6 is only used for the Ben Nevis/Glencoe area following the lead given in the recent Cicerone guide. There are many climbs graded 5 in other areas that are of similar difficulty but so far no further attempt has been made to introduce Grade 6.

Climbs indicating some advance in difficulty or concept have been selected from the main areas. In new or developing areas, important new routes have been noted, whatever the grade. Records of early ascents in Wales and the Lake District are virtually non-existent. The difference between summer and winter climbing having been blurred by many early ascents of climbs in semi-winter conditions. Judging by the climbs that have been recorded, it seems likely that standards of ability have been roughly the same as those in Scotland. It should be stressed that this list is merely a 'selection' of the main events. Many other routes of quality have been done, but in general they consolidated exploration on the cliffs in question.

Other interesting facts and influential developments are recorded in the right-hand column. These may add a further dimension to the list.

**Before 1890**

| Year | Grade | Area | Climb |
|---|---|---|---|
| 1812 | | S/hlands | **Ben Lomond** First known example of step-cutting by Colome Hawker. |
| 1870 | 1 | B/Nevis | **Number 3 Gully** *Coire na Ciste.* |
| 1882 | 2/3 | Lakes | **Central and South-East Gullies** *Great End* First ascent (semi-winter) by W. Haskett-Smith and party. |
| — | | | **Deep Ghyll** *Scafell* First descent (in deep snow) by A. Mumm and J. King. |
| 1883 | 2 | Wales | **West Buttress** *Lliwedd* First ascent (semi-winter) by A. Stocker and T. Wall. |
| 1888 | 1 | S/hlands | **Central Gully** *Ben Lui.* |
| 1890 | 1 | Lakes | **Shamrock Gully** *Pillar Rock* First ascent (semi-winter) by G. Hastings, C. Hopkinson and J. Robinson. |
| 1891 | 3 | Lakes | **B(Great)Gully** *Wastwater Screes* First ascent (winter) by N. Collie, G. Hastings and J. Robinson |
| 1893 | 1 | C/gorms 1 | **Black Spout – Left-Hand** *Lochnagar* First ascent (winter) by J. Gibson and W. Douglas. |
| | 3/4 | Lakes | **Moss Ghyll** *Scafell* First winter ascent by O. G. Jones with back-rope protection on the Collie Step. |
| 1894 | 3 | B/Nevis | **Tower Ridge** First ascent (winter) by N. Collie, J. Collier and G. Solly. |
| 1895 | 2 | B/Nevis | **Castle Ridge** *Carn Dearg* First ascent (winter) by N. Collie, W. Naismith, G. Thomson and M. Travers. |
| | 2 | | **North-East Ridge** *Aonach Beag* First ascent (winter) by J. Maclay, W. Naismith and G. Thomson |
| | 2 | Glencoe | **North Wall of the Chasm** *Buachaille Etive Mor* First ascent (winter) by J. Bell, McGregor, J. Napier and R. Napier. |
| 1896 | 3/4 | B/Nevis | **North-East Buttress** First winter ascent by W. Naismith, A. Kennedy, W. King, W. Brunskill and F. Squance. |
| | 3 | | **The Castle** *Carn Dearg* First ascent (winter) by W. Brown, J. Maclay, W. Naismith and G. Thompson. |
| | — | Meagaidh | **Centre Post** Attempt by W. Tough, W. Brown and H. Raeburn ended when party was avalanched. |
| | 3 | Wales | **Devil's Kitchen Icefall** *Cwm Idwal* First ascent by J. Archer Thomson and H. Hughes using a coal axe. |
| 1897 | 2/3 | B/Nevis | **Gardyloo Gully** First winter ascent by G. Hastings and W. Haskett-Smith. |
| | 2 | C/hlands | **Upper Couloir** *Stob Gabhar* First ascent (winter) by A. E. Mayland and three others (inc. two ladies). |
| 1899 | | Lakeland | **Walker's Gully** *Pillar Rock* First ascent (semi-winter) by O. G. Jones, G. Abraham and A. Field. |
| | 3 | Wales | **Central Gully** *Glyder Fawr* First winter ascent by O. G. Jones, G. and A. Abraham. |
| | 2 | | **Clogwyn Du Gully, Right-hand** *Glyder Fawr* First winter ascent by O. G. Jones and party. |
| 1902 | 3 | S/hlands | **Great Gully** *Creag na Caillich, Tarmachans* First ascent (winter) by A. Mackay, S. Gillon and G. Winthrop-Young. An epic ascent with a late start and a finish in the dark. |
| 1904 | 3 | B/Nevis | **Central Gully** *Trident Buttresses, Coire na Ciste* First ascent (winter) by H. Raeburn, Mrs W. Inglis Clark and C. Inglis Clark. |
| | 4 | | **North Trident Buttress** First ascent (winter) by J. Maclay, H. Raeburn, C. Walker and H. Walker. |
| 1906 | 4 | B/Nevis | **Green Gully** *Coire na Ciste* First ascent (winter) by H. Raeburn and E. Phildius. Technically advanced. |
| | 2/3 | Glencoe | **North-West Gully** *Stob Coire nam Beith* First ascent by G. Glover and Wordsell. |
| 1907 | — | B/Nevis | **Tower Ridge/Goodeve's Route** Tower Ridge escape. T. Goodeve, C. Inglis Clark and J. McIntyre. |
| | 3 | Glencoe | **Central Buttress** *Stob Coire nam Beith* First ascent by H. Raeburn, W. Ling, G. Glover and W. Inglis Clark. |
| 1909 | 3 | Glencoe | **Crowberry Gully** *Buachaille Etive Mor* First ascent (winter) by H. Raeburn, W. Brigg and H. Tucker. |

**1914–18 THE FIRST WORLD WAR**

**1857** Alpine Club formed. Members actively involved in major alpine climbs until the First World War. By the end of the century these climbs were often difficult and serious and sometimes climbed without guides.

**1880** Railway link to Tyndrum. Further progress to Glencoe and Fort William by horse and carriage on poor roads.

**1889** Cairngorm Club and Scottish Mountaineering Club founded. Both clubs decide to publish regular journals.

**1893** *Snowcraft in Scotland* by W. Naismith published in the SMCJ.

**1894** Railway link with Fort William. SMC Meets at Fort William begin. Munro influences climbers to operate in winter months, outside the sporting seasons.

**1895** SMC establishes policy of regular guidebook publication; William Douglas appointed editor.

**1897** *Rock-Climbing in the English Lake District* by Owen Glynne Jones

**1899** Owen Glynne Jones† Dent Blanche.

**1902** *Ben Nevis* guide by William Inglis Clark published in the SMCJ.

**1905** *Twenty Years on Ben Nevis* by W. T. Kilgour.

**1908** Oscar Eckenstein designs the ten-point crampon.

**1909/10** Climbing guides to *Lliwedd* and *Ogwen* by J. M. Archer Thomson and A. W. Andrews (Lliwedd).

**1914–18** Many experienced climbers killed in action. Tradition and knowledge lost.

| 1920 | 3/4 | B/Nevis | **Observatory Ridge** First winter ascent by H. Raeburn, F. Goggs and W. Mounsey. |
|---|---|---|---|
| 1928 | — | Wales | **Avalanche/Terminal Arête** *Lliwedd* Semi-winter ascent by H. Hartley and A. Chisman. (Hartley) |
| | 4 | | **Great Gully** *Craig yr Ysfa* Earliest-known true winter ascent by J. Longland and A. Bridge. (Longland) |
| 1932 | 2 | C/gorms 2 | **Raeburn's Gully** *Lochnager* First winter ascent by G. Symmers, A. Clark and W. Ewen. |
| 1934 | 3 | Glencoe | **S.C.Gully** *Stob Coire nan Lochan* Earliest known winter ascent by P. Baird, E. Leslie and H. Fynes-Clinton. A Cambridge University party. |
| | 3 | Meagaidh | **Staghorn Gully** First ascent by C. Allen, J. H. B. Bell, H. Kelly and H. Cooper. |
| | 4 | Wales | **Direct Route** *Glyder Fach* First winter ascent by J. Hoyland, A. Serraillier and W. Wand. (Cox) |
| 1935 | 3 | B/Nevis | **Glover's Chimney** *Coire na Ciste* First winter ascent by G. Macphee, G. Williams and D. Henderson. An influential ascent that had a regenerating effect on Scottish winter climbing. |
| 1936 | — | B/Nevis | **Slav Route** *Orion Face* Semi-winter ascent by J. H. B. Bell and C. Allen after an attempt on Zero Gully. |
| 1937 | 4 | Glencoe | **(Garrick's) Shelf Route** *Buachaille Etive Mor* First winter ascent by W. Mackenzie and W. H. Murray. |
| | | | **Agag's Groove** *Buachaille Etive Mor* Semi-winter ascent by W. Mackenzie, W. H. Murray and J. Dunn. |
| | 3 | Meagaidh | **Centre Post** *Coire Ardair* First ascent (winter) by J. H. B. Bell and C. Allen. |
| 1938 | 3/4 | B/Nevis | **Comb Gully** *Coire na Ciste* First ascent (winter) by F. Stangle, R. Morsley and P. Small. |
| | 4/5 | Lakes | **Steep Ghyll** *Scafell* First winter ascent by A. T. Hargreaves, Ruth Hargreaves, S. Cross and Miss A. Nelson. An advanced climb – not recorded in journals or guidebooks. (Cross) |
| 1939 | 3/4 | Glencoe | **Deep-Cut Chimney** *Stob Coire nam Beith* First winter ascent by W. Mackenzie and W. H. Murray. |
| 1941 | 4 | Lakes | **Birkness Chimney** *Buttermere* First winter ascent by W. Peascod and A. Beck. |

### 1939–45 THE SECOND WORLD WAR

| 1947 | 2 | C/gorms 2 | **South-East Gully** *Creag an Dubh Loch* First winter ascent by W. Russell, M. Smith and W. Stephens. |
|---|---|---|---|
| 1948 | 3 | C/gorms 2 | **Parallel Gully A** *Lochnagar* First winter ascent by G. Ross and R. Still. |
| | 4 | Wales | **Hanging Garden Gully** *Clogwyn y Geifr* First winter ascent by J. Brown and W. White. (Brown) |
| | 4 | | **Devil's Staircase** *Clogwyn y Geifr* Earliest known ascent by A. Moulam and party. (Moulam) |
| 1949 | — | B/Nevis | **Orion Face/Zeta** Semi-winter ascent by H. Nicol, D. Stewart, N. Tennent and Mona Macleod. (Nicol) |
| | 4 | Glencoe | **Crowberry Gully, Left-Fork** *Buachaille Etive Mor* First ascent (winter) by C. Smith, R. Taunton and I. Robertson. |
| | 3 | C/gorms 2 | **Shadow Buttress A** *Lochnagar* First winter ascent by W. Brooker and J. Morgan. |
| | 3 | | **Black Spout Buttress** *Lochnagar* First winter ascent by J. Tewnion, C. Hutcheon, D. Sutherland and K. Winram. |
| 1950 | 4 | C/gorms 2 | **Giant's Head Chimney** *Lochnagar* First winter ascent by W. Brooker and J. Morgan. |
| | *4* | | **Douglas/Gibson Gully** *Lochnagar* First winter ascent by T. Patey and G. Leslie. An important ascent originally thought to be the first Grade 5. |
| 1951 | — | B/Nevis | **Zero Gully** Dramatic attempt by H. Nicol and A. Rawlinson which ended disastrously when both climbers fell to the foot of the climb from the final difficult pitch (neither sustained permanent injury). |
| | 4 | Glencoe | **No.6 Gully** *Aonach Dubh* First ascent by D. Munro and P. Smith. |
| 1952 | 4 | B/Nevis | **Observatory Buttress Direct** First winter ascent by D. Stewart and W. Foster. |
| | 4 | Glencoe | **Clachaig Gully** First winter ascent by H. MacInnes and R. Hope. |
| | 5 | C/gorms 1 | **Scorpion** *Cairn Etchachan* First ascent by T. Patey, M. Taylor, G. Nicol and K. Grassick. The first major winter route in the Loch Avon Basin. |
| | 3 | C/gorms 2 | **Tough/Brown Traverse** *Lochnagar* First winter ascent by T. Patey and D. Aitken. |
| | 3/4 | | **Gargoyle Chimney** *Lochnagar* First winter ascent by M. Taylor and W. Brooker. |
| | 4 | | **The Stack** *Lochnagar* First winter ascent by M. Taylor, G. Leslie and T. Fallowfield. |
| | 4 | Wales | **Western Gully** *Ysgolion Duon* Earliest-known winter ascent by J. Brown and R. Moseley. (Brown) |
| | 4 | | **South Gully** *Clogwyn y Geifr* Earliest-known ascent by J. Brown and R. Moseley. (Brown) |
| 1953 | 4 | Glencoe | **Agag's Groove** *Buachaille Etive Mor* First winter ascent by H. MacInnes, K. McPhail; C. Bonington, J. Hammond and G. McIntosh. Steep icy rock-climbing. |
| | 4 | | **Crowberry Ridge Direct** *Buachaille Etive Mor* First winter ascent by H. MacInnes and C. Bonington. |
| | 5 | | **Raven's Gully** *Buachaille Etive Mor* First winter ascent by H. MacInnes and C. Bonington. The climb was in an icy yet slushy condition. Some pitches led in stockinged feet. Crampons and pitons used. The end of a long campaign by MacInnes and the Creagh Dhu. In 1951 an attempt by W. Smith, J. Cunningham and MacInnes ended dramatically when Smith fell the full length of the gully from above Pitch 4 – escaping without injury. Another attempt by MacInnes, C. Vigano and J. Cullen also had an epic conclusion when the party was benighted with MacInnes 10ft. from the top of the Direct Finish. |
| | 5 | C/gorms 1 | **Mitre Ridge Direct** *Beinn á Bhuird* First winter ascent by W. Brooker and T. Patey. A Cairngorm classic. |
| | 4/5 | C/gorms 2 | **Polyphemus Gully** *Lochnagar* First winter ascent by K. Grassick and H. Bates. |
| | 5 | | **Eagle Ridge Direct** *Lochnagar* First winter ascent by T. Patey, J. Taylor and W. Brooker. Important. |
| | 3/4 | | **Look C Gully** *Corrie Fee of Mayar* First ascent (winter) by C. Donaldson and J. Marshall. |
| 1954 | — | B/Nevis | **Zero Gully** Attempt by J. Brown, D. Gray and R. Greenhall repulsed by 'falling blocks of ice'. |
| | 3/4 | C/gorms 1 | **The Corridor** *Creagan a'Choire Etchachan* First ascent (winter) by F. Malcolm and A. Thom. |
| | 4 | | **East Wall Route/Mitre Ridge** *Beinn a'Bhuird* First ascent (winter) by T. Patey and G. Nicol. This was |

| | | | |
|---|---|---|---|
| | 4 | C/gorms 2 | **Gargoyle Direct** *Lochnagar* First winter ascent by R. Sellers and G. Annand. |
| | 5 | Wales | **Schoolmasters' Gully – The Grooves** *Cyrn Las* First winter ascent by J. Brown and R. Moseley. 'The climbing above the final difficult section (in summer) of the Grooves was very hard.' (Brown) |
| **1955** | — | B/Nevis | **Point Five Gully** Christmas week attempt by J. Brown, N. Allen and N. Underwood nearly ended in disaster when Brown and Allen fell and were both held by Underwood. |
| | 4 | Meagaidh | **Central Pillar** *Post Face* First ascent (winter) by T. Patey and K. Smith |
| **1956** | 3 | N/hlands | **Minor Rib** *An Teallach* First winter ascent by W. Brooker and D. Barclay. |
| | 3 | Meagaidh | **South Post** First ascent (winter) by N. Tennent and M. Slesser. |
| | 3/4 | C/gorms 2 | **Eagle Buttress** *Lochnagar* First winter ascent by W. Brooker and M. Taylor. |
| | 5 | | **Parallel Buttress** *Lochnagar* First winter ascent by T. Patey, J. Smith and W. Brooker. |
| | 5 | | **Route 1/Black Spout Pinnacle** *Lochnagar* First winter ascent by J. Smith and W. Brooker. |
| **1957** | — | B/Nevis | **Point Five Gully** Attempt by T. Patey and G. Nicol repulsed by heavy spindrift avalanches. |
| | 3 | | **Cresta Climb** *Little Brenva Face* First ascent by T. Patey, L. S. Lovat and G. Nicol. The first route on this face. Other climbs were added by I. Clough, D. Pipes and others in 1958 and 1959. |
| | — | | **Zero Gully** and **Point Five Gully** Attempts by J. Cunningham, M. Noon and H. MacInnes. |
| | 5 | | **Zero Gully** First winter ascent by H. MacInnes, G. Nicol and T. Patey. A major problem climbed. |
| | 4 | Glencoe | **Deep-Gash Gully** *Aonach Dubh* First winter ascent by J. Cunningham and M. Noon. |
| | 4 | C/gorms 1 | **Route Major** *Cairn Etchachan* First winter ascent by T. Patey and M. Smith. |
| | 5 | | **Sticil Face** *Shelter Stone Crag* First winter ascent by K. Grassick and G. Nicol. The first winter climb on a formidable cliff. |
| | 4 | | **Savage Slit** *Coire an Lochain* First winter ascent by G. Adams, J. White and F. Henderson. |
| **1958** | — | B/Nevis | **Zero Gully** P. Knapp, A. Beanland and M. Morgan killed after falling from the third pitch. Wooden ice axes (used for belaying) snapped – stumps found by MacInnes in snow below the third pitch. |
| | — | | **Point Five Gully** Two attempts by MacInnes and Clough, on the second they were joined by Patey. |
| | 4/5 | Glencoe | **North Face Route** *Buachaille Etive Mor* First winter ascent by R. Marshall and J. Stenhouse. |
| | 3 | | **The Crack** *Stob Coire nam Beith* First winter ascent by L. S. Lovat and N. Harthill. |
| | 4 | C/gorms 1 | **Deep-Cut Chimney** *Hell's Lum Crag* First winter ascent by T. Patey and D. Holroyd. |
| | 5 | C/gorms 2 | **Parallel Gully B** *Lochnagar* First winter ascent by J. Marshall and G. Tiso. The great winter problem of Lochnagar. Technically advanced. Crampons used – at the time most Lochnagar climbers used nails. |
| **1959** | 4 | B/Nevis | **Waterfall Gully** *Carn Dearg* First ascent (winter) by D. Pipes, J. Alexander, I. Clough, R. Shaw and A. Flegg over two days in early January. |
| | 5 | | **Point Five Gully** First winter ascent by I. S. Clough, J. Alexander, D. Pipes and R. Shaw. A five-day sieged ascent of a long-standing problem. A very controversial ascent. |
| | 5 | | **Orion Face** First winter ascent by R. Smith and R. Holt. A new dimension of winter climbing on the Ben – the chimney pitch to turn the Great Slab Rib is still considered very hard. |
| | 4 | | **Hadrian's Wall** First winter ascent by W. Brooker, J. Marshall and T. Patey. Strong team/classic climb. |
| | 4 | | **North Face Girdle** First winter ascent by J. Marshall and T. Patey. An entertaining climb from Observatory Buttress across Point Five, Zero, Orion to finish across the upper part of the Little Brenva Face. |
| | 5 | | **Minus Two Gully** First winter ascent by J. Marshall, J. Stenhouse and D. Haston. A hard gully climb. |
| | 4 | | **Platform's Rib** *Minus Face* First winter ascent by H. MacInnes, I. Clough, T. Sullivan and M. White. |
| | 5 | | **Tower Face of the Comb** *Coire na Ciste* First winter ascent by R. Smith and R. Holt. |
| | 4 | | **Pinnacle Arête** *Coire na Ciste* First winter ascent by R. Sellers and J. Smith. |
| | 2/3 | | **Nordwand** *North Wall of Castle Ridge* First ascent (winter) by I. S. Clough, D. Pipes and J. Porter. |
| | 4 | Glencoe | **Diamond Buttress Direct** *Bidean nam Bian* First winter ascent by J. McLean and M. Noon. |
| | 5 | Meagaidh | **Smith's Gully** *Pinnacle Buttress* First winter ascent by J. Marshall and G. Tiso. A very hard gully. |
| | 4/5 | | **'59 Face Route** *Pinnacle Buttress* First ascent by J. Marshall, J. Stenhouse and D. Haston. |
| | 4 | C/gorms 1 | **South East Gully/Mitre Ridge** *Beinn a'Bhuird* First winter ascent by R. Sellers and G. Annand. |
| | 4 | | **Alladin's Buttress** *Coire an t'Sneachda* First winter ascent by T. Patey. A bold solo climb. |
| | 4 | | **Kiwi Slabs** *Hell's Lum Crag* First winter ascent by T. Patey and V. Stevenson. Ice smeared slabs. |
| | 4 | | **Red Chimney** *Creagan a'Choire Etchachan* First winter ascent by J. Hay and R. Ibbotson. The direct finish was added in 1967 by I. Paterson and S. Hepburn. 'A very fine ice climb and a natural ice trap.' |
| | 5 | C/gorms 2 | **Labyrinth Route** *Creag an Dubh Loch* First winter ascent by R. Sellers, J. Smith and G. Annand. |
| | 4 | | **Labyrinth Edge** *Creag an Dubh Loch* First winter ascent by W. Brooker and D. Duncan |
| **1960** | 4/5 | B/Nevis | **The Great Chimney, Minus Three Gully, Gardyloo Buttress, Observatory Buttress, Pigott's Route on the Comb** and **Orion Face Direct** Six first winter ascents (including two Grade 5s) and the second ascent of **Point Five Gully** (in seven hours) by J. Marshall and R. Smith. These climbs, made on consecutive days in February had an important inspirational effect on succeeding generations of climbers. |
| | 4 | | **Rogue's Rib** *Coire na Ciste* First winter ascent by G. Grandison and I. Clough. |
| | 4 | Glencoe | **Flake Route** *Bidean nam Bian* First winter ascent by H. MacInnes and party. |
| | 5 | Meagaidh | **North Post** First ascent (winter) by T. Patey, J. Deacon, G. Mcleod and P. Danelet. |
| **1961** | 5 | B/Nevis | **Vanishing Gully** *Coire na Ciste* First ascent (winter) by R. Marshall and G. Tiso. Originally graded 4. |
| **1962** | 3 | W/hlands | **Viking Gully** *Ladhar Beinn* First winter ascent by T. Patey and A. Nicol. '. . . compares with the classic Crowberry Gully and can be thoroughly recommended as a winter climb.' A 1,200ft. route. |
| | 3/5 | Meagaidh | **Post Horn Gallop** and **Last Post** First ascents (winter) by T. Patey and R. Brooke. the pair also climbed South Post using the direct entry pitch (first ascent). |
| | 4 | C/gorms 1 | **Boomerang** *Braeriach* First winter ascent by D. Pyper and D. Reid. |
| | 4 | C/gorms 2 | **Route 2** *Lochnagar* First winter ascent by J. Marshall and J. Stenhouse. Another attempt at a girdle. |
| **1963** | 3 | N/hlands | **Trident Gully** *Beinn Dearg Mhor* First ascent by N. Tranter and N. Travers (by the Centre Branch). |
| | 4 | Wales | **Central Gully** *Clogwyn y Grochan* First winter ascent by M. Boysen and B. Ingle. |

Etchachan clubs formed a major force for the next decade: Brooker, Patey, Taylor, G. Nicol, Grassick, Sellers and Annand among those involved.

**1951** *Undiscovered Scotland* by W. H. Murray (Dent).

**1954** *Ben Nevis* guide revised by G. Macphee.*

**1956** Mountaineering Association run ice-climbing courses in Glencoe and on Ben Nevis in collaboration with Hamish MacInnes. Ian Clough an early pupil.

**1957** RAF Kinloss Mountain rescue team attracts climbers doing national service including Alexander, Clough, Pipes, Sullivan and Shaw. Crampons gradually replace nails among Glencoe/Nevis/Meagaidh activists. Many Cairngorm climbers continue to favour nails.
Loosely-knit Edinburgh grouping comprising the brothers Marshall, R. Smith, Tiso, Haston, Stenhouse, Moriarty, Holt, Hughes, and later Campbell and MacNiven involved in high-standard climbing all over Scotland until the deaths of Smith and MacNiven and the departure (to Switzerland) of Haston.

**1958–59** Four articles – *A Winter ascent of Crowberry Gully* and *Scottish Mountaineering* by Tom Weir, *Post-War Winter Climbing in Scotland* by Tom Patey, and *Little Brenva Face* by Ian Clough published in Mountain Craft. Mass circulation magazine used to disseminate up-to-date information.

**1959** Two of the most powerful Aberdeen-based climbers killed in the same summer: Ronnie Sellers† Lochnagar and Jerry Smith† Aig Noire.
*Buachaille Etive Mor* guide by L. S. Lovat.*

**1960** SMCJ edited by G. F. Dutton. Writings of Smith and Marshall given prominence.

**1961–62** *Cairngorms* guide (Vol.1 – North and Vol.2 – South) by Malcolm Smith (assisted by Tom Patey). Two superb guides that were the first to introduce a special grading system for winter climbs.*

**1962** Robin Smith† Pamirs.
Tom Patey moves to Ullapool and subsequently inspires new-route activity notably on Beinn Dearg, Assynt, Coigach and Applecross.

Edinburgh Squirrels group starts. Members include Robertson, Bathgate, MacEacheran and McKeith. Hut built in Glencoe.

Glenmore Lodge introduces winter survival and technical snow and ice courses during the sixties.

| | | | |
|---|---|---|---|
| | 4 | | **Waterfall Route** *Craig y Rhaeadr* First winter ascent by M. Boysen and B. Ingle. |
| | 5 | | **The Black Cleft** *Clogwyn du'r Arddu* First winter ascent by M. Boysen and B. Ingle over three days. An advanced route involving both steep ice and hard, mixed-climbing. Partially sieged. |

---

**1964** 4 C/gorms 2 **False Gully** *Creag an Dubh Loch* First winter ascent by K. Grassick, W. James and M. Taylor.

---

**1965** 3 N/hlands **Penguin Gully** *Beinn Dearg* First ascent (winter) by T. Patey, W. H. Murray and N. Tennent. Together with Inverael Gully (1962) this indicated the possibilities on these cliffs. Six more routes added in 1968.

4 **Gamma Gully** *Sgurr nan Clach Geala* First ascent (winter) by N. Tranter and I. Rowe. The first major winter route on an important new cliff. Originally considered the first Grade 5 in the N. Highlands.

— Skye **The Cuillin Ridge** First winter traverse by T. Patey, H. MacInnes, B. Robertson and D. Crabb. A major expedition. The climb was repeated soon afterwards by J. Moriarty and G. Tiso.

4 B/Nevis **Green Hollow Route** *North-East Buttress* First ascent by J. Marshall and J. Moriarty.

4 **The Chute** *Coire na Ciste* First ascent (winter) by J. Marshall, R. Campbell and R. Holt.

5 **The Curtain** *Carn Dearg* First winter ascent (Mourning Slab) by D. Bathgate and J. Knight.

4 Glencoe **Pterodactyl** *Lost Valley Buttress* First ascent (winter) by D. Crabb and H. MacInnes.

5 Meagaidh **Centre Post Direct** First ascent (winter) by B. Robertson, E. Cairns and F. Harper.

5 **South Post Direct** First ascent (winter) by I. MacEacheran and J. Knight. The final hard pitch is added.

4 **Diadem** *Inner Corrie* First ascent (winter) by T. Patey and J. Brown.

4 C/gorms 1 **The Shroud** *Sgor an Lochan Uaine* First winter ascent by I. MacEacheran and J. Knight.

5 **Djibangi** *Creagan a'Choire Etchachan* First winter ascent by J. MacArtney and W. Barclay. The third Grade 5 in the northern Cairngorm group and a harbinger of the hard mixed climbs of the seventies.

4 **The Talisman** *Creagan a'Choire Etchachan* First winter ascent by K. Grassick and J. Light.

4 **The Great Rift** *Braeriach* First winter ascent by G. Nicol and J. Light.

4 Wales **Slanting Gully** *Lliwedd* First winter ascent by J. Brown and A. Cowburn.

5 **The Black Cleft** *Clogwyn du'r Arddu* Second winter ascent by R. Edwards and E. Wallace and third winter ascent by J. Brown and J. Anthoine. Both parties completed the climb in a day.

---

**1966** 4 C/gorms 1 **Square-Cut Gully** *Creagan a'Choire Etchachan* First winter ascent by M. Forbes and M. Low.

5 C/gorms 2 **Pinnacle Face** *Lochnagar* First winter ascent by K. Grassick, J. Light and G. Nicol. A major climb.

4 **West Gully Direct** *Lochnagar* First winter ascent by A. Fyffe and M. Mowat.

4 B/Nevis **Echo Face, Tower Ridge** First winter ascent by J. Marshall and R. Marshall.

---

**1967** 4 N/hlands **Raeburn's Buttress Direct** *Sgorr Ruadh* First winter ascent by W. D. Brooker and S. H. Wilkinson.

4 B/Nevis **Ruddy Rocks** First winter ascent by J. Marshall, R. Marshall and R. N. Campbell.

4 C/gorms 1 **Trident** *Beinn a'Bhuird* First winter ascent by J. Bower and M. MacLennen.

4 **Flanking Ribs** *Creagan a'Choire Etchachan* First ascent (winter) by A. Fyffe and J. MacArtney.

4 **Phoenix Gully** *Braeriach* First ascent by J. Light, G. McGregor, M. McArthur and D. Halliday.

— C/gorms 2 **Parallel Gully B** *Lochnagar* Second and third winter ascents: A Fyffe and J. MacArtney; M. Boysen and J. Jordan. The first repeats, nine years after the Marshall/Tiso ascent.

4 Wales **Pyramid Gully** *Ysgolion Duon* First winter ascent by M. Boysen and N. Estcourt.

---

**1968** 4 N/hlands **The Blue Pillar** *Meall Gorm, Applecross* First winter ascent by J. Brown and T. Patey.

5 Meagaidh **The Pumpkin** *Inner Coire* First ascent (winter) by N. Quinn, R. McMillan and G. Peet.

4 C/gorms 1 **West Buttress Direct** *Braeriach* First winter ascent by J. Bower, R. Simpson and G. Strange.

4 Wales **Central Gully** *Lliwedd* First winter ascent by D. Alcock and B. A. Fuller.

4 **Shallow Gully** *Lliwedd* First winter ascent by M. Boysen and N. Estcourt.

4 **Ypres** *Ysgolion Duon* First ascent (winter) by D. Alcock and J. Anthoine.

4 **Icefall Gully** *Ysgolion Duon* First ascent (winter) by P. Nunn and J. Street.

---

**1969** 4 N/hlands **Checkmate Chimney** *An Teallach* First ascent (winter) by T. Patey and C. Bonington.

3/4 **Easachan** and **Geodha Ban** *Beinn Lair* First ascents (winter) by Q. Crichton and G. Hunter. Two new 1,000ft. gullies each with several ice pitches and amidst 'grand rock scenery'.

4 **March Hare's Gully** *Beinn Bhan* First ascent (winter) by T. Patey and C. Bonington.

4 W/hlands **Great Gully** *East Face of Garbh Bheinn* First winter ascent by T. Patey, C. Bonington and D. Whillans.

3 B/Nevis **Route Major** *Little Brenva Face* First ascent by I. Clough and H. MacInnes.

4 Glencoe **Mome Rath** *Gearr Aonach* First winter ascent by A. Fyffe and J. MacArtney.

4 **The Wabe** *Gearr Aonach* First winter ascent by J. Hardie and H. MacInnes.

4 **Frostbite Wall** *Gearr Aonach* First ascent (winter) by H. MacInnes, A. Gilbert, P. Debbage, D. Layne Joynt and D. Alright. This and the two previous routes were the hardest of over 25 new climbs made on the cliffs of the Bidean nam Bian massif in 1969 by Glencoe School of Mountaineering parties.

5 Meagaidh **The Wand** *Inner Corrie* First ascent (winter) D. Lang and N. Quinn, G. Hunter and Q. Crichton.

5 **Ritchie's Gully Direct** *Pinnacle Buttress* First ascent (winter) by G. Hunter and N. Quinn.

3/4 **Crab Crawl** First winter ascent by T. Patey. An 8,000ft. epic.

4 C/gorms 1 **Commando Route/Mitre Ridge** *Beinn a'Bhuird* First winter ascent by P. Macdonald and I. Rowe.

4 **She-Devil's Buttress** *Braeriach* First winter ascent by G. Boyd, B. Findlay, R. Simpson and G. S. Strange. The hardest of six new winter routes on Braeriach in 1969.

4 C/gorms 2 **Theseus Grooves** *Creag an Dubh Loch* First winter ascent by J. Campbell, B. Findlay, R. Simpson and G. Strange.

4 **Tough Brown Ridge Direct** *Lochnagar* First winter ascent by N. Keir and M. Rennie.

5 S/hlands **Great Central Groove** *The Brack, Arrochar* First winter ascent by W. Skidmore and R. Richardson.

3 **Taxus** *Beinn an Dothaidh* First ascent (winter) by A. Ewing and A. Trees.

3/4 S/Ulands **Grey Mare's Tail** First ascent by G. Anderson, W. Anderson; D. Bathgate and I. MacEacheran.

---

**1970** 4 N/hlands **Emerald Gully** *Beinn Dearg* First ascent (winter) by P. Nunn, B. Fuller and A. Riley.

4 Glencoe **Summit Buttress Original** *Stob Coire nan Lochan* First winter ascent by K. Spence and guided party.

5 **Raven's Gully Direct** *Buachaille Etive Mor* First winter ascent by Y. Chouinard and D. Tompkins. This ascent demonstrated the effectiveness of Chouinard's curved-hammer technique. Influential.

4 Meagaidh **Trespasser Buttress** *Inner Corrie* First ascent (winter) by H. MacInnes, G. Hunter; D. Lang, N. Quinn.

---

Instructors (temp./perm.) include MacInnes, Haston, Slesser and McLeod. Eric Langmuir appointed Director in 1967. Cunningham, March and MacArtney instructors.

**1963** Graham Macphee† Canary Islands.

**1964** Hamish MacInnes introduces short metal axes and hammers with slightly inclined picks.

Other equipment improvements include: Salewa adjustable 12-point crampons; Marwa tubular ice screws; full length gaitors.

**1965** *Glencoe* guidebook by L. S. Lovat.*

**1966** *Coire Ardair/Creag Meagaidh* guide by A. McKeith (published privately).

Guides to *Easter Ross and Fionaven* by A. Park and P. Tranter (published privately). Record activity of the Edinburgh based Corriemulzie Club whose members also included Rowe, Wright, and Macdonald.

Robin Campbell joins Dutton to edit SMCJ.

Alistair Park† Fionaven. Philip Tranter† road accident in France.

**1966–67** Yvon Chouinard and Tom Frost introduce curved pick axes and hammers and chrome-moly rigid, adjustable crampons.

**1969** *Ben Nevis* guide by J. R. Marshall.*

*Ben Nevis and Glencoe* (winter climbs guide) by Ian Clough (Cicerone).

*Northern Highlands* (Letterewe and Easter Ross) guide by I. G. Rowe.

Road improvements in the Northern Highlands allow easier access to remote mountain groups.

First issue of *Mountain*. Regular coverage given to ice-climbing and equipment developments.

Clog introduce Deadmen and Deadboys.

**1970** Jim MacArtney†, Fergus Mitchell† and Mary Ann Hudson† in avalanche on Italian Climb.

Gunn Clark† in avalanche on Buachaille Etive Mor.

Ian Clough† Annapurna.

Tom Patey† on a sea stack at Whiten Head.

A series of tragedies that stunned climbing circles, and dealt a crippling blow to the active Glencoe group that had developed around Clough.

Yvon Chouinard visits Scotland and meets Cunningham and MacInnes. Ideas on equipment and technique exchanged. Two schools later emerge, one favouring curved-pick, wooden-shafted axes and hammers, the other concentrating on the inclined-pick, metal-shafted

| Year | Grade | Area | Route and description |
|---|---|---|---|
| | 4 | C/gorms 1 | **Hourglass Buttress Direct** and **The Carpet** *Coire na Ciche, Beinn a'Bhuird* First winter ascents by J. Bower and G. Boyd. Short and hard. |
| | 5 | | **False Scorpion** *Cairn Etchachan* First winter ascent by W. March and O. Ludlow. |
| | 5 | | **The Chancer** *Hell's Lum Crag* First ascent (winter) by J. Cunningham and W. March. A steep ice pitch climbed on front points and ice-daggers – a signal of the imminent revolution in technique. |
| | 4 | C/gorms 1 | **Brimstone Grooves** *Hell's Lum Crag* First winter ascent by S. Docherty and K. Spence. |
| | 5 | | **Bugaboo Rib** *Cairn Toul* First winter ascent by B. Findlay and G. Strange. |
| | 4/5 | C/gorms 2 | **Bower Buttress** *Creag an Dubh Loch* First winter ascent by J. Bower and R. Simpson. |
| | 4/5 | Arran | **Beinn Nuis Chimney** First winter ascent by W. Skidmore and J. Crawford. |
| 1971 | 5 | N/hlands | **Hamilton Route** *Central Buttress, Beinn Eighe* First winter ascent by K. Spence, J. Ronayne and K. Urquhart. The first Grade 5 in the Northern Highlands but not recorded until 1979. |
| | 4 | | **Wall of the Early Morning Light** *Beinn Bhan* First ascent (winter) by K. Spence, J. Horsfield, B. Jones and P. Thomas. Not recorded until 1979 thereby superseding the route Moonshine (1978). |
| | 4 | | **Rough Diamond** *Luchd Coire, Seana Braigh* First ascent (winter) by P. Macdonald and I. Rowe. |
| | 6 | B/Nevis | **Astronomy** *Orion Face* First winter ascent by A. Fyffe, H. MacInnes and K. Spence. Terrordactyls used. |
| | — | | **Point Five Gully** Rapid ascents by parties using curved or inclined picks. Geddes and Higham, Rouse and Gillespie, Cunningham and March (in under 3 hours). |
| | — | | **Smith's Route** *Gardyloo Buttress* Second ascent by M. Geddes and N. Rayner. K. Spence later led a party from Glencoe School of Mountaineering up the direct line describing it as 'a good course route'. |
| | — | C/gorms 1 | **Citadel** *Shelter Stone Crag* A two-day attempt (with a bivouac) by J. Cunningham and W. March failed when conditions deteriorated. A. and R. Barley made a semi-winter ascent later. |
| 1972 | 5 | N/hlands | **Sellars' Buttress** *Sgurr nan Clach Geala* First winter ascent by G. Strange and D. Stuart. |
| | 5 | | **Ordinary Route/Slueth** *Fuar Tholl* First winter ascent by K. Spence, H. MacInnes and A. Fyffe. |
| | — | B/Nevis | **Orion Face Direct** Second ascent by A. Rouse and M. Geddes 12 years after the first ascent. |
| | 6 | B/Nevis | **Left Hand Route** *Minus Face* First winter ascent by S. Docherty and N. Muir. |
| | 6 | | **Right Hand Route** *Minus Face* First winter ascent by R. Carrington and A. Rouse. |
| | 4 | Meagaidh | **Nordwander** *Pinnacle Buttress* First ascent (winter) by D. Dinwoodie, B. Lawrie, M. Freeman and D. Stuart. Stuart was seriously injured and disabled after completing this climb. |
| | — | | **North Post** Soloed by M. Geddes. |
| | — | C/gorms 1 | **Sticil Face** *Shelter Stone Crag* Second winter ascent by J. Cunningham and W. March. |
| | 3/4 | C/gorms 1 | **Clach Dain Chimney** *Shelter Stone Crag* First winter ascent by C. Butterworth and A. Frost. |
| | 5 | C/gorms 2 | **Labyrinth Direct** *Creag an Dubh Loch* First ascent (winter) by J. Bolton and P. Arnold. A bold lead. |
| | 4 | | **Hanging Garden Route** *Creag an Dubh Loch* First winter ascent by D. Dinwoodie and G. Strange. |
| | 4/5 | Wales | **Gallipoli** and **Passchendaele** *Ysgolion Duon* First ascents (winter) by M. Boysen and D. Alcock. |
| 1973 | | B/Nevis | **Zero Gully** and **Point Five Gully** Soloed in three hours by I. Nicholson. Startling proof of the effectiveness of the new axe technique in reducing times on the great classic gullies. |
| | 5 | C/gorms 1 | **Devil's Delight** *Hell's Lum Crag* First winter ascent by J. Cunningham and party. |
| 1974 | 6 | B/Nevis | **Minus One Gully** First winter ascent by C. Stead and K. Crocket. |
| | 5 | | **Minus Two Buttress** First ascent (winter) by C. Higgins, B. Dunn and D. McArthur. |
| | 5 | | **Left Edge Route** *Observatory Buttress* First winter ascent by D. Lang and N. Quinn. |
| | 5 | | **Slav Route** *Orion Face* First winter ascent by D. Lang and N. Quinn. |
| | 4 | C/gorms 1 | **East Wall Direct** *Mitre Ridge, Beinn a'Bhuird* First winter ascent by N. Keir, J. Mothersele, R. Smith. |
| | 4 | | **Carmine Groove** *Creagan a'Choire Etchachan* First winter ascent by R. Smith and G. Stephen. |
| | 5 | C/gorms 2 | **Winter Face** *Black Spout Pinnacle, Lochnagar* First ascent (winter) by N. Quinn and D. Lang. |
| 1975 | — | B/Nevis | **Centurion/Route 2** Semi-winter, semi-siege ascent over two days by R. Milward using self-belay tactics. |
| | 4 | C/gorms 1 | **Vulcan** *Braeriach* First winter ascent by J. Bower, J. Ingram and K. Turnbull. |
| | | | **Citadel** *Shelter Stone Crag* A partial winter ascent by A. Rouse and B. Hall finishing up Sticil Face. |
| | 4 | | **Gaffer's Groove** *Coire an Lochain* First winter ascent by J. Cunningham and A. Fyffe. |
| | — | C/gorms 2 | **Eagle Ridge** *Lochnagar* Soloed by N. Keir using a self-belay system on the Tower. |
| | 5 | Wales | **Central Gully Direct** *Lliwedd* Earliest known winter ascent by A. Kellas and party. May have been climbed earlier (Kellas). Not climbed again until 1979 – M. Fowler and T. Jones. |
| 1976 | 4/5 | N/hlands | **Mad Hatter's Gully** *Beinn Bhan* First ascent (winter) by M. Freeman and G. Stephen. |
| | 4 | | **Robertson's Gully** *Sgorr Ruadh* First ascent (winter) by A. Nisbet and N. Spinks. |
| | 6 | B/Nevis | **Astral Highway** *Orion Face* First ascent (winter) by C. Higgins and A. Kimber. |
| | 6 | | **Left Edge** *Gardyloo Buttress* First winter ascent by R. Carrington and A. Rouse. |
| | 5 | Meagaidh | **The Fly** *Pinnacle Buttress* First ascent partially based on the line right of Smith's Gully by A. Wielochowski and D. Nottidge in a three-day siege. This, and the 1959 Point Five Gully ascent, criticised in the SMCJ 'we find it impossible to accept . . . siege tactics are out of place in Scotland'. |
| | 4 | S/hlands | **The Screaling** *Beinn an Dothaidh* First ascent (winter) by I. Fulton and J. Hutchinson. One of seven new routes made here in 1976 by (variously) Crocket, Skidmore, Crawford, Grant, Stead and Gilmore. |
| 1977 | 4 | N/hlands | **Footless Gully** and **Pyramid Buttress** *Liathach* First winter ascents by C. Rowland with Steph Rowland (on Footless Gully) and with D. Jenkins and M. Webster (on Pyramid Buttress). |
| | 5 | | **Silver Tear** *Beinn Bhan* First ascent (winter) by N. Muir and A. Paul. |
| | 5 | B/Nevis | **Minus One Buttress** First winter ascent by N. Muir and A. Paul. |
| | — | | **Orion Face Direct** Soloed by P. Braithwaite. |
| | 5 | | **Rubicon Wall** *Observatory Ridge* First winter ascent by A. Paul and N. Muir. |
| | 5 | | **The Lobby Dancer** *North Face of Castle Ridge, Carn Dearg* First ascent by C. Higgins and A. Kimber. |
| | — | Meagaidh | **The Pumpkin** Soloed by A. McHardy. |
| | 5 | C/gorms 1 | **Cumming-Crofton Route** *Mitre Ridge, Beinn a'Bhuird* First winter ascent by R. Renshaw and G. Strange. |
| | 4 | | *Creagan a'Choire Etchachan* **Dagger** A. Nisbet and A. Robertson; **Bodkin** R. Renshaw and G. Strange. |
| | 4 | | **Cascade** *Stag Rocks* First ascent (winter) by W. March and D. Alcock. |
| | 4 | | **White Nile** *Braeriach* First ascent (winter) by R. Archbold and M. Hillman. |
| | — | C/gorms 2 | **Parallel Gully B** Soloed by P. Braithwaite. |

Terrordactyl hammers and axes. Reported in detail in Mountain. These meetings, and the subsequent equipment developments, climbs and books that followed had a major impact on Scottish, American and world climbing.

**1971** *Cairngorms* (Creag an Dubh Loch) guide by A. F. Fyffe.*

*Scottish Climbs* (2 volumes) selected climbs guide by Hamish MacInnes (Constable). Climbs graded in adjectival terms for winter climbs, and by a numeral system for summer rock climbs.

Comprehensive survey – *Scottish Winter Climbing* in Mountain 14. Contributors include Marshall, Quinn, Campbell and Cunningham.

New Chouinard, Salewa, Clog, Snowdon Mouldings, MSR and MacInnes/Peck equipment (ice pitons, crampons, hammers and axes) become generally available.

Elements in the SMC advocate moratorium on publishing route descriptions for the Northern Highlands.

**1973** Strong Scottish-American film team operating on Ben Nevis including Chouinard, Barber, Jeff Lowe, Cunningham, MacInnes, Spence, Carrington and Nicholson. Further exchange of ideas. Lowe's Hummingbird design influenced by discarded MacInnes prototypes.

*Cairngorms* (Beinn a'Bhuird, Ben Macdui) guide by G. S. Strange.*

*Cairngorms* (Loch Avon Basin and Northern Corries) guide by W. March.*

*Northern Highlands* (Torridon, Applecross) guide by D. G. and R. W. L. Turnbull.*

Expatriate British climbers join Canadians in developing ice climbing in the Calgary area. Many steep ice walls climbed — the ideal arena for the new equipment. Following this Bugs McKeith advocates introduction of Grade 6 in Mountain and SMCJ.

**1974** North Wales (winter climbs guide) by Rick Newcombe.‡

Allen Fyffe summarizes rapid changes in Scottish winter climbing in Mountain 40. Republished in Japan.

Jeff Lowe and Mike Wiess climb Bridalveil Fall in Colorado.

Walter Cecchinel and Claude Jager make first ascent of the Dru Couloir using Simond curved hammers and axes.

Main groups active in Scotland in the seventies:

Ben Nevis/Glencoe Area: After the 1970 accidents disparate groups active mainly from Glasgow and Edinburgh or local residents: Spence, Sykes, Nicholson, Paul, Muir, Docherty, Higgins, G. Smith, Geddes, Cuthbertson, Kimber, Hamilton etc.

Aberdeen: Large group of able and active climbers based here

| Year | Grade | Area | Description |
|---|---|---|---|
| | 3/4 | S/hlands | Activity in several areas. Best discoveries: **Stormbringer** *Beinn an Dothaidh* (Crocket and Fulton), **Monolith Grooves** *Beinn an Lochain* (Clarke and Mackenzie), **The Cramp** *Beinn Udlaidh* (Skelton and Duckworth) and **North Wall Groove** *The Cobbler* and **Right-Hand Route** *The Brack* (Muir and Paul). |
| **1978** | 3/4 | N/hlands | **Cabbage White** and **North Summit Buttress** *Beinn Lair* First winter ascents by A. McHardy and A. Nisbet with J. Anderson and J. Unwin on North Summit Buttress only – 'an excellent route'. |
| | 5 | | **Skyscraper Buttress** *Sgurr nan Clach Geala, Fannichs* First winter ascent by R. Archbold and M. Freeman; J. C. Higham and R. Smith – 'excellent climbing'. |
| | 5 | | **Poacher's Fall** *N E Corrie of Spidean, Liathach* First ascent (winter) by A. Nisbet and A. McHardy. |
| | 4 | | **Diamond Edge** *Seana Braigh* First ascent (winter) by D. Dinwoodie, R. Robb and R. Smith. |
| | 5 | | **Central Buttress Direct** *Beinn Eighe* First winter ascent by A. Rouse and A. MacIntyre. |
| | 5 | | **Fuar Folly** *Fuar Tholl* First winter ascent by R. Archbold and D. Nichols. |
| | — | Skye | **Cuillin Ridge** Repeated by J. Beatty and R. Beighton; G. Cohen, D. Broadhead and G. Macnair. |
| | 5 | W/hlands | **Tir na Og** *Ladhar Bheinn* C. Higgins and A. Foster. The first Grade 5 in the Western Highlands. This was the hardest of eight new routes added to the Ladhar Bheinn cliffs in 1978. |
| | 6 | B/Nevis | **Galactic Hitchhiker** *Observatory Ridge* First ascent (winter) by M. Geddes and C. Higgins. |
| | 6 | | **Pointless** *Observatory Ridge* First winter ascent by G. Smith and N. Banks. |
| | 5 | | **Albatross** *Indicator Wall* First ascent (winter) by C. Higgins and M. Geddes. |
| | 5 | | **Psychedelic Wall** *Indicator Wall* First ascent (winter) by A. Paul and N. Muir. |
| | 6 | | **The Great Glen** *Gardyloo Buttress* First ascent (winter) by P. Braithwaite and P. Moores. |
| | 5/6 | | **Route 2** *Carn Dearg* First winter ascent by M. Geddes and A. Rouse. The Direct Start was added later by G. Smith and I. Sykes. Climbed direct the route is considered Grade 6. |
| | 5 | C/gorms 1 | **Red Guard** *Cairn Etchachan* First ascent (winter) by M. Freeman and N. Keir. |
| | 4 | | **Crucible Route** *Garbh Coire, Beinn a'Bhuird* First ascent by R. Archbold and D. Dinwoodie. |
| | 5 | C/gorms 2 | **Vertigo Wall** *Creag an Dubh Loch* First winter ascent by A. Nisbet and A. Robertson. |
| | 5 | Wales | **Devil's Appendix** *Clogwyn y Geifr* First winter ascent by M. Poynton and P. Kershaw. A coveted route. |
| | 5 | | **Cascade** and **Chequered Wall** *Craig Rhaeadr* First winter ascents by M. Fowler and P. Thomas. |
| **1979** | 4/5 | N/hlands | **Crystal Tripper** *Garbh Coire Mhor, Fannichs* First ascent (winter) by J. Mackenzie and D. McCallum. The hardest of five new routes made on these cliffs in 1979. |
| | 5 | | **The Second Icefall** *Creag Urbhard, Foinaven* First ascent (winter) by A. Nisbit and N. Spinks. The hardest of ten ice routes made here during February by a five-man Aberdeen team. |
| | 5 | | **The Nose of the Fiddler** *Coigach* First winter ascent by N. Keir and R. Smith. |
| | 5 | | **Meanderthal** *Beinn Bhan* First ascent (winter) by A. Taylor and C. Robertson. |
| | 5 | B/Nevis | **Central Route** *Minus Face* First winter ascent by A. Nisbet and B. Sprunt. |
| | 6 | | **Girdle Traverse of Minus/Orion Faces** First ascent (winter) by R. Milward with A. Dilger and S. Parr. |
| | 6 | | **The Shadow** *Carn Dearg* First winter ascent by P. Braithwaite and D. Pearce. |
| | 6 | | **Shield Direct** *Carn Dearg* First winter ascent by M. Fowler and A. Saunders. The first route to be given Grade 6 in an SMC guidebook. |
| | 6 | | **Waterfall Gully/Left Wall** *Carn Dearg* First winter ascent by A. Kimber and A. MacIntyre. |
| | 5 | | **Alchemist** *North Face of Castle Ridge, Carn Dearg* First ascent (winter) by A. Paul and D. Sanderson. |
| | 4 | Glencoe | **Misty High** *Slime Wall, Buachaille Etive Mor* First winter ascent by A. Paul and D. Sanderson. |
| | 6 | | **Elliot's Downfall** *Aonach Dubh* First ascent (winter) by D. Cuthbertson. |
| | 4/5 | | **Heart of Glass, Venom, Viper Start, White Snake** and **The Flute** *Aonach Dubh* First winter ascents by (var) D. Cuthbertson, K. Johnstone, W. Todd, R. Anderson, D. Brown, M. Duff and A. McAllister. |
| | 5 | C/gorms 1 | **Wig-Wag** *Stag Rocks* First ascent by G. Smith and M. Fowler. |
| | 4 | | **Eastern Approaches** *Cairn Etchachan* First ascent (winter) by A. Fyffe and A. Liddell. |
| | 5 | C/gorms 2 | **Link Face** *Black Spout Pinnacle, Lochnagar* First winter ascent by J. Anderson and A. Nisbet. A major ascent – the most important climb on Lochnagar in the seventies. |
| | 4/5 | | **Crypt** *Lochnagar* First winter ascent by A. Nisbet and B. Sprunt. |
| | 5 | Wales | **Bloody Slab** *Clogwyn du'r Arddu* First winter ascent by P. Braithwaite and R. Baxter-Jones. |
| | 5 | | **Silver Machine** *Clogwyn du'r Arddu* First winter ascent by M. Fowler and C. Griffiths. |
| | 5 | | **Central Icefall Direct** *Creag Rhaeadr* First winter ascent by M. Fowler with P. Thomas and C. Griffiths. |
| | 5 | | **East Peak Direct** *Lliwedd* First winter ascent by M. Fowler and M. Morrison (via Yellow Slab). |
| | 5 | | **The Somme** *Ysgolion Duon* First ascent (winter) by M. Boysen and D. Alcock. |
| | 5 | | **Trojan** *Cader Idris* First ascent (winter) by J. Sumner, J. Codling and G. Kirkham. |
| **1980** | 5 | N/hlands | **The Resurrection** *Sgurr Mor, Fannichs* First ascent (winter) by J. Mackenzie and D. Butterfield. |
| | 4 | | **Twisting Gully** *Beinn Dearg Mhor* First winter ascent by M. Geddes, C. Higgins and A. Walne. |
| | 4 | | **Vanadium Couloir** *Coire na Caime, Liathach* First ascent (winter) by A. Paul and D. Sanderson. |
| | 5 | | **Y Gully** *Beinn Bhan* First ascent (winter) by H. MacInnes and C. Williamson. |
| | 5 | | **Der Riesenwand** *Beinn Bhan* First ascent (winter) by A. Nisbet and B. Sprunt. |
| | 6 | B/Nevis | **Interstellar Overdrive** *Observatory Ridge* First ascent (winter) by I. Kennedy and R. Anderson. |
| | 6 | | **Journey into Space** *Orion Face* First ascent (winter) by A. Kimber and C. Higgins. |
| | — | | **Slav Route** *Orion Face* Soloed by M. Duff. |
| | 5 | Glencoe | **Rainmaker** *Gearr Aonach* First winter ascent by D. Cuthbertson and M. Duff. |
| | 5 | | **Tilt** *Stob Coire nan Lochan* First winter ascent by M. Hamilton, K. Spence and A. Taylor. |
| | 5 | C/gorms 1 | **Equinox** and **Boa** *Cairn Etchachan* First winter ascents by A. Nisbet, M. Morrison and S. Kennedy. |
| | 5 | | **Pilgrim's Groove** *Sputan Dearg* First winter ascent by A. Nisbet, M. Morrison, S. Kennedy and E. Clark. |
| | 5 | | **Citadel** and **Postern** *Shelter Stone Crag* First winter ascents by M. Hamilton and K. Spence with A. Taylor (on Postern only). The big Shelter Stone routes are climbed at last. Bivouac on Postern. |
| | 5 | C/gorms 2 | **The Mousetrap** *Creag an Dubh Loch* First winter ascent by M. Hamilton, K. Spence and A. Taylor. Another important ascent. |
| | 5 | | **Goliath** *Creag an Dubh Loch* First winter ascent by A. Nisbet and N. Morrison. |
| | 5 | | **Pink Elephant** *Creag an Dubh Loch* First winter ascent by R. Anderson and R. Milne. |
| | 5 | | **The Straitjacket** *Lochnagar* First winter ascent by A. Nisbet and N. Spinks. |
| | 5 | | **Epitome** *Lochnagar* First winter ascent by J. Fijalkowski and R. Smith. Very strenuous. |
| | 5 | S/hlands | **Captain Hook** *Beinn Udlaidh* First ascent (winter) by C. Calow and D. Cuthbertson. The hardest of 27 routes made here throughout the seventies all tabulated and described in the 1980 SMCJ. |

throughout the seventies (Aberdeen key city in the oil boom) and make major impact on Scottish climbing. Bower, Findlay, Simpson, Dinwoodie, Strange, Keir, Smith, Nisbet, Sprunt, Archbold etc.

Northern Highlands: English climbers living in the region join with Scottish residents to create focal point for activity based on Inverness. Rowland, McHardy, Cain, Macdonald, Mackenzie.

Glenmore Lodge instructors active in the early seventies: Fyffe, Cunningham, March etc.

SMC members with no particular local loyalties: Lang, Quinn, Crocket, Skidmore, Crawford, Stead etc.

Raiding English climbers: Braithwaite, Fowler, Saunders, Rouse, Milward and Carrington.

**1976** SMCJ edited by Bill Brooker.

**1977** New generation of hammers and axes begin to emerge: Mjollnirs, Chacals, Hummingbirds etc. Curved picks droop steeper. Crampon design in constant state of improvement. Textiles and fibres improve: Goretex used for bivi sacks, anoraks, overtrousers etc. Waterproof ropes, proofed sacs, salopettes.

Dougal Haston† skiing in Switzerland.

**1978** *Climbing Ice* by Yvon Chouinard (Hodder and Stoughton). *Cairngorms* (Lochnagar and Creag an Dubh Loch) guide by G. S. Strange and D. S. Dinwoodie.*

Bugs McKeith† Mt Assiniboine

**1979** *The Ice Experience* by Jeff Lowe (Contemporary Books) covers the most modern ice techniques.

Group of French climbers visit Scotland and do many of the hard traditional routes in fast times.

*The Lake District* (winter climbs guide) by R. Bennett, W. Birkett and A. Hyslop.‡

**1980** *Glencoe and Glen Etive* guide by Ken Crocket.*

John Cunningham† Anglesey.

*North Wales* (winter climbs guide) by Rick Newcombe.

Three Polish climbers visit Lochnagar and other Scottish cliffs and perform well.

Aberdeen climbers record (in SMCJ) various permutations of crampons and nails for use in varying conditions. Strap-on tricouni plates (Trampons) favoured by some for mixed climbing.

**1981** *Ben Nevis and Glencoe* (winter climbs guide) by Ed Grindley. Grade 6 used for the hardest climbs.‡

*The Cairngorms* (winter climbs guide) by John Cunningham and Allen Fyffe.‡

*SMC or SMT publications
‡Cicerone publications

# Graded List of Climbs

The climbs in this book fall into three main categories: gullies, mixed or buttress routes and pure ice routes. By drawing on the opinions of a team of experienced climbers, the following comparative table has been produced. This correlates relative difficulty, in mean (average) conditions, using gullies, roughly in order of severity, as the standard. 'Mean' conditions are hard to define when routes can vary in grade daily or even hourly. The table should provide a general comparison, though there could be a five-place error, within or between the columns.

| Gullies | Buttresses and Mixed Climbs | Ice Sheets, Walls, Frozen Waterfalls |
|---|---|---|
| | Route 2 Direct (Ben Nevis) | |
| | Black Cleft (Clogwyn du'r Arddu) | Central Icefall Direct (Craig y Rhaeadr) |
| Labyrinth Direct (Creag an Dubh Loch) | Der Riesenwand (Beinn Bhan) | |
| Minus One Gully (Ben Nevis) | Galactic Hitchhiker (Ben Nevis) | *approx division between Grade 5 and Grade 6* |
| Central Gully Direct (Lliwedd) | Pinnacle Face (Lochnagar) | |
| Minus Two Gully (Ben Nevis) | Sticil Face (Shelter Stone Crag) | |
| Smith's Gully (Creag Meagaidh) | Eagle Ridge (Lochnagar) | The Devil's Appendix (Clogwyn y Geifr) |
| Raven's Gully (Buachaille Etive Mor) | Skyscraper Buttress (Fannichs) | |
| Parallel Gully B (Lochnagar) | Parallel Buttress (Lochnagar) | |
| Point Five Gully (Ben Nevis) | | Cascade (Craig y Rhaeadr) |
| Ebony Chimney (Braeriach) | The Resurrection (Fannichs) | |
| | Mitre Ridge (Beinn a'Bhuird) | |
| | Central Buttress (Beinn Eighe) | |
| | Orion Face Direct (Ben Nevis) | |
| | Passchendaele (Ysgolion Duon) | |
| | Ravenshead (Fannichs) | |
| Mad Hatter's Gully (Beinn Bhan) | The Somme (Ysgolion Duon) | |
| North Post (Creag Meagaidh) | Crystal Tripper (Fannichs) | South Post Direct (Creag Meagaidh) |
| Zero Gully (Ben Nevis) | | Smith's Route (Ben Nevis) |
| Western Gully (Ysgolion Duon) | | Capt. Hook, Peter Pan Direct (B. Udlaidh) |
| Polyphemus Gully (Lochnagar) | Gallipoli (Ysgolion Duon) | Trojan (Cader Idris) |
| The Pumpkin (Creag Meagaidh) | | |
| Scorpion (Cairn Etchachan) | Monolith Grooves (Arrochar) | |
| Central Gully (Lliwedd) | Echo Face (Fannichs) | |
| Central Gully R.H. (Wastwater Screes) | Ypres (Ysgolion Duon) | White Nile (Braeriach) |
| Gamma Gully (Fannichs) | Icefall Gully (Ysgolion Duon) | The Curtain (Ben Nevis) |
| Maria (Gallt yr Ogof) | Plumline (Fannichs) | |
| Steep Ghyll (Scafell) | | The Wand (Creag Meagaidh) |
| Hanging Garden Gully (Clogwyn y Geifr) | | |
| March Hare's Gully (Beinn Bhan) | | |
| No.6 Gully (Aonach Dubh) | Cirrus (Beinn an Dothaidh) | |
| Green Gully (Ben Nevis) | | |
| Slanting Gully (Lliwedd) | | |
| Devil's Staircase (Clogwyn y Geifr) | | |
| Inaccessible Gully (Dove Crag) | Crab Crawl (Creag Meagaidh) | |
| Look C Gully (Glen Clova) | Observatory Ridge (Ben Nevis); | |
| South Gully (Clogwn y Geifr) | North-East Buttress (Ben Nevis) | |
| Comb Gully (Ben Nevis) | Deep-Cut Chimney (Hells Lum Crag) | |
| Emerald Gully (Beinn Dearg) | | |
| Moss Ghyll (Scafell) | | |
| Snowdrop (Snowdon) | Tough-Brown Traverse (Lochnagar) | |
| Clogwyn Du Gully, Left-Hand | Skye Ridge – technicalities only | The Grey Mare's Tail (S. Uplands) |
| Dove Crag Gully (Grasmoor) | Phoenix Buttress (Braeriach) | |
| Deep-Cut Chimney (Stob Coire nam Beith) | | |
| Crowberry Gully (Buachaille Etive Mor) | Central Crack Route (Northern Corries) | |
| Great Gully (Craig yr Ysfa) | East Face Route (Fannichs) | |
| Glover's Chimney (Ben Nevis) | | |
| S.C. Gully (Stob Coire nan Lochan) | | |
| Raven Crag Gully (Borrowdale) | | |
| Central Gully L.H. (Great End) | Prune Buttress (Fannichs) | |
| Chock Gully (Helvellyn) | | |
| Staghorn Gully (Creag Meagaidh) | Tower Ridge (Ben Nevis) | |
| The Vent (Northern Corries) | | |
| Red Gully (Northern Corries) | | |
| Central Gully L.H. (Great End) | | |
| Twisting Gully (Stob Coire nan Lochan) | | |
| Right-Hand Trinity (Snowdon) | | |
| Raeburn's Gully (Lochnagar) | | |
| South East Gully (Great End) | | |
| Central Gully (Glyder Fawr) | | |

# 1 Emerald Gully

by Paul Nunn

**Route** Emerald Gully, Grade 4, 700ft.
**Cliff** The Glensguaib cliffs on the West Face of Beinn Dearg.
**First Ascent** Winter: P. Nunn, A. Riley, B. Fuller, April 1970.
**Map** O.S. 1:50,000 Sheet 20 (248820).
**Guidebooks** S.M.C. *Northern Highlands Area, Vol. 1.* by I. G. Rowe: *Scottish Winter Climbs* by Hamish MacInnes (Constable).
**Nearest Road / Approach Time** A forestry road at Glensguaib (205852) reached from the A835 Garve – Ullapool road from near the head of Loch Broom. Follow good footpath up Gleann na Sguaib. 3½ miles/1,800ft. Allow 2 hours.
**Route Summary / Conditions** Comes into condition quite quickly and usually provides two major ice pitches and sections of steep snow.
**Campsites and Bunkhouses** Accommodation at Ullapool and Inverlael.

*Far right: Emerald Gully. Photo: Tony Riley*

*Near right: The 1,000ft. cliffs of Beinn Dearg's northern flank dominate the upper end of Glensguaib. Emerald Gully is the obvious fold on the extreme right. Most of the other gully lines have also been climbed. Penguin Gully – a fine Grade 3 – takes the extreme left edge of the cliff in this view. Photo: John Cleare*

'Bad weather, bad conditions and aberrations from the right way will provide a guideless party with as many exciting and trying situations as they ought to wish for.'

*R. L. G. Irving,
Alpine Club Address, 1908*

With a big grin Tom [Patey] had promised 'An easy couloir, grand in scale, ignored only because of its remote situation; no-one ever climbs in winter that far north in Scotland.' After an hour's moor-bashing the first névé came into sight. It was perfect for a fast solo front-point to an impasse. Black in the shadows of Quinag's Barrel Buttress, a bergschrund loomed, separating the névé and ourselves from the rock of an unwanted barrier in the gully bed. It was of daunting height and steepness and it looked near-impossible. We all milled about the edge of the black hole. Tom even prodded his axe across at the sandstone doubtfully, but without the benefit of a rope and daylight it looked like a defeat. Even Tom's inexhaustible optimism was dented. It was 1 a.m. and the pit by our feet seemed bottomless in the moonshadow. Tom suggested that a human pyramid might do it; some of us worried about how the tail of the party would make the crossing. Eventually we demurred, unanimously.

At least the long slog back remained moonlit. Quinag sank back into a hump behind, quartz pavements speeded progress, and as usual Tom scurried ahead, ever-anxious to be first to the road. Eventually four oversized men crammed into a battered Skoda, the hero of Tom's extensive medical practice. The car rattled off south on endless single-track roads towards Ullapool. Too near dawn we three bunked down in Tom's garden shed.

That shed was a legend. It was fitted with bunks and cooking space and was used to seduce southern sceptics to the North. Climbers of all descriptions could find a welcome there, a few yards from the sea. Always Tom entertained, for he hated dead time. Most of all he advertised the merits of the northern winter and summer. He had done dozens of climbs alone or with visiting friends. In the shed a campaign map showed the whole of the North, star-rated for quality. It will keep people happy for generations. Over late-night drams the Doctor talked of objectives and prodded us towards those unfitted to his designs. Ideas and suggestions ranged the whole regions with occasional excursions to the Alps and Himalayas and every manner of wild anecdote. Unfortunately we had not quite the numbers or the voice to sing

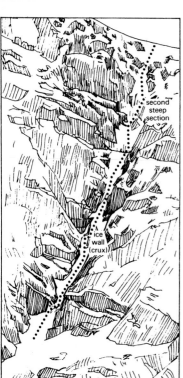

with Tom's squeezebox.

The next morning was dark and we woke late. Tom was off on his rounds. We were armed with verbal details which got us in an hour or so to the base of the cliffs. Spring blizzards blew thick cloud in from the west. Most of the Inverlael Gullies had been climbed by Tom on lone afternoon jaunts. There was little to be seen through the cloud, though we knew that the big mixed face of Beinn Dearg lay to the east. The route to do was unmistakeable, an ice-tube dropping out of the murk with at least two biggish pitches and quite a lot of easier ground. It was already 2 p.m.

Snow fell steadily on the plod into the gully. I set off up the first ice-tube, which was not as difficult as it had looked. The snow-ice was good and easily hewed into fine pigeon-hole steps and mitten-holds. Occasionally a draught of spindrift cooled our work. Like Green Gully I thought, as time passed and progress continued in slow but steady arm-aching effort. A rock-piton on the left improved the view until at last the angle eased back into a gully of fine solid snow. It took the rest of the rope to climb up it to a belay below a beard of icicles, dangling across a steeper part above.

Brian Fuller followed easily and quickly up the step-ladder. After a momentary halt to hand over

Tony Riley's rope, he hacked away upwards towards the icicles while I anchored them both – one above, the other below. By the time Tony came into sight Brian was just a pair of crampon heels high on the right wall. Watching was anxious work as time evaporated and darkness crept in. It would be a long, long fall if he slipped, 50ft. away without protection. But he kept moving up and we were comforted by the knowledge that he rarely parted company with the rock. On a trying bit he swung and poked with the pick for a few moments to no avail. Then his pick found a firm sod – a pull, a scrape, a flash of Fuller's famous fangs, and he disappeared into the grey-black mystery above. Two ropes trailed up behind, one attached to each of our waists. He was our anchor.

When all the rope had gone Tony and I shouted

but there was no reply, so we followed in close file. It was a groping, awkward process in the conditions, especially at the bulge, and we were worried about dislodging one another. Torches stayed off most of the time, in anticipation of terrible times ahead. After the wall a traverse left led back to steep snow and a characteristic long flog for the top. Crampon-bashing up névé completed the trip to the plateau, where the wind howled.

Then the anxious question was, which way from here? To the east the crossing to Beinn Dearg looked too long. Nor did the Pass of the Fools, a feature on that route, sound encouraging. So it was west, aiming for the sea, playing our last card. At least it led homewards. The leader poked along, too near the cornice, peering out and down into mists below with the thin torch beam.

There are gambles and gambles. This one paid off and we were saved a wander by torchlight around the wildernesses to the south. We picked a way round the long Glensguaib escarpment until open slopes led down to the deep heather. Torches flickered and faded for the last leg, then there were a few footprints beyond a stream. We were back on course. One near-extinct torch led on down, looking for the old red van. It eventually found a matching tiny light, the living red end of a cigarette, last of several that night. Tom was somewhere behind, lolling on the Skoda:

'You're a wee bit late. It is gone one and the blizzards are closing the Braemore road. We'd best be off.'

*Left: The initial ice pitch of Emerald Gully during the first ascent. Climber: Paul Nunn / Photo: Tony Riley*

*Above: The direct pitch at the start of Penguin Gully – an entertaining excursion over ice bulges that often banks out in heavy snow. The gully above is rather easier. Climber: Dick Renshaw / Photo: Greg Strange*

# 2 The Corries of the Fannichs

by John Mackenzie

Most climbers have heard of the Fannichs, few know where they are. Find Ross-shire on the map, and then bisect the county between the A832 and A835. Apart from Fionn Bheinn they lie north of Loch Fannich and resemble scaled-down Cairngorms. For winter climbing they have several advantages; they are centrally placed and high, the main corries facing east and north-east, so conditions can be relied on to a greater extent than in more westerly mountains. And further, they are serviced by two main roads, providing easy access.

You are in splendid hill-country, with considerable untapped potential. For climbers, the main interest is centred on the three main corries. Historically, the corrie of Sgurr nan Clach Geala was first attacked. Its cliff has the finest architecture, giving lines of 800ft. and, unlike those in the other two corries, it has deeply-etched gullies. The approach can be problematic, and is worth studying on the map. If a key can be obtained from the first house west of the Grudie track, and if the track is not impassable, a car can be driven past Fannich dam and on to the lodge. A couple of hours' walk up the Allt a' Choire Mhoir leads to the cliffs. Alternatively the longer northern approach starts at Loch Droma, follows the hydro road and after a few permutations leads to Loch a' Mhadaidh. It then crosses the col between Sgurr Mor and Carn na Criche to reach the cliffs.

Here are the finest gully climbs in the traditional mould, of which the best is Gamma Gully. Concentrated difficulties in the first half include narrow chimneys, and a very steep crux above, which is sometimes vertical. On the first ascent, two days were taken due to the obvious technical problems of cutting steps in such steep material. However, front-pointing has altered that and it should now give a good Grade 4.

The schistose rocks have not only weathered into gullies, but into equally fine ribs between. Buttresses 3, 4 and 5 give magnificent climbs, of which Number 4 (Skyscraper Buttress) is an 800ft. Grade 5, whilst Number 3 and Number 5 (Sellars' Buttress) have marginally shorter Grade 4 climbs. Given the daylight and conditions, they are very rewarding; Clach Geala has the greatest concentration of classics in the Fannichs.

Garbh Choire Mor of An Coileachan has a lower altitude but easy access. Using the Grudie track, cars can be left half a mile before the dam, and the corrie reached in 40 minutes. Perfectly curved, this

natural bowl has steep, slabby crags reaching 700ft., with higher walls either side. Ice-climbing here is in the modern idiom and often thin. In summer I remember walking in with Duncan McCallum and falling silent at the prospect of holdless overhung slabs, festooned with dripping black moss. In winter all is different and sheets of ice drape the back walls, which are punctuated by four corner gullies. The monumental left wall has two thin icefalls which, perhaps fortunately, have never reached the bottom. These are bordered by a short gully. Apart from the easy but popular Central Gully the most obvious line in the corrie is the scimitar-like corner on the right.

Until its recent ascent, Plumline drew several suitors, but all failed due to thin ice. Do not be put off, however. If the conditions seem right, the ice-curtain at the cave may be thick enough to climb. It has some excellent positions, with good rock-belays. The one drawback is the easier ground above the crux, but it is still long and satisfying. Perhaps a better and more sustained climb takes the central line on the slabs to Plumline's left. Echo Face boasts no worthwhile rock-belays and ice-pitons must be relied on. It is very deceptive; do not be fooled by the easier-angled slabs between the icefalls as they are most likely to be powder resting on a skin of ice. Though the would-be second ascent failed because of this, it is still the best line here, and comes into condition early in the season. It requires good route-finding and a light tread, and has a fascinating echo which makes conversations quadrophonic.

The central icefalls, when formed, are both excellent. Crystal Tripper at Grade 4/5 takes the left fall, and Ravenshead, at Grade 5, the right. Both are sustained, with scanty protection and lots of exposure, giving a contrast to the confines of the Clach Geala gullies. Care must be taken, as huge slab-avalanches occur in the corrie. We have seen a section stretching half-way up Echo Face leave debris yards deep. Cold weather with little thaw sets up soft slab and January can be a bad month here as elsewhere. If in doubt do Sage's Corner, half-way up Central Gully or, better, Prune Buttress, at Grade 3, which bounds the gully edge and gives similar climbing to North Buttress on the Buachaille.

The next corrie has the biggest route, which, due to its aspect and altitude, is more often in condition than others in the Fannichs. Sgurr Mor, at 3,637ft,

**Route** Gamma Gully, Grade 4, 700ft.
**Cliff** East Face of Sgurr nan Clach Geala.
**First Ascent** Winter: P. N. L. Tranter, I. G. Rowe, March 1965.
**Map** O.S. 1:50,000 Sheet 20 (184715).
**Nearest Road / Approach Time** The A835 Garve – Ullapool road at 235759. Follow a path up the Allt á Mhadaidh. 6 miles/2,000ft. Allow 4 hours. Also from Fannich Lodge (219660). 5 miles/1,700ft. Allow 2½ hours.
**Route Summary / Conditions** Sustained technical interest in the first half with a vertical ice pitch (crux).

**Route** The Resurrection, Grade 5, 1,500ft.
**Cliff** East Face of Sgurr Mor.
**First Ascent** Winter: J. Mackenzie, D. Butterfield, March 1980.
**Map** O.S. 1:50,000 Sheet 20 (203718).
**Nearest Road / Approach Time** As above, from the A835. 5 miles/1,800ft. Allow 3 hours.
**Route Summary / Conditions** Very serious because of insecure belays, high level of commitment and avalanche danger.

**Routes** Echo Face, Grade 3/4, 1,200ft., Plumline, Grade 3/4, 1,200ft.
**Cliff** The cliffs of Garbh Choire Mor.
**First Ascent** Winter: Echo Face – J. Mackenzie, D. McCullum, January 1978, Plumline – R. Brown, J. Mackenzie, January 1978.
**Map** O.S. 1:50,000 Sheet 20 (203718).
**Nearest Road / Approach Time** The Grudie to Fannich Lodge road at 260665. 1½ miles/1,500ft. Allow 1½ hours.
**Route Summary / Conditions** Echo Face is poorly protected. Plumline has a steep, icy cave pitch. Both climbs are prone to avalanche.

**Guidebooks** No complete coverage – routes recorded variously in S.M.C. *Northern Highlands Area, Vol. 1* by I. G. Rowe; *Scottish Winter Climbs* by Hamish MacInnes (Constable); S.M.C. Journals 1979 and 1980.

*Left: The cliffs of Sgurr nan Clach Geala. Photo: Tony Riley*

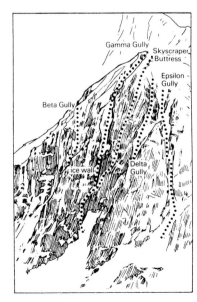

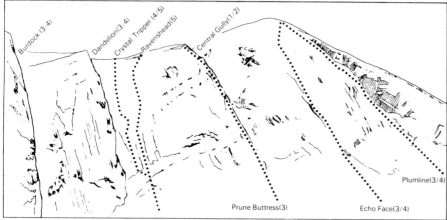

*Above: The snow-rimed, slabby cliffs of the Garbh Choire Mor of An Coileachan. Photomontage: John Mackenzie*

is the highest and most pointed peak in the range. Its north-east face should be approached shyly to savour its truly Alpine appearance. Pick a cold, sunny day, scout round the south-east shores of Loch a' Mhadaidh, and climb the slopes to traverse below the cliffs. Triangular in aspect and hemmed by a lower south wall, they sport three lines. Easter Gully on the left is long and Grade 2, with a vast cornice, sometimes inescapable. On the right, East Face Route follows a runnel cutting up for 1,000ft., giving a Grade 3. The first of several ice pitches

being the crux. In the centre is a complicated mass of lower icefalls with a concave face above. There are two snowfields, of which the lower is larger and less steep than the upper, and separated from it by a central icefall. The upper field abuts a vertical summit wall which in turn is overhung by massive cornices.

To Dave Butterfield and myself, considering the line for the first time, no obvious escape at the top was visible from below! In the sun the whole face shone with a glittering magnificence. We started up the narrow gully-cum-groove left of the icefalls and gained them via a diminishing ledge on the right. The line traversed across bulges to reach a block belay, then followed the icefall up left for a full rope's length to a fixed piton. The piton has a history. It had been generously donated to me by Clive Rowland a long time before, on the condition that it would be left *in situ*. Naturally it was still in use many climbs later, but now, on the very last blow, the head of my Terrordactyl flew off. In situ the peg would remain, but it was not the best of places to lose an axe.

Halfway up the first névé field we heard a mournful dirge. Bill Bridges, a climbing friend, was watching us from below. Up floated his moral

22

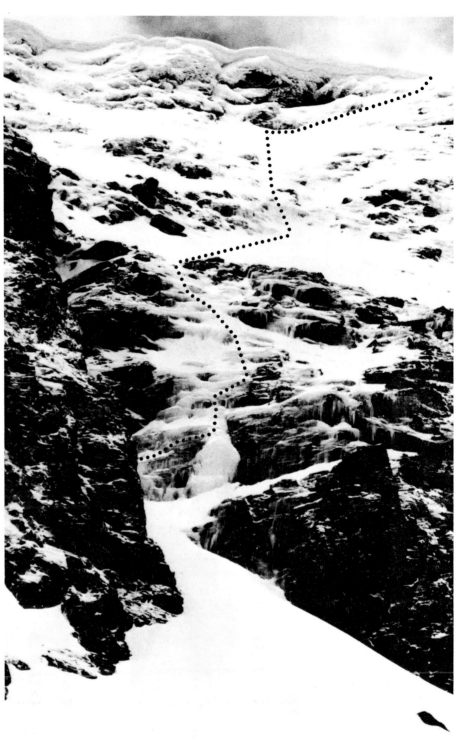

support in broad Glaswegian: 'You're gonnae DIE', and 'You're DOOMED', followed by 'Repeat after me: Our Father which art in Heaven . . .' With a broken axe and a doubtful exit we thought this in very poor taste. I think the tirade finished with the 23rd Psalm being gleefully screamed up at us.

The exposure gradually unleashed itself as the ground became steeper towards the icefall and snow-belays gave more cause for anxiety. The icefall led to a steep scoop and the upper névé, where below the headwall a splendid icicle-fringed cave is to be found. We threw ourselves inside to escape the drop below. The contrast was a tonic. In trouble, it would be the ideal bivouac spot, the only secure haven on the climb. A traverse now led out right on steep ground to another snow belay, past a thin rib; fall here and you won't die alone! Still the outcome was uncertain. We doubted if the headwall would ever end, but it did, and the next pitch was up a short snow ramp to a final belay on the summit cairn itself.

The Resurrection is good, more Alpine than Scottish, though its technical difficulties we considered no more than Grade 4. But the 'high grip' factor and paucity of solid belays increased the seriousness to a point where the merely physical problems of upward progress were effectively dominated by all the other problems. Watch out for three things: soft slab on the snowfields, icicle bombardment lower down (start early), and then those brooding cornices. To be on the lower snowfield and watch them peel off hundreds of feet above, and to realise what's below gives a high insecurity rating to this climb. Do it in good conditions and you'll have no real problems; try it in bad, and your world might come tumbling down.

*Above: The line of The Resurrection (Grade 5) on the 1,000ft. East Face of Sgurr Mor – this climb has many alpine characteristics, including a band of huge cornices above a vertical headwall spanning most of the top of the face. The steep snowfields are prone to avalanche in certain conditions, as they lie on rock slabs and steep grass slopes.*
*Photo: John Mackenzie*

# 3  Beinn Eighe's Central Buttress

by Alan Rouse

**Route** Central Buttress Direct, Grade 5, 1,000ft.
**Cliff** Triple Buttress, Coire Mhic Fhearchair, Beinn Eighe.
**First Ascent** Summer: 1922; Winter: A. MacIntyre, A. Rouse, February 1978 (this was probably the first direct ascent in winter, though there had been a number of earlier, indirect ascents including one in 1971 by K. Spence, J. Ronayne, and K. Urquhart).
**Map** O.S. 1:25,000 Sheet *The Cuillin and Torridon Hills* (945601).
**Guidebooks** S.M.C. *Northern Highlands Area, Vol. 2.* by D. G. and R. W. L. Turnbull; *Scottish Winter Climbs* by Hamish MacInnes (Constable).
**Nearest Road / Approach Time** A car park (960569) on the B858 Kinlochewe – Torridon road. 6 miles/1,600ft. Allow 3 hours.
**Route Summary / Conditions** Essentially an iced-up rock climb, with bulges, ramps, walls and chimneys – will probably be thinly verglassed on the steeper sections.
**Campsites and Bunkhouses** Campsite by stream and ruined buildings (960569), Ling Hut in Glen Torridon (S.M.C.).
**Bibliography** *Arctic Island Climbs* by Alan Rouse (Crags, 23).

North-West Scotland has for me always been the most beautiful part of the British Isles. The harsh grandeur of the rocky hillsides contrasts sharply with the narrow bands of luxuriant vegetation hugging the banks of the many sea-lochs. There is a feeling of permanence and great age about the landscape. For once man has made little impression.

The relatively low altitude of the mountains and their proximity to the sea ensure that good climbing conditions come and go quickly. After making an ascent of Route Two on Ben Nevis with Mike Geddes, it was obvious that Torridon might also have good conditions. The weather was perfect as Tim Lewis drove Alex MacIntyre and myself over from Fort William to Loch Torridon. Next morning Alex discovered that he had left his crampons in Tim's car so we set off for a walk to look at Coire Mhic Fhearchair, on the north side of Beinn Eighe. It was the first time I had seén the Coire, and it amply fulfilled the expectations which had been aroused in me. The three buttresses presented a harmonious and balanced architecture above the frozen lochan. It was certainly one of the most timeless and perfect scenes I had ever viewed. Conditions looked good and we soloed up an easy gully on the right of the main face. That night Tim arrived with the missing crampons and well before dawn the following morning we drove up Glen Torridon and set off on the long walk back to the Coire. The cliff is divided into three prominent buttresses, each about 1,000ft. high. The central buttress appeared to offer the best climbing and the most continuous line.

The climb is in three distinct sections: the first tier of old red sandstone; a steep, short wall of quartzite; and a final buttress of slightly darker quartzite. There was an obvious ramp on the lower buttress, cutting through the steepest and cleanest area of rock. We scrambled up to the foot of it. Alex led off, making good use of Terrordactyls firmly planted in the half-frozen turf. The second pitch began with a small overhang. I took my gloves off and swung about on large flat holds for a minute or two, before making a satisfying lurch over the steep section. Easier climbing led to a broad terrace. The climbing so far had been similar to Welsh winter climbing, but the next pitch was rather like the Alps in winter. The rock was completely clean, although snow was lying on all the ledges and in the cracks. Alex led up, finding

good runners and adequate handholds. I followed with pleasure, enjoying the exposure and relishing the positive moves.

An easy section led to the final steepening. Conditions here were quite different from anything below; hard snow and streaks of ice promised conditions akin to Ben Nevis. I led off on improbable terrain, and was soon standing precariously on top of a rock-spike, clinging by a sidepull to the overhanging wall above. Round the corner to the left was a groove full of loose snow. After much deliberation I performed a disturbingly thin layback-type move and managed to place an axe round the corner. My feet followed reluctantly and finding rock under the snow I moved up quickly to better ice. I drove in a peg runner and went quickly up a series of grooves, using intermittent streaks of ice.

The next pitch was unusual – a narrow chimney coated with verglas and slightly overhanging for the first 15ft. We both tried but the chimney was too narrow to squeeze through and it was almost impossible to get any purchase on the verglas because there was no room to kick at the ice, so that crampons just scarted about, and the ice was too thin for the axe. Eventually, after nearly an hour, I managed to jam my axe between the pick and the adze and lean right out of the chimney. I then shuffled nervously around the main constriction hoping that the axe would hold. By moving on that same axe until it was well below my waist I succeeded in getting firmly lodged above the narrowing, after which a strenuous struggle brought me gasping to a good ledge.

Alex led through in gathering gloom up a steep wall to reach a hanging groove which demanded a couple of points of aid and some determined climbing. We hoped we were nearing the top, although more mountain could still be discerned above by the light of our head-torches. I set off, expecting an easy ride to the top and hoping to use rather more standard techniques than those I had been forced to employ earlier. Soon, losing sight of Alex, I became absorbed by the uniquely Scottish atmosphere of the final pitch before the summit plateau. In traditional fashion a wind got up and whipped the snow around, reducing my world to the few feet in front of my face. I reached a final vertical corner about 12ft. below the top. The crack in the corner was hopelessly iced and offered no protection. I

looked down along the rope, which disappeared into the gloom and snow, uninterrupted by a single runner. I tried bridging, but the right wall was slightly undercut with nothing for the feet. Again I searched for a runner, again in vain. At last, in near desperation, I lay across the corner and with feet on the left wall and hands on the right I made sufficient progress to achieve a rather more orthodox bridge. The climbing ended suddenly on perfectly flat terrain where a strong moon illuminated our mountain, and we sat for a while before a bitter wind sent us scurrying to the valley.

*Above: The Triple Buttress of Coire Mhic Fhearchair on Beinn Eighe. Photo: Hamish MacInnes*

SCOTLAND    Beinn Bhan, Applecross, Northern Highlands

# 4  Mad Hatter's and March Hare's Gullies

by Stuart Smith

**Route** Mad Hatter's Gully, Grade 4/5, 1,000ft.
March Hare's Gully, Grade 4, 1,000ft.
**Cliff** The cliffs of Coire na Poite, Beinn Bhan,
Applecross.
**First Ascents** Winter: Mad Hatter's Gully –
M. Freeman, G. Stephen, February 1976;
March Hare's Gully – C. J. S. Bonington,
T. W. Patey, March 1969.
**Map** O.S. 1:50,000 Sheet 24 (810449).
**Guidebooks** SMC *Northern Highlands Area,
Vol. 2,* by D. G. and R. W. L. Turnbull, *Scottish
Winter Climbs* by Hamish MacInnes
(Constable). S.M.C.J. 1980 has route-
descriptions of recent climbs.

A story came down from the frozen north of
climbing on Beinn Bhan, of ice-encrusted cliffs, of
classic gullies and of fine days. This we remembered as, in silent darkness, Ed Jackson and I
approached Coire na Poite, along the track,
through the heather and up towards the snow. As
daylight tip-toed round the hill great glistening
drools of ice came into sight on the sandstone back
wall. But our objective was the dark cleft of Mad
Hatter's Gully, lurking in the deepest corner.

The name of the gully, the early morning cold,

the usual nagging doubts about confidence, and the
aura created by Patey, who enthused in the SMC
Journal with extravagant claims about this area,
combined to evoke the tingling anticipation which
is the very essence of winter climbing. The
guidebook too enriched the atmosphere: 'Mad
Hatter's Gully—a wide, deep snow-channel
interrupted by a giant ice-pitch halfway up. It
remains unclimbed.' We knew that it had in fact
been climbed but with that background how could a
first-time visitor aim for anything else?

*Above: The corries of Beinn Bhan: (left to right) Coir 'Each, Coire nan Feola, Coire na Poite, and Coire nan Fhamhair. Photo: Hamish MacInnes*

Above the frozen lochan, we were drawn inwards from the open corrie to the gloomy cleft. The walls reared up, sealing off the outside world, while the floor of the gorge rose gradually to be blocked by the object of our ambitions.

With Ed safely belayed, I took the sharp end of the rope up the first broad ice-grooves. Confidence increased with height, a runner adding security, and I reached the haven of an overhang bristling with giant icicles. Ed climbed up and, re-united at the stance, we worked out the traverses used by the first ascensionists to overcome the obstacles above. But Ed delights 'n the obvious rather than the elegant, so with a wicked grin and vigorous waving gestures he pronounced, 'Straight up!'

Wild bridging up and out between icicles, frantic hooking, and 30ft. or so of effort found the bold leader hanging in his harness from a Terrordactyl wedged into a pocket. His balaclava was ripped back over his helmet, confirming the obvious; it was hard. I murmured encouragements. Ed, however, was more concerned about the state of his

**Nearest Road / Approach Time** At Tornapress (834423) ½ mile from the A896 Shieldaig – Loch Carron road. 3½ miles/ 1,700ft. Allow 2½ hours.
**Route Summary / Conditions** Mad Hatter's Gully – a wide couloir blocked by a big ice pitch, only in condition after a long cold spell. March Hare's Gully – a sustained snow and ice climb.
**Campsites and Bunkhouses** Camping at Tornapress (834423).

Left: The main pitch of Mad Hatter's Gully – a 150ft. water-ice cascade. Climber: Dave Jenkins / Photo: Peter Macdonald

Above: The cliffs of Coire na Poite. The main cliff with its major face routes is on the right. Photo: Hamish MacInnes

axe. His 'improvements' were proving to be less than satisfactory because, while the heat-treatment had undoubtedly helped in changing the angle of the pick, it was also probably responsible for its crazy bending. Swinging from a drive-in ice piton, he began hammering the pick back into shape.

Some time later, happy with his axe once again, he set off. Left a little to an icicle, right a little to a foothold, another piton, another rest. On again, up and round, to disappear above. Following the ropes was hard and I was glad of their presence. But what were they tied to? Was the security just an illusion? Best not to think of such things and just

concentrate on the climbing. Eventually the pitch was climbed and the difficulties eased; ice slopes gave out to snow, climbing gave way to walking. On the summit we relaxed in the sun, content, gazed over the water to Raasay and the Cuillins of Skye, and round the vast panorama of the seldom-visited hills of the North West.

The next dawn found us back in the corrie heading for March Hare's Gully, one of the finest Grade 4s in Scotland. Imagine two Green Gullies strung together, take away the crowds, add a certain touch of magic, and that is March Hare's Gully. A 1,000ft. ribbon of beautiful snow-ice falling in a series of steps in a shallow gully. Nowhere too difficult and each step forming a good pitch with an easier slope to belay in between. We moved together towards the top; care was needed

as fatigue set in, but progress was still smooth and steady. It was a fitting contrast to the antics of the previous day. But both routes gave us solitude and superb climbing in perfect surroundings. We went away well-satisfied.

### RECENT DEVELOPMENTS by Andrew Nisbet

Despite earlier reports of massive potential in the corries of Beinn Bhan, development has been slow, as it has with the other great winter cliffs of the North-West. Its vital statistics – four great corries and two miles of uninterrupted cliff up to 1,000ft. high – should have attracted a blitz of activity. It's never happened. Unreliable conditions can't be the answer; these recessed, east-facing corries may be near the coast, but they come into condition quickly and ice abounds. Perhaps the reason is the

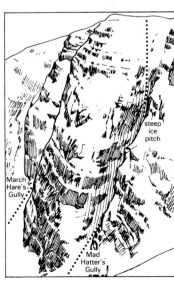

Top right: March Hare's Gully, flanked on the left by Alice's Buttress and on the right by an unclimbed face. Photo: Pete Macdonald

Lower right: The 1,400ft. back wall of Coire na Poite, to the right of Mad Hatter's Gully. A number of climbs have been made here, using the obvious areas of ice e.g. Silver Tear (left) and Wall of the Early Morning Light (centre). Photo: Colin Stead

air of secrecy that has persisted, and the all-too-familiar rumour that MacInnes (or Patey, or anyone else) did a route here and didn't record it.

The main limitation would seem to be the nature of the rock itself. Torridonian sandstone has its own distinctive terrace formation, well designed to disrupt upward progress and turn the natural climbing line into a tortuous series of interconnecting snow ledges. Of course, the gullies are exempt from this criticism but they were the first routes climbed. It's not that the routes lack quality, unlikely on such huge, steep, icy cliffs – just that the potential is much more limited than might be expected.

The back wall of Coire na Poite (right of Mad Hatter's Gully) is the perfect example. It holds the largest area of ice in Scotland, an inspiring 500ft. wide, and high, blanketing out the bottom third of the cliff, superb climbing without doubt. At least four routes have been recorded here, but there seems little point in differentiating between them. You simply climb the face, direct at Grade 5, indirect at Grade 4.

On the left side of Coire na Poite, high on the north face of A'Chioch, is the worthwhile Dormouse Chimney (Grade 4, 1980), a prominent and intimidatingly steep icefall. Alice's Buttress (Grade 3/4, 1978) is the fine looking bastion to the left of March Hare's Gully, but the intimidating wall to the right of the gully is still unclimbed.

The most notable new route on Beinn Bhan is Der Riesenwand (Grade 5, 1980), the first and only penetration, summer or winter, of the colossal, evil face of Coire nan Fhamhair. Like all the face routes hereabouts it suffers from an absence of obvious line. It is not technically extreme, but surely nothing can surpass it for breathtaking exposure. As you hand-traverse on axes past the last bulge, dangling over the abyss, try spitting and watch it fall free, for 800ft. to the base of the cliff. All this on limited protection, suspect belays, and a bivouac on the first and only ascent, make this a route not to be undertaken lightly, or ever forgotten.

Left: The crucial traverse on Der Riesenwand (The Giant's Wall) of Coire nan Fhamhair. Here the use of Terrordactyls in frozen turf allowed sensationally exposed climbing across the cliff linking snow terraces. Poor belays and poor runners gave the pitch an extra degree of excitement. Climber: Brian Sprunt / Photo: Andrew Nisbet

Near right: The snow terrace used for the bivouac on Der Riesenwand. Climber: Brian Sprunt / Photo: Andrew Nisbet.

# 5  The Cuillin Ridge

by Geoff Cohen

**Route** The Cuillin Ridge, Grade 3/4, 14 miles/ 10,000ft. of ascent.
**Location** The Black Cuillin, Isle of Skye.
**First Ascent** Summer: 1911; Winter: T. W. Patey, B. Robertson, H. MacInnes and D. Crabb, February, 1965.
**Map** O.S. 1:25,000 Sheet *The Cuillin and Torridon Hills.*
**Guidebooks** S.M.T. District Guide *The Island of Skye* by Malcolm Slesser; *Scottish Winter Climbs* by Hamish MacInnes (Constable).
**Nearest Road / Approach Time** A863 at Sligachan and minor road at Glen Brittle. North to South: Allow 3 hours (3 miles/3,000ft.) to reach the summit of Sgurr nan Gillean.
**Route Summary / Conditions** A long and demanding expedition, with no excessive technical difficulties but requiring sustained concentration. The route involves long sections of exposed ridge-climbing with a number of abseils. Some sections of the ridge are difficult to quit in the event of bad weather. The route is rarely in condition and requires a long cold spell after heavy snow fall. Allow at least two days for the expedition in clear and calm conditions which are probably essential for success.
**Bibliography** *The Cuillin of Skye* by Ben Humble (Robert Hale); *One Man's Mountains* by Tom Patey (Gollancz) has a classic account of the first ascent; *The Winter Traverse of the Cuillin of Skye* by John P. Beatty (Mountain 65).

*Right: Sgurr nan Gillean's West Ridge at sunset – a view from Am Basteir. Photo: Dave Broadhead*

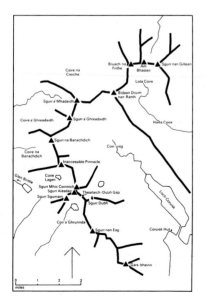

In the very first volume of the SMC Journal in 1891, W. W. Naismith wrote of the Cuillin that 'It is doubtful whether much snow is ever likely to be found on them.' And in the latest edition of the District Guide to Skye, we are told that 'The frustrating thing about Skye weather is the rapid change in temperature in winter. To find winter climbing one must almost live on the spot, or keep trying in the hope of eventual luck.' Even Tom Patey, who was on the spot, relatively speaking, (in Ullapool) only made the first winter traverse of the ridge at his third attempt, after three years of waiting. So who were we to expect good conditions on our first-ever winter visit to Skye?

It was in this frame of mind, notwithstanding the good forecasts, that Gordon Macnair and I set out from Edinburgh one Thursday evening in February 1978. Two weeks before a huge blizzard in Scotland had enveloped a train and left some ten feet of snow in parts of the North East. That same day, while wandering over a very wild Cheviot, Gordon had been persuaded to join a long-standing arrangement that I had made with Dave Broadhead for a half-term trip to Skye. We had booked the BMC Hut for three nights and looked forward to good sport, though we had hardly dared to hope that the ridge would be in condition.

We arrived at Sligachan about 9 a.m., quite unable to believe our luck. Sgurr nan Gillean looked like some peak out of a fairy story, draped in glistening white, while the sun shone from a cloudless sky. But getting ready was no small matter; the agonising decisions on how many pegs to take, which sweaters and so on. Food was remarkably light, thanks to Dave's thoughtful and thrifty commissariat over which he retained sole charge. In case someone began to wonder about the van during our absence we left a note at the Hotel, and at noon we set off.

We got onto snow at about 2,000ft., but only when we reached the col on the South East Ridge of Sgurr nan Gillean did we really appreciate what we were in for. The view of the ridge was breathtaking, impossible to describe save by likening it to the perfection of dreams. But it was also daunting, and it looked an awfully long way. We were still unsure just what the conditions would be like and moved gingerly up through deep snow towards the summit of Sgurr nan Gillean. There we stopped for a bite at 3 p.m. then began the descent of the West Ridge. I rapidly called for a rope, having perhaps missed the

best way, as I found myself front-pointing down steep but excellent snow on the Lota Corrie side. Very soon we were able to move together till we reached the crenellated lower part of the ridge. Here, by an abseil down a chimney, we evaded the famous gendarme and were thence able to dispense with the rope.

The next big obstacle was the descent of the Bhasteir Tooth. Engraved on my mind was Patey's graphic account of the 'Affaire Tiso', in which Graham Tiso had hung suspended upside down by one foot after abseiling off the Tooth. The memory of my own previous visit, on which I had had to solo up Naismith's Route on the Tooth in order to retrieve a jammed abseil rope, added its mite of trepidation too. Our first abseil now, off Am Basteir, was easy enough and then we gingerly traversed round over slabs to the top of the Tooth, where a very exposed ledge gives access to a peg belay at the top of Naismith's route. It was impossible to see whether the ropes reached, and I had to do a series of strenuous crab-like movements on the abseil rope until I was just able to reach *terra firma*. By the time all three of us were down it was well after 6 p.m. and the stars were out. As Dave and I cramponed round to the Bealach nan Lice the wide gully below the Tooth had the huge echoing quality of high mountains at night. Here Gordon, who had gone on ahead, was ensconced between the icy walls of two large boulders. At the time it seemed the perfect sheltered bivouac site, though on subsequent summer visits it has hardly looked so welcoming as it did then. We snuggled down, all three, in Gordon's two-man bivvy sack, but while the others cooked I, for some reason, was dispatched to the airless nether regions of the sack, where the vista of the infinite recesses of space was exchanged for a face-full of clammy wet nylon.

Saturday dawned fine. Once under way we quickly regained the rhythm we had begun to experience the day before. I felt a deep exultation, a sense of lightness and freedom, a blissful movement in space that I wanted never to end. I thought that for the first time I understood what people meant when they spoke of 'walking on air' or 'between heaven and earth'. The névé was frequently perfect and where the sun shone on the rocks and ice it was a pleasure even to look for suitable difficulties, as one might in Summer. The ascent up to Bidean Druim nan Ramh gave steep and exciting climbing leading us finally, in the

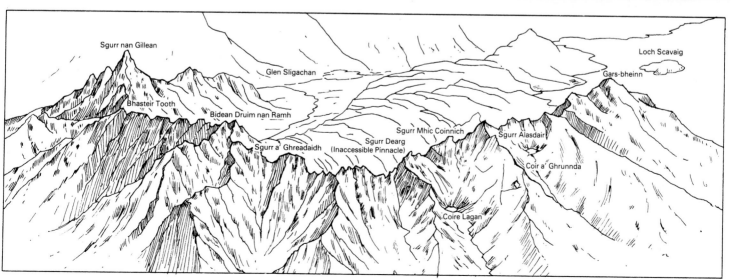

Sgurr nan Gillean

Glen Sligachan

Loch Scavaig

Bhasteir Tooth

Gars-bheinn

Bidean Druim nan Ramh

Sgurr Mhic Coinnich

Sgurr Alasdair

Sgurr a' Ghreadaidh

Sgurr Dearg
(Inaccessible Pinnacle)

Coir a' Ghrunnda

Coire Lagan

shade, up heavy accumulations of fresh snow to a point a little way along the Druim nan Ramh from the centre peak. The descent too looked imposing, but only required a single abseil. Again the peaks of Sgurr a' Mhadaidh entertained us all the way, with climbing of about Grade 3 and a couple of abseils. Moving off from Mhadaidh there was one of the most delightful sections of the whole ridge—a graceful crest of snow so immaculate that it seemed a sacrilege to set foot upon it. A little later we encountered windslab. One piece measuring about 20ft. by 10ft. swished off just below us and there was a suspicious hollow sound as we plunged our feet in as deeply as we could. Progress was painstakingly slow for a while but soon the snow improved, though we did come across one or two more areas of windslab further on.

After a long easy flog from Banachdich we reached Sgurr Dearg a little before dark and began the excavation of another bivouac. It always requires an effort of imagination to see in the

mind's eye a comfortable bivouac under the frozen slopes and so, to begin with, three separate places were tried. But with a convergence of effort on a boulder some 200ft. below the Inaccessible Pinnacle we soon had a large enough platform to lie on and watch the dramatic fading of light in Coire Lagan. Once again I got the berth at the bottom of the bivvy sack while the others sat in the mouth of the sack with the stove lodged in a boot between them. My reward next morning was to be pointed at the Inaccessible Pinnacle on the sharp end of the rope, a dubious privilege. The weather was still fine, but by the time we had waited for the sun it was 9 a.m. and a keen wind was coming across the ridge from the north. The Pinnacle itself looked absolutely amazing, an impossibly savage fang, a fantasy from the Andes somehow transported to reign over this lovely land of low light and water. The north face was fairly free of snow, but the south face and the long east ridge were encrusted with daggers of hoar frost several feet thick.

It was an unsuitable way to start the day and feeling clumsy and nervous I slowly worked my way upwards. There was a choice between removing sufficient hoar and underlying 'sugar-ice' to get to rock-holds or trusting to crampons scrabbling on this unreliable material. The excavation approach was safer, but time-consuming and I eventually used a combination of faith and hope with the barest whisper of technique to get up the first section. I found myself on a level step of the ridge about 70ft. up, with the last 25ft. rise ahead still looking quite formidable. A solitary peg was the best protection I could find but while I stood there mustering courage for the final assault the others summoned me down. They argued, quite sensibly, that by the time we had all got up and down it, it would be very late (I had been over-long already) and that if we wanted to finish the ridge that day we should press on and leave the Pinnacle inviolate. After the ritual grumbling and mumbling that accompanies such retreats, I abandoned my hard-

*Above: Looking south from Sgurr a'*
*Ghreadaidh to Sgurr Dearg and the*
*Inaccessible Pinnacle (right). Sgurr Alasdair is*
*the dominant peak in the centre of the view.*
*Climber: Mike Edwards / Photo: John Allen*

*Right: The Inaccessible Pinnacle from the*
*east. Climbers: Geoff Cohen and Gordon*
*Macnair / Photo: Dave Broadhead*

won position with a mixture of reluctance and relief
and abseiled off the miserable peg. Climbing this
East Ridge of the Inaccessible Pinnacle in summer
it all passes so quickly that it is hard to imagine how
it could seem so huge and difficult. I can only say
that on this occasion it was a formidable obstacle.

It was now about 11 a.m. and we had yet to
advance from our bivvy site. Seeking perhaps to
salve our consciences we took a more direct route
than necessary, abseiling straight down the crest of
An Stac instead of just following the diagonal
snowfields below the cliffs. Having climbed up
again to Mhic Coinnich we had our next dramatic
abseil, down King's Chimney. Here the wind was
blowing hard and we found ourselves balanced on a

convex slope of hard névé at the brink of the
corner, trying to dig out a suitable abseil point
before being swept down by air power alone! The
walls of the corner were covered with great plates
of water-ice, which shattered as our crampons
skated down. Looking across to Sgurr Thearlaich,
the route seemed tricky and we decided to rope up;
but in the event two pitches of Grade 3 climbing
saw us to the top.

Since time was still short we missed out Sgurr
Alasdair and headed straight on to the Thearlaich-
Dubh gap. One more abseil brought us into the
gap, where the short side leered under a covering of
verglas. After a brief attempt on it, lack of suitable
protection, plus the ever-present time-factor,

persuaded us to press on down the gully on the south side of the gap. This proved quite easy and was probably a time-saver as the climb back up to the ridge is short. Now we were past all the difficulties and the last mile and a half of ridge was sheer, unadulterated pleasure. The continuous movement which is the most wonderful thing about the whole route here quickened to a race with the sun. As the great orb sank into the west it grew perceptibly larger and more full of colour, casting a swathe of rosy pink over the sea towards us. At the very moment we climbed onto the summit of Garsbheinn it touched the horizon and we were able to sit there in silence, drinking in the peace and the incomparable view, trying in vain to realise what it

*Above: Looking back to Sgurr Dearg, the Inaccessible Pinnacle and An Stac from Sgurr Mhic Choinnich. Photo: Dave Broadhead*

*Right: Descending the south-west ridge of Sgurr a' Ghreadaidh. Photo: John Beatty*

meant.

From Gars-bheinn you could almost dive into the sea. But the slopes to Glen Brittle are long, though our exultation carried us almost effortlessly down, pausing only to gaze at Soay and Rhum floating on the gathering gloom. It was still freezing hard even down at sea-level and the track round to Glen Brittle was a thread of clear ice, not very suitable for tired feet in vibram soles. However, the moon came out and then we could crunch our way through the grass beside the path, while our eyes wandered to the silvered waters of Loch Brittle. I felt supremely grateful for a mountaineering experience which nothing in Britain could surpass.

# 6  Minus One and Minus Two Gullies

by Ken Crocket and Pat Littlejohn

## MINUS ONE GULLY by Ken Crocket

If the Orion Face of Ben Nevis is overpowering in scale and appearance, then Minus One Buttress and Gully are elegant court companions. Defining the Orion Face on the left, the buttress begins as little more than a broad rib, swells to its maximum breadth at half-height, then tapers spectacularly to a finish at a giant flake which is reluctantly connected to the main mass of the North-East Buttress by a rickety arête. Minus One Gully soars in an apparently undeviating line up the right flank of the buttress, and until February 1974 had never had a winter ascent. It was the last of the great Nevis gullies to fall.

At some point in their genesis the lava flows forming the Minus Face must have been disturbed, for a band of more irregular rock crosses the face at one-third height. This band results in a series of overhangs and bulges, one of which effectively barred all previous attempts on Minus One Gully. (26 attempts, according to one local expert.)

Particle physics shows that we can never know exactly what reality is; our knowledge will forever be imperfect. What follows then is an imperfect account of a perfect day. Somewhere in between I found a personal reality, one that gives pleasure still. And that's one better than anything the physicists have so far managed.

'Minus One Gully hasn't had a winter ascent,' interjected Colin as we sped northwards along the side of Loch Lomand. As the last of the Nevis gullies, I thought, there must be a good reason for its virgin state. We accelerated along a straight, and I returned to musing and studying the stars.

A typical cross-section occupied the hut: a noisy beard, a bald head, a pair of unabashed youths. A unique hut; a stone-coated cigar-box with galloping damp, at its best in a full gale howling demonically out of Coire Leis, keening a strident climbers' requiem on rough stone edges.

Saturday dawned as forecast, with firm snow at the hut. Colin was footling around inside like a fussy old bachelor, nervously packing and repacking. Finally I could stand it no more and left without a word, struck dumb by my own nervous anticipation—two different reactions to the same stimulus. I was rounding the foot of the Douglas Boulder before the silent hut spawned a dark figure

*Left: Approaching the overhang on Minus One Gully. Climber: Tony Saunders / Photo: Mick Fowler*

and the hunt was on.

Ahead, the Minus and Orion Faces grew in stature as I approached, crossing Tower Gully and the foot of Observatory Ridge. I stopped to absorb the scene, and the massive indifference radiating from the great cliffs. A shout broke into my pilgrim's thoughts – was Colin. His cries were muffled by the snow but he was obviously concerned about our destination. His seed of last night had germinated and I shouted back:

'Minus One!'

The hunter had sighted the prey. I entered the gully to find a ribbon of good snow framed by steep rock walls. Momentum carried me up the ribbon and over a steep wall to a snow step. The next stretch was of patently poor snow and ended in a loose cone beneath a massive overhang. Time to gear up. By the time Colin arrived I had calculated that the next pitch would be a relatively short one up the crumbly snow wall, leaving me the overhang. I offered him the lead. He accepted with some surprise and clanked off like an arthritic knight, laden with superfluous ironware. Much too cunning an iceman, he avoided the lower section by back and foot work until a widening forced a move onto the snow. Deep punch-holes and ungainly straddlings gained the summit cone, where all my calculations were shredded by the pronouncement that he was continuing.

The flow of time now divided, carrying Colin along the faster main branch whilst leaving me stranded in a sluggish backwater. I patrolled my miserable snow ledge for half a lifetime as he gnawed at the overhang like a beaver at a tree. The circumstances were admittedly intriguing. The gully ended in a solid rock overhang. The slight leftwards tilt to the gully which followed the general tilt of the face, explained an ice-boss filling the left corner of the overhang. The right wall and corner were bare, while the left wall was speckled with small lumps of snow, as though after a children's snowball fight.

He was making no progress with the overhang and to my impatient eye seemed to be tiring. A loose suggestion to use a screw ended in technical failure as he made a soft landing on the snow-cone. Finally, caught between my impatience and the improbable left wall, he announced a tension-traverse. I was impressed when he admitted it was his first. Of all the places to learn. Reluctantly I closed the camera case and inched out the ropes as

**Route** Minus One Gully, Grade 5/6, 900ft. Minus Two Gully, Grade 5, 900ft.
**Cliff** The North Face of Ben Nevis.
**First Ascent** Minus One – Summer: July 1958; Winter: K. V. Crocket and A. C. Stead, February 1974. Minus Two – Summer: 1950; Winter: J. R. Marshall, J. Stenhouse and D. Haston, February 1959.
**Map** O.S. 1:50,000 Sheet 41 (166723).
**Guidebooks** S.M.C. *Rock and Ice Climbs in Lochaber and Badenoch* by A. C. Stead and J. R. Marshall; *Scottish Winter Climbs* by Hamish MacInnes (Constable); *Winter Climbs – Ben Nevis/Glencoe* by Ed Grindley (Cicerone).
**Nearest Road / Approach Time** The A82 Fort William – Spean Bridge road at a layby (137763) or the Golf Club car park. A path leads across the golf course to a stile, and then up a steep, wooded hillside to the Allt á Mhuilinn. 3½ miles/2,800ft. to the C.I.C. Hut. Allow 3 hours to the hut and further ½ hour from there.
**Route Summary / Conditions** Minus One Gully – the most difficult of the Ben Nevis gullies, with a hard cave pitch low down followed by sustained mixed climbing. Rarely in condition and requires a heavy build-up of snow. Minus Two Gully – a sustained climb with ice pitches and long sections of mixed climbing in chimneys. Also requires a heavy build-up of snow.
**Campsites and Bunkhouses** C.I.C. Hut (S.M.C.) below the cliffs and Steall Hut (J.M.C.S.) in Glen Nevis (prior booking essential for both huts). Youth Hostel in Glen Nevis. Camping in Glen Nevis and in the Allt á Mhuilinn.
**Bibliography** *One Below the Belt* by Colin Stead (S.M.C.J., 1974) – an illustrated account of the first ascent of Minus One Gully; *Minus Two Gully* unattributed (Rocksport 3 – new series, c. October, 1974) – a curious account of an early ascent; *Ben Nevis 1970-78* by Alan Rouse (Crags 17).

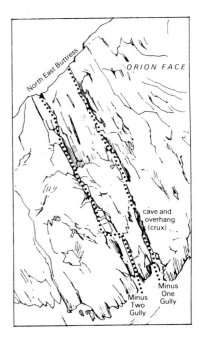

he launched himself leftwards. Fascinated, I watched an apparent revolt against gravity as he teetered across from snow lump to snow lump, outlined starkly against a lowering grey sky. The climbing was obviously impossible – yet he was succeeding. At last he reached the gully edge, and hooked a pick into snow beyond. Mercifully it was good, and as he pulled over and out I let out the whoop I had been holding back and began to breathe again.

It was a great moment, but quickly tempered by the realisation that I would be unable to follow the same route. Colin had gone back right above the overhang and as he had been unable to fix a runner out left the ropes now draped mockingly over it. Moreover, he had shouted down that the belay was so poor he would be unable to give me much help. The overhang would have to yield, and by my efforts alone.

I reached the foot of the ice-boss and deepened my breathing in anticipation. I decided to risk all in one attempt, and having made that commitment everything seemed to become calm and crystal-clear. This was no place for a series of studied moves. The angle was such that arm-strength was a limiting factor. It was equally no place for a wild flailing of picks – the belay was obviously non-existent and the penalty clause for careless climbing much too severe. I quietly warned Colin to watch the ropes. They were of psychological use only, but I was winding myself up for the effort ahead.

On rock, it would have been a respectable bulge. Smeared with ice it was a formidable obstacle. The ropes tightened as I stepped up off the snow cone. I could see my crampon points on the initial moves only, thereafter I was kicking blind. The ice was tough, but good, and with each good swing the picks were biting deeply enough to satisfy my needs. Several strenuous moves later the gamble paid off. I was past the overhang to reach more normal angles above. A short shuffle left, a final upward section and on to Colin's highly dubious but welcome belay. We were up and out. Only then did we become aware of a fine drizzle, as a front swept over and our world was drawn in by thick, swirling curtains of mist.

The remainder of the gully was exciting, if anticlimactic. I traversed left under a bulge in the open gully – it was now more of a scoop – and found a steep wall of hard snow. I still had an adrenalin high from following the overhang and clumsily smashed a fingernail on a protruding lump of ice. A string of not-so-muffled curses embarrassed a rope of old boys over on Observatory Ridge. The belay was even worse than the preceding one (I hung my sack from an axe in preference), but confidence was bubbling irrepressibly as I thrust chocolate into Colin's hand. I cheekily remarked how the next pitch would suit him fine. And straight up he went, baring a menacing set of crampon-points up a beautifully-defined corner on steep and still-hard snow to land in an easing of the gully.

Two more pitches through the spectral mists and we ran up against a terminal wall separating us from the crest of the North-East Buttress. All through the last pitch I had been hearing faint, alien sounds, and I feared some form of euphoria. Then I realised that Colin, not usually prone to emotional display, was so happy he was singing to himself! As I mantelshelfed carefully onto the final rickety arête, we knew we had snatched one of the glittering prizes. Even an abortive attempt to descend the North-East Buttress in thick mist, followed by a quick scurry upwards again, was undertaken cheerfully, by-passing the dreaded Mantrap by the exposed slabs on the right. It was somehow more appropriate to finish on top.

When I eventually wandered back to the hut, Colin having gone on ahead, there was no immediate desire to go in. I sat outside removing crampons, reluctant to release the moment. Finally I pushed open the door and entered its steamy confines, ready to face the music.

## MINUS TWO GULLY by Pat Littlejohn

Ice didn't take to me at first. Perhaps it was my first attempt at front-pointing, in the early seventies on a tree in Snell's Field, Chamonix. This ended when both Terrordactyls ripped simultaneously 10ft. up, depositing me on my back bruised and winded amongst a small, amused audience. Or the time six months later when Keith Darbyshire and I were soloing in the Northern Corries. Keith got bored with the gully and shot off up an ice-plastered arête, obliging me to follow. Thin ice and 200ft. of exposure produced a feeling of insecurity such as I had never known on rock. I meekly asked for a top-rope, only to be reminded that it was in my pack. Moments of pure trauma followed, and I decided you had to be a bit crazy

to enjoy ice-climbing.

The seventies wore on and I must have got crazier, for suddenly I had a very strong desire to climb ice. Luckily Chris King, my regular climbing partner at the time, felt likewise. Armed with Ian Clough's old guidebook, we headed for Ben Nevis and, we hoped, the frozen North.

*Left: The upper part of Minus One Gully. Climber: Tony Saunders / Photo: Mick Fowler*

*Above: The distinctive slanting lines of the Minus Face stand out in a light snow cover. Photo: Bert Jenkins*

We camped by the lochan above the tourist path, a level, frozen wasteland just before the Ben rears up in a great whaleback for its final 2,000ft. Not the ideal spot for getting to the climbs but perfect for getting off them, with a 1,500ft. glissade straight back to the tent. Day One was frustrating but fun. We retreated from a pitch and a half up Point Five in the face of incessant spindrift avalanches, alarming to the uninitiated and unprepared, then soloed Tower Ridge before glissading back to base whooping like a couple of kids. Next day we thought we should do something half-decent:

'Formidable, unrepeated, and probably technically the hardest of the Nevis gullies.'

Those wonderful, foreboding, but fatally attractive descriptions in the old guidebooks! It had to be Minus Two.

Peering across from beneath Observatory Ridge, we thought we could make out the line. Not the vague, shallow smear which must be Minus One Gully, unclimbed for all we knew, but the slanting, ice-filled groove system leading to a secure-looking chimney which finally emerged on to North-East Buttress. We had identified it but could we get to it? The slope below was chest-deep powder set at a fairly steep angle, clearly avalanche-prone. And being really keen, keyed-up and unwilling to turn back, we were just the sort of party Scottish avalanches like to save themselves for. I put on the rope and set off, using a combination of breast and butterfly stroke. Like I said, you have to be slightly crazy to enjoy ice-climbing. Chris followed in the huge trench I'd created. The first pitch was

*Top Left: In the lower part of Minus Two Gully. Climber: Rab Carrington / Photo: Paul Nunn*

*Bottom left: Wide bridging in the upper chimneys. Climber: Chris King / Photo: Pat Littlejohn*

*Right: Minus Two Gully, generously filled with ice. Photo: Alan Rouse*

surprisingly enjoyable – delicate and intricate climbing with reasonable rock protection, exactly what we'd come for. Chris led through up an equally fine pitch, similar in quality and difficulty to the first. So this was Scottish Grade 5 – give us more! At this point we became aware of another party above us. Strange, for there had been nobody on the face when we started. We later learned that it was Bob Millward and partner beginning their epic, multi-day traverse of the Minus and Orion Faces. The leader seemed to be hacking out a massive stance directly above us and a continuous stream of snow and ice-chunks whistled down our gully, persuading me to break out on to the left wall. It was a big mistake – regaining the gully was very difficult and time-consuming. We were now at the base of the chimney, and it looked mouthwatering. Clean rock on the right wall, gleaming bulges of good ice on the left. Chris set off and got into some alarmingly wide bridging positions on the bulges which, with my short legs, I could never hope to emulate. At one point his left crampon grated down the chimney wall, stripping off a plate of ice and leaving smooth, bare rock. A couple of straight arm-pulls got him out of trouble. To my mind the climbing in the chimney was as good and interesting as any below, and I was sorry that the difficulties lasted for only one pitch.

Once on North-East Buttress the mists closed in, reducing visibility to a few feet. Easier climbing brought us to The Mantrap, an infamous obstacle which was to live up to its reputation. Seeing no way of tackling it direct I traversed around to the right, as prescribed, and chose a likely-looking groove to follow. After running out 90ft. of rope, with no protection, I finally found a poor spike above which the climbing looked desperate. The problem was that the snow-cover gave out. Whether I was on route is doubtful, as the next few moves were harder than anything on Minus Two proper. The cloud really thickened for the last few pitches, destroying any sense of scale and making route-finding a matter of sheer luck. We were just beginning to wonder when on earth it was going to end when suddenly it did, just a few steps from the summit. It was not a place to linger – gear was stuffed into sacks, ropes coiled, then we were off on our compass bearing towards the tiny life-support system which would sustain us for a few more days on this big, inhospitable mountain.

# 7  North-East Buttress

by Paul Nunn

## THE HISTORY OF EARLY ASCENTS

North from Glencoe's tops one bold mountain structure looms above all else. From here Ben Nevis *is* North-East Buttress. A dazzling white shoulder sweeps down into the arc of the Carn Mor Dearg Arête and disappears behind the shadows of the Mamores. Right of the arête, on its northern flank, a few jagged black rocks sprout from the icy reflections of the face and merge into the 1,500ft. cliff of the North-East Buttress itself. In between is the Little Brenva Face.

A view from north of Ben Nevis reveals other complexities. To the west of the Buttress a formidable face is thrown into the Observatory Gully. This is the Minus/Orion aspect. In summer it is a soaring mass of rock slabs and buttresses. Winter transforms it into an ice-plastered mass scarcely scratched by three vertical slots, misnomered 'gullies', which all end on the North-East Buttress. Beyond is the hanging White Spider of Orion Face, then the verglassed slabs of Slav Route and at last the proud plume of ice that is Zero Gully.

In September 1892, two days after making a descent of Tower Ridge, John Hopkinson and his son Bernard, made the first ascent of North-East Buttress. Hopkinson, who was an extremely active alpinist, had previously made a determined attempt to *climb* Tower Ridge, failing on a hard chimney on the right flank of the Great Tower. He later noted 'The climbing on this [North-East] ridge is interesting but much easier than the central [Tower] ridge.' A few days later, with his brothers Edward and Charles joining the party, he climbed the rock face of the Douglas Boulder. Modesty or Victorian reserve may have been the reason for a delay in recording the routes, and it was not until three years later that they briefly noted their activities in the Alpine Journal (A.J. Vol.17, p.520).

In 1894 Norman Collie, Dr. Joseph Collier and G. A. Solly, attending an SMC Easter Meet at Inveroran, made the first *ascent* of Tower Ridge. SMC interest in the Fort William area was, at that time, minimal. As one member noted 'the suggestion that the Club should have its Easter Meet there was received with dismay'. One reason for this reluctance may have been the difficulty in reaching the area but with the opening of the West Highland Railway in 1894 access to Fort William eased. Another SMC Meet was held the following Easter but this time Ben Nevis was in full winter condition. Collie, Naismith, Travers and Thomson made the

first ascent of Castle Ridge, but Tower Ridge and North-East Buttress were thought too hard in the conditions. Two members, Brown and Tough, decided to return to attempt North-East Buttress, and did so on the Queen's birthday in May. They had a suitably Scots epic described entertainingly in *Mountaineering in Britain*:

'They took the overnight train [from Edinburgh] to Kingussie, arriving there on a grey Saturday morning at 3.50 a.m. They then mounted their bicycles and for two hours pedalled through the rain and mist until "a sudden report recalling the simultaneous opening of six bottles of Bouvier announced the puncture of one of Brown's tyres" . . . Thirteen miles lay between them and the nearest point on the West Highland Railway, Tulloch Station. "Tough mounted the remaining bicycle, with a pyramid of ropes, axes and rucksacks piled up on his shoulders, while his fellow traveller half-walked, half-trotted alongside." Thus they arrived at Tulloch, and thence by train to Fort William [arriving at midday] . . . .

'They reached the foot of the rocks at 5.30 p.m., were drenched by a minor cloudburst for ten minutes, and then saw their buttress blotted out by the mists. However, these soon rose, and at 6.15 they put on the rope. They easily reached a ledge now known as the First Platform, continued upwards by a succession of small chimneys and gullies, and reached another ledge – the Second Platform. "Here the really interesting work may be said to begin," Brown wrote later, "for the ridge is fairly narrow, and, besides being very steep, is broken into all the delightful incidents of this form of architecture. There are little towers up which the leader had to scramble with such gentle impetus as could be derived from the pressure of his hobnails upon his companion's head. There are ledges (not very terrible) where it is convenient to simulate the grace of a caterpillar. A sloping slab we found, too, where the union of porphyry and Harris tweed interposed the most slender obstacle to an airy slide into the valley." Higher still a smooth overhanging wall was reached; "these slabby rocks are the mantrap of the ridge" – a phrase which has stuck – and Tough spent three quarters of an hour among them before finally turning the difficulty.

'Daylight was already ebbing and there was still some few hundred feet of ridge above them.

**Route** North East Buttress, Grade 3/4, 1,500ft.
**Cliff** The North Face of Ben Nevis.
**First Ascent** Summer: 1892. Winter: W. W. Naismith, W. Brunskill, A. B. W. Kennedy W. W. King, and F. C. Squance, April 1896.
**Map** O.S. 1:50,000 Sheet 41 (172716).
**Guidebooks** See page 41.
**Nearest Road/Approach Time** See page 41.
**Route Summary / Conditions** A long mixed climb with a problematic crux, the Mantrap, in a high and exposed position. The climb is committing, with no easy escapes, and will require a long retreat, with the likelihood of an involuntary bivouac, if the Mantrap cannot be overcome.
**Campsites / Bunkhouses** See page 41.
**Bibliography** *Mountaineering in Britain* by R. W. Clark and E. C. Pyatt (Phoenix House). has some interesting passages dealing with early ascents (in summer conditions); *Mountaineering in Scotland/Undiscovered Scotland* by W. H. Murray (Diadam) contains a good description (Chapter 18 of *Undiscovered Scotland*) of an ascent in the thirties, *Big Four* by Colin Beechey (Climber and Rambler, January, 1982) – a short account of an ascent in good conditions.

*Left: North-East Buttress from Carn Mor Dearg. Photo: Hamish MacInnes*

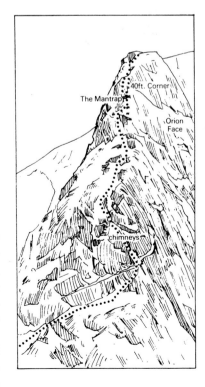

*Above: Moving up to the steep cliff above the First Platform. Climber: John Kingston / Photo: Ken Wilson*

Hopkinsons three years earlier.

'As was common, once the spell of inaccessibility had been broken, other men quickly followed the pioneers. Eight days after Tough and Brown's ascent, another was made by Hastings, Howard Priestman and Cecil Slingsby . . . a few days later yet another ascent was made by Napier and Green.'

These ascents, made in spring or summer conditions, indicated the trend for the future, for their originators were alpinists who saw Scotland as an alpine training ground. It is not surprising to find that winter ascents soon followed. The first ascent of North-East Buttress in winter conditions was made by Naismith, Brunskill, Kennedy, King and Squance on April 3, 1896. This ascent went unnoticed by generations of chroniclers and the facts were only recently resurrected from early SMC Journals. Robin Campbell sifted the evidence in the 1972 SMCJ:

'[Naismith's] . . . greatest achievement was the first winter ascent of the North-East Buttress . . . Something of Naismith's well-known self-effacement and of the Victorian climbers' attitude to winter climbing is known by [William] Brown's matter-of-fact report [of the SMC Meet]:

'"The North-East Buttress was only ascended by one party. It held a good deal of ice, and was reported to be in a rather difficult condition. The gully above the First Platform was paved with blue ice, and had to be left severely alone. Higher up also, below the last 'peeler', the summer route was impracticable for the same reason, and a new line had to be struck out up the rocks on the left."

'Thirty years later, Naismith "admits" that it was he who made the ascent:

'"This was a long day, for we were on the buttress for nearly seven hours. The party was a jolly one, but rather large for speed. The rocks were plastered with ice and snow and distinctly difficult. At one or two places the route followed by the first climbers [Tough and Brown] was impossible and had to be varied . . . a pitch that Brown had climbed with difficulty was now found to be iced and hopeless; but by crossing to the left side of the buttress, we followed a narrow gully, at first hard ice but afterwards good snow, which led us past the last obstacle . . ."

'In fact, this astonishing early ascent was so little noted at the time that our present

Luckily, the worst of the difficulties were over, and at 10.05 they were received by the staff of the Observatory on the summit plateau. After warm drinks and an hour's nap they set off down the path, reaching Fort William by the light of the new day. At 4 a.m. they were in the mail-gig for Kingussie; and, after 45 hours of continuous travelling, back in Edinburgh.

'Then, before the description of the ascent could be published, a note appeared in the Alpine Journal recording the first ascent by the

guidebooks either fail to mention those responsible for it or list them as "unknown".'

## A RECENT ASCENT

In February 1970 ambition's pull was towards Point Five Gully, Hadrian's Wall, Gardyloo Buttress or the Orion Face. It was an odd transition period, the year in which I first used a Terrordactyl on a big route. Yet the limits of these tools were only being tested; all I knew was that I was becoming too weak to cut steps for 12 hours at a stretch. But there was no question of venturing on open faces or snow-packed gullies this day. Deep-crusted snow plastered the Allt a'Mhuilinn valley right down to below the edge of the forests. To reach the CIC Hut at all was a long plod, knee and deeper, until in frustration we ploughed up to join some tracks from Glen Nevis, crossing several avalanche scars below Carn Dearg. Geoff Arkless was in the hut, a cheerful high-pitched Geordie voice, with a gaggle of clients. If he knew that I was one of the recent 'banned' he did not let on. Perhaps he knew of the spurious nature of the charge – feeding tea to a rescuer who should not have been allowed into the hut. The subsequent indictment from the SMC read: 'had he not tasted the tea before your descent with the casualty (the victim of a fall from Observatory Ridge) he would not have felt so motivated to re-enter the place by breaking down the door upon his return to camping outside – so you are required to comply with a ban on using the hut for a year.'

Four of us squeezed into the bunks and everyone agreed that conditions were wild and poor.

Meringue-like cornices hung over the gullies and along the ridges, the product of heavy snow about a week before. In between there had been high wind and low temperature, with scarcely any thaw. Windslab had been widespread a day or two earlier and little had happened since to change things. Snow lay about in freakish quantities, much of it at a high angle, yet still unconsolidated. Worst omen of all was a bad accident only a day or two earlier – Jim MacArtney, Mary Anne Hudson and Fergus Mitchell had been swept to their deaths from Italian Climb by a powerful avalanche. In these conditions, if we must climb, it had to be a ridge.

In the morning an odd quartet set out. I, a hefty 13 stoner, was climbing with Bob Toogood, ageless, small and wiry, happiest when the commitment was total and retreat impossible. Tony Riley is lean and tall, with a Hasselblad camera in his rucksack, and masochistic in his pleasure in the discomfort of winter. He climbed with Trevor Briggs, another small, wiry man, at once enthusiastic and anxious.

Snow devils whirled over the powder crust in Coire Leis and a stiff wind was chill even in the valley. Reaching the First Platform involves a traverse which is usually straightforward. Today fickle crust broke off in slabs and slid away in man-sized chunks. At each step axe and arms plunged to the armpits, another move consolidated, another foot won. When we reached the little col of the First Platform Bob cursed as we strapped on our crampons – he had left his behind.

At first the ground ahead appeared daunting. A big cliff barred the way and it was not clear how this

*Above: A party using combined tactics to overcome the Mantrap in heavy powder-snow conditions. This photo is taken from an identical position to that on page 51. Climbers: Bob Toogood and Paul Nunn / Photo: Tony Riley*

was to be overcome. We moved up to some ledges
on the right and from there were able to see a line of
gullies and chimneys leading up through the cliff. I
started up a little gully, then there was a step right
to a shelf of snow. Another runnel followed and
then some small ice-crystalled and snow-plastered
ribs. Eventually we emerged on an easier part of
the ridge above the cliff. The edge of the buttress
was now a jumble of icy blocks which resisted our
efforts. Each difficulty tended to push us to the left,
only to regain the crest after 40 or 50ft. The wind
was a problem on exposed sections, but we found
shelter in little runnels and gutters. A snow shelf
emerged at a steep angle from the Minus Face, and
we wondered how we would have felt had we
gained the ridge by one of the Minus gullies.

Speculation, daydreams, they are symptoms of
ease, of a relaxation which might seem inappropriate to the Ben's biggest ridge in winter. But for a
time we were lulled by this iced beauty as no particular difficulty demanded concentration. Then,
after an easy section, a short block barred the way.

The Mantrap has done exactly that to many a
party, and some have had to suffer rescue from
below this intractable barrier. It is short, not more
than 10ft. from bottom to top, and many must have
wondered at its base if they ought not, zen like, to
will themselves up it. But it lacks those accommodating spikes which civilize many a famous obstacle
on the Ben and above, a flat shelf affords little
purchase for hand or axe. When the snow is good it
is usual to outflank to left or right, rather than to
tussle with the little meany of the block itself.

My first reaction was to get a good belay, a piton
brayed in low down below the block to secure us
from any Owen Glynne Jones-style collapsing
pyramids. Bob fastened on while I examined the
step. A few arm wavings and futile pawings proved
that nothing much was attached to the rock. The
wind had blown most of the snow away and only a
skittering of powder decorated a smooth wall. On
top of that a further mound of loose powder offered
no assistance. I took to the slabs on the right,
jutting out over the Orion Face, in the hope of an
easier passage. Time was already deserting, the
wind scoured the exposed ridge and Tony and
Trevor shivered below with Bob. This right-hand
route was scarcely an improvement – nothing was
attached to anything, and I realised that this was an
action replay of Murray's experience:

'We looked round the flanks in search of some

*Top right: Looking up to the Mantrap in lean conditions.*
*Climbers: Mike Banks, Richard Brooke and Dave Viggers*

*Bottom right: The '40ft. Corner' pitch above the Mantrap.*
*Climbers: John Gillespie and Bob Richardson / Photo: Colin Stead*

avoiding move. On the left flank the rock was quite clear of fog crystals, which at this point had been wind-blasted. The rock fell away in smooth convex slabs which rose to near verticality at the wall beside the Mantrap. The only semblance of weakness there, was a shallow chimney filled from side to side with a twist of thick black ice. Its ascent was not possible . . . We examined the right flank. There was here a much greater and more open expanse of rock . . . . On this face it might be possible to cut out a traverse and regain the ridge higher up – it *might* be possible . . . but again, no rock belay, a 1,200ft. cliff below, at least an hour of cutting . . . I turned and went back.'

Frankly I could not even remember how Bill Murray had overcome this section so, as is usual when descent is long, time and light short and the weather wild, we took to guile.

Scraping with the axe I excavated a rope thread above the piton belay and, being a coward, firmly attached myself asking Trevor to give Bob and me a back-up belay from below. Bob then sat on my shoulders while I crouched on the edge with bent knees. I was glad as I stood up to gain height that he had no crampons, and even more so when he stepped onto my shoulders and asked me to 'jerk him upwards'. But he knew what he was doing, even if I didn't, and he levitated onto the ledge above with an elfish spring, before skipping up to a belay in a mound of powder. I followed quickly on a firm line, then the others had the benefit of a hawser-like rope held by the two of us. Stiff inside icy anoraks after the best part of an hour's wait in the gale they were ready for off. We all were!

The 40ft. corner ahead looked uninviting so we tried to avoid it on the left. A ledge offered a possible route to reach what appeared to be a gully or groove but there was so much soft snow that it pushed me out of balance as I fought to get round the corner into the groove. The problem was solved by a floundering technique, with arms and legs penetrating as much puffy snow as possible. Once gained, the groove was steep for a bit but it led to the easier ground above, and so on towards the top with ropes blowing out in sabre curves. There was even the luxury of a little grey light before descending. A later encounter brought different conditions but the climbing was still appropriate training for the snow-covered slabs of the Barnaj, high and remote in the Himalayas.

# 8  Orion Face Direct

by Dave Wilkinson

**Route** Orion Face Direct, Grade 5, 1,400ft.
**Cliff** The North Face of Ben Nevis.
**First Ascent** Winter: J. R. Marshall and
R. Smith, February 1960.
**Map** See page 41.
**Guidebooks** See page 41.
**Nearest Road / Approach Time**
See page 41.
**Route Summary / Conditions** Despite its
name, a devious and intricate mixed climb
of great quality. The more icy the conditions
the easier the route becomes. Serious,
because of position, length and paucity of
good protection and belays.
**Campsites / Bunkhouses.** See page 41.
**Bibliography** *The Games Climbers Play*
(Diadem) has first ascent accounts by Smith
('The Old Man and the Mountains') and
Marshall ('The Orion Face'); *With God On
Our Side* by Terry King (Crags 6) – a
humorous account of a guided ascent; *Winter
Dreams* by Ken Crocket (S.M.C.J., 1976).

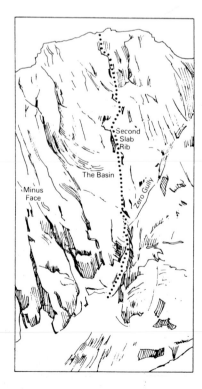

It was Easter 1975 and the green of spring was well advanced by the shores of Loch Linnhe. But higher up, white was the dominant colour, for winter had lingered late on the Ben that year. The Orion Face, for which we were bound, still had a reputation for great seriousness, for although we had heard rumours that it wasn't too hard, we had also heard that it had poor belays, and complex route-finding. It was also long. In the event we found these rumours were true, but its reputation for quality was fully borne out.

I was with Rob Ferguson. Prior to this trip we had only climbed together once before. He impressed me with his quiet, gentle, but determined disposition. After ascents of Comb Gully Buttress and Creag Meagaidh's Pumpkin we felt ready for this greater challenge.

None of the CIC Hut luxury for us sassenachs, but a drive from our tent in Glen Nevis to the Distillery and the full walk up from there. As we plodded up to the crag our doubts nagged. Perhaps it really was too big a thing for us. How about the conditions? There had been a little thaw recently, and a fresh snow-fall. The weather was clear now, and frosty as we walked up on hard old snow covered with a dusting of fresh powder. Ahead loomed the face, with an ample white coating, but whether of good snow-ice or fresh powder, we could not tell.

The line was not immediately obvious. More than any other British winter route, with the possible exception of those on the Little Brenva Face, Orion looks and feels Alpine. It is closer to the big Oberland North Faces, both in appearance and in the climbing, than it is to the traditional Scottish gully. When you try to fit the route description to the face, it seems complicated. Try climbing it and it fits. Short grooves, bits of gully, buttresses, a face and a rib or two, all link with a subtle simplicity which is not easily spotted from below. Each feature, once embarked upon, leads naturally on to the other, as happens only in the very best of routes. There are even a couple of snowfields, Eiger-like and only slightly less spectacular. And right at the top, above the Orion version of the White Spider, there is a crest of steep rock which looks as if it might provide a sting – so there's even that Alpine nag at the back of your mind the whole way up. By the purest Alpine standards Orion may be short on stature, but by all other criteria it's a mighty route, a fine and intricate

line. You'd have to climb far and wide to find better.

Rob led a small pitch up an icy groove just left of Zero Gully and took a peg belay where the face steepened, My turn. The first big pitch loomed – a shallow groove running up the face, well-plastered with the as-yet-untested white stuff. I moved across and hit it with an axe. The pick stuck in an inch and

stopped without hitting rock. Certainly not fresh powder. I moved up, still a little nervous. This was the first serious climb with my recently-acquired Terrordactyls, tools which were not yet fully accepted south of the border. The picks seemed very narrow, and I feared they might cut through and slip out of the névé-like material. Therefore before wandering too high I gave them a thorough

try-out, hung all my weight on one pick and swung about. It held, so with equipment and conditions thereby checked and approved, I set off in earnest.

The white stuff turned out to be near-perfect snow-ice and confidence grew as I gained height. Then my qualms started to return. The ice was too soft and too thin to take screws and I noticed the length of rope hanging down to my man. He was

*Above: The cliffs of Ben Nevis, heavily snow-covered. The Orion Face is the prominent wall in the centre. Photo: Colin Stead*

**53**

gazing absently at the distant sea, and seemed strangely unconcerned with my progress:

'Can't get any runners in up here, Rob!'

'Oh dear.'

His mild-mannered answer brought little comfort. Where was the staunch second with his helpful suggestions and confidence-boosting rope-side manner? I continued on my lonely way with growing doubts about the security of the ice. Then I made a great discovery. The groove had closed to a crack and was blocked at the front by a lump of ice. There was just room to thread a sling round the back. I sighed with much relief. Suddenly the texture of the ice seemed firmer. Conditions were, after all, perfect:

'That's what I call a runner.'

'Oh good,' came his calm, understanding reply. Yes, he was the ideal climbing partner. None of that interfering second stuff with unhelpful suggestions and only semi-audible interruptions. Just trust – a calm support that left me to get on with the job. As the groove continued the ice became more glassy, then more snowy; now steepening, now easing back. Marshall's words echoed in my mind:

'..and whooped the way up over grand bulges...'

I gained a snow patch with room for both feet and started the great hunt for a belay. Half an hour later I had excavated a lot of slabby rock and several blind cracks and attached myself to an assortment of unconvincing anchors; a screw in some hollow crust, a tied-off knife-blade and a small wire nut pivoting on two corners in a flared crack.

Rob passed my insecure perch with no sign of concern and climbed up towards the bulging ice which barred direct access to the Basin. But then he sneaked cunningly round the rib on the left into a hidden gully. The rope ran swiftly out. Again Marshall, describing Smith:

'. . . after he moved from sight, a horrible flow of oaths seared down the sterile slopes; I thought he was in a cul-de-sac, but no, he had climbed into easy ground with the way to the Basin clear and the share of labour too small . . .'

I led on up the easy snow of the Basin and then Rob did a minor ice pitch to a smaller snowfield just above. A feature of this route is the inaccuracy of its name. It is not really direct at all, but twists and turns, taking the natural line up the face; and it's full of surprises. The original route up the Orion Face, climbed by Smith and Holt in 1959, slants left

from the Basin up an icy chimney to the crest of North-East Buttress. The main wall above the Basin is split by a number of groove-lines which seldom hold ice. Here lie the true Orion direct routes, the recently-climbed Astral Highway and Journey into Space, the work of Con Higgins and Alan Kimber in 1976 and 1980. But this day there was nothing there but powder-dusted rock, so another crafty evasion was called for. I peeped round the buttress on the right and found the missing ice draining from the upper snowfields. Once more Marshall's words fitted the situation perfectly:

'. . . an exploratory traverse 10ft. round the corner disclosed a well-iced wall, shining green in the evening light . . .'

Another feature of the route which will appeal to the climber who habitually schemes to hog all the good leading (or to avoid it) is that if alternate leads are taken using longish run-outs the same climber gets all three best pitches. Marshall had all the joy on the first ascent, as I did on ours. The wall out of the Basin was the second of the three, and gave superb exposed work with steep moves on ice-banked shelves.

Two delightful easier pitches followed, slanting left by iced slabs and grooves which took us up a snowfield and the final steepening. This gave me the third big pitch, up an icy chimney then left below an overhang and up an iced wall to the top. I climbed in a sort of drug-like trance. Gone was the earlier nervousness. Picks and front-points felt like extensions of my limbs as they moved from one icy lodging to the next. My mind had somehow become detached; a spectator as the body performed alone.

We landed on the very top of the North-East Buttress, just a step to the summit of the Ben and an easy, dreamy, contented shamble down after one of the most enjoyable days of our lives.

*Top left: The lower part of Orion Direct, where a groove followed by face-climbing leads up into the Basin. Photo: Ray Simpson*

*Bottom left: 'Steep moves on ice-banked shelves' – one of the devious pitches above the Basin which enable climbers to by-pass the steep, upper rock buttresses. Climber: Ronnie Richards / Photo: Ken Crocket*

*Right: A view across the lower part of Orion Face from Zero Gully. Photo: Calum Fraser*

# 9  Zero Gully

by Allen Fyffe

'The winter ascent is a serious expedition and should only be attempted by parties experienced in advanced snow and ice techniques. The lower section of the gully presents sustained high-angle ice-climbing with minimal natural protection and exposure to spindrift avalanches in wind.'

'It is a good climb, not technically hard but poor belays make it very serious. It is exposed to spindrift.'

These quotes from SMC guides to Ben Nevis refer to the same route, but they could be describing different climbs. The first, from J. R. Marshall's definitive Nevis guide, refers to an old-style ascent; the second to the route as it is now climbed. In between, step-cutting gave way to front-pointing with curved or inclined picks, the single most significant advance in snow and ice-climbing. A boom in Scottish winter climbing soon followed.

The routes most affected by this change in style were those where steep ice presented the main difficulties. Thus attitudes to climbs such as Zero Gully, one of only eight Grade 5 routes on the Ben in the mid-60s, changed overnight. Like its companion, Point Five, The Curtain and Orion Face, the once mighty Zero toppled from its position as a reputation-route to a soft touch at Grade 5; a shattering of myths that changed the face of Scottish winter climbing. Nothing ever filled the gap. No modern winter climb excites the same awe, and what was involved in those early ascents is easily forgotten.

Then, the ascent of any Grade 5 was a notable event. Zero was immortalised by Tom Patey in his story 'The Zero Gully Affair'. The attempts by the top climbers of the day, the failures, the epics, the vertical ice and continual spindrift avalanches all contributed to its reputation and loomed large in any mind contemplating an attempt at Zero in those days. MacInnes's ascent with Patey and Nicol in only five hours was regarded as one of the great achievements in Scottish winter climbing.

So it was with some trepidation that we approached the Ben that night in 1967. Jim MacArtney and I had our eyes on Zero; a secret plan, little spoken about. Our experience of Grade 5 routes was limited to the 'Gorms', home territory for Aberdeen climbers such as ourselves. But the Ben was bigger and badder than anywhere else and we knew little about it. This guaranteed that the

walk up the Allt a' Mhuilinn was worse than it need have been. The path lost, the bog found, it was early on Saturday morning by the time we sneaked into the CIC Hut. Even the hut was different then, with no trouble in staying unbooked and no bouncers or fortifications to keep you out.

The Saturday dawned cold, blustery, grey and cloudy. We dawned about noon, in a similar condition. Not a Zero day. We needed plenty of time. Since its first ascent Zero had averaged about one ascent per year and most had taken the best part of a day; so Jim and I left for the Brenva Face for an easy day and a look at conditions.

The next morning the weather was little better but at first light we left for the route. Tension fought an abdominal battle with greasy indigestible fry-ups and little was said on the approach. We geared up, a simple task then; Grivel crampons, ice-axe (cut-down Stubai ladies' model) attached by a piece of cord, peg-hammer, slings, krabs, pegs and our first two tubular ice-screws. The route reared above us, not so much a gully as a huge groove where the Orion Face angled into Observatory Ridge. An easy initial pitch led to the first steepening, where I took a stance and belayed to a vertical axe, noting that it was unlikely to hold. Jim came up and through. Above was a half-round chute which ran into an ice-pillar on the right and faded into rock on the left. It was closed by overhangs at the top. The pitch succumbed to a combination of bridging and step-cutting with help from the occasional rock-hold. Protection consisted of a piece of line poking out of the ice at 80ft. and a poor ice-screw at 100ft.; then Jim was below the roof. The pitch had taken an hour; the belay took almost as long. Even then it was another vertical axe and tied-off peg. An instruction not to fall off inspired little confidence in the belay, whilst the denial of tension when it was requested a few minutes later inspired weightless care. I teetered up on minute steps until I stood quaking below Jim. Holding his ankles while he draped the gear round my neck, I looked up at my pitch. The way seemed to go right to a steep ice-wall, onto the front of the ice-pillar, and then straight up and out of sight.

Now traverses are hard on step-cutters. The steps are difficult to shape and separate sets are needed for hands and feet. And when it comes to turning a corner and cutting blind it is harder still. The secret is to make every blow count. Use the adze; chop down into the hole formed by the first

**Route** Zero Gully, Grade 5, 1,000ft.
**Cliff** The North Face of Ben Nevis.
**First Ascent** Summer: 1955; Winter: H. MacInnes, T. W. Patey and A. G. Nicol, February, 1957.
**Map** See page 41.
**Guidebooks** See page 41.
**Nearest Road / Approach Time** See page 41.
**Route Summary / Conditions** A serious and exposed climb with poor belays and protection. Exposed to spindrift avalanche. It requires a good build up of snow and ice and hard frost conditions for a safe ascent. In unconsolidated snow or melt conditions the route is particularly hazardous.
**Campsites / Bunkhouses** See page 41.
**Bibliography** *One Man's Mountains* by Tom Patey (Gollancz) has a classic account of the first ascent; *Ben Nevis 1970-1978* by Alan Rouse (Crags 17); *Nightshift on Zero* by Dougal Haston is an interesting account of an early ascent (E.U.M.C.J. 1962).

*Left: The Orion Face, Zero Gully and Observatory Ridge. Photo: Alex Gillespie*

*Above: The initial 'chute' pitch of Zero Gully. Climber: Tobin Sorenson / Photo: Rob Matheson*

*Top right: Mixed ground at the start of the second pitch. Climber: Rob Matheson / Photo: Matheson collection*

*Bottom right: The snow/ice bulge on the fourth pitch which marks the end of the major difficulties. This pitch is often very serious because of insecure belays, unconsolidated snow, and poor protection. Climber: Dave Robbins / Photo: Al Morgan*

blow, then cut deeper into the back to form a lip. Study the ice for changes in colour, no matter how subtle, that indicate patches which are hollow or soft. Unless you're built like a gorilla you'll need all the help you can get.

I hacked my way onto the front of the ice and then up to slightly easier ground where balance could be found in rare places. Runners, however, were less easily discovered. At the first attempt the screw broke; at the next our second screw fell from a krab whose gate had frozen open. The belay was a sling on a rounded spike.

Jim came up and led through again on a similar pitch. He weaved a way up vague easings, always leaving a line of holes, while resting on snow-patches and seeking rocks for protection. At last, at the end of our third full pitch, we unearthed a secure belay.

We were in a big bay, belayed to a huge block. It was well into the afternoon and a major pitch still lay between us and the easier upper slopes of the gully. My turn again, and I was feeling the strain mentally and physically. A bulge had to be surmounted. Again the cutting was awkward, demanding either my weak arm or cutting across the body to fashion steps that had to be jugs, but which were almost impossible to cut into. A final desperate swing, when all that seemed to keep me on were gloves frozen to ice, and we gained the top of the main difficulties.

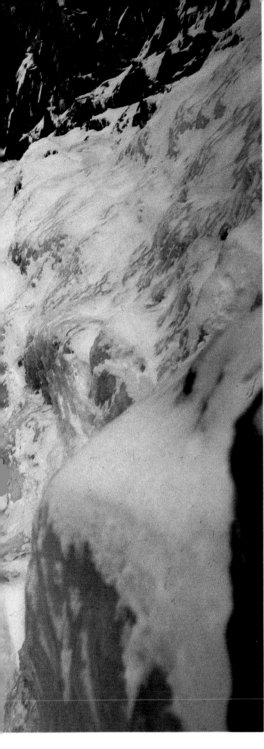

The gully now eased off, but every pitch seemed to present its own little problem to slow us. One pitch, I remember, had a 20ft. ice bulge that was completely hollow, a sheet of ice over nothing but air. The climbing was easy but precarious, rather like cutting steps up the side of a huge bottle. Then snow, followed more easily, on steps that could be kicked, to a small cornice. And we were out; eight hours in Zero Gully, exhausted, elated and glad to be out.

That was the old Zero. The new Zero has been soloed in under an hour, used for time-trials, raced up, queued for, and suffered the indignities of countless ascents. In spite of all that, Zero remains a great ice-climb.

Four photographs that illustrate typical situations on the classic Ben Nevis buttress routes:

*Left: Approaching the Mantrap on the North-East Buttress. Tower Ridge and Carn Dearg Buttress are in the background. Climber: Nick Tritton / Photo: Rob Collister*

*Top right: An icy overhang near the end of the main difficulties on Observatory Ridge. Climber: Rab Carrington / Photo: Alan Rouse*

*Near right: The left flank of the Mantrap – a difficult variation that can be used to turn the normal direct line. Other more circuitous variations exist to the left and right. Whichever option is chosen, gaining the ridge above the step can be both problematic and time-consuming. Climber: Martin Barnicott / Photo: Rob Collister*

*Far right: On the crest of Observatory Ridge where the route joins Zero Gully. Climber: David Bennet / Photo: Donald Bennet*

*Left: Two climbers tackling the fourth pitch of Point Five Gully. The gully is hemmed in on the right by Observatory Buttress – taken by Left Edge Route (Grade 5, Lang and Quinn, 1974) at this point. The iced rocks to the left of the gully provide two Grade 6 routes – Pointless (Smith and Banks, 1978), and Interstellar Overdrive (Kennedy and Anderson, 1980). Photo: Mungo Ross*

*Above: Ice-sheathed steps that provide the main difficulties at the start of the Direct Route on Observatory Buttress. Climber: Rob Ferguson / Photo: Rob Collister*

*Right: Starting the second pitch of Point Five Gully. Photo: James Divall*

# 10  Point Five Gully

by Colin Stead

Probably the most famous ice gully in Scotland, perhaps in the world – that's Point Five. Such is its pull that Americans cross the Atlantic to climb it and Continentals regularly brave both our climate and the malevolent bogs of the Allt a'Mhuilinn with Point Five as their sole objective. Even the name is unique. Where else but on Ben Nevis are there gullies so unimaginatively, yet so evocatively named and numbered from Minus Three to Plus Five?

Its history is almost a microcosm of Scottish winter climbing. Bill Murray was interested in the thirties, but the main assaults began in the fifties and the route really sprang to fame when it contemptuously gave Joe Brown and party a firm and spectacular brush-off, tossing them several hundred feet to the slopes below. Brown was attempting the second pitch when the ice gave way. Neither his ice-peg runners nor second man, Nat Allen, could hold him, and they were both fortunate to be stopped by the third man, Nip Underwood. Brown was uninjured, but Allen had damaged a knee. With typical fortitude they carried out their own rescue. Recording the event in the CIC Hut Book with pawky humour, Brown noted that 'the party descended, at the terrible rate of 32ft. per second, 300ft.' Thereafter, the leading Scottish climbers of the day were choked off by the spindrift avalanches which are Point Five's secret weapon, poised to cascade whenever a hopeful leader is in a suitably committed position. The route earned more attention than any other major climb and its eventual subjection by five-day siege remains controversial to this day. Dignity was restored when second ascentionists Jimmy Marshall and Robin Smith cut up it in seven hours, a time some would find respectable with modern gear. Its reputation in no way diminished, Point Five remained the pinnacle of most winter climbers' ambitions. In 1971 John Cunningham and Bill March convincingly demonstrated the effectiveness of front-pointing techniques with their two-and-a-half hour ascent. In so doing they did much to convert the traditional step-cutting Scots to the inclined picks. Finally, Ian Nicholson soloed the route in something under an hour, a far cry from the 29 hours climbing time of the first ascent; it has since been soloed many times.

Poised between Observatory Ridge and Observatory Buttress, at the apex of treadmill snow slopes above Observatory Gully, Point Five rises 1,000ft to the summit plateau. With no jinking about, and inescapable in its crucial bottom half, it knows no peer as an ice-gully for position and quality. Such a tremendously classic climb is inevitably popular and sometimes even crowded. Recently, as two climbers retreated by abseil, the leader of another party hurtled past them, fortunately at no severe detriment to anyone! But the dirtiest trick ever played by the gully was to one of a successful Inverness rope who, untied and apparently well back from the edge, was hurled to his death when the cornice gave way.

Back in the early seventies Ken Crocket and I sallied into battle one beautiful March day. But the big bulge barring access to the main chimney gradually collapsed, so that after much wallowing I slowly subsided level with the belay. There was no option but a nervous abseil from two *in situ* ice-pegs, our tails very much down. Resident icemaster Neil Quinn, fresh from the third ascent of Orion Direct, consoled us with the fact that it took him five attempts to climb the gully, having been beaten back each time by spindrift, even on one occasion from above the major difficulties on the fifth pitch. We looked like having to serve a long apprenticeship!

Next winter we were back in the CIC Hut at an SMC meet, having confided in two non-attending friends that we were hoping to do Point Five. It became clear from various whispered conversations as successive parties crashed into the hut throughout that sleepless Friday night that we were not alone in that ambition. Les Brown muttered to his partner that 7 a.m. was early enough to set the alarm. Ours went two hours earlier and as we stumbled from our beds the whole hut erupted in a frantic dash for cooking space. I grabbed a cup of cold water and a flaming piece of toast and fled after Ken who was out of the door ahead of me. Quinn fell about laughing. Such unseemly behaviour was a new departure from the normal Club decorum.

We ground up to the foot of the climb. Surely those weren't lights ahead of us? They were, and we arrived breathless to discover our two friends stealing a march on us. They had left the road at an unearthly hour and crept past the hut. There was a nasty silence, anger on one side, embarrassment on the other, and we took second place in the queue. Somehow, despite the sun glinting off the Great Tower in a clear, windless sky, the day had gone

**Route** Point Five Gully, Grade 5, 1,000ft.
**Cliff** The North Face of Ben Nevis.
**First Ascent** Summer: 1955; Winter:
J. M. Alexander, I. S. Clough, D. Pipes and R. Shaw, 12-16 January, 1959.
**Map** See page 41.
**Guidebooks** See page 41.
**Nearest Road/Approach Time** See page 41.
**Route Summary / Conditions** The classic gully climb, often in condition and giving sustained difficulties on ice in the lower 500ft. and two or three smaller ice pitches thereafter. The difficulty varies greatly with the state of the ice and the weather. Any wind causes regular mini-avalanches of spindrift to funnel down its narrow lower section. Good belays and protection.
**Campsites / Bunkhouses** See page 41.
**Bibliography** *Point Five, A Ben Nevis Saga* by Ian Clough (S.M.C.J., 1959) – a detailed account of the first ascent; *The Games Climbers Play* (Diadem) has a brief account of the second ascent in 'The Old Man and the Mountains' by Robin Smith; *Squirrels on Point Five* by Brian Robertson (S.M.C.J., 1966); *Point Five Gully* by Rob Collister (Mountain 28) – a graphic description of an ascent in poor conditions; *Ben Nevis 1970-78* by Alan Rouse (Crags 17).

*Left: At the start of the steepest section of Point Five Gully. The lean conditions seen here are usually found at the end of the season. Climber: Dave Walsh / Photo: Terry Storry*

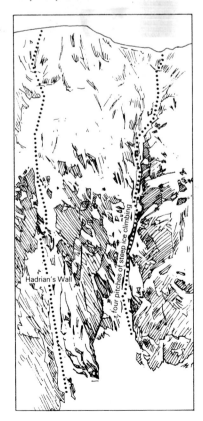

*Above: Point Five Gully and the western flank of Observatory Ridge. Photo: Paul Nunn*

*Right: A heavy spindrift avalanche on Point Five Gully, conditions that can make an ascent impossible. Climber: Jean-Franck Charlet / Photo: Jean Marc Boivin*

resolved when a foothold gave way, leaving me dependent on the new technique. The ice in the chimney felt incredibly steep. I seemed to be rubbing my nose on it as I moved slowly on with a churning stomach and dry mouth. The psychological barrier of our first Grade 5 was proving harder to overcome than I ever imagined. But suddenly there was a good peg in place on the right wall for a runner and the nervous tension and the fear evaporated. With confidence surging I moved happily on to easier ground and ran out the rope to the bottom of the Cave pitch. It looked beautiful, gleaming blue ice with a horizontal rippling; and it was Ken's lead. Up he went, with a pause for an ice-screw runner. The top looked very awkward, his stretchy legs were going all over the place. Suddenly, with a hiss, down came the first spindrift. Out of the line of fire, I took a photograph as his bad language was silenced by the liquid misery. Then he was over the top.

The upper gully was packed with snow to form a great wall. There were no more ice pitches, indeed little of note as we steamed on and crawled happily through the remains of the cornice before the critical gaze of half the Club, who were sunning themselves on the summit. Jimmy Armour trotted round:

'Done half a gully then?'

Three years later I felt the call of Point Five again. This time conditions were very different. A lean winter had left the gully a gleaming smear of ice contained by rock walls which were as bare as in summer. The mountain was quiet and there was no need to rush to be first in the queue. The approach could be leisurely and the climbing likewise.

The first pitch was mine. The only problem was my complete inability to find a belay. Others can find the rusty old bolts of the first ascent, but I've never seen them. Above, a great bulge of green ice gave my companion pause for thought and a drive-in, before gaining the bottom of the chimney. This time there were no nerves, just a steady rhythm, trying not to bang the knuckles on the hard ice. So good was the ice that the picks thudded and vibrated each time they went home. Dave led the crux, but there was no snow wall above, just pitch after pitch of superb ice all the way to the cornice. I was totally content as we coiled the rope on the plateau. This time the gully had given of its best and nothing had marred the day. On a great climb that is how it should be.

sour.

Ken won the first lead up a steep slab and over a bulge to a belay at the foot of the chimney. There were no complaints about the quality of the snow this time. It was impeccable. The trouble was, we didn't really know how to use it. We were at the awkward transition from step-cutting to front-pointing, but wholly committed to neither. Progress depended on frightening lurches from one big foothold to another. This dilemma was abruptly

# 11  Galactic Hitchhiker

by Mike Geddes

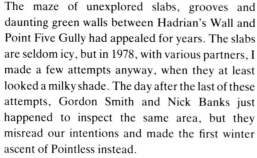

**Route** Galactic Hitchhiker, Grade 6, 1,000ft.
**Cliff** The North Face of Ben Nevis.
**First Ascent** Winter: M. Geddes and
C. Higgins, April 1978.
**Map** See page 41.
**Guidebooks** *Winter Climbs – Ben Nevis and
Glencoe* by Ed Grindley (Cicerone).
**Nearest Road / Approach Time** See page 41.
**Route Summary / Conditions** A hard mixed-
climb; up ice-glazed slabs and corners. Close
attention to the state of the ice build-up and
weather is required to catch it in good
condition.
**Campsites and Bunkhouses** See page 41.

The maze of unexplored slabs, grooves and
daunting green walls between Hadrian's Wall and
Point Five Gully had appealed for years. The slabs
are seldom icy, but in 1978, with various partners, I
made a few attempts anyway, when they at least
looked a milky shade. The day after the last of these
attempts, Gordon Smith and Nick Banks just
happened to inspect the same area, but they
misread our intentions and made the first winter
ascent of Pointless instead.

So Con Higgins and I arrived at the still virgin
slabs rather late one day. The key to the route is a
series of prominent corners high up. We hoped to
climb the initial steep slabs just left of the fall-line
from these corners to gain the foot of the long,
vertical face, which stretches almost to Hadrian's
Wall, and move across beneath it into the corners.
Con true to his civil and sensitive nature, let me
work out my impatience on the first pitch. I was
well 'psyched-up', and grated steadily up the initial
groove. There was a good runner at 60ft., then the
route left the groove for a steep slab. The first 40ft.
led easily to a clutter of loose blocks where I rigged
up a series of dubious runners, reasoning that they
might slow a fall, I carried on. A reasonable crust
lured me on. But it took me into the precarious
situation of dwindling one-inch snow with little
crust remaining, and a 70° slab beneath with no
holds to be found. With my heart in my mouth, I
teetered on, delicately cutting slots in the snow for
handholds, putting as little weight as possible onto
my feet as they moved into the same slots. Just as
the rope tightened. I scrambled into a shallow cave.
It took an exasperating hour groping in powder
snow to find barely satisfactory pegs and a sling.

Con followed with his customary panache and
went on to a more substantial groove, before
breaking up left to below the long, vertical wall. (A
later alternative start comes in here from the left.)
His stance was in a fabulous situation, back to the
steep wall and overlooking 300ft. of slab and the
steep snow slopes below.

I traversed a massive block with great pleasure,
for you could swing safely above the slab, then
scuttle into a good stance. The first prominent
corner of the face lurked above. It held no ice, but
the stance had a dream belay.

I explained to Con that we shouldn't miss this,
that the rope might not be long enough, and so on.
But Con is much too wise – I was forced onto the
right wall, and balanced above his head, clearing

snow and heading for an apparent break in the lip
of the wall. Finally I made the last big hold, about
12ft. below a ledge which led back into the corners.
I tapped our precious knife-blade into a vertical
cracklet. It had to be tied off, and was the only
runner on the wall. I could only just reach the snow
dribbling down from the ledge, and my axe barely
held. It wouldn't do. I tried to use the rock better,
and to place them better, but to no avail.

By now the sun had gone down, and the weather
had blown up. All other climbers had long since left
the hill except Con, stoically huddled out of sight
50ft. below. The only option short of retreat was to
use the peg for aid. I could neither place more
securely, nor test it properly. I just eased onto it.
The exposure was sickening – a fall down to the
slabs would be awfully free.

More snow was now within reach, but it was
pretty poor. I wished for the scoop-like adze of a
Terrordactyl. Up and down I went on that awful
peg, searching for adequate holds until my strength
and warmth were mostly gone. Finally I found
enough, and pulled over onto the ledge. There was
no runner to protect Con, so I had to move back
into the corners and up to an easy groove till the
rope ran out. I collapsed on a funny rounded spike,
and watched Con perched on the lip of the wall,
white with blowing snow, backed by the shadowy
lines of Observatory Buttress.

The first 10ft. of the next corner were bare and
Con scrabbled at it fearlessly before getting
established on the first real ice of the day. I
unpacked my headtorch. The yell came at last, and
I lunged up in bobbing pools of light, to join him at
the Girdle Traverse ledge, where the angle
changed. We finished by several pitches of 2 or 3.

Gordon was up there two or three days later, true
to his competitive mood, out to climb the 'real' route.
But it thawed like hell during that period, so there
can't really have been much white stuff left. And of
course, if he had found the face thick with good ice,
that would have been out of condition too . . . .

*Near right: The third pitch of Galactic Hitchhiker – at the start
of the corners. Climber: Wil Papsfield / Photo: Tony Saunders
Far right: The west flank of Observatory Ridge. Photo: Mike
Geddes*

# 12  Observatory Ridge

by Paul Nunn

**Route** Observatory Ridge, Grade 3, 1,300ft.
**Cliff** The North Face of Ben Nevis.
**First Ascent** Summer: 1901. Winter:
H. Raeburn, F. S. Goggs and W. A. Mounsey,
April 1920.
**Map** See page 41.
**Guidebooks** See page 41.
**Nearest Road / Approach Time** See page 41.
**Route Summary / Conditions** A rocky
buttress followed by an icy upper face.
Exposed mixed climbing on the lower part
of the route varies greatly in difficulty
according to conditions – the combination of
powder and verglas making it extremely
problematic. Hard snow or ice is sometimes
encountered on the upper section. In this
garb it is the most difficult of the classic Nevis
ridges.
**Campsites / Bunkhouses** See page 41.
**Bibliography** *Fourteen Hours on the
Observatory Ridge* by W. M. MacKenzie
(S.M.C.J. 124, 1938) – an account of an ascent
in very difficult conditions; *Mountaineering
in Scotland/Undiscovered Scotland* by W. H.
Murray (Diadem) has some valuable technical
comments; *A Progress in Mountaineering* by
J. H. B. Bell (Oliver and Boyd) – more sage
comments; *Big Four* by Colin Beechey
(Climber and Rambler, January, 1982)
describes an ascent in average conditions.

*Right: The Ben Nevis cliffs — from North-
East Buttress to Tower Gully. Photo: Alex
Gillespie*

Between the ice-chutes of Point Five and Zero
Gullies a narrow snow-ridge plunges down from
the summit cornices to a slight shoulder, hesitates,
then bursts into a looming and steep-sided buttress
above Observatory Gully. This is Observatory
Ridge, harder than most and companion to North
East Buttress, though not quite as long or as
difficult. The buttress-like lower ridge is slabby at
first, and then cut by a shelf which extends from the
lower slopes of Zero Gully. Above this short, steep
walls bar easy access to the medial snow-ridge,
beyond which the route becomes indefinite and in
certain circumstances a traverse left into Zero
Gully provides an easy way out.

The wind thumped around the outside of the CIC
Hut. Most of the bunks were occupied and the pot-
bellied stove was burning down in the morning
gloom. In the shadows the greasy gas rings stood
silent, their legs dipping into the squalid spillage on
the cooking bench. Up to my nose in the sleeping
bag I dreamed of Antarctic Expeditions I had read
about, of good dinners, and of the birds at the
Rosthwaite Dance in Borrowdale. We were sick of
Scots austerity.

A föhn-like thaw ruled. Observatory Gully had
avalanched, but there might be more. A gale blew
on the plateau. No-one moved. One unlucky
inmate groaned miserably with broken ribs
incurred falling from top bunk to table in the early
hours.

But if others were dormant, Pat Fearnehough

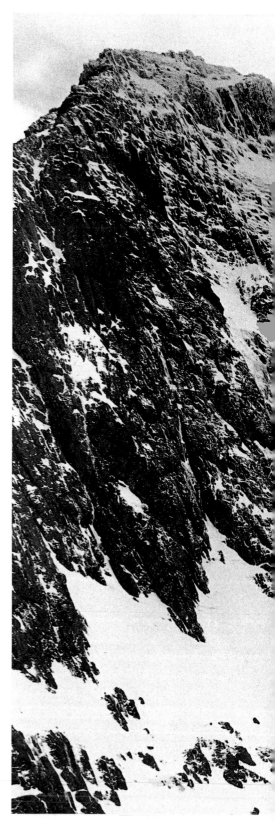

*Above: At the base of the final rock step on the lower section of Observatory Ridge. The ridge here provides an excellent viewpoint for Orion Face on the left, and Point Five Gully and Observatory Buttress on the right. Climber: Dave Viggers / Photo: Colin Beechey*

*Top right: A view from below the Minus Face to Zero Gully (left), and the lower section of Observatory Ridge. Photo: Alex Gillespie*

*Bottom right: The snow/ice arête that marks the end of the lower section of Observatory Ridge. At this point the route comes close to Zero Gully (right). Climbers: Richard Brooke, Mike Banks and Dave Viggers / Photo: Colin Beechey*

never was. There had to be some action each day and usually there was. In bad conditions we had climbed Tower Ridge again, Comb, Green and Gardyloo, and some longish bit of the Little Brenva Face. But it was not enough. With an Alpine season not too far away we practised holding falls on ice-axe belays, falling alternately from the base of the first pitch of Zero to the debris at the bottom. The red sweater went on and so did the kettle. Bacon and eggs were meticulously arranged in the pan. With a bite of bread and marmalade and a second mug of tea we were on our way.

Though conditions were repulsive we went light. It was to be a technical test, climbing with as little gear as possible. One 9mm rope, three slings and karabiners, one straight axe each, no crampons.

Blocks of snow filled the back of Observatory Gully. Crossing them, we took to the slopes leading up in the mist towards the Ridge, kicking steps in damp snow. It was a relief to be out of the gully lines in such conditions. Once on the rock it was a zig-zag progress up the front of the ridge, pleasant enough, with the occasional runner. Some short walls and icy ramps were more difficult, with little pulls up icy sections of rock. We moved steadily, always making steps for our vibrams, to the snow-ridge above the lower rock difficulties. We sensed the day's shortness as the light faded behind thick, swirling clouds. Step-cutting led on and on to more rocks. The last few hundred feet were plastered and blasted by squally gusts, and in the storm it was hard to decide on any particular direction to follow, or even see where step-cutting might be possible on the complex, runnelled face. So we plumped for the apparent ease of the top of Zero, over to our left, hoping to escape the savage wind.

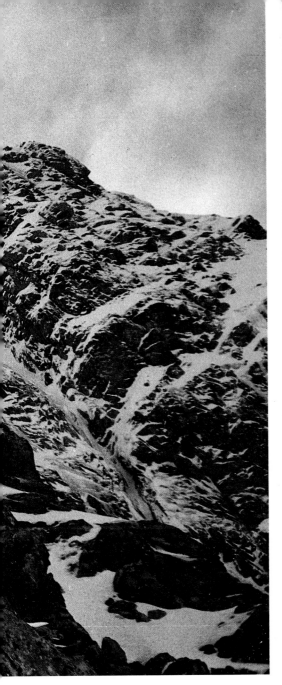

At first all went well; steep, neat, little ladders of steps on undisturbed névé. I hewed out a stance under some bulging ice, planting the axe as a dubious belay. Pat came up for the attack, but just as I expected him to launch out he stepped back in retreat. Spindrift poured over the bulge, coating our anoraks in ice and sliding through the holes in my elbows:

'The snow above is loose slops. It's going to be the one-axe pull.'

Pat's uncramponed feet scraped uneasily in the shallow ice-slots of the bulge. Using an ice-jug on the left, he thwacked the axe over the bulge, so hard that I thought he might break the second shaft of the week. Now the axe was in. The die was cast. Standing in two icy footholds, I leant on the axe-belay, which met ice only a few inches below the surface, intoning the old rule of ice-climbing – the

*Above: The upper part of Zero Gully gives an alternative and straightforward finish to Observatory Ridge by-passing mixed ground to the left. Climber: Richard Brooke / Photo: Colin Beechey*

leader must not fall. Below was the full length of Zero Gully.

His feet bridged up to former handholds, vibram edges braced on ice. After what seemed an age, those legs were levered up out of sight and the stiff rope followed, yard by yard through icy mittens up the ice-bulge into the grey mist and the dark. It tightened and I heaved out the axe-belay. Snow-glow just illuminated the edges of the steps. I shivered. A few optimistic bridging movements on thin crust led to the bulge. The pick went in above, but everything else gave way. Rope and axe pulled me into the gully above.

Pat was hulking. A shadow in the dark, rather spent, feet disappearing into a bucket step. We weren't out yet. It was a question of skimming the soft surface stuff away and hacking into the solid underlayer. Always a step or two ahead, with the odd handhold too. There was a sense of near-total isolation from the other man on the rope. Pat came up, missing all the holds in the dark, then led on, suddenly breaking onto the plateau. Almighty relief. It was 8 p.m. in February.

In the mist and wind we groped from cairn to cairn, roped and keeping the cornices well away to the right. We turned away from the gale and aimed

for the bivouac hut, at that time sited at ground-level near the top of Tower Gully. A hole appeared and Pat went for it like a dog for a bone.

The bivouac hut of red corrugated tin was completely buried, but we knew it had been excavated recently. There we feasted on bread and cheese, and dried peas that we found on the floor. We serenaded the grey man howling outside with our complete repertoire of songs, a few hymns included. Of no great help was a Gideon Bible thoughtfully left for Lost Souls – we hadn't a match. Eleven hours later it still blew as dawn came and we hopped straight over the cornice into Tower Gully to escape the gale. It was still necessary to nick out steps for 1,000ft. to make a safe descent.

Hours later, as we luxuriated in the hut, Dougal Haston's wild figure burst in with bad news. At 10 p.m. Pat, Dougal and myself set out to scour the whole of the base of the North-East Buttress from high in Observatory Gully to the bottom of Carn Mor Dearg Arête. For hours we probed and prodded for tangled bodies. Nothing came to light, and as we cramponed back to the very door of the hut we heard that they had turned up elsewhere. What a fraught black mound the Ben can be

74

# 13 Smith's Route, Gardyloo Buttress

by Ken Crocket

'For the purpose of becoming familiar with the balance and 'feel' of an ice-axe . . . the axe may be thrown into the air, caused to revolve a determined number of times, and caught on the descent, in either hand, as a good step-cutter should be ambidextrous.' *Harold Raeburn*

'Then I lost my grip of the axe and it started somersaulting in the air with both my arms windmilling trying to grab it and my feet scarting about in crumbly holds.' *Robin Smith*

I dropped my single axe once only during my step-cutting days, and that was from near the top of the first pitch of Point Five Gully. It embedded itself next to my amused partner, quivering like its hapless owner. How the pitch was finished belongs to another story. The point is that those of us who began winter climbing in the late sixties, were very aware of the heritage left by Patey, Marshall, Smith, *et al.* A young entrant to the Scottish scene quickly buried his nose in the pages of the SMC Journal, where blurred photographs of legends on twilit ice walls quickened the pulse and sustained the excitement from one weekend to the next. Patey moved fast over mixed ground; Marshall didn't like wrist slings on his axe; wrist slings were slow and clumsy anyway. And Smith — I never met.

Strength and endurance were major factors in the years before the early seventies, when climbing ice meant hanging on with one Dachsteined hand while chopping holds in stubborn ice with the other, all with a usually ill-balanced, cut-down axe, twice as heavy as some modern tools. A good step-cutter had to be ambidextrous, to permit cutting on either side and to allow the alternate arm to recover its strength. But if the effort was high, the rewards were higher still. Each pitch was a route in itself; to be worked out and worked on. The climber on a hard route was constantly aware of the fine line between satisfied fatigue and dangerous exhaustion.

None of this should be forgotten when considering the hard winter classics climbed in the step-cutting era. All of the Smith and Marshall routes fall into this category, including the toughest little gem of them all, Smith's Route on Gardyloo Buttress. But new technology hasn't dulled all the old excitement. Harder routes have been opened up, as have variations to existing routes. And, occasionally, conditions can spring a nasty surprise.

Gardyloo Buttress, at an altitude of over 4,000ft, is one of the highest in these Isles. Standing imperiously at the head of Observatory Gully, its name derives from Gardyloo Gully on the left, which was used as a rubbish dump by the former observatory. (Gardyloo, of course, is a corruption of the French *Gardez l'eau*, and was the traditional cry of Edinburgh householders when tipping refuse into the streets below.)

The Buttress drops two edges into Observatory Gully, with a steep face draped between. At three-quarters height the rocks lie back and the twin ridges are seen to enfold a short gully. This embryonic gully is responsible for any plating of snow and ice on the very steep central wall, while the lowest rock of the buttress form a steep convex slab with grooves cutting into its right flank. These grooves are capped by an overhang, above which a narrow hanging ramp cuts up and left to join with the top of the central wall. In good conditions, ice descends from the foot of the ramp to form an icicle-fringed cave just right of the central wall. The first ascent, so graphically described in the twin essays of Marshall and Smith, started up the grooves, traversed left beneath the small cave, then climbed the steep central wall to gain the final gully.

By February 1975, when Chris Gilmore and myself stepped onto the buttress, we knew of only four ascents since the first some 15 years earlier. All these ascents, to the best of our knowledge, had taken the original line. And until we began climbing that blue, sunny day that was our intention too.

From below, the cave looked like a hospitable refuge which might provide a belay. We could also see a hanging ramp above the cave, but although it looked like an interesting line, from our angle it appeared to be too well-defended. A quick solo up the first 20ft. brought us to a ledge beside a groove. On the few windless days it can be very difficult to judge the temperature. It had been thawing at the hut, but here we were not so sure. There were no tell-tale dripping icicles and the ice-wall in front seemed dry. So we carried on.

The first pitch went steeply but steadily until just below the cave. Here the ice steepened to the vertical and developed a disconcerting booming sound. With relief I broke through a rapidly-thinning skin of ice to topple into a constricted hollow. The psychology of a frightened climber is interesting – three useless belays suffice where one

**Route** Gardyloo Buttress (Smith's Route), Grade 5, 500ft.
**Cliff** The North Face of Ben Nevis.
**First Ascent** Winter: R. Smith and J. R. Marshall, February 1960.
**Map** See page 41.
**Guidebooks** See page 41.
**Nearest Road / Approach Time** See page 41.
**Route Summary / Conditions** A sustained ice climb with poor belays. As it is high on the mountain, the original line comes into condition in most winters; the Ramp variation usually takes longer to build up.
**Campsites and Bunkhouses** See page 41.
**Bibliography** *The Games Climbers Play* (Diadem) includes accounts by Marshall ('Garde de Glace') and Smith ('The Old Man and the Mountains'); *Winter Dreams* by Ken Crocket (S.M.C.J., 1976) *Climbing Ice* by Yvon Chouinard (Hodder and Stoughton) has several good photos of the climb including the jacket illustration.

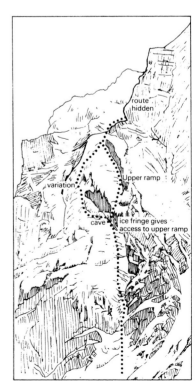

will not. From left to right my best efforts were a big nut in the ice, a loose screw half-in (that repeatedly fell out), and funniest of all, a dead man that I had to stand on to keep down.

By the time Chris appeared, laden with a bulging sack, I had regained my confidence. The hanging ramp now looked easier; the traverse left appeared most uninviting. The ramp it would be. One small detail remained — it was guarded by an overhang. Chris looked at the belay and showed the whites of his eyes. Rather me than him I felt, at least I could engage in some activity. A few moves right led to the bulge, and a few moves left back to the belay again. Chris was dubious, but I reassured him and borrowed a long sling, for I had spotted a weakness in the ice-curtain. Hooking an arm behind an icicle and leaning out right, in several sorties I cut and battered at the curtain. Finally the axe broke through into space behind. A similar opening, picked through higher up, and I had a thread runner. If the ice held we had a belay. I returned for another rest. The next sortie saw me poised on the overhang with a beautiful left hand-jam, hammering a drive-in ice-screw above for more protection. Things were looking better. A final breather in the cave, a cheerful farewell to Chris, and I danced out right again. The left hand clenched between two icicles, my right pick swung overhead onto the ramp above. A vibrating shaft in solid snow was like music of the spheres to me, and I pulled over the bulge and onto the ramp.

We should have known better, of course. Loose ice-screws and wet gloves seldom lie. Water surreptitiously oozed through the ice behind a façade of drier snow. Only on the ramp did it make its presence felt. To ease my companion's passage on the overhang I had leaned down and removed the drive-in screw by hand. I felt I might need it higher anyway. The overhang at my feet not only concealed the belay, it hid from view the rest of the buttress below, so that the view beyond was an aching plunge down the length of Observatory Gully. I didn't look down much after that.

A few moves up and the picture became all too clear; a few inches of loose, wet, snow-ice overlying the water-ice below. A freeze would probably transform the pitch into something more pleasant. Unfortunately I had to deal with it now. A little voice within whispered retreat, but the thought of a difficult and ungainly scrabble down the overhang was too repugnant. I tried for jams in the corner

Left: Gardyloo Buttress. Photo: Ken Crocket

Below: Moving up on to the lower slab of
Smith's Route. The climber is wearing a
'hairy' sweater which gives extra adhesion.
Climber: Ken Crocket / Photo: Crocket
collection

where the ice had separated from the rock; it was
too thin and snapped off. So it was picks all the way.

The water-ice was plating on impact, and several
times the front-points of my left crampon slid down
sickeningly until they caught on the ice again. The
ramp was pushing me out leftwards and as the ice
was thin near the corner I was relying heavily on the
left axe and foot to maintain contact. A few more
hesitant moves up and my mouth was dry. A
worried Chris had sensed the bad vibrations
coming down the line, but for him there was no
reassurance. I gained a paradoxical comfort in
knowing how helpless he must be feeling. The
hidden face of teamwork. The little voice
whispered again – fear and panic this time. But
that path leads the wrong way and I rebelled. 'Get a
grip of yourself,' I said, 'Make the moves as best
you know how.' Left pick up; scrape away the
rubbish; hit the ice; feel the pick bite; trust it.
Repeat with the right. Kick the left foot in, trust it,
step up. Concentrate on the moves – suppress the
imagination. And so I inched towards the final
bulge. To climb 20ft. took a lifetime. Calf muscles
protested and forearms knotted from the
continuous strain, but finally the bulge was
reached. With the arrival of an icicle-runner
confidence began to trickle back. I was able to take
my first rest since the foot of the ramp. I could
wring the water out of my gloves before the final
move. The bulge had shrunk to a manageable size,
and with a high step out left and a pull I was up the
wretched ramp, wallowing in soft snow at the foot
of the final gully. A rock outcrop was typically
crackless, and for the second time that day I sat on a
dead man to bring up my long-suffering
companion. I was flying high on natural opiates,
and laughed as Chris rolled over the bulge with a
gasp of relief and a comment about craziness.

I offered the final lead to Chris, but as he
generously suggested that I finish the job, I
continued up the beautiful little gully. The snow
was well-drained and perfectly firm. I ran out a
rope's-length and belayed below a sun-rimmed
cornice. Ice-crystals danced in the sun as Chris
broke through above me. We met again in the glare
of the plateau and indicated our respect for the
route by shaking hands. Formalities over, I
attempted a somersault, and danced around
shouting 'Gardyloo Buttress!' and 'Smith lives!'

And, in a metaphysical sort of a way, I felt that
we had gone no little way towards meeting him.

# 14  Tower Ridge Rulebook

by Robin Campbell

I first made the acquaintance of Tower Ridge in 1958. At that time my idea of correct footgear was a pair of what may have been duck-shooting boots, abandoned in a golf clubhouse, retrieved by me and banged full of clinkers, tricounis, etc., which you could get mail-order from Blacks for a few pence. Somehow I got these over the Carn Mor Dearg Arête one summer from Steall and sparked my solitary way up the Ridge, my head full of the Bill Murray brand of German Romanticism. I made a terrible mistake and traversed left too soon below the Eastern Traverse into a zone of bottomless slimy corners. Of course I thought this *was* the Eastern Traverse. It was pure luck that I got up. That's Rule One: climb the Great Tower until it gets really steep before traversing left.

The next time I saw it was in February 1960. I went up the Allt a'Mhuilinn with John Proom and Jim Gillespie from Perth. The Ben was in immaculate winter condition (I've only ever once seen it so good) and Tower Ridge glittered in the full moon like a colossal iceberg. In the Hut were Smith, Marshall and others. At breakfast a grubby arm reached down to remove a sausage from my plate:

'Yuh're surely no goin' tae eat a' that by yersel , laddie?' Its owner enquired.

Their gear lay all over the hut floor – short ice-axes, baby nylon, alloy karabiners, crampons. They seemed to have no plans to get up. I had no conception that such people climbed. German Romanticism could encompass them only with difficulty. We chopped our way carefully up Tower Gully over snow hard as frozen turf. I noted that my heroes (for they were already that) had whizzed up behind us in their Grivels and were now, despite their lengthy sojourn in bed, whizzing up Observatory Buttress. The whole thing captured my imagination completely. It led me to go to Edinburgh with the primary object of seeking these men out and learning how to participate in this splendidly unwholesome style of climbing. This is all by the way, of course.

Eventually I climbed Tower Ridge properly. I can't remember much about that day except that we (whoever we were) got into a mess at the Gap and wasted ages buggering about in the half-dark trying to fiddle round it on the right. This is Rule Two: go straight across the Gap. Step down onto a ledge on the Tower side, lean (fall!) over to the Ben side, and clear the huge spike that's hidden there

under the fog crystals or whatever. Lots of people don't know this rule.

Another time, in 1965 or thereabouts, a great squad of 'Squirrels' and I attacked the Ridge in unfavourable conditions of wettish powder, verglas, etc. We took ages on the lower bits and then chose an enticing line of grooves just left of the crest on the Little Tower. These look easy but are actually hard (horrible pull-ups on sloping ledges) and darkness got the better of us. We retreated by abseil, which is fairly difficult on a ridge. A shambles from start to finish and all because we broke Rule Three: climb the Little Tower by the crest, not by these nice easy-looking grooves on the left. Lots of people don't know this rule either; read Bill Murray, for instance.

Rule Four is never, never, never start off by climbing the Douglas Boulder, that 'pretty little pinnacle' (to use William Brown's description in the 1896 SMC Journal) at the foot of the Ridge. The Douglas Boulder is quite hard, about Grade 4, extremely large, about 600ft. and has a nasty sting in its tail — the descent to the Gap.

Number Five isn't really a rule or even a recommendation, but if there's a lot of you or if you're not much good, it may be as well to climb onto the Ridge above the first steepening beyond the Douglas Gap. That steepening can provide in icy conditions difficulties greater than anything above.

**Route** Tower Ridge, Grade 3, 2,000ft.
**Cliff** The North Face of Ben Nevis.
**First Ascent** Summer: 1892 (in descent); Winter: J. N. Collie, G. A. Solly and J. Collier. March 1894.
**Map** See page 41.
**Guidebooks** See page 41.
**Nearest Road / Approach Time** See page 41.
**Route Summary / Conditions** With good snow conditions and on a fine day this is, perhaps, the finest one-day mountaineering expedition in Britain, but in poor conditions it can be a tough proposition. Long, complex and committing but with no particular technical difficulties in good conditions. Care should be taken to avoid an involuntary bivouac.
**Campsites / Bunkhouses** See page 41.
**Bibliography** *Divine Mysteries of the Oromaniacal Quest* by J. N. Collie (S.M.C.J., September 1899) – a strange first-ascent account; *Four Days on Ben Nevis* by W. Inglis Clark (S.M.C.J., September 1899); *Mountaineering in Scotland/Undiscovered Scotland* (Diadem) by W. H. Murray; *A Progress in Mountaineering* by J. H. B. Bell (Oliver and Boyd), *Call out* by Hamish MacInnes (Hodder and Stoughton) and *Mountain 8* contain descriptions of the fatal accident on Italian Climb in 1970, with comments on slab avalanche conditions; *Big Four* by Colin Beechey (Climber and Rambler, January 1982).

*Left: Looking down to the Great Tower of Tower Ridge from the summit plateau of Ben Nevis. Climbers: Stanislaw Handel and Michael Momatiuk / Photo: Mark Hutchinson*

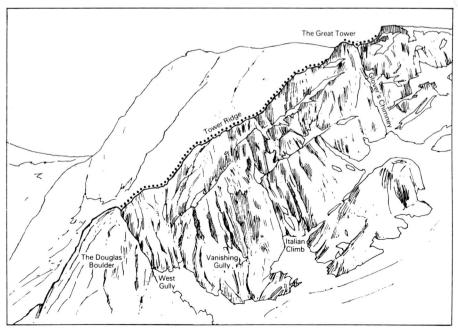

Nowadays everyone can climb Tower Ridge (especially if you follow these rules) and enjoy the best day's climbing to be had in these islands, on the biggest single piece of rock, on the highest mountain. This is just as it should be, since Tower Ridge was climbed in winter in 1894 by Norman Collie and his friends, twice in a week. Collie thought it was tremendous – like the Italian Ridge of the Matterhorn, he said. The early SMC thought so too. At their Easter Meet in 1896 five different parties climbed it. They also worked out all sorts of little wrinkles on the Great Tower (nowadays you only ever see people on the Eastern Traverse – a discovery, made some years later, of Willie Naismith's) and various dodges. One of the most interesting ones is that the Eastern Traverse ledge continues past the fallen block into Tower Gully. In the first place this provides a simple escape route from below the Great Tower, a blow to German Romanticism. In the second place it can be used to make an entry onto the Great Tower, allowing an

ascent of the most spectacular section of the Ridge after an early afternoon breakfast, let us say. In the third place it permits an easy but exciting girdle traverse of the Ridge from Coire na Ciste. Go up Broad Gully from the top of the Garadh na Ciste and then the gully between the main and secondary Tower Ridges to gain the Great Tower. Now traverse off into Tower Gully! This bizarre excursion is well-suited for miserable weather or incompetent parties.

Between the wars people worked out various ways up the enormous north-western flank of the Ridge, the so-called Secondary Tower Ridge. Vanishing Gully and the Italian Climb are probably the best of these routes, and they were climbed in winter by the brothers Marshall (one apiece) around 1960. Above these routes it's usual to go left to join the Ridge below the Little Tower. Then you can press on up or down the Ridge or simply traverse off into Observatory Gully by East Wall Route (I wish I'd known this in 1965!). If it's terribly

late you don't even need to go onto the Ridge –
just keep on up the Secondary Ridge until you
reach Broad Gully and go down this to Coire na
Ciste. Right up at the top of the north-western flank
are two splendid climbs, for my money the best
ways of approaching the Ridge. The first of these is
Pinnacle Buttress of the Tower. Marshall nearly
fell off this when figuring out a so-called 'Difficult'
route on the crest of the buttress while working on
the guidebook. If you go this way you get 1,000ft of
concentrated climbing up to the Ridge, over the
Great Tower, the Gap, etc., without any of that
dreadful fiddling about with coils. I don't know that
anyone's actually *been* that way in winter. Donald
Bennet climbed the Pinnacle Buttress in the winter
of 1957, but by an inferior line to the right. To the
right of Pinnacle Buttress is Glover's Chimney
which leads directly up to the Tower Gap. This is
disappointing to begin with but the final pitch up to
the Gap is a brute and well worth the trip.

  Whether you climb the Ridge honestly, from the

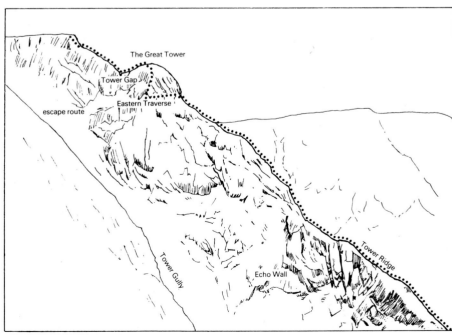

*Left: Tower Ridge from North-East Buttress. Photomontage: Tony Riley*

*Above: Two photos which show the approach to, and crossing of, the Tower Gap – straightforward climbing in clear, calm weather, but a formidable obstacle in storm conditions. Photos: John Allen and Ken Crocket*

*Above: Climbers on the final section of Tower Ridge above Tower Gap. Photo: Mark Hutchinson*

Douglas Gap to the plateau in a straight line, or deviously by one or other of its many back entrances, be sure to arrange things so that you get to the Gap just as darkness is falling (take that extra hour in your bed). If you are lucky the whole thing will be sheathed in ice and/or fog crystals, and a vilely cold wind will be whistling through it. There is no more intimidating sight on the Ben (except possibly the Allt a'Mhuilinn path from below), and what a relief when it turns out to be a real piece of duff!

Oh, I forgot. Rule Six: don't under any circumstances decide to spend the night up there and finish your climb in the morning. This luxury from the heady days of German Romanticism is no longer available. The local Mountain Rescue team will be up in a flash buzzing round with dogs and helicopters and you won't get a wink of sleep. Not a wink. Press on and take your chances.

# 15 Comb Gully

by John Barry

Jeez, they were arrogant, those lads. All the arrogance of youth and more besides – the arrogance of those whose vaulting ambition has yet to stumble on a pair of front-points.

They were mighty pleased with themselves too. After all, they had just climbed Smith's Gully as their first-ever Scottish winter route. True, they had been fooled by MacInnes's adjectival winter grades into thinking it was akin to a summer VS. But even so, hadn't they just romped up it, one pterodactyl between them, through the rain and a couple of respectable avalanches? And hadn't a hastily convened Clachaig tribunal declared this *débâcle* to be the third direct ascent? They were pleased with themselves all right.

What about Point Five? They zoomed up that in a couple of hours, and Zero the next day before swapping crampons for PAs to scamper up Centurion and Sassenach. All this in one week . . . of course they were arrogant. Why, this very day they had scratched about for the new route they now felt was their due, and pounced on a little line somewhere right of Glover's which, with rare modesty, they graded 4. (It is doubtful whether their arrogance would have been dented one whit had they known that Raeburn had done the route 50 years earlier, and grade it 1.)

When they thought, which wasn't often, they saw themselves as young gladiators, or a self-appointed Praetorian guard to winter climbing. Too lucky in their narrow experience to need the crutch of romanticism; unbeaten, unbattered, unthinking, they could climb mountains but were not yet mountaineers.

Despite their brand new Grade 4 it was still only 10 a.m. so they cast about for something else to occupy them till opening time. One of them, I can't remember which, and it hardly matters now since they were both fools, found that Comb Gully was just down the road. Neither the route-description nor its star-rating excited much interest, but their attention was caught by a note: 'Since Dougal Haston climbed it solo in 20 minutes, its reputation has declined'.

To arrogants such as these this was a Dachstein thrown down in challenge. Not that they knew much about Dougal Haston, or cared. Nor did they care that Comb was a little gem tucked away amongst the castellated towers of that part of the Ben. No, they cared only about the challenge, and they knew a race when they saw one because they

were young and, Oh! so arrogant . . .

Helter-skelter down No. 2 Gully to the foot of the Comb. Toss for position, set a watch and off again. Go! A gallop up the first snow slopes. A canter to the bay where a startled team were belaying. A trot to the final bulge, where their presumption gave best to steepness and they climbed for a minute or so before a final idiotic charge to the summit plateau where they collapsed, feeling ever so slightly silly. 'Seven minutes,' gasped one to the other.

Why? 'Dunno . . .' one said. 'Why not,' said the other. If they had reflected then, as they have since, they might have argued that since the game of mountaineering doesn't bear rational examination for more than a couple of minutes it wasn't worth thinking about. They might have done, but they didn't.

They are wiser now. Slower too, ten years on. And sorry. Sorry because they treated a great wee route badly; sorry because they remembered little of it; sorry because seven minutes is too quick to savour any gift that the goddess of all mountains dispenses as a favour; sorry because they're less daft now.

That was years ago. Since then they have both been back to do the decent thing. Climbed it, that is, with all the accoutrements of modern ice and in more decent haste. Enjoyed it too – and found it, here and there, rather less than straightforward. Best of all, they arrived at the top several spindrifted hours after 'go.'

Wiser men, they now know that climbing on the Ben belongs to a tiny élite of games best consumed in a slow passion with the conscious accumulation of pleasure as insurance against that day the passion, or the power, deserts.

Do I know these lads? Sure. We all do. There are two at every crag still vying to bear that standard for the Praetorian guard. I know. I tried to carry it once myself, for seven daft minutes.

**Route** Comb Gully, Grade 3/4, 450ft.
**Cliff** The North Face of Ben Nevis.
**First Ascent** Winter: F. G. Stangle, R. Morsley, and P. A. Small, April 1938. Summer: 1958.
**Map** See page 41.
**Guidebooks** See page 41.
**Nearest Road / Approach Time** See page 41.
**Route Summary / Conditions** A short gully in fine surroundings with a steep 20ft. corner pitch and some small ice bulges. Good belays, but sparse protection. The approach slopes can be troublesome, even avalanche-prone.
**Campsites / Bunkhouses** See page 41.

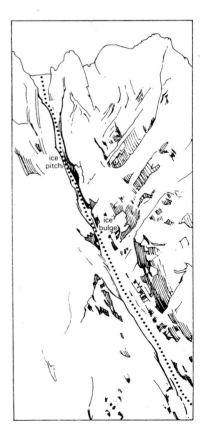

ice pitch

ice bulge

Left: *Comb Gully, with Comb Buttress to its right. Two winter routes have been made up the buttress: Hesperides Ledge (Grade 3, 1959) and Pigott's Route (Grade 4, 1960). Photo: Colin Stead*

Right: *The steep groove which is the crux of Comb Gully. A bolt (not obvious) on the left wall provides a belay anchor, but some leaders prefer to use it as a runner and leave the second positioned lower down. Climber: John Barry / Photo: Barry collection*

# 16  Green Gully

by Robin Campbell and Harold Raeburn

**Route** Green Gully, Grade 4, 400ft.
**Cliff** The North Face of Ben Nevis.
**First Ascent** Winter: H. Raeburn and E. Phildius, April 1906. Summer: 1958.
**Map** See page 41.
**Guidebooks** See page 41.
**Nearest Road / Approach Time** See page 41.
**Route Summary / Conditions** A steep and sustained ice gully (four main pitches) which is usually in condition. Difficult to protect. The approach slopes can be troublesome and sometimes avalanche-prone.
**Campsites / Bunkhouses** See page 41.

Green Gully marks the right edge of the central bastion of the Comb in Coire na Ciste. It has a special place in the history of Ben Nevis because it was the scene of a futuristic ascent by Harold Raeburn in 1906 and was surely Raeburn's most significant winter climb on the Ben. The gully runs straight as an arrow and usually consists of a succession of short, steep ice pitches. There is often a short entry pitch where the frozen watercourse crosses a steep rock band. With a heavy build-up of snow this will hardly be noticed but late (or early) in the season this pitch may prove a formidable obstacle. It may, however, be bypassed by following the obvious ledge rightwards below the central wall of the Comb. Apart from this pitch, a steep pitch halfway up and the exit will normally provide the main difficulties, though it is possible to traverse left to join the arête of the Comb from below the exit pitch.

Raeburn's ascent, although reported at length in the SMC Journal passed unnoticed by post-war climbers, perhaps because Raeburn described it as an ascent of the Comb. It should, of course, have become known as yet another 'Raeburn's Gully,' and perhaps the best of them at that! Raeburn's two winter ascents of Crowberry Gully on Buachaille Etive Mor suffered the same fate and in the first guidebooks to Glencoe and Ben Nevis, Green Gully is attributed to a rope led by J. H. B. Bell in 1937 and Crowberry Gully to W. M. Mackenzie's party in 1936. There is really no adequate explanation for these oversights but it is tempting to speculate that Bell and Mackenzie found these gullies so hard that they couldn't conceive of the possibility that they might have been climbed in the Edwardian period.

We still lack a thorough evaluation of Raeburn's contribution to climbing in Scotland. However, it is already clear that he was climbing at the turn of the century at a standard which was not surpassed until the renaissance of Scottish climbing led by Marshall and Patey in the fifties – a judgement fully sustained by examination of Raeburn's prowess in the Alps which included such exceptional ice-climbs as the Spigolo Inglese (sic!) on the North Face of the Disgrazia, climbed with Willie Ling in 1910.

To set the record straight, then, here is Raeburn's own account of the climb from his article 'A Scottish Ice Climb' in Volume 9 of the SMC Journal, January 1907:

The Comb

four ice pitches

'Among the climbs prospected at the memorable summit meet on Nevis in Coronation Week of 1902 was that of the ascent of the Comb, a steep ridge projecting into the lower or Coire na Ciste corrie of Nevis. The foot of this ridge overhangs, but means of access could apparently be obtained on the north side by climbing a gully on the left wall. This gully, however, proved very steep and slabby, and was not seriously attacked.

'All SMC members and their friends who took part in the Glencoe Meet of 1906, will remember the wonderful weather of early April, extending, alas, only into the first day of the meet. The Rev. A. E. Robertson, who had spent these days at Fort William, reported the rocks of Ben Nevis in perfect conditon. During the meet, and for a full fortnight thereafter, Atlantic cyclones raged, and when I came to Fort William, through rain and snow on April 22 to keep a tryst with Robertson, he reported the rocks heavily iced. Robertson, greatly to his and my regret, found that, owing to a slight indisposition, he would be unable to accompany me. I was saved the necessity of climbing the Comb

*solus,* however, as he introduced me to a Genevese gentleman, a member of the Swiss Alpine Club, Monsieur Eberhard Phildius, who was staying in Fort William, and who proved a pleasant companion and a keen and capable climber.

'During the night the wet sou'wester had given place to a strong cold wind from the north-east. Sweeping up the Allt a' Mhuillin, it carried with it flurries of snow. As our party passed below the great overhanging cliffs of the Carn Dearg Buttress, coat collars turned up, and hats well down on the back of the head, the snow, hitherto flying past in large soft flakes, turned hard and powdery in the grip of the increasing cold. Many feet of snow lay in the deep chasm below the Tower Ridge, and sheets of snow-ice covered the *roches moutonnées* below the glacier-planed lip of the Lochan na Ciste. Where a small streamlet trickles down these rocks, we swung our ice-axes to cut ourselves steps and seats, and to hollow out a crystal basin which the bubbling water quickly filled. It was a clearer interval, and we utilised it to scan our route ahead.

'On our right, as we looked down, rose above us

*Above: Green Gully, flanked on the left by Comb Buttress. Photo: Alex Gillespie*

the jagged arête of the Tower Ridge, but how different from its summer aspect!

'And through the drifts the snowy clifts
   Did shed a dismal sheen.'

Just like a great iceberg it was, or perhaps more like a mass of rough marble, all the dark rock hid by a plating of ribbed and embossed dull white snow-ice, with here and there streaks, ribs and columns of pale green water-ice from a few inches to several feet in thickness.

But the mists were again creeping slowly down from the heights, and presently everything was blotted from our ken but a few yards of the steepening slope of hard snow up which we were now making our way. We had, however, got our bearings for the foot of the Comb.

'My plan was to ascend the icy lower slopes of No. 2 North Tower Ridge fully till under the great overhanging beak of the Comb, traverse across a snow ledge below it to our right, and then cut up till

*Above: The final ice pitch of Green Gully.*
*Climber: David Howard Jones/*
*Photo: Grindley collection*

amateur axe, which, by the way, is nearly useless for real hard ice work, stands a strong chance of being broken. The only way to make an impression on this toughest of snow is to cut a groove with the blade and then drive the piece out with the pick. There is one advantage about the toughness for the climber, that handholds and footholds once made can be relied upon. They are practically as good as if cut out of rock.

'Soon leaving the gully we reached the rocks below the beak of the Comb, ice and snow-covered as was everywhere. The ledge noted was traversed, steps kicked and scraped, round to the right, then up a steep slope of soft snow, lying from one to two feet deep on hard icy stuff. The angle was pretty steep, and avalanching-off highly probable, so it was necessary to dig down to and cut steps in the underlying hard snow. Now we found ourselves looking up, so far as the mist and the descending cataracts of snow-dust would permit, the steep gully which should give access to the ridge. Then began the real struggle. Keen frost reigned, and a biting wind moaned among the icy battlements impending over the great moat of the Corrie na Ciste. We two, stormers of one of the salient towers, felt the blast strike us now and again as it swept round the angle of the Comb. The worst was that the snow-batteries were opened on us from both above and below. From above one could, to a certain extent, take cover beneath the shield of our cone-pointed, brim-turned-down felt hats, but occasionally the snow that fell mixed with the seldom-ceasing stream that poured down the gully, was caught by the powerful ascending eddy and rushed up, thus taking us behind our defences. The pain of a stream of icy snow in the face is so great that work must stop, and the face covered till breath is regained. Fortunately those underhand tactics were never long continued, and the interrupted sapping and mining was soon renewed.

'To speak of angles of ice or snow is always dangerous if these same angles have not been actually measured by clinometer, but two of the pitches we now encountered, if we make a distinction in what was practically one great pitch, were what is usually known as perpendicular, i.e., probably 70° to 75°, with small portions approaching 90°.

'It was of course only due to the peculiar tough quality of the snow-ice curtain hanging down these steeper portions that they were climbable at all. At

we gained the foot of the slabby gully prospected in 1902. Then to cut up this, going out to our left to the arête whenever possible. As we ascended the steepening snowfield, here and there projected from the smooth slope large masses of half-buried fragments of cornice. Evidently fallen while the snow slope was soft, these tenacious blocks had sunk in and stopped. They exhibited in a high degree all the qualities of Scottish névé in late spring. Struck by the pick of the ice-axe no result is produced; the pick merely sinks in and remains. If levering out is attempted, the ordinary Swiss

angles such as these it is impossible to remain in toeholds in ice without holding on as well, and it is impossible to hoist the body up unless the handholds are cut so as to give a 'pull in.' These icy curtains allowed of this being done; frequently the pick broke through to soft snow or black vacancy, backed with green bulbs of ice, and 'pigeon-hole' holds resulted.

'Ice-work of this kind is, however, particularly cramping and exhausting, and progress was slow. To hang on with one hand, while that long two-handed weapon, the modern ice-axe, is wielded in the other, is calculated to produce severe cramps in course of time, and did so now. It is much harder work than the free, open swing on the hard, splintery ice-slopes of the Alpine peaks. I suggest for climbs such as this our going back to the original Swiss icemen's tools, the iron-shod straight *baton,* and the light tomahawk-like hatchet stuck in the belt when not in use. The second of these pitches almost stumped us, but yielded at the third attempt, and the reserves, in the person of Monsieur Phildius, were now brought up, and took their place in the van.

'It was at this height evidently possible to traverse out to the left and thus reach the arête, but the sharp edge of this was so fringed and crowned with unstable-looking cornices of ice and snow that we judged it better to continue straight up.

'Round the top of the gully — rather a shallow scoop now — up which we were cutting, stretched the threatening line of the summit cornice. This did not look very high from farther down, but on approach was seen to rear its breaker-like crest, more than two-man height above the slope. Obviously our only chance here was to traverse out to our right where a rib of ice-covered rock ran up to meet the cornice, reducing it to half the height, and where it was only slightly overhanging. This way eventually went but the Comb was game to the last, and I must confess to a feeling of helplessness for a moment as I stood on my ice-axe, driven horizontally into the vertical snow wall, so many hundreds of feet of little-less-than-vertical, ice-plastered rocks stretching away down into the depths of the mist beneath, while my fingers slid helplessly from the glassy surface of the cornice névé, in the vain endeavour to find or make a hold by which I might haul myself up. The problem was solved by a retreat, until Phildius was able to pass me up his axe. Then the ice-plating was quickly

shattered, and with fingers well crooked in the tough névé, a steady drag landed the body over the cornice lip, and Phildius soon followed.

'Objections may be made to this climb that it is not the actual climb of the Comb. This is true, for we were never once on the exact arête. But what does this really matter? Phildius and I came out for a climb, and we got one, up one of the steepest cliffs on Nevis, in as icy conditions as I have ever seen the old berg. We were both pleased and enjoyed it every bit, except perhaps when under the hottest fire of the rear batteries.'

*Above: A view down Green Gully. The climbers are starting the fifth pitch, above the ice pitches in the narrows below.*
*Climbers: David Howard Jones and Cynthia Grindley / Photo: Paul Moores*

# 17 The Curtain and Glover's Chimney

by Colin Stead

**Routes** The Curtain, Grade 4, 300ft. Glover's Chimney, Grade 3, 450ft.
**Cliff** The North Face of Ben Nevis.
**First Ascents** The Curtain – Summer: 1961 (Morning Slab); Winter: J. Knight and D. Bathgate, February 1965.
Glover's Chimney – Summer: 1902; Winter: G. G. Macphee, G. C. Williams and D. Henderson, March 1935.
**Map** See page 41.
**Guidebooks** See page 41.
**Nearest Road / Approach Time** See page 41.
**Route Summary / Conditions** The Curtain – a short, technical, water-ice climb that comes into condition rapidly during a freeze. Good belays. The ideal training route for inclined pick technique. In the old style, it was a strenuous and difficult climb. Glover's Chimney – a popular climb with a steep entry pitch leading to a long snow couloir topped by an awkward verglassed chimney. The approach is often arduous and sometimes avalanche-prone.
**Campsites / Bunkhouses** See page 41.
**Bibliography** *First Ascent of the Curtain* by D. Bathgate (S.M.C.J., 1965); *Ben Nevis 1970-78* by Alan Rouse (Crags 17); *Days On Ben Nevis* by G. C. Williams (S.M.C.J., 1935) describes the first ascent of Glover's Chimney; *A Progress of Mountaineering* by J. H. B. Bell (Oliver and Boyd).

The Curtain is a great tumble of green ice which drapes the lower left flank of Carn Dearg's Great Buttress. In most reasonable winters it forms and persists for long periods, but not if hard frosts follow a dry spell. For the purist, it is a great non-route, as it skulks round the side away from the imposing challenge of the Buttress face and ends only part way up the cliff, on Ledge Route, allowing a quick slope-off down into No. 5 Gully and safety. It does, however, have the advantages of being short, on pure ice, and accessible being only 15 minutes from the CIC Hut. It has become very popular as a training climb, a route for a short day or dubious conditions.

Its first ascent was an important one, as it involved a prodigious amount of step-cutting on the hard ice, meriting a grading of 5. Nowadays, modern picks make it a more modest 4. It starts innocently enough as a gentle iced slab at the angle of those of Etive, but as you advance a full, runnerless rope-length, the exposure suddenly grips you and you gratefully belay in the shallow cave at the top of the corner. The climbing is now sterner, as the ice rears up, smooth and hard. A left, right, left movement is necessary to gain the vertical wall of ice which slopes up and left to the edge. This is a popular proving ground for ice-screws. As you hang on your picks, spare a thought for Dave Bathgate, cutting left-handed across this on the first ascent:

'After making the normal incut hold, I chipped the sides away, leaving a mound of ice like half a tennis ball sticking up in the middle of the hold. Fingers could then spread and the thumb grip. . . My left arm was as strong as a wet newspaper by the time I reached the rock ledge.'

From the comfort of a good perch on the left edge, an exciting traverse leads right to the steep barrel of knuckle-bruising ice which tapers away to a groove as it gradually falls back to the haven of Ledge Route. Having completed The Curtain, there is ample time to stroll round into Coire na Ciste to climb a gentler and older classic, Glover's Chimney, which slashes down the side of Tower Ridge from the Tower Gap to the top of Garadh na Ciste. The route-bagger can gain this point by an ascent of the short Garadh Gully which divides Tower Ridge from Garadh na Ciste and offers two straightforward pitches at Grade 2/3.

The first winter ascent of Glover's Chimney in 1935 was led by the indefatigable Graham

Macphee, who commuted from Liverpool when engaged in compiling the first guidebook to the Ben. This required some enthusiasm when you consider the roads of the time and the 700-mile round trip. It was a modest milestone, as little of note had been added in winter since the days of Raeburn. The climb took eight hours of fine effort and, in keeping with tradition, the crux was climbed in the dark. Some minor discord occurred during the lunch-break, when Macphee produced firelighters instead of the hoped-for sandwiches.

The middle section of the climb had been descended from the base of the Great Tower in December 1907 by the party of Goodeve, Inglis Clark (after whom the CIC Hut is named), and McIntyre, who had been unable to find the Eastern Traverse (a not-infrequent event even nowadays), during an attempt on Tower Ridge. Caught in darkness, they failed to descend the bottom icefall of Glover's Chimney, and re-ascended by a new way up the right wall to gain the summit plateau. Their troubles were compounded when their navigation went awry and they finally met an SMC rescue party near Steall in Glen Nevis, and gained safety after 30 hours on the mountain.

My first acquaintance with the climb, on a day of youthful incompetence, paralleled that of Goodeve's party in that, unable to agree on what was the Eastern Traverse on Tower Ridge in the thick cloud and gathering gloom of a December night, we too descended Glover's Chimney to the icefall. Courage failed us after much contorted downward step-cutting, with our suddenly-useless short axes, illuminated only by a tiny pocket torch which proved incapable of penetrating the blanket of mist and night. We eventually returned to the Ridge to bivouac unpleasantly in the drizzle. Next day our line of holds could be seen to end only a few feet above the bottom of the initial icefall.

Steep to begin with, then falling back, the first ice of Glover's gave a pleasant, long pitch (with no runners) in the days of step-cutting. Modern techniques reduce this to a few minutes of unexacting effort to a belay on the left. Thereafter, a long section on mostly easy snow in what is more of a gully allows the mind to relax and appreciate the scenery. The final, narrow chimney springing abruptly to the Tower Gap comes as a rude shock. This is the crux. At first its ice is comfortably thick, but it thins suddenly, just as the exposure becomes impressive. I find the best way is to chimney up, but

*Below: The Curtain. Photo: Robin Campbell*

*Right: The initial slab pitch of The Curtain, showing a thick veneer of water-ice on the slab surface. Climber: Richard Zorab/ Photo: Mungo Ross*

other solutions are possible. Runners on the left wall are utilised gratefully until you gain the inhospitably draughty base of the Tower Gap. The downward views are spectacular, as you hasten to belay. Leaders should not relax too soon, as the far wall of the Gap gives the proverbial sting, before the easy terminal slopes of Tower Ridge and the summit. For those unable to sustain a frontal assault on the short wall of the Gap, a cheating way exists by the rocks down and round to the left. This knowledge may prevent any repetition of the verbal and physical tug-of-war I once witnessed here between a successful leader and recalcitrant second.

On a rare day of good visibility, wander from the summit by the graceful arête to the top of Carn Mor Dearg, and enjoy the view of the Ben's cliffs as the sun sets down Loch Linnhe.

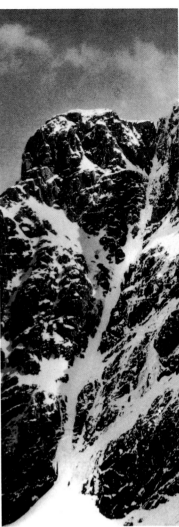

*Left and above: Two views of Glover's Chimney, one showing climbers on lower icefall. Photos: Alex Gillespie and Wil Hurford*

*Right: The final section of Glover's Chimney. Climber: Pete Long / Photo: Ed Grindley*

Three views of The Curtain:

*Above: Nearing the end of the initial slab pitch, with ideal snow/ice conditions. Climber: Dick Peart / Photo: Peart collection*

*Top right: The final moves of the leftward traverse to gain the second stance. Climber: Ian Sutherland / Photo: Ian Sykes*

*Bottom right: An overall view of the route with a climber on the second pitch. Photo: Ed Grindley*

*Top: The bivouac shelter on the summit of
Ben Nevis. Photo:John Beatty*

*Bottom: Ben Nevis and the Carn Mor Dearg
Arête from Aonach Beag. Photo:
Ken Crocket*

*Above: The bastions of North East Buttress and Tower Ridge dominate the northern flank of Ben Nevis above the CIC Hut.*
*Photo: John Beatty*

# 18 Route 2, Carn Dearg

by Alan Rouse

**Route** Route 2, Grade 6, 800ft.
**Cliff** Carn Dearg Buttress, Ben Nevis
**First Ascent** Summer: 1943; Winter:
M. Geddes and A. Rouse, February, 1978
(the direct start was climbed a few days later
by G. Smith and I. Sykes).
**Map** See page 41.
**Guidebooks** See page 41.
**Nearest Road / Approach Time**
See page 41.
**Route Summary / Conditions** A committing
and sustained mixed-climb. Usually climbable
in cold conditions but best reserved for
optimum conditions (rare) which occur when
a heavy snowfall is followed by periods of
thaw and freeze.
**Campsites / Bunkhouse** See page 41.
**Bibliography** *Ben Nevis 1970-1978* by Alan
Rouse (Crags 17); *Arctic Island Climbs* by
Alan Rouse (Crags 23).

For years climbers have looked at Carn Dearg Buttress trying to imagine the superb climbing that good winter conditions would bring; and for years they have been disappointed, for the great natural lines of Centurion and Sassenach rarely hold more than a sprinkling of snow while ice never seems to form in any quantity. But in 1977, as Mike Geddes and I walked up to the CIC Hut in perfect weather, the buttress was for once well-plastered.

We got up quite early the next morning but Mike, a stickler for tradition, refused to budge from the hut until 11.30 a.m. When I suggested leaving at 9 a.m. Mike countered with 'Och, if we leave now we might finish before dark.' He was keen to emulate the Smith—Marshall tradition, by which you started late and finished well after nightfall. He could quote verbatim from original articles describing such epic first ascents as Gardyloo Buttress and the Orion Face Direct. Since the north side of Ben Nevis is a very special place I was happy to wait, enjoying the anticipation of some exciting climbing ahead.

The idea was to climb the buttress by any route, but on inspection only Route 2 seemed feasible and in good winter condition. Route 2 was the first to tackle the main part of the Buttress and was climbed in June 1943 by Kellet and Russell. It sneaks in from the left and traverses right across the buttress, neatly and naturally avoiding the great overhangs which cut through all the other natural lines. Its exposed slabs defy the overall verticality and offer a very reasonable summer rock-climb through serious and severe terrain. Today the line was obvious, picked out by a continuous ribbon of snow which led across temptingly to the right arête of the buttress.

From the base of The Curtain we walked right along a snow-ledge to reach the chimney-line of Route 1. I led off up the chimney, hesitantly at first until after 30ft. I began to feel at home again. The reassuring bite of crampons in frozen, snow-covered turf and the finding of a good hold buried under two feet of loose snow brought great pleasure. A small overhang fell to a little muscle on a cold but secure hand-jam and I soon reached a stance at the start of that crucial traverse. Mike came up and led through, though it took him a while to launch out onto the smooth, snow-covered slabs to our right. It was obviously going to be a hard pitch. The snow would not support our weight unless, by chance, crampons bit on a

rugosity beneath while sloping handholds allowed only leaning moves to clear the next few feet. It was time-consuming and strenuous on the calves. Standing on sloping footholds in crampons needs precision, and some luck! Especially when the handholds supply no more than balance.

I followed the traverse, grateful that the main holds had been cleared. Although we had only completed two pitches, we were a long way above the ground and retreat would not have been easy. I led off towards a giant icicle that emerged from under the prominent band of overhangs. The ice was friable and, worried about the lack of protection, I climbed slower than the difficulties necessitated, cutting the occasional foot-ledge to rest until I found a good belay tucked under the overhangs, near where Centurion breaks through. Mike came through and tried to continue in the

*Right: Approaching Carn Dearg's Great Buttress from the CIC Hut. Photo: Alan Rouse*

same line, but all the holds seemed to slope the wrong way and he came back. There was another possibility: it looked possible to drop for 15ft. to join a lower traverse line. I protested at the prospect of seconding this descent and encouraged Mike to try the upper way again; but no luck. Reverting to the lower line, he descended the 15ft. and found a good runner before making some disconcertingly difficult moves rightwards which led back to the main traverse line. When my turn came I decided to leave a runner in place for some degree of protection. Descending difficult moves always enhances the exposure to an alarming degree, and the exposure here was considerable anyway. We were perched between overhangs of indeterminate extent. Those above clearly defined the margins of our world, and focussed attention more sharply on the void below.

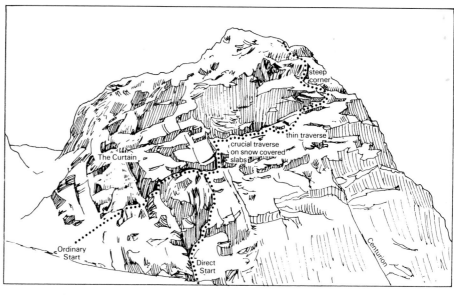

*Above: On the upper section of the climb where the final pitches of Sassenach provide a direct finish from the end of the traverse. Climber: Gordon Smith/Photo: Ian Sykes*

*Right: On snow and ice-glazed slabs at the start of the crucial traverse on Route 2, just after crossing the chimney of Route 1. Climber: Mike Geddes/Photo: Alan Rouse*

Another traversing pitch brought us to the edge of the buttress, which I naïvely assumed would mark the end of the difficulties. Darkness fell as we climbed easily over big icy blocks until Mike belayed before a steep groove, down which a fierce wind and a torrent of spindrift were whistling. Steep grooves, spindrift and darkness are ingredients which have greater appeal to Mike than me, so I did not object when he was keen to lead on. Before setting off he dived into his sack and produced a flask of coffee from which he poured a cup with a fingerless gloved hand and a demonaic grin. The groove was vertical and choked with rotten snow, but underneath spikes and icy cracks provided runners and comfort. I crouched, with hood up and sack over my head, at the base of the groove as Mike's efforts added to the already healthy spindrift, and soon I could only see a feeble head-torch beam some incalculable distance vertically above me. He took ages, and when my turn came the holds were buried again,

waiting to be rediscovered. I struggled up, nearly blinded by snow behind and in front of my glasses. Occasionally, just as further progress seemed unlikely, I would bury my arm to the hilt and find a welcome spike. By the time I reached the stance my hands were frozen but I led through, thinking surely now things would be easy. The angle eased but the holds disappeared and I was suddenly 50ft. above Mike on smooth, snow-covered slabs. I was sure there was an easier way but I could not find it so I carried on chimneying up an open groove, trying desperately to see something and hoping that I would find a runner. Eventually I emerged onto easy open slopes.

Traversing across the top of the buttress we found No. 5 Gully and ran on down to the hut and, as Mike had to be in London the next morning, we continued to the halfway dam, where we had left the car. Unfortunately, by the time we had negotiated a couple of locked forestry gates, it was already light when we reached the road.

# 19 Crowberry Gully

by Jimmy Marshall

The elegant sight of Buachaille Etive Mor's rise from rich brown moorland to majestic, frosted crown of winter splendour is a vision unique in the Central Highlands, a blatant display of mountaineering challenge sounding a clarion call to climbers' aspirations.

Doubtless Harold Raeburn felt the same appeal, perhaps welcoming an opportunity to dismount his heavy bike and rest his battered seat whilst pleasurably pondering on a possible ascent of Crowberry or Gully B as it was then known. It was he who led the earliest ascents, no less than three times into the gully to achieve both winter and summer ascents to his satisfaction. Thereafter the climb remained virtually unsullied for over 25 years until a new generation of ice-climbers from Glasgow discovered its exciting qualities, when they added the final major pitch above the junction to complete the winter climb as it is known today.

Murray's belated but stirring account of his experience roused post-war ambitions and interest in winter climbing but endless benightments or failures by strong parties of the day tempered my youthful ambition for Crowberry with caution. Eventually, one *dreich*, snowy day, a serious attempt was joined but it ended in failure as the leader descended or flowed down the 'Thincrack Chimney' in a minor avalanche, cunningly to halt his decadent progress by anchoring his Tricouni nails deep in my frosted pate. This experience and the ensuing retreat did much, however, to contribute to success on the next visit, when as a rope of three we chopped our way up in marvellous conditions which left me with a great empathy for the mountain and the Crowberry Gully in particular.

I've been back often since; during the heyday of step-cutting it was hell; the ice was hacked to pieces, a virtual ladder to the summit. Fortunately, taste and techniques change, for today the hard men rush past Glencoe in favour of Nevis, Meagaidh or the far North, leaving Crowberry and its satellite climbs uncluttered for the delectation of a few old men or the teething of Pterodactyl chicks.

The gully is endowed with distinctive scenic qualities, with its huge, overhung wall impending on the left and great cataracts of ice encasing the slabby right wall. The bed twists and turns with each successive pitch succeeding in difficulty and exposure to form a delightfully orchestrated natural happening which will always fill the climber with joy in exercising his skill amongst such marvellous surroundings.

The reputation of Crowberry stems from the days, of ice-clogged, nailed boots, frozen mitts and stiff hemp ropes, when it was a redoubtable ascent within the capabilities only of a few bold men. Today the climber will not be pressed. The delicate progression on front-points and hammers leaves him free of trauma to enjoy the delights of superb scenery and exposure in much the same manner as climbers savour the pleasure of situation on warm classic summer rock.

The climb can vary dramatically according to the level of snow-cover during a season, and therein lies a factor which should be used to fully enjoy the route in relation to one's experience. This variance is further compounded by the fact that little snow in a normal season equates with little light. The chimneys of Crowberry, lightly-filled, verglassed, and deluged in spume, can be very leavening places. You won't raise eyebrows in the pub saying 'I've done Crowberry'; but you'll know you've extended yourself to get down for that drink.

However, for the moment, it should be assumed idyllic weather and median conditions prevail on our ascent, in February or March we've strolled up from Jacksonville, maybe even breaking sweat; if we have a few climbs under our belt we'll pick our way up the frozen waterslide and upper slopes to a ledge under the East Wall of North Buttress where we can see into the gully and know the tournament

**Route** Crowberry Gully, Grade 3, 1,000ft.
**Cliff** The North East Face of Buachaille Etive Mor.
**First Ascent** Summer: 1910; Winter: H. Raeburn, W. A. Brigg, H. S. Tucker, April 1909. Left Fork, Grade 4: C. M. G. Smith, R. J. Taunton, I. C. Robertson, March 1949.
**Map** O.S. 1:50,000 Sheet 41 (228548); S.M.T. 1:20,000 Sheet Glencoe.
**Guidebooks** S.M.T. *Glencoe and Glen Etive* by Ken Crocket; *Winter Climbs – Ben Nevis and Glencoe* by Ed Grindley (Cicerone); *Scottish Winter Climbs* by Hamish MacInnes (Constable).
**Nearest Road / Approach Time** The A82 Crianlarich – Glencoe road at Altnafeadh (221563). 1 mile/600ft. Allow 1 hour.
**Route Summary / Conditions** The great classic Scottish gully with a succession of varied pitches, the most difficult being high on the route. Optimum conditions occur after a good build-up of snow and a prolonged period of cold weather. In lean conditions, under vérglas the route is much harder, and has been experienced as a Grade 5 expedition.
**Campsites and Bunkhouses** S.M.C. Hut, Lagangarbh; Creagh Dhu Hut, Jacksonville; L.S.C.C. Hut, Blackrock Cottage; Grampian Club Hut, Inbhirfhaolain in Glen Etive; Glencoe Youth Hostel; Macall's Bunkhouse, Clachaig Inn; Campsites at Kingshouse, upper Glen Etive and in Glencoe.
**Bibliography** *Mountaineering in Scotland/Undiscovered Scotland* by W. H. Murray (Diadem) has a superb account (Chapter 20) of an eventful early ascent; *The Day We Didn't Do Easy Gully* by C.M.G. Smith (C.U.M.C.J., 1949) – an account of the first ascent of Left Fork; *A Winter Ascent of Crowberry Gully* by Tom Weir (Mountain Craft, Spring 1958) describes an ascent of the gully in hard conditions.

*Left: Buachaille Etive Mor. Photo: Hamish Brown*

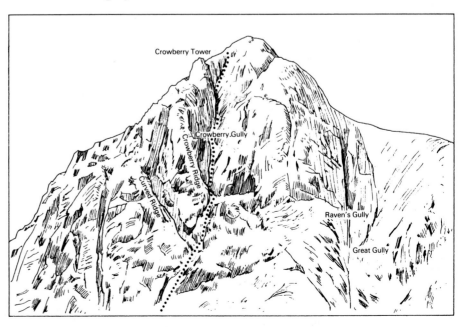

*Below: Two views of the Thincrack Chimney
– the first difficult pitch of Crowberry Gully.
Climbers: Unknown (left) and Reg Pillinger.
Photos: Ed Grindley and Ken Crocket*

*Far Right: Looking down Crowberry Gully
from the Junction. Photo: Tom Weir*

is about to begin. So relax, have a bite or smoke, sort out the gear then push on up about to the first cave to rope up and arrange leads. About here, for some time, there was a purloined road sign, fixed to the left wall with the somewhat laconic warning 'ICE'.

Already the scenery is impressive, but the first step is only a gentle loft — just enough to get the legs uncrossed and waken up. Then simple treading leads on to another comfortable cave, where you can appreciate the beautiful colour combination of rock and icicle. The next pitch is much the same, but sharper, likewise the snow above as it steepens to a narrowing of the gully.

There are two ways above – straight up a thrutchy chimney, or by a groove and traverse in on the right. Either way is stimulating and will get your mettle up. Steep snow above leads to the base of the 'Thincrack Chimney'. The view down the gully is now superb. Dark overhung walls frame the vision on the right, delicate runnels and ribs of rock

Right: The difficult pitch from the Junction where a rightwards traverse across icy slabs allows access to the (easier) right fork of the gully. Climbers: Chris Gilmore and Dave Gundry / Photos: Ken Crocket

Left: A view looking directly into Crowberry Gully. Photo: Hamish MacInnes

whole party can lounge in a fankle of ropes and relax. The view out the window is superb, blue sky, plummeting rock and sparkling spume.

Once more it's by the right wall, steep but blessed with inches of healthy ice. Enjoy the exposure and company till out over the lip, then it's bridging, steep and exposed ice in isolation. Spindrift sifts down to fill the neck and sleeves, but there's no weight, it's only wind-blown powder from the summit slopes. A few awkward moves lead to the snow above and it's cracked; then up to the base of a mini-pitch to wait.

This and the funnel above are shambled up to take a belay, happy in the experience of a perfect day. It's unlikely, even on a nice day like this, that you'll unrope; it's coiled in hand to the summit to divest yourself of irritating paraphernalia and enjoy the superb views over Glencoe to silvered sea-lochs shimmering in the evening sun. A great climb!

An ascent by Left Fork alters the whole character of the route, not only because it is more demanding but possibly because it disrupts the escalation sequence of the 'Voie Normale'; for once in Left Fork's chimneys, things change radically. Unlikely ever to fill out with snow or ice, they call for old-fashioned thrutching up verglassed walls, exhausting but safe, deep within the dark recesses of the mountain. Ultimately, after much slipping up and down, a chockstone perch is gained high up and impressively out over the main gully, a superb spot; but up above, the great capstone fringed with icicles is begging the question. From here, on the first ascent, the leader made a desperate but successful assault; the second followed via the head of the third man, who in turn was unable either to climb or be pulled up over the capstone. So they abseiled down to complete their day — no doubt a very exciting and memorable experience.

Today the means of protection are infinitely improved and the roof is accommodating on this score so persistence should prevail. A contorted effort leads up and out to the lip, whence the icicled fringe plummets out into the impressive maw of the gully. There's a tendency to fling yourself despairingly over the lip, but progress is maintained by back-and-foot till secure anchorage is obtained. Only then, with points well home, can the truly impressive drop be relished with equanimity. A very exciting climb, not quite up to the traditional route, but certainly well worth doing.

and ice sweep down on the left to the warm brown and golds of the moor; from here it seems you could do a Cresta down the beautiful blue chute, right onto the A82. But up is the operative word of the day and the 'Thincrack' generously provides thick ice on the right wall, ideal for pick and stick and you gain the rocky grotto of the chimney of Left Fork. Not much in the way of belays here and much damaged rock from the passage of vandals.

Now you're at the epic-making crux of past generations – no sign of it today, however. There's enough ice for the axes and a simple, rising, rightwards traverse out on ice or névé is all that's required; the exposure certainly increases on the way out though, almost enough to make you cower back in! But lean out, enjoy it, look at that swoop of the gully. Whoosh, down comes a wave of powder, but there's nothing to it; just a small indicator of what could be, and so up and on to belay on rock by the steep continuation of the gully. The next rope length on snow leads into a superb cave where the

# 20  Raven's Gully

by Rab Carrington and John Barry

**Route** Raven's Gully, Grade 5, 500ft.
**Cliff** The North East Face of Buachaille Etive Mor.
**First Ascent** Summer: 1937. Winter: H. MacInnes and C. J. S. Bonington, February 1953.
**Map** See page 107 (225546).
**Guidebooks** See page 107.
**Nearest Road / Approach Time** See page 107.
**Route Summary / Conditions** A gully with mixed climbing characteristics: with steep ice, snow-covered rock-climbing and gigantic chockstones. Sustained difficulties which can be increased by adding the Direct Finish. A good plastering of snow is essential to bring it into condition.
**Campsites and Bunkhouses** See page 107.
**Bibliography** *I Chose to Climb* by Chris Bonington (Gollancz) has an account of the first winter ascent.

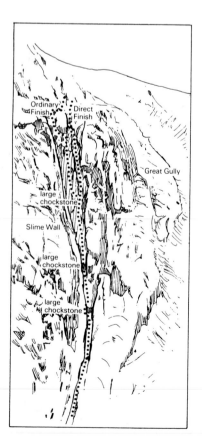

## AN EARLY ASCENT by Rab Carrington

It must have been January '69 or '70 because I was still at university in Glasgow and Big Ian was at the Building College. I had it badly organised that year with lab. practicals every Friday afternoon. So it wasn't till gone six that I got off the blue train at Balloch and started the long hitch up to the Coe.

The hitching spot was deserted, cold, I remember. Maybe even a chance of getting a route done this weekend, a bit of a rarity in Glencoe. The hitching went well that night, as it always does when you're in no particular hurry. The lochside was as black as ever, then swinging up over the hills above Tyndrum the hills suddenly lit up as the moon rose and set the frosty snows twinkling.

At the Kingshouse I got out and padded down to the hotel – maybe Big Ian and some of the lads will be in and we can have a bit of a bevvy together and a game of darts. But the pub was deserted, quiet as the grave and almost as cold. The barman came through from the obviously warm lounge to serve me near-frozen pints of Heavy. Just before closing time Jimmy Weed from up the road called in and we had a bit of a blether about skiing conditions on Meall a'Bhuiridh. Not that I knew anything about it, or was particularly interested in it. It was just nice to talk to someone. Closing time in Scotland, and the doors were thrown open; an icy blast hit the inmates and reminded them it was time to leave.

Typical, I thought – freezing weather, skies clear as a bell, conditions perfect, and me stuck here with no-one to climb with. I left the road and followed the faint track down to Jacksonville. The moonlight sparkled knowingly on the stepping-stones and I took care not to skate off one into the icy river. The 'Ville was as dark and silent as it always is when you are on your own. I stepped inside the doorway and stopped. The typical musty smell came to my nostrils. I let my eyes adjust to the darkness, then felt my way round the walls till I came to the first stub of candle, which, when lit by fumbling fingers, cast an eerie light round the square, bare room. In the corner was a pile of gear – Ian's. A black brew pan hung from the roof and nothing else. Well, if Ian's gear is here he must be here too; probably hitched up early and decided to go on down to the Clachaig to see what the crack was – obviously better than the Kingshouse. Put a brew on – he'll be glad of that after walking back up from the village. No chance of a lift at this time of night. Brew finished, I doss down on the bare

boards, no airbeds allowed here, and go to sleep.

A thin layer of ice has formed over the tea before Ian staggered in. It was 3.30 but he still woke me up to tell all about this fantastic bird he picked up in the Clachaig; got a lift with her back to her place in Kinloch and he reckons he was on to a promise tomorrow night – pity about the 15-mile walk back to the 'Ville. Still, a little thing like that never bothered Big Ian.

'What about a climb tomorrow?' I queried.

'Why not,' said Ian. 'What d'you fancy?'

'Raven's,' said I.

Next morning, with sleeping-bags hunched up over shoulders and steamy glasses over mugs of tea, Ian told the full tale. He'd not really come up with big routes in mind, and after all, Raven's hadn't had many winter ascents. In fact all he had with him were boots, axe, and one crampon. The other one he had lost out of the back of the car when he was returning from climbing the Eiger North Face. Still, we should be able to do it he said, laughing.

The first pitch leading up to below the chockstone was straightforward, and we soloed up to it and set up belays. The year before I'd watched as Les Brown had struggled inconclusively on this pitch. With spider-like legs he had desperately tried to bridge up past the chockstone with very little success. Having two crampons, I was in the lead and concentrated on the more conventional left wall. Scraping a couple of flimsy footholds in the thin icicle allowed me to jam the shaft of my axe in a crack. Without a thought of the consequences I feverishly grabbed the axe and with legs threshing wildly and absolutely no technique I found myself above the chockstone and looking for a belay. Ian followed, snapping all before him; footholds went crumbling into space, icicles spun useless over his shoulder, but Ian came up full of it and grinning. So happy was he that I quickly ushered him into the lead before he had time to have a proper look at it. Gear changeover didn't take long; two half-round Cassin ice-pegs, a Leeper, and a Chouinard angle was our full complement of equipment. I'd been relying on Ian to supply the gear for this little sortie.

Ian performed like a snow-plough, cutting himself a trough in the soft snow, 30ft., then 40ft. of rope was paid out, and no protection. I glanced automatically at the belay – let's hope he finds something soon. 70ft. and still nothing. Suddenly Big Ian disappears from the gully above and is

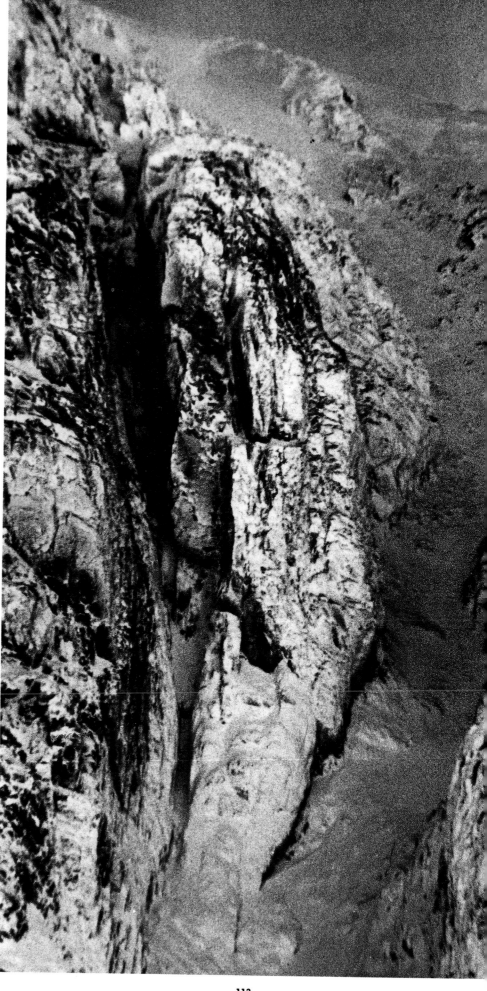

replaced by a black hole. Seconds later this was filled by Ian's toothy grin: 'Come on up, it's a great doss up here.'

Just when Ian had been wondering what to do about protection the snow had collapsed in front of him and he was deposited in a tiny ice cave complete with belay.

The next few pitches were a doddle and we were romping. Great bellows of laughter swept up the gully as we constructed conversation-pieces for the pub – 'Where have you been today, lads?' 'Ach, we went for a bit of a walk up the Buachaille. Nice day out you know. Raven's Gully we did, and Big Ian with only one crampon. Piece of piss really.'

We were sharply brought back to reality by the sudden appearance of steep black walls. Help mammy, daddy, I don't like the look of this. Ian uses his crampon excuse again and throws the pegs at me. Above there's a choice; straight up via the Direct Finish or a wee traverse left then up thin verglassed grooves to the top of the steep section. I smash one of the ice-pegs in a boss of ice and elect for the traverse. Chipping nicks for hands and feet I shuffle across leftwards to crouch at the foot of the grooves. Slowly, coldly I cleared snow-covered holds and chipped nicks for the feet. At 30ft. I got the angle in – the next 10ft. seemed easy with the security of the peg. Then, as the security of the peg dwindled, so did my confidence. I didn't feel safe climbing in gloves so I took them off, fingers scrabbling in the icy cracks. I became desperate after 20ft. and banged the Leeper into a poxy patch of snow. Inspired by this dubious protection I continued upwards then crabbed across to the right to a snow patch. At last there was proper ice. I smashed in the last ice-peg – safety. I belayed. Ian set off half-heartedly; one crampon was not going to be of much use to him on the traverse, and so it proved. Almost immediately he swung off and crashed into the other side of the gully. By dint of muscle power Ian reached the belay, not laughing so much by now.

Above was the final slot, where MacInnes is reputed to have spent the night wedged during the first ascent. I'd had enough of leading and sent Ian and his one crampon into the lead. By jamming various parts of his body into the verglassed groove Ian managed to scrape his way to the top. We'd done it, there was no more route left. We slid off down the traverse into Great Gully and shot off down to Jacksonville.

## RAVEN'S WITH THE GREAT MAN
### by John Barry

We parked by Altnafeadh and bundled out, six of us, in a welter of gear. Then the boot door was hoisted skywards, triggering an avalanche of equipment. The accoutrements of modern ice are awesome. I watched the Great Man with interest – and some nervousness. After all, here in our very midst was one of the *glitterati*, the embodiment of *jeunesse dorée*; and BMC National Officer to boot. We would watch and learn. I knew little about the Man except that he had climbed Everest whilst still a virgin, was reputed to be a nice bloke, and like all nice blokes was popular with grannies.

The five of us waited, respectfully allowing Pete first shot at the mountain of gear that lay strewn half across the A82. If, as I think we did, we expected him to crisply gird himself like some latter-day gladiator we were to be cruelly disappointed. Indeed he paraded woefully ill-equipped, lacklustre even, standing before us sporting not much more than odd stockings, two very pedestrian axes and a supreme indifference to the arsenal which lay all about. 'Don't forget the ropes,' he said and set off toward Great Gully, a painfully thin sack flapping in the wind.

That wind! It was a wild day even down here and Raven's did not look friendly. See it for yourself on one of those raw Rannoch days and you will assuredly agree. This is the Buachaille's bad side; black, malevolent, and the slit of Raven's blacker still. Not friendly. No flirt here with a fine lace of chantilly ice, nor any smile of firmly compliant, sparkling névé beckoning to a summit altar. No, Sir. Black walls and a black-eyed gully trapped in a bleak embrace between Slime Wall (what horrors that name conjures for the PA-shod) and Cuneiform Buttress. Hobson's choice. But Raven's was one and we were six, so we had the advantage of her.

Then the wind did for two of them. The wind and an escape ploy that would have graced Patey's pages: 'I live here,' protested Allan, 'I can afford to wait for better weather. Do it any time.' His partner quickly clipped into the same gambit and they turned with the wind and ran goose-winged back to the car. I envied their sanity, admired their courage, looked askance at Pete. The Great Man, his face set in an expression of frozen insouciance, resolutely plodded on, lugubrious to the last but betraying no sign of the hangover that should have

been beheading him while I suffered for all four.

In an hour we gathered at the foot of a gully of steep, soft snow that drowned the first three (summer) pitches and led straight to a chockstone roof which forms the summer crux. Pete surged forward. If I half-expected a Red Sea parting of the powder to allow him unimpeded passage I was, for a second time, disenchanted. The Great Man flailed, grunted and swam – the last a badly co-ordinated butterfly stroke – in a distinctly mortal fashion to collapse in a terrible wrack of panting just below the chockstone. We three followed easily up a well-bulldozed trough. Here Martin Burrows Smith, who instructs these things, suggested that it might be a good thing to rope-up. He joined with Pete, I with Paul Moores.

Pete, now recovered, went at the crux, the wall to the left of the chockstone. It spat him back. Obviously there was even more to Raven's than met the eye. 'My dad did this in 1945 in army boots,' I observed, trying to sound helpful. Whether Pete believed me (and it's true) I have never discovered, but it goaded him to a fury, galvanised him. He charged full frontal to the breech and squeezed up the full 5a of it, axes and crampons sparking where his bludgeon laid bare the rock. The rope ran out at an alarming rate.

I followed, leading my half of the team. It was hard. Jams for the right arm and foot, left axe anxiously searching skyhook incuts. Left front-points despairing a lack of ice, and crampons complaining cacophonous on bare rock. Just when I thought I might be off – downwards – a careless knot in Pete's rope caught between my left front points and lent me that tiny tug which measures the mile between up and down. Such was the Great Man's surge up the easy slope beyond that he was unaware of his 12-stone parasite.

I joined him at the mouth of the cave below a second enormous chockstone. It was wilder here. As wild as Smith or Marshall could have ever asked for. Wilder than we wanted, 'wild above rule or art'. The moor had been rough, but this was something else. A vortex of omnidirectional, supersonic spindrift that numbed the senses and stung the flesh. Straight to the vein like Stones' chords or Sibelius' crescendoes – go to Raven's on a wild day and you will feel what I mean.

The four of us crawled deeper into the cave and found an eerie haven. Martin produced a flask of coffee, Paul a great nugget of chocolate, I a packet of biscuits. Pete, without so much as a *noblesse oblige*, tucked into all three simultaneously. 'The sports plan is this,' he said at length in superstarspeak, 'there are three or four gigantic chockstones at intervals above this one. With luck they'll all provide a cave just like this. One of you will lead and fix the rope so the rest of us can use it to save time. I've already done the crux for you so you should be OK now. Anyway, I'm a greater-ranges man myself.' Sips of coffee then, 'Now you go first Paul.'

Paul steeled himself and crawled back to the maelstrom. He had not gone 10ft. before we lost sight and sound of him, but 30 seconds later he was back, gasping like a pearl diver:

'What's the problem?' Asked Pete, into a mug of coffee.

'Can't breathe out there, or see a thing either.'

'Take a deep breath and just keep going upwards – the line's obvious,' advised Pete through a biscuit. 'And give the rope a couple of tugs when you want us to come up.'

Poor old Paul. He huffed and he puffed and he puffed and he huffed; and he hyperventilated. Then over the top. Pete kicked a dozen coils toward the entrance. 'Enough for him to be going on with.' The minutes ticked by as we chatted comfortably over our coffee and biscuits. From time to time one of us, following the Great Man's example, would foot a few yards of rope to the void, scuttling quickly back to the sanctuary and a sip. 'Much like this on the summit push on the Big 'E',' Pete observed casually, adding with equal nonchalance, '28,000ft higher on Big 'E' of course.' Difficult to follow that, and though I struggled for a riposte none came within 20,000ft.

At last the rope went tight and two tugs signalled an end to our coffee break. Out we went, Somme-style. The weather was daunting; this surely was Armageddon. The wind tore at you. Tore into you. Snatched the breath from between your teeth before you'd barely tasted it. Buffeted the brain insensate and knocked at the heart and challenged, 'Climb me if you dare.' And where or what are you? What pleasures are the draught of this moment? To be sure there's no space, no freedom, no grace or joy in movement. The world ends three inches in front of your face and limbs go where they can, where they will stay – and you seldom see where that is. Can this be the same game that we play in the sun on those slabs a few miles away

around the corner? That gambol in shorts with chalk and rubbers. The one a series of narcissistically-deliberate moves, like physical arithmetic; the other a blind, wanton struggle – a gravitational gamble. Can this be the same game? The brain says, 'NO, not at all!' But the soul shouts to be heard — 'Yes it is!'

Martin's turn. Out he goes. Out come the coffee and biscuits. And so we went on. When my turn came I struggled upwards for 20 minutes with little

*Above: On the steep ice leading to the crux of Raven's Gully. Climber: Tony Saunders / Photo: Mick Fowler*

*See also colour photo on page 154*

115

*Left: Two views of Raven's Gully, showing typical, near-vertical terrain with snow covered bulges and chockstones. Climber: Roger Wild / Photo: Mick Tighe*

idea where I was until I found myself in the lee of an enormous chasm, 100ft deep. I cast about, looking for the gully continuation which refused to reveal itself, fixed the ropes and tugged. The others quickly joined me, Pete looking greatly exercised:

'This is the Direct Finish,' he said, 'Chouinard did it. Chimneyed it, and he's even shorter than you.' I didn't believe him. Still don't.

'Got to do something for the second half of your pitch.' The comment chided me down and across left to where I found the groove of the original finish. The climbing was steady, pegs here and there and an occasional glimpse over the left shoulder through to the storm to Slime Wall and an evil-looking Shibboleth. A winter ascent of that lot? From the imagination springs such sweet horror! I hugged at my groove and fought back the images that shivered involuntary across the inward eye, sowing a seed in the sub-conscious. It lingers yet, barren, I hope.

There's a landing 15ft. from the top, where we joined. Then a convoluted corkscrew of a problem pitch and it's all over. We were out. Out of the vortex, gone from the maelstrom, with nothing worse than the scraich of the wind and a scoot down Great Gully to worry us.

The Great Man spoke and I waited for a leg-pull: 'That's the best day on the hill I've ever had.' His face creased with pleasure and four huge smiles exploded far wider than that Direct Finish. Raven's had beaten badinage.

POSTSCRIPT:

I wrote this on the bus coming back from Chamonix. A few minutes after I had put down that last full stop we pulled into Victoria where I bought a newspaper. Peter Boardman, it told me, was dead on Everest. Stricken, I returned to this story and hacked at all that now seemed in bad taste. Daft, of course, but understandable I hope. Most of it is back now, as it should be. As he would have asked.

The sad thing is that he had wanted to write about Raven's for this book. It was his best day on the hill, he repeated. I refused to budge for reasons I can scarcely admit even to myself. If only I had.

I wish that this were a story of such merit as to match Pete's best day, a best story for his best day. Alas the gift is not mine to give. But it was a great day on a fine climb with a great mate – and a marvellous memory.

# 21   S.C. Gully and Twisting Gully

by L. S. Lovat

From the Study in Glencoe above the Meeting of the Three Waters, the eye travels from the green meadows about Loch Achtriochtan in the floor of the glen upwards over the dark, rocky hulks of the Three Sisters to the high corrie of Stob Coire nan Lochan, that most beautiful of the entourage of peaks surrounding the great Bidean nam Bian. Even the most jaundiced eye must brighten at the sight of the north-east corrie of Stob Coire nan Lochan. The pyramid of the main peak, with Summit Buttress below, is flanked to the right by a line of elegant buttresses divided by steep gullies and all poised above a scatter of small lochans at the base of the screes at about 2,700ft. The magnetic attraction of this curtain of cliffs intensifies as the climber reaches the corrie. There is adventure here for novice and expert in a high place unsurpassed in the Central Highlands. Coire nan Lochan is miniature in comparison with the corries of Nevis or Lochnagar, but it presents a compact grace and nobility of form which is unique.

On the left flank of South Buttress, Twisting Gully winds upwards from a deep recess to a wide fan below the cornice. South-Central or S. C. Gully is the narrow and deep incision between the South and Central Buttresses. These climbs are unlikely to come into condition until mid-January, and the rot often sets in by mid-March. But one must not be dogmatic. Conditions in Glencoe are defiantly erratic.

Irrespective of the weather or the mood of the party, a climb may cast its own spell. For years after the Second World War, S. C. Gully retained a fierce reputation. First climbed in 1934 by Baird, Leslie, and Fynes-Clinton, whose account in the SMC Journal was succinctly objective, it had been blessed by W. H. Murray in a gripping description in *Mountaineering in Scotland* of an ascent in 1939, and positively consecrated by the same high priest with an exciting account in *Undiscovered Scotland* of another ascent in 1947, when the gully presented 250ft. of ice followed by 250ft. of hard snow. Like many others at that time, I held the gully in awe, and after three ascents of it I still have much respect for it as a route of quality.

On the first day of February, 1953 we hopped over the ice-carapaced rocks of the river Coe and went up to Coire nan Lochan in a keen wind. Stob Coire nan Lochan stood ghostly against the grey pallor of the sky. As soon as we reached the frigid, hushed entrance of S. C. Gully, it cast its spell on us.

We roped up for our first ascent with a sort of taut eagerness. The gear was the usual post-war assortment – balaclavas, ex-WD anoraks, trousers tucked into stockings, shapeless boots with tricounis, heavy full-length ice-axes and 120ft. of medium nylon rope. I had also a slater's hammer with the pick flattened to an adze. Keen men carried these, for working on steep ice. In those days some eccentrics even wore head-torches and a fanatic might carry an ice-piton like a badge of office.

Watched by a second party, I started up what should have been the first ice pitch but my axe clanged against bare rock through thin, floury snow. A short and unpleasant rock-climb followed before I embarked on the steep, soft snow of the second pitch. It led to the foot of the crucial ice pitch. We all assembled before it – the second party had roped up to us – and looked at it uneasily. The gully was now very narrow, and the rocks ahead, masked with snow, reared up to an overhang at about 70ft. I wondered if there was any ice below that veneer of snow. I was to take the right flank of the gully, get on to an icy ramp rising steeply to the right of the overhang, and gain the snowy bed of the gully. The right traverse to the ramp proved unsafe due to the extraordinary conditions – here the ice was dependable, there it was not; here the snow held, there it did not. Frozen turf provided an occasional hold.

Then came the ramp. Far from being the solid ice-fall which it usually is the ramp was an ugly blend of insecure ice and snow. Never had I teetered more tentatively, nor committed myself so positively to such mean holds. When I got close to the snow-slope above, I made a baleful attack on the final ice-bulge. The ice-splinters flew past my sweating face and scuttered down to the silent circle of watching faces. Mercifully, the upper snows were hard-frozen, and I started to bring up the first of four men from a stance and belay which I excavated some distance up the gully.

Here was an eagle-high niche made for contemplation! The gully, hemmed in by great projecting walls, was very narrow and steep, plunging down to the invisible company far below. I looked out to the north beyond the spiky wall of the Aonach Eagach ridge to the peaks of the Mamores and the dominating massif of Nevis. An icy breeze swirled round the gully walls bringing to the nostrils that indigenous whiff of rock, snow and

**Routes** S.C. Gully, Grade 3, 500ft.; Twisting Gully, Grade 2/3, 500ft.
**Cliff** The North Face of Stob Coire nan Lochan.
**First Ascents** S.C. Gully – Winter: P. D. Baird, E. J. A. Leslie, and H. A. Fines-Clinton, March 1934.
Twisting Gully (Left Fork) – Winter: W. H. Murray, D. Scott, and J. C. Simpson, December 1946.
**Map** See page 107 (148549).
**Guidebooks** See page 107.
**Nearest Road / Approach Time** The A82 at the Meeting of the Three Waters (175567). 1 mile/2,000ft. Allow 2 hours.
**Route Summary / Conditions** S.C. Gully – a fine gully set in impressive rock scenery, with short ice pitches and steep snow. Usually in condition between January and March. The grading of the climb assumes normal snow-ice conditions, but the ice pitches are fickle and can become glassy and hard. Twisting Gully – a snow/ice climb, with odd rock-steps which provide the difficulties.
**Campsites and Bunkhouses** See page 107.
**Bibliography** *Mountaineering in Scotland/ Undiscovered Scotland* by W. H. Murray (Diadem); S.M.C.J. 1934, Note by P. D. Baird (p. 284).

lichen which fans up the gullies.

Short work was made of the hard snow of the upper gully, which runs for about 250ft. The cornice is seldom formidable and was quickly surmounted. We scampered down Broad Gully, the easiest descent, well-satisfied with a memorable and rather dangerous day. My later ascents were on secure ice and snow, and were testing without being dangerous.

On 11 April 1954, Tom Weir and I were relishing the sights and sounds of Spring as we made our way up Coire Gabhail, the Lost Glen. Willow warblers had colonised this wooded ravine, and the delicate, falling cadence of their song could be heard on all sides. We traversed over to Coire nan Lochan. The gullies and upper slopes of the buttresses were gleaming white in the sun. We blessed our lot with our usual vehemence.

Twisting Gully was the ideal route for such a day. Commencing as a deep-set groove, and involving a

traverse and mantelshelf, the gully opens out pleasingly and meanders up the left flank of South Buttress to the cornice. When W. H. Murray and party made the first ascent in December 1946, conditions were difficult and the climb was pretty challenging. It is a mixed snow, rock and ice-course on a miniature scale and on a sunny, tranquil day there is an Alpine charm about it. Tom and I cut steps up the first 100ft. to the small crag which divides the gully. We took the left fork and shot up a short rock-chimney until the angle suggested a leftward move onto a ledge on the vertical, left wall. The ledge had to be traversed leftwards to the outside edge and so up to the crest. The traverse, although short, was rather icy and awkward but the sun was warm and the mood ebullient. Immediately above, the little rock-mantelshelf was clear of ice and we were soon over it. Its grade is about Very Difficult but in uncongenial conditions it can cause delay.

Tom was now chanting Sherpa canticles as he swung his axe methodically on the shining snows. The glare was such that it was a relief to look rightwards at the big andesite columns of South Buttress. As the gully snaked upwards and fanned out to a small but radiant cornice, I outclassed Weir with a fine burst of oratorio and we went over the top with panâche. As on two other occasions when I have climbed Twisting Gully, our ascent had been light-hearted, not out of any blasé complacency, but induced by the open and varied character of the place. The time taken, without speeding, was an hour and a quarter. Two hours might be a reasonable time unless there are very difficult conditions. Where the gully fans out on the upper slopes, there might be a risk of avalanche if the snow be inferior.

In early Spring it is possible to climb the East Face of Aonach Dubh by routes of quality and finish in the grand style by a classic snow and ice-route on Stob Coire nan Lochan. The opportunities are rare and the young mountaineer must seize them before he reflects, as I do with Louis MacNeice:

> For now the time of gifts is gone —
> O boys that grow, O snows that melt
> O bathos that the years must fill. . .

## 22  No. 6 Gully

by John Mackenzie

**Route** No. 6 Gully, Grade 3/4, 800ft.
**Cliff** The North West Face of Aonach Dubh.
**First Ascent** Winter: D. H. Munro and P. D. Smith, March 1951.
**Map** See page 107 (143555).
**Guidebooks** See page 107.
**Nearest Road / Approach Time** The A82 at the road junction near the end of Loch Achtriochtan (138567). ½ mile/1,200ft. Allow 1 hour.
**Route Summary / Conditions** A low altitude route which requires a long, cold spell to bring it into condition. Straighforward, scenic, and interesting climbing on a succession of ice pitches. The first pitch varies in difficulty: in lean conditions it will be a long ice pitch; in heavy snow it might bank out altogether. There is a choice of three exits, the central, or direct, being the hardest.
**Campsites and Bunkhouses** See page 107.

*Right: The main pitch of No. 6 Gully.*
*Climber: Keith George / Photo: Colin Foord*

No. 6 Gully is one of those climbs which the advent of front-pointing has brought within reach of the majority.It is no longer considered a *tour de force* involving hours of step-cutting, where stamina as well as strength was needed to hack out a stairway up its monumental crux. It has lost something special. The barrier of self-doubt which assailed most people when confronted by its large ice pitch was a prudent reminder of frail mortality and made successful ascents less frequent than today.

Despite the greater chances of success nowadays, No. 6 should not be considered as just another route, a tick in the guide, rapidly assaulted and soon forgotten in the rush to the pub. It is worth more than that and deserves some reflection over its former reputation.

On the 30 March 1951, long before curved picks were heard of, D. H. Munro and P. D. Smith cut their way out of the confines of the gully and onto the open slopes of Aonach Dubh. Subsequent ascents only served to confirm their grading of Very Severe for the big pitch. Since the number of winter climbs of that grade in Glencoe was few, the climb immediately attracted an aura of difficulty. Thus it was a route to aim for after a suitable build up of arm-strength gained on other epic classics such as Crowberry and S. C. Gullies, or Deep-Cut Chimney, and represented a tangible but difficult goal.

So much for reflection. The gully is still as it was then and the big pitch no smaller. Only our methods are different and instead of a four to six-hour battle you should average between one-and-a-half to two hours in good conditions. Because of its relatively low altitude the climb is prone to sudden thaw, and this may have a disastrous effect on the ice. The crux does occasionally collapse, being an icefall, so if you are on it and water spurts out of every hole you make, beware! There is a story of two Irishmen who, having just completed the pitch, watched with dismay as the whole edifice crumbled beneath their feet and obliterated the lower section of the gully in its fall. With a good hard frost and not over-much snow the ice will form very quickly indeed. Rarely will you get the continuous run of ice mentioned in the guidebooks. More often there will be three or perhaps four pitches, (five if you include the Direct Finish), separated by straight-forward snow at a much gentler angle. Topographically the gully is tucked away on the right-hand portion of the West Face and, unlike the

prominent gashes to its left, veers to the right. From the road its shallow walls permit a good view into the interior and with binoculars you may assess the conditions. It is not much of a walk to its base; you are barely halfway to the climbs starting on Stob Coire nam Beith, let alone Bidean. Because of this the West Face has become popular, especially if the going above is bad. Moreover, the lower altitude enables the climbs to form rapidly under cold, dry conditions when their higher brethren are suffocated by yards of powder resting loosely on unconsolidated ice.

The climb starts pleasantly enough. A small pitch may form in the lower watercourse, or it may be a snow slope. Either way the gully proper is entered by a reasonable pitch which leads to snow. It is at this point that you will notice the gully's biggest drawback. It is far too open. The walls are low, decorated with the occasional tree. It has not the vigour of a soaring architecture to divert the mind between pitches. Still, it is what nature has produced and should be enjoyed for its own sake. Another bump of a pitch in some narrows leads you to the *raison d'être* of the whole climb. Because of the lower openness of the gully, the effect of the 150ft. icefall is all the more stunning. The walls either side now rear up sternly. This is a climb whose merits are confined to this one unavoidable pitch, a white barrier to further progress.

There is a belay on the right, after which you go out left and up steeply to an easing of the angle beneath the vertical left retaining wall. When I reached this point I remember being amused by a pathetic little piton only just in place in the wall. It was moveable and gave only half-hearted moral support as a runner. But a runner is needed. The ice funnels up vertically, so the best line of progress is to bridge up this crux section. Take time and savour the situation. Your second now looks tiny, is shrunk in his cave, and the rope will sweep down alarmingly free of worthwhile protection. All in all this is not a good place to fall off. A few feet more and a belay can be fixed up on the left. Above, the snow stretches to an easy left-hand exit, whilst below the immediate horizon is cut short by the plummeting ice.

You may well decide to opt for the left-hand and most popular exit. But why follow the herd? Go for the centre, the true finish. It is no use saying it's avoidable, therefore artificial. All climbing is avoidable and therefore artificial, so make the most

*Above left: The first pitch of No. 6 Gully, a long ribbon of ice that often 'banks out' after heavy snow fall. Photo: M. Griffiths*

*Above right: No.6 Gully. Photo: Ed Grindley*

of what there is. A near-vertical and narrow runnel of ice rears above, giving 40ft. of impeccable bridging. Some think it provides the best climbing of the route, perhaps because it comes as a bonus, a final rounding-off after the main course.

Disappointingly, you arrive in the middle of nowhere and still a long way from any summit, so a good alternative to wondering what to do is to go right then descend steeply back to the base, which can be followed until you reach Chaos Chimney. If you have time, climb it. A couple of short ice-steps take you to a cave and a fine 80ft. ice-pitch on its left. There are more slabs of ice above but the whole climb is soon completed and will polish off your day nicely.

Ours had a different ending. We had almost finished when a tremendous crash was followed by massive blocks of ice spinning down to our left. The icicle of No. 5 Gully (Elliot's Downfall) had collapsed with a party climbing on it. It took us only a few minutes to unrope and hurtle down to the path and around the base of No. 6 to gain the line of fall. Yard-deep blue-green blocks stretched up the hill to where, amongst the debris there stood a rather shaken threesome. The leader had been left suspended as the ice sheared at his feet, narrowly missing the second and third men. Perhaps the most amazing thing was that the leader's ice-screw runners had all pulled as the icicle collapsed, thus relieving him of the onerous task of supporting several hundred tons of ice by two arms. Such is the luck of the hill!

# 23  Deep-Cut Chimney

by L. S. Lovat

On a bright and frozen morning in January 1958 we stood to the west of Loch Achtriochtan in Glencoe, contemplating the scene. A heron trod fastidiously in the shallows. Behind us the River Coe was brawling and glucking over the stones, but our eyes were drawn upwards to Stob Coire nam Beith, silent in the cold, clear air. It is the archetypal mountain, embracing within its rugged, pyramidal form a cluster of tapering buttresses riven by gullies and converging to a narrow summit. Dominating the Clachaig aspect of Glencoe, Stob Coire nam Beith stands guard in front of the highest mountain in Argyll, Bidean nam Bian, from some angles seeming to dwarf it and from others masking it entirely from view. Although there are rock-climbs to be enjoyed on the buttresses, Stob Coire nam Beith has its time of glory when snow and ice delineate its beauty and character, and offer challenging lines to mountaineers of differing capacity. What a paradox it is that such an accessible peak has been so much neglected, even when clad for a winter battle.

It was battle which we sought that morning, not meditation. Two weeks before I had enjoyed a jubilant ascent of the Crack Climb on the edge left of Deep-Cut Chimney. Today the target had to be the Chimney, a narrow gully of formidable repute, rarely climbed and holding within its recesses a mysterious and faintly sinister ethos. The first winter ascent in April, 1939, by W. M. Mackenzie and W. H. Murray, had been an epic, and is recorded for posterity in the pages of *Mountaineering in Scotland*. My companion was a visitor to Glencoe, I had never climbed Deep-Cut Chimney and knew no one who had (other than Mackenzie and Murray) – so the scene was set for a day of ice and spice. We pounded up the steep ground close to the burn which drains the corrie, pausing occasionally to admire the palisades of icicles which fringed the waterfalls. The sun shone fitfully as we gained the lip of the coire and surveyed the six buttresses which form this 1,300ft. north-facing pyramid.

We traversed left past the shallow North-West Gully, immediately left of which is No.4 Buttress, until we saw further left No.3 Buttress, the highest and broadest of the buttresses. Our route was the slit between these two. We kicked steps up the snow-covered screes and went in the narrow entrance. Conditions were ideal. Apart from a veneer of dry powder deposited by recent high

winds the steep snow beneath was reassuringly hard. We could see the first two ice-pitches barring our way, their apparant verticality shortened by a banking of snow.

Even in halcyon conditions there is a purgatorial element in ice-climbing; a temporary suffering from which one will often emerge elated, if unpurified. My companion, unused to ice, opted to tackle the first pitch – about 12ft. of steep, white ice – and he laboured mightily with a heavy hammer-axe. He came close to demolishing the whole structure. I had to remind myself that this was a natural product of anxiety and inexperience while I endured a barrage of particles as I stood below in frigid immobility. When I joined him he told me that the pitch had not been to his taste and that I was welcome to lead anything similar which might lie ahead. These were not his precise words. As he spoke, I saw above a steep section topped by an unmistakable ice pitch of about 30ft. I hacked up to it with a sense of irony. If 30ft. of ice is ever straightforward, this was straightforward. The ice was just right for cutting and it was possible to avoid the odd bulge and to rest with hot face nine inches or so from eye-level handholds. When my companion reached the stance he confirmed the insanity of the whole exercise while I assured him that he had enjoyed it.

Wind and snow had combined to present us with a ramp, designed for climbing, on the left wall of the third ice pitch. A big cone of snow-ice led to an extraordinary pillar of crystalline ice, rough and rippled as if adapted for my vibram soles. I could glimpse the steep little amphitheatre above, and when the angle of the pillar abated and I had stamped over pinkish rock to a comforting stance I fairly enlivened the sepulchral walls with the old cheering shout of 'On you come!'

Every ice-climber knows that wave of exhilaration. 'That was terrific!' Said my companion, now converted to the true faith.

Concentrating on holds, we had not noticed the greying of the sky until surprised by a flurry of rice-like snow and an icy breeze. We quit the small, steep bay of the amphitheatre by the left fork which is the true continuation of Deep-Cut Chimney. Stretches of hard snow, interrupted by exposures of clean rock and a gradually relenting angle made for rapid progress in a gathering storm. We arrived at the summit of No. 3 Buttress and by unspoken agreement sped away down to the left, contouring

**Route** Deep-Cut Chimney, Grade 3/4, 1,500ft.
**Cliff** The North Face of Stob Coire nam Beith.
**First Ascent** Summer: 1936. Winter: W. M. Mackenzie and W. H. Murray, April 1939.
**Map** See page 107 (140548).
**Guidebooks** See page 107.
**Nearest Road / Approach Time** The A82 at the road junction near the end of Loch Achtriochtan (138567). 1½ miles/2,000ft. Allow 1½ hours.
**Route Summary / Conditions** A fine gully and chimney climb, which is often in good condition. The upper part of the climb is on open ground amidst magnificent mountain scenery.
**Campsites and Bunkhouses** See page 107.
**Bibliography** *Mountaineering in Scotland/ Undiscovered Scotland* by W. H. Murray (Diadem) contains an account of the first winter ascent.

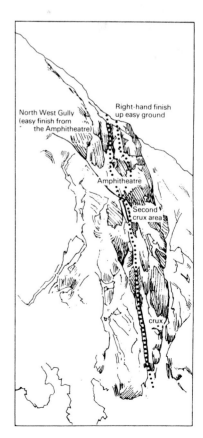

*Above: Stob Coire nam Beith, with the cliffs of Bidean nam Bian in the background. Deep-Cut Chimney takes a diagonal line up the cliff from its lowest point. Photo: Hamish MacInnes*

*Left: The North Face of Stob Coire nam Beith. Photo: Hamish MacInnes*

*Right: On the pitch below the crux of Deep-Cut Chimney. Climber: Larry Taylor / Photo: Mungo Ross*

the fan of snow above Arch Gully and descending easy rocks beyond to the corrie. Shoals of big snowflakes were swirling down in great soughs of wind. We bounded down to Clachaig where within half an hour the day was tranquil again and a wan sun glimmered through a curtain of mist.

Deep-Cut Chimney will often provide a harder climb but seldom a more intensely enjoyable one. Further south, I heard my companion preaching to others about the virtues of winter climbing in Glencoe. No mere convert, he was now an evangelist. I smiled the tolerant smile of a Father of the Early Church.

# 24  Smith's Gully

by Jimmy Marshall

**Route** Smith's Gully, Grade 5, 600ft.
**Cliff** The cliffs of Coire Ardair, Creag Meagaidh.
**First Ascent** Winter: J. R. Marshall and G. Tiso, February 1959.
**Map** O.S. 1:50,000 Sheet 34 (436877).
**Guidebooks** S.M.C. *Rock and Ice Climbs in Lochaber and Badenoch* by A. C. Stead and J. R. Marshall; *Winter Climbs – Cairngorms* by John Cunningham, revised by Allen Fyffe (Cicerone); *Scottish Winter Climbs* by Hamish MacInnes (Constable).
**Nearest Road / Approach Time** The A86 Spean Bridge – Newtonmore road at Aberarder Farm (483875). 4 miles/1,300ft. Allow 2½ hours.
**Route Summary / Conditions** A continuously steep and sustained climb, with poor protection and belays. Exposed to spindrift and cornice avalanches. The climb takes time to come into condition and the crux pitch (pitch 5) can be very trying if it is unconsolidated. This pitch can be avoided by traversing along the Appolyon Ledge.
**Campsites and Bunkhouses** Camping possible at Aberarder Farm. Howff under large boulder below the Pinnacle Buttress. Bunkhouse accomodation at Fersit, west of Loch Laggan.
**Bibliography** S. M. T. District Guide *Central Highlands* by Campbell R. Steven.

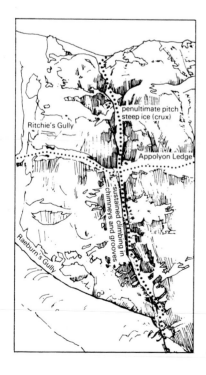

The cliffs of Creag Meagaidh lie discreetly hidden some four miles from the main road. Perhaps this contributed to the lack of interest shown during a period of otherwise great activity by the early mountaineers. More likely it was the aura deriving from the repulse of their strongest party when avalanched out of the Centre Post, and their infamous quip that the route should be named 'Post Mortem'! Whatever it was, the cliffs remained unsullied for over 30 years, till the pawky Bell gardened and grovelled his way about the corrie, endeavouring to raise enthusiasm among his contemporaries (without success) but at least making a few good winter ascents before a curtain of anonymity fell upon the mountain once more for 20 years.

My first visit was in July 1951. I'd never heard of the place and was amazed on entering the upper glen to see the massive array of crag. How could such a place be anonymous? It was Pinnacle Buttress that caught my attention; it was superb, but the illusion soon faded on making contact with the rock! Great scope here for gardeners. We thought the chimney-gullies further up might yield a climb, but no, they were dripping wet and ruled out, but noted as a possible bet for winter.

Good lines were plentiful in these days, so it wasn't until February 1957 that I joined a JMCS bus meet to look further into the chimney-gullies of the pinnacle. The day turned out fine, though a strong wind whipped up the soft, new-fallen snow. We ploughed our way under the magnificent encrusted cliffs, for the main face was of no interest to me. I was committed to the Pinnacle, with its few difficult but fine lines. As Ritchie and I toiled through the deep powder and wind-whipped mini-blizzards in Raeburn's we were suddenly confronted by the sight of young Smith hacking his impertinent way up the fierce introductory icicles of what I considered my gully. We sat and jeered, watched him for a spell, comforted by the cataracts of powder thundering on his head, then moved on to traverse into the left-hand gully above the initial ice-fall. The ensuing ascent was exciting and dangerous enough, climbing apparently vertical powder in white-out conditions, furrowing a long groove to find the ice, wondering all the time when the whole gully would shoot out to frighten the life from Smith toiling below. We named that route after my partner, and later on meeting a defeated Smith decided to name the right-hand gully after

him, once the route was in the bag.

The pace was quickening; winter-climbing had taken off, so we were back next winter, fresh from a great climb on Lochnagar. Arriving late we stayed in a freezing cold open barn, and I awoke in the morning to find that a big icicle from a slung water-bag above had grown to encase my hair and sleeping-bag in its icy grasp.

In fact, the following day was probably the coldest I ever experienced. It pained our faces as we raced along to the gullies; sadly, though they were in wonderful condition, there was no way we could have attempted a climb in the face of such gripping cold. We had to be content with a tour of the mountain just to keep warm.

A year later we were back, this time thanks to my memories of the cold and the kindness of the farmer we were comfortably esconced in the bothy at Aberarder, with a bed and all. The party comprised Stenhouse, Haston, Tiso and myself. 'Typhoo' only had the week-end, we others were out for a week and jumping fit. We couldn't believe our luck when the next day dawned frosty, cloudless, and calm, so we tore off up the glen, stripped to our waists, enjoying the brilliant sunshine and snow. The weather had obviously been this way for a week or more, for the steep rocks were stripped of snow with ice runnels everywhere.

We rested awhile by the frozen lochan, enjoying the magnificent sight of Meagaidh's winter crags, then Jimmy and Dougal, being apprentices, were despatched to straighten out Bell's Centre Post whilst Typhoo and I followed the now-familiar track up to the chimney-gullies of the Pinnacle.

Our luck was still holding. The conditions could not have been bettered; masses of ice poured down the gully and the sun still shone, so without delay we launched up the route. In these prehistoric times, it was a case of cutting steps and this was a perfect icefall to apply the skills of economic fashioning and positioning. No thundering, blinding spume today, only firm névé and steep, dry ice.

The run-outs were long but protection was found on the rock walls of the gully. After a few rope-lengths Typhoo took over a pitch, as he was getting second-man blues with the exposure, both cold and visual! The following rope-length was superb, narrow and bulging, even more than below. I was convinced it was the crucial section, and chopped

on with a will to struggle over the top into an icy bay, grateful to find a little rock platform in the midst of a sea of green shining ice. Unbelievably, up above was a huge bulge barring the exit to the gully. Quite taken aback, I felt trapped and looked around for an escape and there it was, up on the left and out, but that didn't seem right for such a royal route. Further scrutiny of the wall above revealed a faint groove, just left of the offending prow, which could go if the arms held out. After all, there was a way out on the left if that failed. I hauled my partner up. He huffed and puffed up the bulges below with some trouble, obviously tiring but like me thought the effort worthwhile as the route was

Top left: *Steep ice above Raeburn's Gully bars access to Smith's Gully. Climber: Peter Surfleet / Photo: James Divall*

Bottom left: *The fifth pitch of Smith's Gully. Climber: Jean Marc Boivin / Photo: René Ghilini*

Right: *A party on the second pitch of Smith's Gully. Photo: Paul Nunn*

in the bag, then eventually landing on our little rock oasis he had time to look about at the bulging headwall and was overwhelmed:

'Christ, where do we go now?' Feverishly searching about he spotted the escape route on the left and yelled, 'Let's get the hell out of here.' But I demurred and pointed up.

He nearly had a nervous breakdown (this was only his second decent route). However a handful of collar and a few firm words resolved the situation, and I made off up the little groove. The ice was perfect, reflecting the last shimmering light of day in stark emphasis to the drop below. The ice stayed thick all the way, but the familiar flapping axe, spent arms, and frantic, stomping front-points were all in evidence in the final ungainly crawl to the security of the snow-hollow and belays above.

Typhoo came up fast, doubtless glad to quit the awesome stance below, then we rolled about revelling in the luxury of free movement, delighted with our new climb which had been six exciting hours in the making. Tired but happy we sloped our independent ways off the mountain into the gathering gloom of night and a long tiresome stumble to the comfort of our new-found home.

We found Dougal and Jimmy more than a bit dischuffed when we got back, they hadn't managed to straighten out Bell's line, but earlier that morning I had spotted another fine line on the Pinnacle, so in consolation for their disappointment we three enjoyed a delightful alpine-style ascent of what is now the 1959 Face Route, whilst Typhoo made the long weary way home to work.

In the period preceding inclined picks and screw-pegs, Smith's Gully was a climb of extreme severity in the Grade 5 category. Today it and other, even more notorious gullies have been overtaken by a technology which reduces insecurity and times, rendering such icefall ascents no longer in the realm of very serious expeditions; consequently they could be graded as 4/5s and available to a wider range of climber.

Although winter climbing has advanced far beyond these levels on the superb, difficult face routes of Nevis and Lochnagar, the climb is still rated as one of the hardest gullies in Scotland. But bear the foregoing in mind, await the heavy snowfall followed by a cold, sunny spell, then tear off to Meagaidh, for the gullies and the unclimbed spaces between will surely be ripe for the picking, if you'll pardon the pun.

# 25  North Post

by Mike Geddes

An early start: 5 a.m., and still dark. I gulped some milk, shouldered my rucksack, and swung on to my bike for the ride across Cambridge. Leaving it in a convenient cycle shed, I started hitching.

Thus began one of several long CUMC weekends to Scotland in the winter of 1972. The first one had featured a party of five, plus gear, crammed into a hired Morris 1100 driven mostly in the outside lane without being overtaken for 900 miles up the A1 and back. And ending in a write-off! Another led to the second ascent of Orion Direct. As for the weekend in question, Alan Rouse and I rendezvoused in Edinburgh with Geoff Cohen and Graham Hardie before driving to Loch Laggan. Once there, we set off immediately up the path to Coire Ardair of Creag Meagaidh and its bothy.

I have never managed to reconcile myself to this particular path, and this dark night was no exception. We were soon into the cloud, it was snowing hard, and we faced a long slog into the wind to reach the corrie. Alan and I were feeling the effects of our long day, but fortunately Geoff, always a strong walker was ahead breaking the trail. We arrived at 3 a.m. and slept. The early morning sound of wind-driven snow is not always unwelcome. We were able to recover with a prolonged fester until early afternoon. Then the snow stopped and the cloud base lifted to the upper part of the crag. Alan rapidly marshalled some gear and scurried out of the hut, intent on solo climbing. I followed, through black boulders and deep clutching snow-holes. Then up, passing under the fantastic roofs of Pinnacle Buttress, adorned with vegetation, before crossing Easy Gully, intending to prospect the Post Face. A look over my shoulder revealed Alan already well established on the first pitch of '59 Face Route, a small blue figure dwarfed by the immensity of the buttress. I considered trying South Post Direct, but the upper pitch hung ominously over the face, drooling long, wide columns of vertical green ice without an obvious route through them. So I settled for North Post. We had seen people on it a fortnight before, it couldn't be too bad I thought.

The difficulties of North Post are concentrated within the middle part of the climb – a narrow, steep gully parallel to the wider Centre and South Posts on the left. One of a number of possible starts leads to a snowfield which allows access to the foot of the gully. This has several pitches, particularly noteworthy being a difficult section around a chockstone and a corner pitch above. At the top the gully is overlooked by a steep wall. The best route crosses this wall before finishing by easier open climbing. The first ascent was made in 1960 by a party comprising Tom Patey, 'Zeke' Deacon, G. K. Mcleod, and a Swiss guide, Pierre Danelet.

It was getting late, so I lightened my load by hiding my rucksack in a miniature bergschrund, taking what gear I could about my body. I discovered that I'd left my head-torch at the bothy. Too bad. I carefully tightened my crampon straps, and set off. The first pitch had good ice and was enjoyable. It was followed by step-kicking up and across the snowfield to the foot of North Post. Then steepening névé led into the first pitch of Grade 3 ice. At least that's what it looked like, but halfway up I began to wonder, as the angle pushed me back and I had to concentrate my wandering thoughts into a rhythm: lightly but firmly tapping my front points onto a ripple in the ice, fairly high if possible, stepping up, moving my hammer or my axe, bridging, padding, making use of old steps, creeping upwards till the angle eased and the first pitch was behind. I moved slowly up the steep snow, searching the gully walls for cracks or spikes which might prove handy in case of retreat. There were none. Soon the snow steepened and deepened into one of those horrible cones which form under a chockstone: you have to punch deep with your hands, commando-crawl upwards, and somehow compress a strong enough step; but you can't lean out far enough to make a good job.

The cave hung dark green above, and there was no obvious route. The way was out to the right, up 20ft. of bulging ice, threatening at the bottom where it was steepest, welcoming at the top where it lay back in a shallow groove at the level of the cave roof. Icicles streamed over the cave, trickling to an end somewhere behind my head.

I made several forays onto the ice, usually getting higher but always having to retreat from the search for secure places for my picks while I still had strength. Each time I eased myself back to a more doubtful refuge in the cone of pitted snow, and clutched it more grimly with thick dachsteined hands. Then I remembered that ice is never as steep as it looks, and searched around for something to show the true angle and calm my nerves. Only this time it didn't work, in fact I wished I hadn't looked, for a small icicle hung out from the ice. Below, the snow-cone led my eyes down the gully, plunging

**Route** North Post, Grade 5, 1,500ft.
**Cliff** The cliffs of Coire Ardair, Creag Meagaidh.
**First Ascent** Winter: T. W. Patey, J. H. Deacon, G. K. Mcleod and P. Danelet, February 1960.
**Map** See page 126.
**Guidebooks** See page 126.
**Nearest Road / Approach Time** See page 126.
**Route Summary / Conditions** A varied and difficult climb that is best attempted when liberally coated in snow and ice (infrequent).
**Campsites and Bunkhouses** See page 126.
**Bibliography** There are brief first ascent comments in A. J. 1960, *One Man's Mountains* by Tom Patey (Gollancz) and S.M.C.J. 1960.

*Left: Approaching the crux ice pitch of North Post. Climber: Philip Mangham / Photo: Bill Ryan*

snow pattered on my cagoule. Steep snowfields and short boulder pitches loomed out of the misty gloom. The need to control my exuberance, lest all be lost. A cornice somewhere above, and a descent route to be found.

The cornice proved easy, and I felt my way onto the plateau. But there was no cause for celebration; I had been in the lee of the cliff, but up here the wind was blowing cold, there was snow in the air, and the cloud was thicker. Navigation would be very difficult in the imminent white-out, and within ten minutes it would be too dark to read the map or set the compass. A night out was unthinkable and the ridge to Aberarder impossible to navigate. The only alternatives were to head for The Window, or for Easy Gully. The Window offered a good chance, if only I could reach the fence posts before dark. There was less chance of finding Easy Gully, but if I tried that and failed I could always continue roughly south, and hit the Loch Laggan road. So I took a bearing for the top of Easy Gully.

Soon the white-out, or black-out, became complete. My feet were lost from view, and the angle of the ground became difficult to judge. I thought I felt the short steepening before the bowl of the gully top, and the timing seemed about right, so I turned left, but after a few yards I lost my balance as the ground steepened alarmingly. The feeling of total disorientation was harrowing. I groped back until I was on the plateau again (perhaps), followed the bearing a bit more, and turned left again. This time I backed down on all fours so that with luck I could follow the steepening over the crest and into an uncorniced Easy Gully. Then my feet went away from underneath me again, leaving me clinging to my axe and hammer.

That was enough. You'd better stop fooling about, I told myself, and cramponed up the way. I headed south, thankful for the fluorescent dots on my compass. The plod in deep snow seemed endless; a lightening of the gloom hinted at an outside world for a while, but then I was back to my own isolated plodding. The walking became easier – the ground must be steepening, I thought, yet there are no cornices in this corrie, just isolated outcrops. So I turned round again, and cramponed on downwards for a good while. Then I fell a short distance, and carried on in a suspended, detached world. The weight on my arms grew, I was on all fours again, I could stand up, consult the compass,

over the first pitch, bouncing down the 500ft. of buttress below, and out onto the powdered ice-sheet of the lochan. Eventually I went out onto the ice again, nursing my waning strength, telling myself that panic or haste were just not allowed. The hammers bit securely, I took the plunge, and moved on through to easier stuff. The feel of my ice axe stabbing into the solid ice of the final groove was heavenly.

The next pitch passed in a daze; it reminded me of the top chimney of Hadrian's Wall. I considered avoiding the exposed traverse by taking the easier-looking face on the right, but decided that with night and snow closing in, the situation was bad enough without exploring new ground. Beyond the traverse, I felt exhilarated, and drank deep of the adventure. The surroundings were grey, enveloped in cloud, with just enough light to pick a route, yet no view to the left or right, up or down. A little

Above: The Post Face of Creag Meagaidh.
Photo: Colin Stead

and walk again, still southwards.

The clouds cleared, some hillsides came into view. I came to in the middle of a loch – a frozen corrie loch. The cliffs looked good, but I wished they'd been those of Coire Ardair, not Moy Coire!

I was now only one mile from the bothy as the crow flies, but was faced with a ten mile round trip. Even out of the storm, the night was a dark one, making the stumble through heathery snow down to the road particularly trying. I took a detour to Moy Lodge to look for a telephone, but without success. After the 'road section', and with conditions higher up still looking wild, I had my doubts about continuing beyond Aberarder. There was still a light on, but they refused my request for a doss in one of their sheds. I ended up in the cold tin box of the Morris van. First light saw me on the path back up to the corrie, hungry for some breakfast.

Alan had been out during the night looking, shouting, and flashing lights below the climb. He'd found my sack and concluded the worst. In searching for the other remains he had fallen through the ice of the loch and had a bit of an epic getting out. His climb had also had some exciting moments, including a lengthy jump to safety from a false start above Appolyon Ledge. It did finish more suitably on the slopes of Easy Gully however.

They were all outside when Graham spotted me coming up the path. We re-convened in high spirits, with ribald jokes about the share-out of my gear: axe to Geoff, crampons to Alan, hammer to Graham. . .! Graham and Geoff went out for a climb, but Alan and I, after our nocturnal adventures, rested up in preparation for the long hitch home.

I recommend the climb, but not the style.

# 26 South Post Direct

by Mick Tighe

**Route** South Post Direct, Grade 4, 1,500ft.
**Cliff** The cliffs of Coire Ardair, Creag Meagaidh.
**First Ascent** Winter: Original Route – N. Tennent and M. Slesser, February 1956; Direct Start – T. W. Patey and R. F. Brooke, March 1962, Pitch 3 Direct – I. A. MacEachern and J. Knight, March 1964.
**Map** See page 126.
**Guidebooks** See page 126.
**Nearest Road / Approach Time** See page 126.
**Route Summary / Conditions** Two spectacular, steep and exposed ice pitches linked by an easier section. The climb comes into condition in all but the leanest winters.
**Campsites and Bunkhouses** See page 126.
**Bibliography** S.M.C.J. 1957 has brief first ascent notes.

Aberarder was bathed in moonlight as we tiptoed silently past the sleeping cockerel, careful not to wake him, lest he in turn alerted the dogs to send us howling on our way up the path. The alarm had jingled us into wakefulness at 5 a.m. and we'd tumbled downstairs to find the thermometer reading 14° below, with stars twinkling merrily in the night sky. Hard-frozen snow beyond the farm made for rapid progress, whilst all around us glittered millions of hoar-frost crystals.

We soon came to the upper edge of the northern woods and paused for a breather. Norman Tennent and Malcolm Slesser had camped here over 20 years before, blending pemmican and rice over an open fire and contemplating a new route on the towering cliffs of Coire Ardair. A big freeze on the final night of their little expedition had made climbing possible and they'd pioneered a route up the South Post in a fine tradition and style, creating a lasting monument for a future generation of climbers.

Our intrepid trio made its way into Coire Ardair, bound for South Post Direct. Cor Arder is the old Gaelic spelling, meaning 'corrie of the high water'; hence Aberarder, 'meeting of the Arder stream'. We were made welcome on this occasion by the sun as it peeped over a shoulder of Carn Liath. The frozen waters of the lochan gave us direct access to the foot of Easy Gully and we scrambled up this to belay below the first – direct – pitch of South Post, a towering 120ft. pitch of fine blue ice. A belay was quickly located, and Bob led off. He was soon greeted by some small spindrift avalanches, whispering down from the plateau above and eliciting vague whimpers of discontent from the female contingent. He coped well, though, scampering upwards between the salvos to find a belay in the gully proper. Mumbled reassurances about the avalanches and a quick lesson in the use of Terrordactyls for Linda, and she was launched onto her first Grade 5. No problem for a Glasgow lass, though, and pretty soon we were all ensconced in the gully proper.

That tireless progenitor of routes, Tom Patey, had passed this way in 1962, thereby constituting the first direct ascent; yet another memorial to the ubiquitous doctor. The original route comes in from the right a little higher, having gained access on the initial rocks of the Central Pillar.

The gully looked a little easier as it ascended towards the Narrows, and I set to with alacrity.

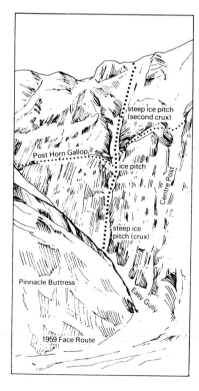

Before long, however, Burns's words came to mind: 'The best laid schemes o' mice an' men gang aft a-gley.' I wondered if he had ever been a climber. The fine blue ice of the first pitch had given way to a welter of crusty snow, that served only to hold sugary granules in place, and wrench my knee-joints mercilessly. Having eventually reached the Narrows, (a short, narrow ice-defile at mid-height) I proceeded to demolish it with one mighty blow of the Chouinard, and as two tons of ice rattled off down the gully, the remaining 20ft. of bare rock

were negotiated in a very short space of time.

We toiled on upwards, taking a long, long time and noting a distinct deterioration in the weather. Eventually a non-existent belay was reached below the second direct pitch and a moment of reckoning was at hand. Discretion, of course, is always the better part of having no belays, so we opted for the easier original route around to the left. However, half an hour of thrashing about in a quagmire of ice, punctuated by the odd tussle with gravity, decided me that valour might yet win the day and the direct version got a second reading. It seemed that the only good ice to be found was at an angle of 80° or more, and this 90° pitch looked in fine condition, so off I went. I put two ice screws in low down to satisfy the fall-factor merchants and set off into the now-omnipresent mist. The rope came tight just as the angle eased, but a good 'deadman' saved the day. Bob came next, followed by Linda, with one or two rather unladylike comments – something about bashing her knuckles on the ice. They do have a way with words, these Glasgow girls.

*Above: On the first pitch of South Post Direct with climbers employing 'traditional' step-cutting tactics during an early ascent. Climbers: Allen Fyffe and Jim MacArtney / Photo: John Cleare*

The rest of the route was pretty straightforward, but the reception on the plateau was unexpected, as the relative calm of the gully gave way to ferocious winds sweeping in unimpeded from the Atlantic. No place to linger, but neither was it a place to make a false move. We estimated Easy Gully to be about 600 yards south-east, but how to get there? We edged along, leaning Lowry fashion into the wind, and eventually found the gully, there to slide down out of the wind again, and make for the local alehouse.

It must have been around 6.30 p.m. when the 'phone rang, as the mince and tatties were bubbling away merrily on the stove, ready for the evening meal:

'Hello, Mick. Fort William Police here, we have a report of a missing climber on Creag Meagaidh. Can you get up there right away?'

It was the kind of night that you might well have spared the cat its night out, and it was with faint heart that I ventured forth to Aberarder. It appeared that two lads had climbed the South Post, and whilst descending had mistaken the declivity at the top of Last Post for a similar one on Easy Gully. Whilst investigating this, one of them had slipped and disappeared down into the gathering gloom. His companion, having found the correct descent, had later searched the gully below, but found nothing other than the contents of a rucksack strewn about on the snow.

The remainder of the rescue team would be some time coming from Fort William, so Ian Sutherland and I set off up the path alone with the sense of foreboding that comes only with darkness on a wild winter night coupled with the thought of an injured climber lying somewhere above. We were soon at the ruined hut in the boulder field, lungs heaving and clothes dripping, but took reassurance from the pinpricks of light showing in the valley below, heralding reinforcements, both mental and physical. A stumbling, cursing traverse took us from the hut to Easy Gully, and we were soon engulfed by its leering walls. Forlorn items of equipment were scattered about in the snow below. A couple more of the boys joined us, and in the benign belief that the owner of these remnants was lodged somewhere on the face above, we made for the summit plateau. Hasty belays were arranged on our arrival as the wind blasted us with its full force.

The perilous footprints could just be discerned under the spindrift, leading to the edge of oblivion, disappearing into the night. I was lowered into the black abyss and, silent now, I hung out of the wind like a spider on my braided filament. The only interruptions to this world of quiet verticality were curt instructions on the radio to regulate progress. Each sweep of the power beam brought a fear of what might be revealed, but on reaching the gully 1,000ft. below, I had discovered nothing.

It was now 2 a.m. and there was little more we could do before daylight. More of the team had assembled by this time and we all retired to a cramped night of wet, dripping misery in the hut, made worse now by the inadvertent upsetting of a creosote can which managed an amazing, brushless paint job on everything from crampon to duvet.

We were on the plateau again at dawn, jousting with a wind that had called up all its reserves in a renewed effort to effect our expulsion, but we resisted and once more set up the belays. Back down to the vertical world I went on my kernmantel umbilical, dancing and bouncing back to reality. A huge pendulum took me into the familiar gully of the South Post, where bucket steps in the rotten ice marked the previous day's progress, but there was no visible human presence here today. A Sea King helicopter arrived with a roar in the corrie below, anxious to do his bit, and together we searched that desolate wall of ice for signs of life, but to no avail.

Alighting once more in Easy Gully I looked around in despair for some sign or clue as to his whereabouts. Something blue under the snow caught my eye and frantic digging revealed the inevitable body, three feet under the snow in which he had landed the previous evening. We had passed him by three times in the night, and could do nothing more now but wish him well in a new life hereafter.

*Right: Pinnacle Buttress and the Post Face. Photo: Andrew Wielochowski*

*Left and top right: At the top of the first pitch of South Post Direct. Climber: Colin Wornham / Photos: Jim Loxham*

# 27  Staghorn Gully

by Malcolm Slesser

**Route** Staghorn Gully, Grade 3, 1,500ft.
**Cliff** The cliffs of Coire Ardair, Creag Meagaidh.
**First Ascent** Winter: C. M. Allen, J. H. B. Bell, H. H. Kelly and H. Cooper, April 1934.
**Map** See page 126.
**Guidebooks** See page 126.
**Nearest Road / Approach Time** See page 126.
**Route Summary / Conditions** A diverse climb with a long and exposed approach ramp to reach a fine, gorge-like gully with several short ice steps. Often in condition. Belays are difficult to find – Deadmen may be useful.
**Campsites and Bunkhouses** See page 126.
**Bibliography** *Missing the Last Post* by Norman Tennent (S.M.C.J. 1960).

*Top right: A view of the approach ramp to Staghorn Gully with the Inner Corrie and the Window on the right. Photo: Nigel Shepherd.*

*Bottom right: Staghorn Gully. Photo: Hamish MacInnes*

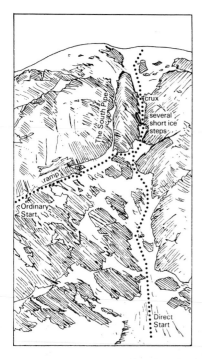

Coire Ardair has always been one of my favourite places, perhaps because it is so secret, hidden away from tourist eyes. It is almost an hour's walk from Aberarder farm before the great eastern face comes into view, and a further hour of steady approach leaves the mind ample time to explore the possibilities, weigh up conditions, and decide upon a route. Then there is the marvellous excuse for a long pause at the lochan to work out the day's plan in fine detail.

It's a great place for the experienced to bring their acolytes. To the beginner the eastern face, the one with the Posts, seems utterly impregnable and gives you the pleasure of showing how the mountain, close up reveals a depth of form and feature, and how its weakness may be exploited to find a relatively easy way up the face. And so, over the years, I must have done Staghorn Gully on half-a-dozen different occasions, each time with a new companion.

I made my first ascent of the climb in 1956 quite inadvertently, with Gordon Waldie, a couthy southerner from Hawick who took to climbing late in life. We had neither crampons nor pitons and it was almost his first winter climb, apart from a few floury gullies in the Merrick hills, and Great End in the Lakes. He was duly impressed, and after a sniff at the snow under the Posts and consulting again the old SMC Central Highlands Guide which rather stressed avalanches, we closed the book and took the line of least resistance up the face.

The Posts in the east corrie are topped by a flat plateau, from the right-hand side of which a large messy buttress falls steeply to the east and a little less steeply to the north. There is a shoulder halfway up this mass, accessible by a snow-covered ramp, easy enough going even for the days when you belayed with an axe and cut steps up hard névé for hours on end. Six or seven rope-lengths brought us to the shoulder. It was a marvellous position. To the right was the north corrie, with great ice-bulges oozing out of the gullies. Above a pair of gullies broke through steep rock to an uncorniced slope above. Below a waterfall of ice dropped steeply for 300ft. It never occurred to us that this route was unascended, for it seems so obvious. We chose the right-hand of the two gullies and on good snow-ice chopped our way up. We found it a little steeper than it looked and at one point were forced to breast vertical ice which led to a steep but easy slope on to the plateau.

Strangely, I have no vivid image of that climb or that day. Later, with other companions, I can recall almost every step. I first came to believe that it might have been a first ascent when the SMC Journal carried news of Patey and Deacon's claimed first ascent in February 1960. It had a brief existence as the North Pipe, but quickly became known as Staghorn Gully, I think as a result of a slanderous article written by one of my regular winter companions, Norman Tennent, whose amusing piece 'Missing the Last Post' is one of the classics of the SMC Journal of the sixties. It was only later that I discovered the route had been ascended in 1934 by Allan, Bell, Kelly and Couper, a fact that for some reason escaped me whilst I was challenging Patey's claim.

Tennent and I arrived at Staghorn Gully one January day after an abortive attempt on the North Post. We had already done the South Post the year before and felt honour-bound to attempt the North Post too. But I think it was out of our class. Anyway, on that bitterly cold January day the North Post was little more than frozen turf with a ribbon of water ice, so we very quickly escaped to the north and found ourselves on the shoulder, with the gully, the Staghorn, (as yet unnamed), above us. And so, retrieving something from the day, up we scampered.

Norman and I, though old buddies (in spite of a tendency to slander each other in print) have very different views about belaying. Being a salvationist in the pure Patey tradition, I take belaying seriously and expect my companions to make my safety their main concern. Tennent is a ritual belayer. There is nothing metaphysical about this. A rope binds two climbers together, till death do them part, and the leader has no business falling off.

As it happened, it fell to me to hack my way up the vertical section while Tennent was cowering in a scoop, peering out like a puffin from his burrow, more or less shielded from the shower of ice-chips. I had taken no chances, and had personally attended to his belay. So you can imagine my indignation when I saw that he had abandoned the rope and was busy with photography. Tennent declares that I threw my ice-axe at him. If so, I certainly failed to hit him, but I do recall climbing down and throwing the coils of rope around his neck and taking over his place. Tennent, of course, made an effortless ascent and while belaying me up

he pitch, he formulated the first of many
slanderous phrases about me that he planned to
publish in the mountaineering press. In his version
he had so concerned himself for my safety as to
make himself into a 'Staghorn bollard.' Hence the
name.

On a later ascent of Staghorn with a newcomer to
ice-climbing we were passed by two pleasant types,
front-pointing. It was impressive, and the first time
I'd seen it at close quarters. They made perhaps
three times our speed, and with a fraction of the
effort. For them, Staghorn was not so much a climb
as a way up. Next week I went out and bought my
own Chouinard axe, but before I had a chance to
try it out, I learnt that my two erstwhile
demonstrators had perished the following weekend
- whilst front-pointing. Staghorn is perhaps the
ideal Creag Meagaidh climb for the salvationists. It
is relatively safe from avalanches, you can retreat,
and it rarely has a serious cornice. And yet it is a
subtle route.

# 28  The Crab Crawl

by Sam Crymble

I knew the instant the car stopped at Aberarder that our route wasn't on. The sky, dank and dark over Loch Laggan, offered scant promise of the cold conditions we needed.

Bob Barton is stubborn. He hates giving up, pronounces hurriedly that it will still be freezing higher up, grabs his gear and shoots off up the lane before I can change his mind. I follow without conviction, thinking up excuses. The farm dogs bark as if in reproach, and cursing Yorkshire grit I sweat in his wake, across the fields, up through the birches, round the corner and into the bleakness of Coire Ardair.

We arrive with the dawn at the lochan and pant beside it, our mood mirrored in its blackness. We debate; the mild weather offers little hope of success on Smith's Gully. It's a long way up just to walk down again, and it's early yet.

Alternatives are presented and in turn rejected:
'59 Face Route?'
'Wasn't complete last week.'
'Pumpkin?'
'Too far to walk – it'll be out of nick anyway!'

We have psyched ourselves for the big one and now nothing quite fills the gap. Maybe we should have a day off, nip up Raeburn's, and see what Smith's looks like for next weekend. We could traverse in from the side – a bit safer than stumbling up the gully. Or we could do the Scene, nip across, have a look at Smith's and Ritchie's, then up to the top and back down the ridge. At least then the day wouldn't be wasted: 'we'll do the Scene.'

Snow-free ramps lead easily left and up to Bellevue Buttress. Cramponed now, we guess our location and trend rightwards up grooves and short walls to a horizontal break. Along the ledge; below us the crag drops away, above it rears up and out. We climb behind a veil of intermittent drips and rattling ice-particles. The ledge narrows and disappears tantalisingly around the corner to the right. The Scene is set – in undramatic style the players traverse right. The choreography is different; shimmy right, up one, down one, and right again. Cocooned in cloud, the outside world and the exposure go unnoticed while the steps become familiar and we settle into a rhythm.

A breeze on our faces indicates that the shelter of the buttress has been left behind. A bleary sun momentarily pierces a tattered grey sky and swings a spotlight onto Stage 2 – Appolyon Ledge.

'Who was Appolyon anyway? Some Greek?'
'Don't know. Classics weren't my subject.'

The ubiquitous Bell optimistically named this a ledge when he crossed over the Pinnacle Face in 1937. We follow him in search of our own Holy Grail. Ritchie's Gully is crossed on wet, slithery snow clinging to soft, green ice. Smith's Gully arrives. We pause, look up, look down; feeling like intruders we cross over. Feet follow as imaginations race ahead. A germ of an idea is mulled over. The Traverse! Unspoken thoughts are interrupted abruptly as the ledge narrows and disappears just ahead. Reluctantly we abdicate our independence and rope up. Bob leads an exposed pitch, his steps puncturing the snow through to the turf. The rope arcs unhindered downwards and draws our eyes and imaginations with it. The exposure is mind-

**Route** The Crab Crawl, Grade 3/4, 8,000ft.
**Cliff** The cliffs of Coire Ardair, Creag Meagaidh.
**First Ascent** Winter: T. W. Patey, March 1969.
**Map** See page 126.
**Guidebooks** See page 126.
**Nearest Road / Approach Time** See page 126.
**Route Summary / Conditions** A traverse of unique length, exposed but not particularly difficult. It is usually climbable for most of the winter but is best in consolidated snow conditions. After blizzards there may be a risk of windslab avalanche.
**Campsites and Bunkhouses** See page 126.
**Bibliography** *One Man's Mountains* by Tom Patey (Gollancz) contains an entertaining account of the first ascent.

*Left: The Scene — the first section of the Crab Crawl, the mammoth girdle traverse of the Creag Meagaidh cliffs. Climber: Bill March / Photo: John Cleare*

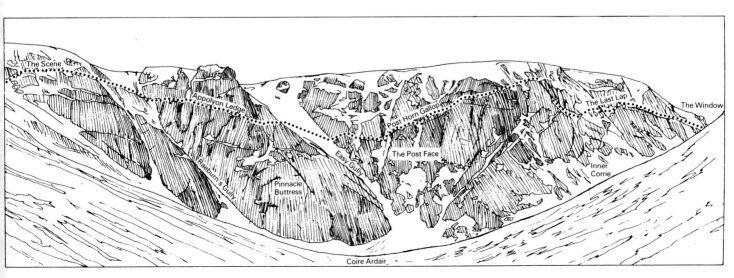

*Above: Crossing the Appolyon Ledge.*
*Climbers: Ian Howell and Bill March/*
*Photo: John Cleare*

blowing, distracting; more Dolomitic than Scottish. I follow his steps and lead easily on. Moving together now, we choose a descending traverse line and arrive at the shoulder of Pinnacle Buttress with the rope dangling uselessly between us. We focus on the Post Face and our doubts:

> 'The Girdle Traverse of the cliffs of Coire Ardair . . . is certainly the longest potential expedition of its kind in Great Britain.'
> *Bugs McKeith, 1967*

'Do we have time? It's eleven now and we're about halfway!'

'Why not!'

'Why not!' Whillans' rebuke of Patey is recalled:

> 'You want to team up with a crab. It's got claws, walks sideways and it's got a thick 'ead. This isn't a climb, it's a bloody crab-crawl!'

It may not be a climb but it's certainly good exercise. I wonder what Bob would look like boiled and garnished in Thousand Island Dressing. I retreat into my own shell and plough a trench across to Easy Gully.

There's an urgency in our pace now. A clearing

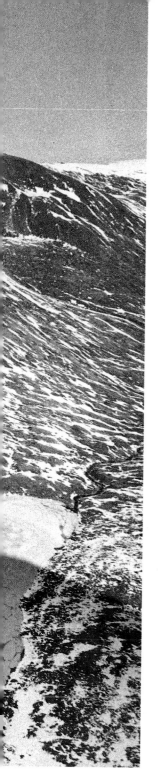

sky gives an unexpected crispness to the snow. Steeply on good solid névé we climb out of the gully and meander, on independent lines, through isolated outcrops and slabs to the open, icy, lower pitches of Last Post. We carry on across the buttress lost in our own private, snowy world. I find myself in the deep recess of South Post, which stretches steep and icy above. Our line takes a diagonal ramp and looks straightforward enough. I start. My first two steps collapse under me and I scuttle back, deflated, to excavate a belay on the gully wall.

Bob arrives, grabs the proffered rope, and launches himself at the ice. The ramp is rotten and hollow, forcing him steeply up and left above my head. He claws up, staccato but efficient, and moves out of sight. The rope slicks up and I follow. Earlier rhythm is lost and I move woodenly, a front-pointing Pinocchio. Bob unties from his belay and rockets on diagonally across a snowfield. I dig out the deadman and clank along behind. The rope is relegated to the sack, only to be produced again minutes later after a peer into North Post. I look across at the steep, exposed pitch,

*Top: On the Post Horn Gallop at the point where the route crosses below the headwall of Centre Post (Direct Finish). Climber: Ian Howell and Bill March / Photo: John Cleare*

*Above: The line of Post Horn Gallop across the upper part of the Post Face. Photo: Colin Stead*

*Below: Crossing North Post near the end of the Post Horn Gallop. Climber: Ian Howell / Photo: John Cleare*

the awkward ground beyond, and glance surreptitiously at the easy slopes to the cornice above. Bob's tail is up. He stitches me to the belay and scrapes his way down and across a blank slab to the back of the gully. The rope jerks uneasily; shadows creep up the coire.

'There's an old peg here.'

'Didn't Patey lower himself on a peg about here?'

A frantic beating at the back of the ledge and grunt of satisfaction. Bob moves cautiously down. His feet scrape twin grooves down the slab, bulldozing the snow into space. A flurry of movement and snow, a mad lunge to impale a turf and he hauls himself onto a ledge beyond. I watch horrified: he grins back. 'There's a good belay here.'

Scratching the remaining snow, I lift his peg from the turf with my fingers. Flakes of rusty metal guard the only possible solid place. I reach down tentatively, at full stretch, only to jar my crampons on bare rock. Lurch back to the peg. It looks better now. My rope is threaded through the rusty ring. I drive my picks downwards at knee-level and slide scraping down the slab. A wild sideways lean, picks flailing and Bob pulls me up to his feet.

Reluctantly the rope is declared redundant again; time is short. Like anxious commuters, we tick off the stations as they pass, Staghorn, the Pumpkin, the Sash, the Wand, the route then is unclear; where to now? As in the game of snakes and ladders we climb ramps and slide down gullies. Imagination fits the features to the description. The climbing is mixed, dramatic and always demanding. It may not be the Quasimodo Traverse or Positively 64th Street, but there's a sting in the tail all right. Like rabbits caught in headlights, we fling ourselves heedlessly at anything vaguely horizontal. It has to go.

Imperceptibly our rhythm changes; we become anthropoid, awkward pedestrians learning how to walk again. A buttress appears in the gloom opposite; we're in the Window, we've arrived. The terminus. A defiant wave westwards to the last red feathers of daylight and a whooping crazy plunge down to the corrie.

# 29   The Wand and the Pumpkin

by Neil Quinn

Development on Creag Meagaidh was slower than on most of the major winter cliffs in Scotland. Even so, it was remarkable that two lines of the quality of the Wand and the Pumpkin had not been climbed before. Many fine climbers had walked past, but for some reason had ignored them. I can still remember my first sight of the Pumpkin. After an early rise and a beautiful walk into the Inner Corrie in magnificent weather, there it was; 300ft. of ice pouring down the corner in a blue and green cascade, and above, the chimneys leading to the summit snows.

I gazed at it with a deal of apprehension. After all, I had been brought along as the step-hacker. I had never climbed with Gerry Peet or Bob McMillan before, and realised that Gerry's generous invitation to come along on an attempt at a first ascent wasn't because I was a nice chap. Fear the Greeks, I thought, when they come bearing gifts.

We roped up and as I was ready first I decided to go up to what looked like a good belay spot. Fooled again. After a struggle I reached the stance, belayed, and brought Gerry up. He led off up the next pitch but after about 30ft. decided it was a bit steep and looked for a belay. After all, he was getting old even then. The next pitch was probably the crux. The ice was very steep but curved enough to permit bridging. After a bit, even bridging was not enough to permit balance while cutting and I put in an ice-screw as high as possible and Gerry gave me tension while I cut up the steepest section. Gerry was impressed, though rather disappointed that I had not fallen off. The exit from the icefall was barred by some ice-bulges but I was able to wend my way between them to arrive at the ledge which forms part of the girdle traverse. Above, ice spewed out of a leftward-slanting chimney. As I had by now assumed the role of leader I sent Gerry up to cut the first part of the chimney while I had a rest. He belayed at about 60ft. and brought me up. The steepest section called for left-handed cutting, which meant three or four little forays up to cut at a hold before retreating for a rest. Up and down until the job was done. A frantic mantelshelf on the top hold brought easier ground. We gathered below the final chimney, which was full of poor snow and ice at a relatively easy angle, then in no time at all we were enjoying the sunshine at the summit. Walking down the track we discussed a name for the route in keeping with the others in the Inner

Corrie. Simultaneously Gerry and I said, 'the Pumpkin'.

The Wand is a different type of climb. Short and steep, it shares a start with Diadem and the Sash. Viewed from the corrie floor, the ice-fringed bulges of the Wand appear to lean beyond the vertical for most of their height. It is an optical illusion. When I first pointed out the Wand to Doug Lang he thought I was mad, but closer inspection proved it to be not as steep as it looked.

The climb starts easily up the Sash to the foot of the icefall, then follows the corner close to the right-hand edge of the ice, next to the buttress. Several small caves form in the corner between the rock and the ice, which can be used for belays or a rest.

Doug and I, accompanied by Graeme Hunter and Quinton Crichton, gathered at the foot of the icefall. Our steps from an attempt the previous week which had been thwarted by poor conditions, were still in place and only required clearing. After a bit of messing about Graeme took a belay at 60ft. in the first and largest of the caves. I climbed our old steps and pushed on up the second pitch. A fantastic jammed boulder provided a bombproof runner and boosted confidence for climbing a steep part. I reached the abseil peg from which we had retreated the week before and belayed to it, jamming myself in the second cave, a much smaller affair than Graeme's 40ft. below. Once inside it was a very secure little refrigerator. Doug was making impatient noises so I brought him up quickly. He

**Route** The Pumpkin, Grade 5, 1,000ft. The Wand, Grade 4/5, 680ft.
**Cliff** The cliffs of Coire Ardair, Creag Meagaidh, (Inner Corrie).
**First Ascent** Pumpkin – Winter: R. McMillan, G. S. Peet and N. Quinn, April 1968. The Wand – Winter: D. F. Lang, N. Quinn, G. N. Hunter and Q. T. Crichton, February 1969.
**Map** See page 126.
**Guidebooks** See page 126.
**Nearest Road / Approach Time** See page 126.
**Route Summary / Conditions** The first 200ft. ice wall of the Pumpkin can feel difficult in less-than-perfect conditions as belays are hard to find and protection sparse. The rest of the climb is mixed in character. The Wand is a steep, sustained ice climb and is frequently in condition.
**Campsites and Bunkhouses** See page 126.
**Bibliography** *More on Creag Meagaidh* by N. Quinn (S.M.C.J. 1970).

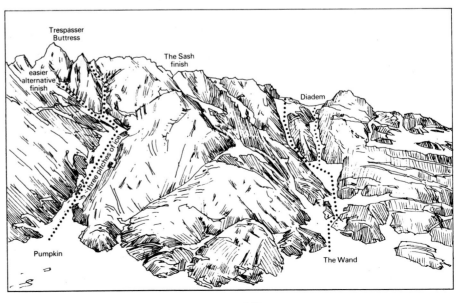

gave me the pack and threw himself enthusiastically at the third pitch. Now when it comes to climbing steep snow and rotten ice Doug is second to none, but he is slight of build and not the strongest ice-hacker around, and here the ice was about as easy to cut as granite. After a few feet Doug decided it was a bit too much like hard work. He cut a large double foothold high enough to let him reach over the top of the main bulge, then reached as high as possible and planted an ice-screw, attached an étrier, cut a few small handholds and in no time at all he was over and heading for the last small cave. A remarkable effort.

After Graeme joined me I left him to bring up Quinton. A few pirouettes later I joined Doug at his cave. As the stance was almost non-existent I wasted no time in handing over the pack and moving out into a steep groove. Some spectacularly airy bridging landed me at the top of the icefall and on easy ground. The difficulties were now over and we very quickly gained the plateau. It was clear and bitterly cold, with views for miles. We headed for the Window, and back down the track for afternoon tea at the lay-by.

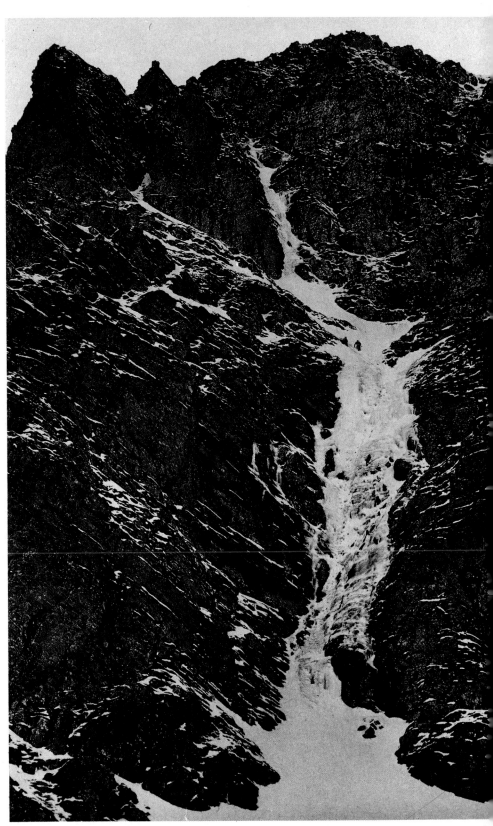

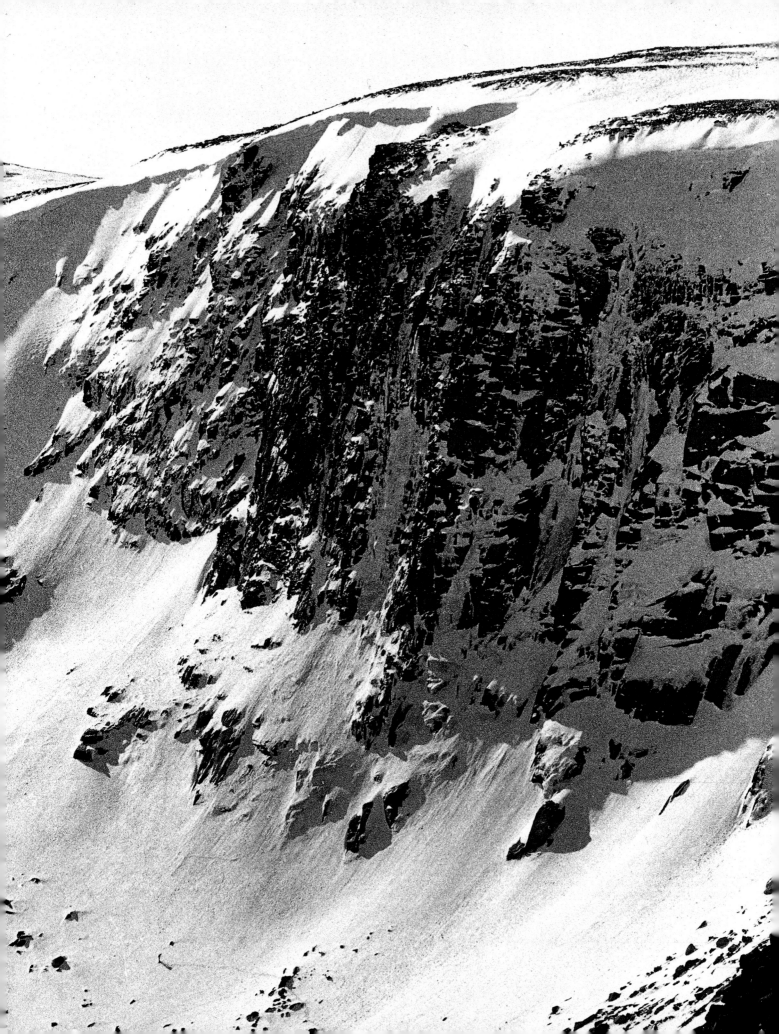

# 30  Deep-Cut Chimney, Hell's Lum Crag

by Allen Fyffe

The setting of Deep-Cut Chimney can hardly be faulted. It lies deep in the Cairngorm range, on Hell's Lum Crag at the head of the Loch Avon horseshoe. The crag itself faces south-east and is basically a straight granite face steepening from bottom to top. This sun-facing aspect ensures that in winter the springs that seep down its walls alternately freeze and thaw, producing quantities of ice. In addition the great amphitheatre at the loch's head is a natural snow trap and the cliff is frequently heavily banked. These factors combine to make Hell's Lum one of the most consistently good winter-cliffs in the area. True snow and ice ascents have been made here as early as October and as late as May. The only drawback is that in sunny weather, a rare occurrence, there can be avalanche and ice-fall danger.

The day we went to do Deep-Cut was a rare day of perfect weather; the air bitter and blue, the snow cold and deep. We took the usual approach from the north, skirting the edge of Coire an t-Sneachda to the col at the head of Coire Domhain. Then we headed down the broad, open slopes, taking turns to break trail in the crusted snow. Where the ground steepened we stopped and geared up. The cliff lay profiled on our right. As we would return the same way, we had the luxury of being able to leave our sacks. Traversing below the crag, we eyed up other lines: Escalator – easy and ice-choked; Devil's Delight, the crag's hard route, which hadn't yet built up; and then the obvious Deep-Cut Chimney.

Above and left a narrow black line split the cliff; the buttress on its left was grey and rough, the slabs on the right sheathed in ice. In summer the chimney starts with a strange diagonal fault which runs across the central third of the crag. This right-to-left diagonal is buried in normal winter conditions so there is a choice of approaches – any line from the diagonal fault to straight up. Tony Shepherd and I picked our own routes, front-pointing and flat-footing up the initial easier-angled ice, with the occasional steeper step across the overlaps – an enjoyable 200ft. introduction. Then we reached the foot of the main vertical fault and belay. The angle had crept up on us, and the diagonal approach had taken us out, away from the slabs, to overlook a more serious prospect.

*Left: Hell's Lum Crag from the Cairngorm plateau. Photo: John Cleare        See also colour photos on page 155*

To begin with, the chimney is fairly shallow and about five feet wide. It goes up in a series of steps. The first, just by the belay, held ice which gave perfect security and runners, a rare treat on winter granite. The next step is a bridging problem and the one after is overcome by chimneying; all on excellent ice. The pitch seemed so good I tried to stretch it, but 150ft. just saw me into the deepening. Above, the chimney cut back even further into the cliff and curved slightly, cutting off the view ahead.

Tony came up and led through, but soon the curve took him out of sight. Belayed across the chimney I regretted not having stopped in a more sheltered spot lower down. Anything cleared or knocked from above was channelled onto me. Then it was time to go; moving up, but deeper into the cliff. No elegant crampon work here, rather scrabble, scrape and fight whilst hanging onto shafts driven deep into the unconsolidated snow. Then Tony and I were united again. He was wedged across the chimney in an unlikely but safe and comfortable belay. I wondered about the next pitch, the crux and a surprising one at that.

The chimney, which had been cutting back deeply, suddenly ended, blocked off by a roof of jammed boulders. This extended for about 20ft. from the back and was about 40ft. above the belay. Straight out from the belay, but another 20ft. away on the outer edge of the chimney a huge chockstone marking the start of easier ground. There were two solutions to the problem; either out to this block or turn the roof.

Going straight out was the first, but a short-lived choice. The gradually diverging walls made back-and-footing increasingly precarious and I eventually returned to the belay. So, back to the chimney. Up over another snowed-up chockstone with a perfect runner, and easy snow to below the roof. Then comfortable back-and-foot work, more runners, and jams appeared; little ledges for the the front-points as I slowly sidled out facing right till I could embrace a square-topped flake on the right. There I crouched near the roof's lip whilst constructing a bombproof thread round the blocks. Now which way to face? I settled for facing in and bridging. Down at first, then out, and at last back up. Here, the left wall slid away a foot and I was at my limit for a few moves. Then I leant left, axe in and lurched onto easier snow. A couple of kicked steps and the ground was flat, a dramatic and unexpected end to the route.

**Route** Deep Cut Chimney, Grade 3/4, 500ft.
**Cliff** Hell's Lum Crag, Cairn Gorm
**First Ascent** Summer: 1950; Winter: T. W. Patey and D. Holroyd, January 1958.
**Map** O.S. 1:50,000 Sheet 36 (995018).
**Guidebooks** S.M.C. *Cairngorms Area, Vol. 1.* by W. March; *Winter Climbs – Cairngorms* by John Cunningham, revised by Allen Fyffe (Cicerone); *Scottish Winter Climbs* by Hamish MacInnes (Constable).
**Nearest Road / Approach Time** The Coire Cas car park, 9 miles south-east of Aviemore (990059). 3½ miles/1700ft. Allow 2 hours. The walk can be shortened by using the Cairngorm chair-lift from the car park. 2½ miles. Allow 1 hour.
**Route Summary / Conditions** Conditions on this climb vary because it is south-facing and therefore prone to rapid thaw. With a good covering of hard-packed snow it is enjoyable and not particularly difficult, but in lean conditions, on verglassed rock, it can be hard.
**Campsites and Bunkhouses** Youth Hostels at Aviemore and Loch Morlich. Camping at the Glenmore campsite. Shelter at Hutchison Memorial Hut in Choire Etchachan (023997) and bivouac at the Shelter Stone (001016).

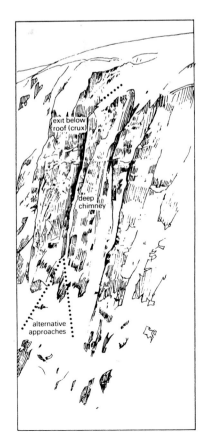

# 31   The Northern Corries of the Cairngorms

by Rusty Baillie

**Route** Central Crack Route, Grade 3, 350ft. The Vent, Grade 3, 350ft. Broken Gully, Grade 3, 450ft.

**Cliff** The cliffs of Coire an Lochain and Coire an t-Sneachda, Cairn Gorm.

**First Ascent** Central Crack Route – Summer 1931, Winter: T. W. Patey, 1958; The Vent – Winter: J. Geddes, E. M. Davidson, R. F. Stobart, Miss Macbain, April 1935, Summer: 1948. Broken Gully – Winter: T. W. Patey, J. MacArtney, J. Cleare. February 1967.

**Map** O.S. 1:50,000 Sheet 36 – Coire an Lochain (986028), Coire an t-Sneachda (993031).

**Guidebooks** See page 149.

**Nearest Road / Approach Time** The Coire Cas car park, 9 miles south-east of Aviemore (990059). Coire an Lochain – 3 miles/1,300ft. Allow 1½ hours. Coire an t-Sneachda – 2 miles/1,300ft. Allow 1 hour.

**Route Summary / Conditions** The Northern Corries offer good easy and middle-grade climbing in normal winter conditions. After heavy snowfall there is a high avalanche risk in both corries, particularly in Coire an Lochan, which is also prone to slab-avalanche during spring thaw.

**Campsites and Bunkhouses** Youth Hostels at Aviemore and Loch Morlich. Official campsite at Glenmore (expensive). Jean's Hut, below Coire an Lochain (981034), is only suitable for emergency shelter.

As one of the 'Thin Blue Band' at Glenmore Lodge, it seemed a good idea to learn the local climbs and so, one fine day that first winter, I set off with Stu Allen. Stu is a New Zealand guide, used to trogging huge distances over Mount Cook.

'Quality, not quantity is what Scotland has,' I pontificated. 'We'll have a go at Central Crack in Coire an Lochain. That'll give some sport on mixed rock and ice, and the spice of technical difficulty. You need a rest from all that walking.'

It was a glorious sunny day. Not the full-coloured too-good-to-be-trueness of High Colorado, but the eerie pastel-shaded hues of the Scottish Arctic. A brooding melancholy that tugs at the heart-strings of an exiled Scotto-Rhodesian. We dawdled up. The Northern Corries are nice friendly places, as mountains go. Not too remote or too big. Challenging, but not demanding. A place to climb like a gentleman, between a good breakfast and high tea. Of course, because of this they kill a great number of people.

The Great Slab of Coire an Lochain enlivens the approach to the upper climbs and, well-warmed-up, we arrived at the bare rocks of Central Crack. Unfortunately, the thaw-freeze had not been hard enough or long enough or whatever to provide any useful ice. Merely a thin verglas layer, producing something too thick for vibrams, too thin for crampons. The climbing was hard but not stylish. There was not that satisfying click as crampon-points bit firmly into the ice-cover. There was instead a lot of scratching and clattering and I even took one crampon off for a stage – the ultimate in bad form on a Scottish winter climb. It all

underlined my heretical theory that the main protagonist in Scottish winter climbing, the thing that gives it its mystical aura of impregnability and other-worldness, is not sheer difficulty, nor the vile weather, the dreaded white-out, nor even the bogs, but merely the fact that most often the winter route simply does not exist.

Winter did return on the summit snow slope and I was proud of the intimidating cornice which was not my lead. Then that strange moment of exiting from vertical climb to horizontal plateau: 'What are these, mountains or what?'

The day was much too good to waste on a descent by the northern snow slopes so we found the exit of Y Gully Right Hand, plunged through the cornice and surveyed the scene. The snow felt funny, sort of slabby, and we stayed roped together, taking rock belays. That way we could test-ski the slope and transfer our problem to those below us.

With such a fine day it seemed a shame to scurry home. When you don't know when the next meal will come you savour what you have! 'The quickest way back is definitely up the Vent,' I suggested. 'We can then nip along the plateau and take the chairlift down; easier on the knees!'

The Vent is like a huge hourglass, with a fine little ice pitch in the narrows. We put the rope away and trotted merrily upwards. Conditions here were superb. Good classical snow-ice, so rare, the stuff that made Zero Gully possible in the good old days. The plateau above appeared much too soon. A cruel return to the confines of gravity.

As we wandered along the serrated plateau rim, swotting up on our cairn recognition, we found ourselves at the head of Red Gully above Coire an t-Sneachda:

'Let's go down here.'

It seemed a good idea, and so we made our easy way down the steep, narrow slot that stretches the definition of a gully. There was a funny little bulge, probably quite straightforward on the ascent, which needed a cold-blooded lower-over-the abyss on a single axe, the feet dangling free. Fun enough.

Now the end of Red is conveniently close to the start of Broken Gully, a route put up by three good friends of mine, two of whom later died in these

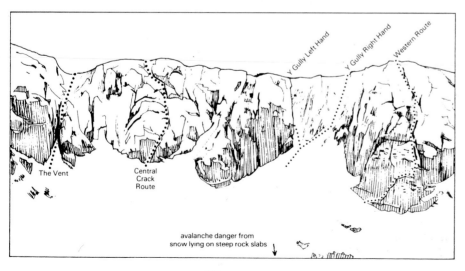

The Vent          Central Crack Route

avalanche danger from snow lying on steep rock slabs

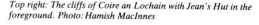

*Top right: The cliffs of Coire an Lochain with Jean's Hut in the foreground. Photo: Hamish MacInnes*

*Bottom right: The Coire an t-Sneachda cliffs: Alladin's Buttress is on the left and Broken Gully and Red Gully take lines on the right flank. Photo: Hamish MacInnes*

hills. Up we go, following the good snow, propelled and protected by our Karma; too involved to think, we plumb the depths of thought. And once again the view – shadows settling into Glen Avon, faint colours sighing, and the plateau sastrugi playing balefully with a fading light.

The chairlift had stopped. Besides, it now seemed inappropriate. Instead we picked our way down Goat Track Gully. A last lingering caress. A reluctance to give up this privilege of free movement. The guidebook says there's a rock pitch at the bottom. Probably there is.

Two notorious cave pitches on Buachaille
Etive Mor (see articles on pages 107 and 112):

Above: The Great Cave Pitch of Crowberry
Gully. Climber: Jim Lawrence / Photo: Andy
Hyslop

Right: The crux of Raven's Gully where it is
necessary to climb an ice-glazed wall (5a in
summer) to turn a huge chockstone.
Climber: Rep Bruce / Photo: Calum Frazer

Two photos of Deep-Cut Chimney on Hell's Lum Crag (see article on page 149).

Left: A view up the deep inner recesses of the chimney.
Climber: Tony Shepherd / Photo: Allen Fyffe

Above: The crux, at the top of the route. Here the chimney is blocked by a roof and back-and-foot techniques are required to work out of the bed of the cleft to gain easier ground.
Climber: Eileen Stroud / Photo: Sam Crymble

# 32  White Nile

by Rob Archbold

**Route** White Nile, Grade 4, 400ft.
**Cliff** Garbh Choire Mor, Braeriach.
**First Ascent** Winter: M. Hillmann and R. J. Archbold. March 1977.
**Map** 1:50,000 Sheet 36 (940980).
**Guidebooks** *Scottish Winter Climbs* by Hamish MacInnes (Constable); *Winter Climbs – Cairngorms*, by John Cunningham, revised by Allen Fyffe.
**Nearest Road / Approach Time** At the Coire Cas car park (990059). Follow path via Chalamain Gap and the Lairig Ghru. 9 miles/ 1,750ft. Allow 4½ hours.
**Route Summary / Conditions** A steep, strenuous ice climb that is often in condition. Large cornices, remote location and, in poor visibility, difficult plateau route-finding combine to lend an extra dimension of seriousness to the Braeriach climbs.
**Campsites and Bunkhouses** Youth Hostels at Aviemore and Loch Morlich. Official campsite at Glenmore (expensive). Garbh Choire Hut (959986), Corrour Bothy (981958), Sinclair Memorial Hut and Bothies (958036).

'. . . the great hollow forming the innermost recesses of the Amphitheatre – perhaps the most intriguing corrie in the massif on account of size, remoteness, wildness allied to beauty, and above all climate. Here are found the snowfields of summer – our nearest approach in this country to the névé of higher mountains.'

'A large headland thrusting out from the plateau divides the corries into two subsidiaries, each of great interest and character. These are Garbh Choire Mor and Garbh Choire Dhaidh. Their cliffs are the least known in the massif – a situation at once disappointing yet delighting their devotees.'

*Malcolm Smith*
*Climbers' Guide to the Cairngorms Area*

My first visit to Braeriach was made at the end of March, 1974 – the start of a lengthy spell of settled weather which marked the spring of that year in Scotland. The snow had receded into the highest corries, yet each night still produced a slight frost before the sun came and took its toll. We arrived in dribs and drabs from Aberdeen, first Dennis King, and then a day or so later Raymond Simpson and myself. Last to appear was Greg Strange, exam-weary but happy to be back. We rose at 4 a.m. and by dawn stood beneath an ice-groove in Garbh Choire Mor which had caught our attention the previous afternoon by its resemblance, from the bothy, to a streak of jagged lightning in the brown, surrounding rocks. Our start was none too early, for even by 9 a.m. as we neared the top, the power of the sun was causing the ice to soften and run with water. Stripped to the waist, we ambled gently round the plateau rim towards the slanting descent on the west side of the Corrie of the Chokestone Gully. Looking back at the climb, we noticed instead a glistening candle of water-ice between the middle and right-hand buttresses of the Pinnacles trio. It was perhaps as well that it was incomplete in the upper section, for the prospect of trying to cut steps up it the next day would have sent disturbing currents through our sunny idyll. We spent the rest of the day sunbathing by the burn.

I returned briefly in the heatwave of 1976, seeking to escape a while from the rigours of the Dubh Loch. My companion on this occasion was Alison Higham, one of the few lady members of the Etchachan Club. We began in Coire Brochain with Braeriach Direct and West Wall Route, a little-known but excellent Severe. Away to the left lay

the short dark slit of Ebony Chimney, with its cavernous through-route, recently climbed in winter by Charlie Macleod and Andrew Nisbet – another icy jewel in Braeriach's crown. We descended into Garbh Choire Dhaidh and climbed the Great Rift. I made a mental note to put it on the list for winter; at that time I had heard of only one ascent of what must be a superb ice climb.

The following year Miles Hillmann and I made the long journey to Braeriach. We spent the night at Corrour, oppressed by the looming hulk of Devil's Point, and next morning moved on up to the bothy. After a second breakfast we set off again and turned into Garbh Choire Dhaidh. The cliff was bare apart from some thin smears of ice in the Rift. Facing south, this natural ice-trap had clearly

trapped a fair amount of sunshine too. We began to consider the alternatives. I had already climbed Chokestone Gully, but just to the right stood the impressive Bugaboo Rib, while out of sight in Garbh Choire Mor lay Vulcan, She-Devil's Buttress, and several other attractive routes, many of them still unrepeated. Somewhat uneasily, I remembered the candle of ice.

Although the Dee runs out of Dhaidh, Garbh Choire Mor is recessed even further westwards into the plateau. Entering the Cairngorms from Braemar, this is probably the farthest you can go without crossing a watershed – truly the end of the line, with nothing beyond but the vast plateau running west to Einich and Feshie. Mist was rolling over the rim as we approached, but we could see

the lower half of the route, looking this time more like a high-angle gully than an icefall. The snow-ice was perfect, perhaps a gift from the management in recognition of all the faithful service on powder, slush and impenetrable water-ice. I had recently acquired two Terrordactyls, but I still excavated a ladder of footholds, ostensibly to ease the strain on Miles's leg, only a week or so out of plaster, but in reality for myself. The picks felt so secure that pulling up seemed almost like using aid compared to the old-style free-climbing on carefully fashioned handholds.

After the first steep section, and the jink right at the top of the ramp above, we made our stance by the heavily-iced sidewall of Phoenix Buttress. From here the line is direct, but farther on a hint of

Above: Deep in the Cairngorms — a view from the slopes of Ben Macdui, across the Lairig Ghru, to the glaciated bulk of Braeriach. The cliffs at the back of the shadowy bowl of Coire Bhrochain are capped by huge cornices formed by the blizzards that sweep across the plateau. An Garbh Choire is on the left. Photo: John Allen

**157**

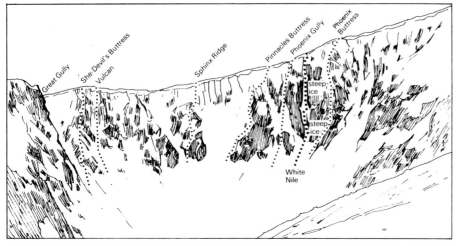

*Above: The cliffs of Garbh Choire Mor.*
*Photo: Greg Strange*

relief; rock protection on the route had been sparse and mediocre in quality, and our supply of four ice-screws was barely adequate.

The wind was only average by plateau standards, but cold enough to remind us of the pressing need to descend. In order not to lose the rim I kept within a perilous 15–20ft. of the edge, while Miles held the ropes and walked parallel further in. An abrupt turn through 90° indicated that we'd reached the ridge between Mor and Dhaidh. It was guarded by a short headwall of steep, unstable snow, and Miles's calm reasoning eventually persuaded me to continue instead with our nerve-wracking progress round the rim. Slowly the landmarks passed by: the dip where the infant Dee plunges into Dhaidh, and then the riser over the top of the Rift. As we moved on between Dhaidh and Bhrochain the edge became less defined and we angled downwards cautiously, for even on this slope a wicked cornice can form a little lower down. The tension seemed endless as we constantly peered ahead to detect slight steepenings, and then we suddenly came out of the mist and could see the dark shape of the glen below. The pace quickened as we dropped hundreds of feet to the burn and stumbled along its bank searching for the bothy. At one point we thought we'd overshot and I cast back, but within a few minutes Miles had found it lower down. We tumbled through the door; I lay motionless and glassy-eyed while the lion cooked a feast.

jelly in the arms caused our route to deviate slightly up a groove on the left. There followed a delicate traverse left, using ice-ripple underclings beneath the overlap, until good ice on the slab above permitted the upward heave. Ironically, this detour provided the technical crux. At the belay, Miles casually revealed that he had a bicycle torch as well as a headtorch – and that both were in the bothy. I moved right in the gathering gloom and began to work up towards the hidden cornice. We expected the worst, recalling how the first ascent description of the neighbouring Phoenix Gully had spoken of a huge cornice 40ft. up and 20ft. out, but eventually my torch picked out a snow-rib on the left which angled gently to the plateau. Surprise mingled with

# 37  Polyphemus Gully

by Paul Nunn

In the Alps 6 a.m. jars the senses, but if it is bright and clear the pleasure soon takes over. Crouching in a Scottish bothy as the wind wails and the snow sifts in through the door is quite another sensation.

Somehow a pan gets to the primus, bacon sizzles, more bodies stir and groan. Long before the real awakening (there is the secret) it is a long plod by the snow-drifted path towards Lochnagar. Mound upon mound of boring heather. Mile upon mile it seems, always with clouds holding back the dawn. How can it be barely freezing when the wind buffets so hard? There is a temptation to go back, but what has Ballater, or even Royal Braemar to offer the likes of us, still half-city-slickers from Manchester, Britain's counter-capital?

Wet-warm at the col, the wind comes from the south-west, a hot winter gale from somewhere in the Canaries. Still it seems better to press, for any other approach achieves nothing in the North. A little frost from a mid-week freeze remains as incentive. Will it be enough?

The great chute of Raeburn's Gully is barely visible in a driving mist. Not knowing the cliff well we use it to locate Polyphemus. A swathe of ice droops in from the left out of some unseen recess behind. That must be it. Despite forgotten complex descriptions the way looks obvious, as far as we can see, which is not beyond a first 100ft. or so of steepish ice. More worrying is a trickle of water emerging from under the ice. The south-westerly is at work already. Companions go different ways. Some go back.

I sort out a belay below the ice and Bob Toogood sets off up an ice-chute and then by a delicately-carved traverse right to an upper fall. An overlap steepens it all. A solitary ice-piton gives a hint of security but Bob prefers to trust his workshop-made hammer, a ferocious tomahawk-like object which bites firmly despite the melt. Leader and rope disappear in murk. The waiting game leads to cold feet, hands and a shiver or two. A duvet would have been nice. 'Have we anything to eat?' 'Not much.' Melt water soaks through a porous old anorak. He stops, obviously taking his time to engineer a thorough belay. Then the slack rope goes out quickly and without a call. It is my time to go.

The melting ice crunches a little under the crampons. The new slightly-curved implements seem to work, but lack security. They have too few teeth or is it the lack of angle? After all, they are ten years old already — it's hard to tell. The pitch is not too steep, but there are awkward steps and some traversing. At the stance Bob is well-satisfied, grinning in elfish pleasure.

Some easier stuff follows, nice but unremarkable. Then the gully rears and Bob takes a stance out on the right wall. A wind howls above but only sends the occasional whumph of spindrift upon us. No problem on easy ground. But Bob does not like his belay. It's solid but I weigh thirteen stones to his nine. The prospect ahead concentrates the mind wonderfully as the upper gully tilts into sight 25ft. above; a hanging gutter. Some rocks between us are steep and almost devoid of snow or ice. Black and naked, short but mean. Our investigations reveal no outflanking move, so up it is. Grade 4/5, like any other, can mask a multitude of sins, especially of omission.

A very long Lost Arrow piton, materializes in my left hand, brought for just such circumstances. I beat it into a crack at face-level. It sinks in as far as the very finely engineered little eye. In goes Bob's rope for a belay and mine on an extra karabiner as a runner. Things look better. Stiffly I move up into a corner. I'm icing up with the wet and cold, building up for a rheumy old age. A few little rock ledges take crampons and five or six feet are won. There's nothing much for the implements. Scraping up carefully in a bridged position allows a long left-hand reach with the axe. The pick swings upwards and lodges in God-knows-what, but it holds, though the spindrift makes it hard to see what is going on. Bob huddles into his hood. It is a familiar scene. It is now a question of using the axe and bridging to gain a little more height. Then the hammer should go in too and all should be well. With luck.

Carefully feet are worked up on precious little, front-points splayed wide on rock. Then the right hand freed to make a longish swing with the hammer, the target safely a foot or two above the axe. The right wall is in the way and it is awkward. The hammer fails to lodge. Feet are braced harder, axe grip tightens and another hammer-blow at a different target area. As the hammer swings something shifts. The axe! Whoops! It's too late. The axe parts company from a bit of ice to which it had feigned attachment. Straddled legs remain momentarily frozen in position and my body tips over backwards before crampons skate off the rock walls and the gully below approaches at speed. One

**Route** Polyphemus Gully, Grade 4/5, 600ft.
**Cliff** The cliffs of the North-East Corrie of Lochnagar.
**First Ascent** Summer: 1933; Winter: K. Grassick, H. S. Bates, January 1953.
**Map** See page 172.
**Guidebooks** See page 172.
**Nearest Road / Approach Time** See page 172.
**Route Summary / Conditions** The degree of difficulty varies according to the amount of snow. In lean conditions as many as six hard pitches may be encountered, but with a heavy snow build-up some of the pitches will be banked-out. There are normally two difficult sections: the first pitch, and two difficult mixed pitches in the upper half of the route.
**Campsites and Bunkhouses** See page 172.

*Left: Shadow Buttresses A and B and Eagle Ridge divided by Polyphemus Gully and Douglas-Gibson Gully. Photo: Bert Jenkins*

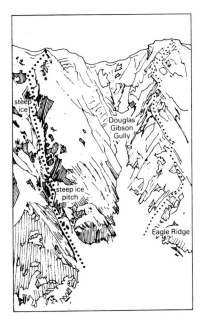

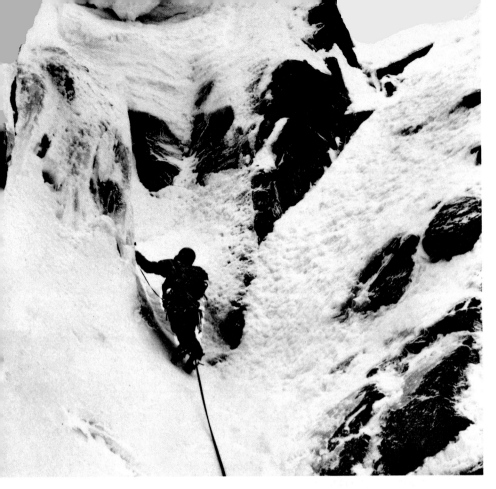

*Top left: Starting the first hard section of Polyphemus Gully. In these conditions the scoop above the climber gave 50ft. of precarious bridging up a groove lined with powder snow. Climber: Dave Wilkinson / Photo: Wil Hurford*

*Bottom left: Halfway up the first crux — in lean conditions with a less-than-average build-up of snow and ice. Climber: Rob Archbold / Photo: Greg Strange*

unfortunate foot catches the wall and is yanked round, splaying crampon points in all directions.

'Anything broken?' enquires Bob as I hang there. 'Maybe.' Is all that I could manage in reply.

Fortunately Toogood is a cool customer, and for him climbing only gets interesting when he is totally committed. This was not yet the case. It was evident that the top was near and as light was short, up might yet be the quickest way. I struggled back one-footedly to the belay, feeling painfully sick and dependent, and remembering a broken leg on Monte Civetta. We had got out of that, so why not this? 'Good thing about the peg,' we agreed. It winks, unmoved, as Bob prepares to lead. Darkness looms and I am glad he is a potholer.

After swopping ropes he moves up into the corner a little rustily, working up his concentration and brandishing the great, black, Sheffield tomahawk. His wiry legs stick out precariously in much the same position that I had achieved. Shivering with shock I grip the rope. There is no messing. The tomahawk whips backwards and slams into the ice, then Bob follows as if attached to it by a string. I sigh with relief despite the pain and the dark. There is little to see above, but the ropes keep going out until Bob camps under a biggish cornice to belay. With a tight rope I wobble, mostly on one foot, up the steep section, leaving my beloved piton behind, half-hoping that some future sufferer might also find it useful.

The cornice takes no time. Bob digs and shovels and ferrets a way into the arm-deep slops before moving out into the maelstrom above. It is a cold thaw and a white-out, and about six, late in January. A compass helps the way down, but a bent ankle does little to aid judgement, and for hours we seem to plod trackless wind-blown snow. Just as we are convinced that we have lost the route we hit the path to Glen Muick. Long after midnight, on the motorable path below the Loch, I go to sleep until Bob gets back with the red van. At the bothy Ted Howard adds insult to injury, regaling us with tales of booze and dance in Ballater:

'One of the best Saturday nights the lads have ever had.'

# 38  Parallel Buttress*

by Jerry Smith

. . . We descended into the corrie, Patey racing towards the rocks like a sheepdog recalled by its master. Bill Brooker and I, the two submissive sheep, followed for a while, then, thankful that our tormentor had left us, made best possible use of the respite: Bill got out his sandwiches and I delved in my sack for a tin of peaches.

'What's that fanatic doing?'

Tom was two-thirds of the way up the first pitch of Parallel Gully A.

'It looks as if he's soloing Parallel A. Have you got a tin opener, Bill?'

He hadn't. But we managed to prise the tin open with one of his 'secret weapons' — home-made ice-pegs — and then passed the tin between us, spearing the fruit slices with pitons. Suddenly our peace was shattered again.

'For God's sake get a bloody move on! We haven't got all day.'

'What are you going to do?'

'Parallel Buttress of course.'

We collected our wits and within a minute were running across the lumpy snow of the avalanche cone below Douglas-Gibson Gully.

The pitch that Tom had just climbed was what any decent mountaineering author from Geoffrey Winthrop Young to Hermann Buhl would call vertical snow: that is, it was soft enough to kick steps and punch armholes, and so steep that snow had to be cleared away before one could bend a knee. 'Quite a good pitch, about V.Diff,' was Tom's verdict, though I can imagine Frank Smythe having had more to say about it. Tom, 50ft. above, was making fast progress towards the right-hand side of the buttress where the 'great difficulties' would start. In the main it was easy snow, but often ice or frozen turf outcropped and we stepped in his rough nicks. A month before I had watched Bill and Dod Adams laboriously chip their way over glazed rock where now we were moving unroped; in half an hour we covered more ground than they did then in four hours.

Tom had disinterred a rock bollard when we arrived with the ropes, and while we tied ourselves to the various ends a discussion started as to who should lead. Finally Bill allocated Tom the first groove, and himself the two succeeding slab pitches; I would tackle the Tower. Meanwhile Tom had already led the first 30ft. of glazed rock and was tugging for me to follow. Having started in the lead

he was in a position to stay there as long as he pleased, since as soon as I joined him, he pronounced the stance unsafe for three, and he must move on before Bill could start. Tom is a very experienced mountaineer.

The steep groove above is in summer a slab pitch of Very Difficult standard about 70ft. high. Now the rock was obscured by layers of tough ice. Fresh crystals of hoar frost had stuck here and there to this surface, though the patches of white and grey bore no relation to the configuration of the rock beneath. Above, on the left of the groove, was the ring-spike from which Tom and Alan Will had abseiled a week previously. Tom reached the peg and started to traverse a sloping ledge back into the groove, sweeping away masses of powder. Having exhausted the handholds, he asked me to hold the rope tight while he crossed the ledge supported by tension from the piton. Thus he stood for fully 15 minutes, occasionally poking down a chip of ice with his axe. I couldn't imagine what was keeping him for there appeared to be perfectly adequate holds. But I said nothing; it wouldn't do to rush the chap, for the leader often has to be nursed up a tricky bit. At last he stepped across, the tension in the rope slackened and he was on his own. Slowly he worked up the slab and from the amount of his sole visible I saw that it must be quite delicate. I shuddered to think that if he came off those steel spikes would crash on my head.

The rope ran out quickly as Tom reached easier ground. As far as the ring-spike I found easy, but the traverse was indeed poor in handholds. I asked Tom for all the slack rope and grasping a loop threaded through the ring, shuffled across to the groove where I placed my right toe on a frozen divot. Still clutching the reassuring handful of rope I stood for ten minutes contemplating the next move, feeling as I did the first time that I dived from the 30ft. board at the Uptown baths. 'Well, here goes! Pull like hell!' I balanced across and letting go of the rope, I watched it snake through the ring until there was a pleasing tension from above. But there was no retreat now. The holds were minute and widely spaced. I hesitate to call them infinitesimal, for these ice-steps half an inch wide would be jug-handles on a warm slab, but numbed fingers encased in leather gloves need something correspondingly more finite to curl round. I was scared stiff. That left toe was just stuck onto the ice and with the slightest wobble would go. I pulled up

**Route** Parallel Buttress, Grade 5, 900ft.
**Cliff** The cliffs of the North-East Corrie of Lochnagar.
**First Ascent** Summer: 1939; Winter: T. W. Patey, J. Smith and W. D. Brooker, March 1956.
**Map** See page 172.
**Guidebooks** See page 172.
**Nearest Road / Approach Time** See page 172.
**Route Summary / Conditions** An intricate line up a series of chimneys, grooves and slabs, the Tower and finally a narrow ridge. The first ascensionists used the first pitch of Parallel Gully A and a diversion into Parallel Gully B to speed progress, but a direct line (see diagram) was later established. The climb will be difficult if not generously coated with snow and ice (rare).
**Campsites and Bunkhouses** See page 172.
**Bibliography** *Sestogradists in Scotland* by Jerry Smith (C.C.J. 1957) is an amusing account of the first ascent, most of which is published here.

*From 'Sestogradists in Scotland', *Climbers Club Journal*, 1957

on a snowball squashed against the slab. More panic, and a fight to regain my balance as a piton I grabbed came out in my hand; I fancied I heard Tom chuckle at the success of this macabre joke. A glove pressed against the ice froze to it giving me courage to step up again, and by a series of such desperate manoeuvres I finally emerged at the top of the pitch.

The stance was very small, so to avoid unnecessary crowding, Tom decided to lead on at once. The promising snow-slope that he started to climb turned out to be the slightest veneer of powder over perfectly smooth rock. Plainly he wasn't sure where the summer route went; in most summers he climbs in the Alps keeping his hand in for winter climbing in the Cairngorms.

When he had climbed down again he consulted my watch. There were another three and a half hours of daylight, and many more difficult pitches. 'As we're pretty hard pressed for time, I think that we had better avoid the next two pitches by climbing this middle section of Parallel B, and traversing back at the Necklace. The snow in the gully looks in terrific condition.' No sooner had Tom said this than he plunged to his armpits in snow as soft as eiderdown. He led out the full length of the rope, then waited while I brought up Bill. It was deathly cold in the gully. Clouds of spindrift sweeping down from the plateau penetrated my several layers of windproof clothing, numbing my body. This frozen Scotch mist crystallized onto my clothes, hair and

eyebrows; even my day-old beard had a bead of ice hanging from each hair. I chewed some chocolate, but could not find sufficient heat in my mouth to melt it. Only this time tomorrow I would be well-fed and warm in a thermostatically controlled laboratory.

When Bill discovered that his two pitches were being by-passed he was very angry. In a few terse phrases the denigration of Patey was complete. I commiserated with him as best I could, though I thought this possessiveness over pitches hardly in the true tradition of pioneer climbing. I found Tom half-buried by the drift and looking cold, his hair matted with snow, his face, where visible, shades of mauve and green. I learned that he had left most of his kit at home and had borrowed the clothes that he had stood in, which were inadequate.

A horizontal belt of snow breaking the steep gully wall enabled us to traverse back onto the buttress. It was an exposed pitch, though a landing in the gully would more likely have resulted in suffocation than a broken bone. The soft powder was crossed by distributing weight as evenly as possible on all nine points of contact; if one step slid down a few inches, support had to be transferred smoothly to knees, fists and chin until a new equilibrium was reached. At the end of this dangerous traverse it was disconcerting to find Tom safeguarded only by his axe driven a few inches into snow with the consistency of confetti. Bill and I spent some time trying to improve the security with a piton, but when at last a 'secret weapon' had been driven into an extra-wide crack, Tom had already led up the next exposed pitch, and it was time to remove it again. I climbed 15ft. of ice and stepped onto the wall overlooking the gully. Luckily it wasn't iced and beneath the hoar frost were good rock holds. It was the first rock-climbing of the day.

One more pitch with a delicate stride from a rock pillar to a steep bank of ice led to the foot of the Tower. The sepulchral walls of rock, suppurating verglas, looked uncompromising. I knew that it was going to be trying on the nerves, and probably dangerous, and started the attack feeling like a soldier who performs an act of gallantry not through any love for his country, but because it has been ordained in Daily Routine Orders.

Soon a useful piton sprouted from the corner crack. With it I could hoist myself fully three feet from the ground, but no more holds came to hand. I asked Bill to give me a shoulder, and standing first on his neck, then on his head, swept away masses of snow until he roared with agony. At last I thought of the solution; returning to the ledge, I pulled from my sack two étriers. This would make the editorial page of the *Cairngorm Club Journal* hum. Clipping one into the peg, I climbed it until I rubbed shoulders with the bulge from the second rung. That was a much better base for further exploration. At the back of the upper groove was a crack that ought to assist the high step to the ledge on the left. Finding it solid with ice, I drove in a twelve-inch ice-piton, glad for the opportunity to use one of these white elephants that I had bought at the start of the winter, and with it I pulled onto the ledge.

So far, so good; I was up the steepest part of the groove. Next came the part customarily climbed with the aid of a piton. At Bill's direction I swept away more powder until I found the horizontal crack that was to take the peg. It was full of ice, and only after several attempts could I hammer my shortest piton into the deepest part. I clipped in an étrier and after climbing and descending it a few times, clumsily changing feet after each, I stood with my left toe on the top rung. Still that wasn't high enough. With my right limbs pressed across the groove, I stooped down and mantelshelved onto the piton, a movement of such ghastly delicacy that at once I wanted to reverse it. But now the steps of the étrier were flat against the wall and I could not go back. I called to Bill asking him where to look for holds, but had to wait while he

photographed Tom, a shot that he hoped would rival Rébuffat's 'Après le second bivouac' in conveying the atmosphere of this climb. Apparently there was a good flake under the overhang above me, but first I had to remove several cubic yards of compact snow, my left toe quivering unsteadily on the peg all this while. At last, jamming my axe behind the flake, I swung over to a bank of snow on the left.

Arriving on easy ground at the end of a fierce pitch is one of the great joys of climbing. The bank of steep snow where I found myself seemed as cosy as a warm fireside. It appeared that the climb was almost over, since the snow continued round to the

*Left: Jerry Smith on the Tower: 'I started the attack feeling like a soldier who performs an act of gallantry, not through any love of his country, but because he has been ordained by daily routine orders.' Photo: Bill Brooker*

left covering the smooth impassable slabs of summer. Thus we could avoid the last 30ft of the Tower which undoubtedly would have been as hard as the first. I shouted down this good news, which was received with rejoicing for already it was getting dark.

Tom came up quickly, the only incident being when he discovered that the second piton was loose. I couldn't resist smiling as he thrashed the air with one arm in an effort to keep his balance. He passed me and traversed the steep snow. Sure enough it provided a straightforward route to the neck behind the Tower. When he had led out about 80ft., Bill removed the pegs and climbed the pitch by a ladder of slings and étriers. We moved across the traverse together to where Tom was crouched beneath a great wall of snow, still shivering, but exuberant. 'The most exciting thing about a winter ascent is to climb pitches that are impossible in summer.' While he elaborated on this theme with examples from every corrie in the Cairngorms, I led on up a 20ft. high wall of snow. It was very steep but of a fine consistency; you could thrust in an arm to the shoulder, kick steps with feet and knees, or drive in the axe as a snow-piton. I emerged on a sharp ridge of snow which, in spite of near-darkness, I could see stretched for another 30ft., gradually steepening to merge with the corniced edge of the plateau. There was no doubt about the outcome now, and when the others arrived all precautions were cast aside as we chased each other up the last 100ft. like children dashing out of school. It was a beautiful snow ridge, the finest that Bill had seen in the Cairngorms, but already it was too dark to appreciate the position.

There was no question of continuing to the summit for we only had an hour and a half to catch our taxi. We coiled the ropes and started to run. As circulation returned, pockets full of snow thawed and the melt water trickled down my legs. In 50 minutes we were at the Spittal, where we collected our rucksacks. We pressed on down the glen and found the taxi waiting after only two miles. At last there was someone else to talk to about the climb, and to a wide-eyed audience we relived the whole expedition, each 10ft. of the route taking us a mile nearer home. In the warmth of the bus I found it impossible to stay awake; the last proclamation that I heard was: 'Every inch a Grade 6.'

But the pundits say that Parallel Buttress is only 5 sup.

# 39  Parallel Gully B

by Martin Boysen

The van stopped at last. We had reached Loch Muick, and we scrambled out into the searing cold and black, star-studded night. I was dog-tired but my stomach tightened with excitement – we had hit lucky. The 400-mile drive would surely have been worthwhile if we could do Parallel B. It was February 1967, and I was with my wife Maggie and Judd Jordan for a Scottish winter weekend. A few hundred yards from the road we spied out a wooden hut. It was open, and we thankfully slumped down on the heather floor. Sleep came almost instantaneously.

I awoke next morning with a start; bright beams of light streamed across the gloomy interior through chinks in the wood. I flung open the door and shouted to the others to get up and take a look. It was what we could scarcely have expected, a perfect day. We breakfasted, hurriedly packed our sacks, and set off up the road. The frosted air was already perfumed by rising smoke from a birchwood fire in the keeper's cottage as we trudged up the track. It was far too late, of course – past 11 a.m., and with a long slog ahead we were unlikely to get our route in, even though it was February and the days were getting longer. Somewhere at the back of my mind, however, the faint hope lingered . . . .

This was my first visit to Lochnagar, but I had often read about it, glowingly described by one of its greatest pioneers, Tom Patey. I could hardly wait to reach the col of Meikle Pap, where I knew it would first be displayed to our view. Parallel B was one of the last 'great' gullies to be climbed. It is not really a gully at all, but a series of chimneys and grooves with a gully section in the middle. Patey first climbed it, as a summer VS. Thereafter it became one of the obvious and desirable goals for a winter ascent. Jimmy Marshall and his faithful chauffeur, the Birmingham Scot Graham Tiso, succeeded on it in February 1958. It was a marvellous bit of route-poaching – the local Aberdonians had one of the finest jewels of the East stolen from under their noses. The rivalry between the East and West Coasts was intense, and in those heroic times they even climbed in different manners. The Aberdonians stuck doggedly to tricouni-nailed boots, whilst the West Coast faction used crampons, which, I suppose it could be said, added points to the rivalry.

After Marshall's ascent, the route remained unrepeated for nine years, despite numerous attempts, and more than any of the other hard classics of the fifties and early sixties, it held a powerful reputation. I badly wanted to do it, and ruminated on our chances as we hastened up to the col. Judd and I had already climbed several of the great Scottish winter routes, and we knew that to capture the second ascent of this one would be a real prize. Judd is the archetypal strong, silent type. His strength in the arms and legs was immense – no doubt developed through his job of standing on ladders cleaning windows. This strength of his was combined with an almost unnerving composure, which I had first learnt to value when we found ourselves climbing Zero Gully one late afternoon with no equipment other than an ice-axe between us and a single rope. I could rely on him utterly, and though he tended to silence we communicated well enough and enjoyed each other's company.

Suddenly the view opened out. Below us was the lochan, set in a perfect corrie dotted with tents, whilst all around curved the stately cliffs of Lochnagar – an elegant array of buttresses, towers, and gullies, all sparkling with snow. As we made our way round to the foot of the cliffs, we picked out the features of which we already knew so much. But the one to which our eyes continually returned was Parallel Buttress, the cliff's recessed centrepiece, bounded on its right by the compelling line of Parallel Gully B. We put on our crampons and charged down to the foot of the climb, determined to give it a go.

Over to our left two friends from Manchester, Eddy Birch and Dave Little, who had been camping in the corrie, were engaged on the first difficult pitch of Parallel A. We looked up and studied the detail of our route. A shallow, verglassed chimney broke the continuity of the lower slabs, running up in a direct line for 250ft. to end in an open scoop where the Tough-Brown Traverse crossed our route. It was uninviting, but to the left I spotted an alternative line, a ramp leading back into the chimney. I started up it and straight away, to my intense disappointment, came across recent crampon marks. Swinging my axe at a sod of frozen turf, it slotted into a ready-made hole. So someone had been here before us. We discovered later that Jim MacArtney and Allen Fyffe had made the second ascent (and the first Aberdonian ascent) a few days before. But these few marks on the first pitch were the only signs of their passage.

The pitch was intriguing and delicate. I scuttled

**Route** Parallel Gully B, Grade 5, 700ft.
**Cliff** The cliffs of the North-East Corrie of Lochnagar.
**First Ascent** Summer: 1952; Winter: J. R. Marshall and G. Tiso, February 1958.
**Map** See page 172.
**Guidebooks** See page 172.
**Nearest Road / Approach Time** See page 172.
**Route Summary / Conditions** A mixed route with considerable technical difficulty. It is easiest in consolidated snow and ice conditions. Sustained difficulties for the first 300ft. with several hard pitches after that.
**Campsites and Bunkhouses** See page 172.

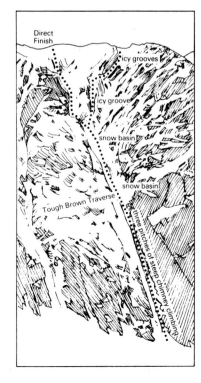

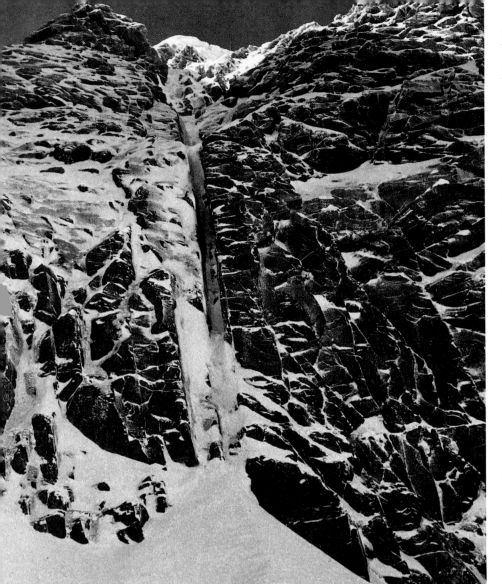

across icy slabs from one grass tuft to another until I reached a tiny cave about 50ft. up in the main chimney line, where I belayed, hung up my axes, and took in the slack to Judd, who was already climbing. He led through up a vertical, iced crack, masterfully dismissed by his powerful and precise climbing style, above which he disappeared into the depths of the central chimney. I was so keen to follow that I left behind one of my axes – a cut-down vintage model over 80 years old, given to me by an old Russian family-friend who had used it in the Caucasus before the First World War. I felt a pang of loss, but it was too late to worry. Above was the iced chimney, curiously scooped in shape, and capped by a large overhang. It was a marvellous pitch, long, hard, but with perfect protection. The overhang was every bit as difficult as it looked, with awkward bridging followed by a tricky pull round. Once above it, we landed in an easy-angled gully filled with névé. With three difficult pitches behind us, we were not much more than a third of a way up the route.

The gully above the scooped section where we stood curved round, narrowed, and disappeared from sight. I knew from the guidebook that 'three huge pitches' lay somewhere above. We rushed on until stopped by an ice-fall, up which Judd cut his way. The gully carried on for a while before ending abruptly beneath a capping mass of overhanging rock draped with huge icicles. For the first time on the route, I felt nervous. We were no longer cosily confined, the way was no longer obvious, and the possibilities looked extremely hard. The light was fading and we were tired, having been hard at it since leaving the bothy.

A gleaming groove of grey ice running up the right wall seemed the best escape. I started up it, balancing precariously on ice-nicks chipped in the inch-thick verglas. The groove continued thus, steeply, for a runnerless 100ft. before my eyes fixed on a tuft of grass which promised a ledge and the end of the pitch. There was no belay and hardly a stance, but I bashed a channel-peg into some grass and called on Judd to follow, and to take things gently. Safely and methodically, he adjusted his way up the pitch. I was thankful to have such a sound companion on the rope. Darkness crept up the pitch behind and by the time he joined me the light had almost gone. A brief moment of appreciation was all we had time for before Judd set off, feeling his way, tapping his axe like a blind

man. Sparks and scrapings marked his slow progress up what I could vaguely make out as a 40ft. rock pitch, caked with snow. Suddenly disembodied but familiar voices floated down through the still air. It was Dave and Eddy who, having finished Parallel A, had waited on top when they realised that we would be benighted. I heard snatches of conversation between them and Judd, and then his shadowy form disappeared from view.

'We've done it, Mart!'

I plucked out my belay, scrabbled up onto a delicately-sculpted snow arête, and tramped past Judd without stopping. Torches shone out like searchlights as Eddy and Dave greeted us at the top. We coiled ropes, all urgency behind us now. It was quite windless. There was no need for haste. The four of us stumbled across the plateau in the inky blackness, searching for the icy drop to Meikle Pap, bubbling about our respective routes. I was ecstatic and even Judd was moved to make the odd enthusiastic comment. The praises rang out into the uncanny stillness of the night:

'What a fantastic route that was . . . what a great climb . . . it had everything, just everything . . . the best route I've ever done.'

And even after all these years, they are opinions I've had no reason to change.

*Above: Jimmy Marshall at work in the chimney of Parallel Gully B during the first winter ascent in 1958. Photo: Graham Tiso*

# 40 Raeburn's Gully

by Richard Gilbert and G. F. Dutton

**Route** Raeburn's Gully, Grade 3, 600ft.
**Cliff** The cliffs of the North-East Corrie of Lochnagar.
**First Ascent** Summer: 1898; Winter: G. R. Symmers, A. W. Clark and W. A. Ewen. December 1932.
**Map** See page 172.
**Guidebooks** See page 172.
**Nearest Road / Approach Time** See page 172.
**Route Summary / Conditions** Straightforward gully climbing with one ice pitch and a large cornice barring the exit. The ice pitch can be difficult early in the season until the snow has banked up. In thaw conditions the cornice presents a serious avalanche hazard, and hidden sections of it sometimes remain to fall later. The photograph shows the gully in late season, prior to the cornice collapse.
**Campsites and Bunkhouses** See page 172.

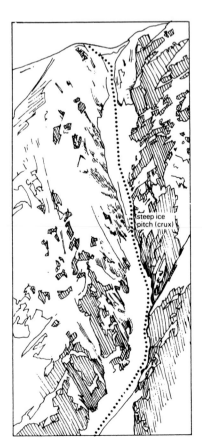

steep ice pitch (crux)

## CLASSIC STYLE by Richard Gilbert

As I pushed open the door, I was met by a blast of hot air and an acrid smell of burning pine logs. Through the smoke-haze I could make out several tousle-headed figures sitting on a rough bench before a blazing fire. Others, including some girls, were lying on sleeping-bags up against the walls. Those by the fire in their bulky sweaters and grease-stained duvets, looked huge and wild, but after a casual glance in my direction, they resumed their contemplation of the flames.

'So you've made it at last. Come and sit down old chap,' drawled a familiar voice from a dark corner at the other end of the room. I jettisoned my pack and joined my friends on the earth floor. Bothy law is simple but tough. First come – pole position by the fire. Thus the husky Aberdonians roasted themselves red while we battled with the draughts that swirled under the door.

The scene was Lochend Bothy, Glen Muick, and the year was 1959. The occasion was the OUMC President's Meet, where so-called hard men, specially selected by the President himself, proved themselves (or died in the attempt) on the ice-cliffs of Ben Nevis, Lochnagar, Creag Meagaidh, or some such precipice. 1959 was an unusual year in that three freshmen made up the party of eight, a horrific accident toll in the previous two years having depleted the ranks. I remember the party well. The President was John Cole, then there was Kim Meldrum, Mike Binnie, Roger Putnam, Jim Murray, and the three freshmen, Colin Taylor, Alan Wedgwood, and myself. Kim had climbed the Andean peak Pumasillo while a schoolboy at Marlborough; Jim, an American studying spiders, had just climbed Tom Tower on Christchurch; Mike Binnie had recently recovered from broken ribs following a fall whilst attempting to mantelshelf into the loft in Helyg.

The weather was perfect the next day as we followed the narrow path through heather and rocks to the Meikle Pap col, where the northern corrie of Lochnagar bursts into view. On this March morning the cliffs were gleaming white in the sunshine and even from the old fat, red SMC Guide to the Cairngorms (the only guide available) we could easily pick out the lines of the Black Spout, Raeburn's Gully, Parallel Gullies A and B, Polyphemus Gully, Douglas-Gibson Gully and the Tough-Brown ridge. A 'recce' along the cliffs and a quick crampon up Black Spout Gully was enough

to tell us that the snow was in perfect condition for a more ambitious climb tomorrow.

As an avid reader of mountaineering literature I had to experience a Harold Raeburn climb for myself. Raeburn was a giant amongst Scottish climbers for over 30 years, and a prolific author. Thus it was that Colin and I roped up at the bottom of Raeburn's Gully in a smoothly-sculptured scoop of snow which was sheltered from the wind. Colin, who thrived on challenge, read out with glee from the guide 'The gully was first climbed by Harold Raeburn in 1898, it is 600ft. in length, ice is often found in considerable quantity and the top can be heavily corniced.'

Raeburn would have approved of our equipment and method. Six turns round the waist with hemp line followed by a steel karabiner and, for Colin, a Tarbuck knot. I could never get the hang of the Tarbuck so I used a figure-of-eight instead. With crampons on, and 75cm Aschenbrenner axes firmly grasped, we were ready. One last glance down to the corrie loch, the ice cracked and patterned like a patchwork quilt, and beyond to the distant browns of the Ballochbuie larch forests, and then we entered the blue shadows in the gully. Chill took over, and our world was reduced to hoar-frosted rock and hanging icicles.

Prior to 1940 the main feature of Raeburn's gully was a vast boulder which choked the whole width of the gully forming an overhanging cave. Raeburn's party first tried combined tactics to surmount the cave. This failed and they had to resort to more desperate ways. Raeburn wrote:

'What was now done was, I fear, unorthodox in the extreme, but Lochnagar appears somehow to lend itself to the unorthodox in climbing. The ice-axe was now employed, the pick was hung upon the edge of the block. The right hand of the leader found a crevice which admitted of its being inserted and half-clenched, then pushing down with the right arm and pulling hard with the left, the body was raised high enough to allow of the left hand being thrown up to catch the edge of the jammed block. Instantly the right hand joined it, then a pull, and the right knee was thrown up on the slope of the overhanging chokestone, the body thrust for a second against the slope of the left wall, while the hands were transferred to an upper block. The ice-axe, the moment the steady pull was relaxed, slipped off, and bounded away down the gully and was lost. The second man

then passed the pitch, stepping lightly from the airy pinnacle of the last man's head, who then followed, actuated solely by the gentle moral suasion of the rope.'

In 1940, following a collapse of the upper part of the gully, the great chokestone was swept away leaving the climb somewhat harder than before. The characteristics of gully climbs change year by year and month by month. In March 1959 the crux was a 60ft. bulge of rather brittle ice, caused by a frozen stream passing over a smooth wall of rock. It was pitch three and Colin's turn for the lead. Colin was new to steep ice, but he adapted his technique brilliantly and this pitch gave him no trouble. A few hefty blows with the axe and a chunk of ice would bound away leaving a perfect jug-handle hold between the inside of the ice and the rock. It was easy and satisfying climbing. Securely belayed by a combination of ice-axe thrust into the snow and an array of nuts on the side wall, I felt no fear.

Arias from *Rigoletto* echoed round the walls, interspersed with the occasional dogmatic comment: 'Scottish climbs make excellent practice for the Alps but they cannot be considered ends in themselves.' Comments which Colin knew would provoke me to reply, for he loved an argument.

Above the ice wall the gully twisted and turned in its bed for 300ft. We climbed rapidly, leading through, cutting nicks in the frozen snow for neither of us had lobster-claw crampons. The snaking of the gully certainly reduced the feeling of exposure and contributed to my peace of mind. The gully opened out at the top and there appeared to be several exits. Just below the cornices the angle steepened to near-vertical, and I longed to gain the sunshine of the summit plateau.

'There could be an alternative exit on the right,' shouted Colin. 'It looks interesting, shall I investigate?'

Very conscious of his meaning of the word 'interesting', his 50ft. run-out without protection, my poor stance and my frozen fingers I yelled, 'No, for Christ's sake take the easiest line and let's get up onto the plateau.' The sun was now striking the top of the rocks and rimming the cornices with gold. Icicles were tinkling down the walls of the Tough-Brown Ridge on our left. Colin moved back to the easier line and hacked through the cornice, the powder-snow sparkling with rainbow colours in the sunshine. A stab with the axe, a big heave and the climb was won. Our first Scottish winter ascent.

Blinking in the bright sun we coiled the rope, experiencing that vivid contrast between light and shade, freedom and restriction and space and closure. We had time in hand to trot over the White Mounth to collect another Munro, and then to examine Creag an Dubh Loch for a future climb.

Finally, as the evening wind ruffled the surface of Loch Muick, we lengthened our stride for home. The Aberdonians were away, having had a God Almighty grip in Polyphemus Gully. It would be fireside seats for us tonight. Daylight was fading and there was much wood to be gathered.

Why do we remember certain climbs above all others? Why can I recall that superb March day on Lochnagar as vividly as if it happened yesterday? The reasons are complex and deep. Certainly one reason is the change in the Loch Muick area which horrifies me every time I return. Lochend Bothy was burnt down in 1963, some say by the factor to discourage climbers. Loch Muick is now a wild life sanctuary with information centre, nature trails and car park. The hills are scarred by brutish Land Rover tracks bulldozed out of the heather with no thought to landscaping, and all to facilitate deer-stalking on the Balmoral estate.

But above all my memories are stirred by the companionship of Colin Taylor. A climb with Colin was always memorable, his enthusiasm was infectious and his zest for life was irrepressible. Sadly, Colin was killed on the Obergabelhorn in 1974, but his many friends will always be grateful for the happy memories which remain.

### A STIFF UPPER LIP by G. F. Dutton

'It certainly could be an aid,' agreed the Doctor. We were discussing the Apprentice's most recent acquisition, a moustache, in the not displeased presence of the new owner. It had germinated in response to his latest girl friend's desire for more public evidence of virility. It was indeed robust, disguising his normally sardonic upper lip with coils of easy splendour. He had grown it remarkably quickly.

'Could be very adherent on steep ice: should steady you, cutting out of balance,' continued the Doctor. 'You could lick it, to freeze in front of you; then breathe it off again and move up.'

The Apprentice swore it was not in the least an artificial aid. 'Grows naturally. Shaving's artificial; that's an aid. A right hairy bearded guy could just get stuck in Parallel B: never get up, whiskers

jamming one side then the other, freezing on as fast as he's breathing 'em off. Shaving's the real Aid.'

Parallel B was coming that weekend. But when we arrived there, a violent freezing wind and snow squalls sent us up Raeburn's instead. The girl friend was Munroing nearby and we would all meet that night in the Inverfyvie Arms.

Raeburn's Gully is reasonable on a foul day and the Apprentice stormed it bravely, moustache as spinnaker. I gathered metal at the blunt end. The Doctor makes an excellent second on such middling routes, being tall, thin, and multi-jointed, and his long, prodding axe and nimble tricounis ran many messages.

Halfway up, just on the steep ice, came a prolonged halt. I peered through drift. My companions were crouched together on a minute stance, examining something inside the Doctor's anorak. Hell of a time. I shouted. No reply. I tugged. A tug back. Then the Doctor's eager beckoning. They had found something interesting.

Too interesting to take in the rope. I clambered up, cursing and coiling, points exploring powder snow. When I reached them, they were still in earnest conclave, the Apprentice fixedly eyeing his companion's bosom. The Doctor, looking down in a curiously strained position, explained.

A krab had jammed with ice. To thaw it the Apprentice had unzipped the Doctor's anorak and thrust the metal against his warm Shetland jersey. He had breathed on it to speed the process. Just then, both were drenched in a flurry of snow from above. Both had crouched farther, and the Doctor had instinctively zipped up his anorak . . . Muffled roars indicated that he had zipped it up into the Apprentice's moustache . . .

Painful trial had proved it jammed, not just frozen. Though, since then, tears and other secretions had welded the jam. The Apprentice was too sore to speak, and any attempt to move, let alone continue the climb as a joint lead, when so intimately and inconveniently mated, was clearly impossible. Yet they couldn't stay there. We had to think quickly, or permanently disfigure our leader.

As we had all forgotten to bring shaving things, I produced an ice-dagger. The Apprentice gurgled and clutched his companion appealingly. But I couldn't insert between whiskers and lip, and the zip was tough metal. So, to the Apprentice's howls and the Doctor's cries of horror ('. . . it's *quite* unobtainable now!') I sawed through expensive

Grenfell and cut, tore out, the offending zip. It dangled free, and the Apprentice now bore a mandarin-like extension of moustachios. But he clutched his pegs with relief and straightened up, sobbing with drool.

The Doctor wrapped the ravaged garment about him and grinned at his leader. 'Looks just like that damn great catfish I caught on the Arkansas. Marvellous beast.'

It was impossible to stow the two ends away without painfully restricting movement, so the zip dangled freely as the Apprentice raged up the rest of Raeburn's, fleeing from our merriment and roaring when, as often, an end jammed suddenly in a crack. ('Try a tension . . .' the Doctor would call up, unfeelingly.)

An hour later, he burst on to the plateau, through a goosefeather cornice. His moustachios now carried a fair weight of ice and snow and his appearance unnerved the two elderly climbers sheltering behind the cairn (we *had* to get to the cairn; the Doctor always insisted). We explained it was a special kind of moustache. (The Apprentice had signed us not to betray his shame; he was very sensitive by now.) They seemed to understand. 'It'll be a prob . . . prob . . . *feelers*, like? For finding the way? Like insects, like?' We nodded. They were relieved and offered us hot broth from a flask. We sipped gratefully. The Apprentice, however, went aside and proceeded to pour his share sideways onto his face. But the zip did not thaw; it was jammed. Instead, the broth froze; carrots and peas and things were added to his burden. He gesticulated at us as if imploring the kiss of life. But he was most repulsive, and only to be embraced by the desperately hungry.

It seemed he particulary desirrghed a drinnghk – 'cogghle'? We smiled, as at some defective, and patted him. 'Never mind; when we get down.' The Doctor, unusually, was whiskyless that day.

We roped down an easy chute. Descent was uneventful, though one tended to tread on the moustache at narrow places. Afterwards, an unhappy sojourn in a dense sitka wood. The Doctor, as always, encouraged the sufferer. 'Damned useful, in a place like this; how cats hunt at night. You know your own width exactly.'

At the edge of the wood we met a large party. The Apprentice being nearly all in, I approached them for tools – a hacksaw or nail scissors – for zip or whiskers respectively. Neither; they stared, wondering. Feeble groans of 'cogghle' again. Alcohol? Was that it?

The victim nodded vigorously, holding his ends, by now long, icicled, white and stiff. No wonder the others were startled. Their leader reluctantly opened his rucksack and, amid mild protests, handed over a well-furnished half-bottle of whisky. The Apprentice, to louder protests, scuttled off with it and, to violent protests, was seen pouring it over – not into – his face. Even the Doctor was irritated. 'That won't unjam the thing; it's a shocking waste – even of a blend.'

But the Apprentice continued to pour and began to tug at his adornment. He tugged and poured, tugged and poured until, by the end of the bottle – and to the stupefaction of everyone – he had tugged off all impediment: zip *and* whiskers . . .

'Good Lord,' exclaimed the Doctor.

It was a fake. A false moustache. Beautifully made, expensive, cemented by an alcohol-soluble gum. That explained the speed of growth – and possibly the short-term romantic intentions of the owner.

Who had been punished enough. He returned, nursing his lip, promising whisky at Inverfyvie. The Doctor meanwhile wrenched out his zip; it seemed more injured than the moustache. He pressed the latter to his own lip. Wonderful sight – a moose among seaweed. It fell off. We cheered. He rubbed it in some resin on a sitka trunk and pressed it hard once more. It stuck. It preened itself, if a bit squint and somewhat de-feathered. As the late bearer refused even to look at it again, the Doctor wore it proudly all the way back to the car.

We entered the Inverfyvie Arms. Noise, lights. Then silence. All eyes on us. Eyes especially from some posh persons in tweeds and from a jazzy-looking wee smasher. The Doctor met the gaze of the next-of-kin of a wealthy patient he had just recommended for psychiatric treatment: and remembered he was wearing a squint moustache. The Apprentice met the gaze of his girl friend: and remembered he was not. Panic seized both. Both leapt at the misplaced appendage . . . .

Next Thursday at Daddy McKay's, they drank much and spoke little. Each fingered thoughtfully a small pink and white memento of surgical plaster.

# 41  Pinnacle Face

by Greg Strange

Back in 1966 Pinnacle Face was still thought to be one of the most difficult rock climbs in the Cairngorms, and its ascent in winter was rightly heralded as a breakthrough – a hint of what Scottish winter climbing might be like in the eighties. Ken Grassick's experience, together with his intimate knowledge of the climb in summer, enabled him and his two companions, Jerry Light and Graeme Nicol, to overcome the steep snow and ice-bound slabs. Yet 300ft. of climbing occupied some 12 hours and darkness forced a retreat to the Black Spout without continuing to the plateau via Route 1. If you must have your winter climbs sheathed in ice or banked with firm snow you will probably have a long wait for Pinnacle Face. But in such conditions and with today's techniques you will wonder what all the fuss was about.

The cold light of a March morning found Rob Archbold, Ian Dalley, and myself at the foot of the Black Spout Pinnacle. Above us smooth, boiler-plate slabs reared up steeply and disappeared into the mist. Light snow fell, and trickles of spindrift ran down the face. It looked much steeper than we had expected. A hint of uncertainty, even dissent, crept into our conversation. For once I was decisive and set off up the first groove. It was perfect névé and easy. The climb goes diagonally leftwards for about 120ft. and by some topographical quirk a feeling of exposure seems to be present right from the start. Beyond a little chimney, the line traverses steep slabs to a small ledge below an overlap. On the traverse the ice was wafer-thin and hollow; but the angle was reasonable so that the strain was more on the nerves than on the calves. It took a while to hack a stance, but the belay was good.

The next pitch was to be Rob's. It is only about 50ft. but it is probably the crux. It involves a delicate friction move right onto a steep slab before slightly easier climbing leads back left to a steepening and a large ledge. Depending on the quantity and quality of the snow or ice on the slab, a peg may be required for aid. Being a mathematician by profession, Rob climbs with calculated precision. He is a master of delicate footwork, even in crampons, and this pitch was well-suited to him. Once the initial bulge had been overcome a long, runnerless 40ft. on shallow ice led to the welcome security of deep névé. I enjoyed a great heave over the steep ice-plated bulge just left of the peg, and marvelled at the water-ice drooling down the rock, for the Pinnacle has no natural watercourses.

We were now at the junction with Winter Face. Here the summer line of Pinnacle Face goes left, steeply up cracks and across a flake-traverse to below a slightly overhanging corner. Subsequent ascents have taken an obvious groove which leads more directly to below the corner. By rights it should now have been Ian's lead. And I doubt that he was convinced by my claim that it would save precious time if I went first because I knew the way ahead, but being a gent he let me through.

The groove was bare and awkward. A couple of picks swung into frozen turf, and once behind a little flake, bridged the gaps in the snow-cover *en route* to a snow slope below the corner. It was up there in darkness and desperation that the first ascent team had resorted to 'combined triple tactics' and where in 1972 the young Dougie Dinwoodie ended his second ascent bid with a 40ft. fall. He returned two years later to make the second ascent. On our ascent the corner was entirely devoid of snow and ice. Fortunately we knew that the easier Lang/Quinn variation would lead us round to the long fault of Route 1. It was simply a question of finding the correct level at which to traverse the prow of the buttress. The solution lay some 15ft. lower in a little groove and a ledge system. We had made steady progress and even as a party of three we had managed to reach the upper pitches of Route 1 with a few hours of daylight to spare.

As we climbed the final 300ft. of ice-encrusted pinnacle the cloud became thicker. There was a surprise left in store for us. The long chimney-fault was a continuous run of green ice – like the classic Grade 4 gully. Ian led. Rob and I followed in tandem. It was difficult to believe that it was the same place where six years previously Bob Smith and I had floundered in deep snow on Route 1.

Another rope-length took us past the exit of Route 2 to the crest overlooking the Left-Hand Branch. The summit was a short distance above. Darkness caught us as we gathered on the knife-edge· of snow at the col above Pinnacle Gullies 1 and 2. It was mighty thick on top, so not wishing to repeat my stunt of the previous week when I fell through a cornice on Braeriach, we set our compass and our crampons towards the south-east and hurried off back to Glen Muick via the Glas Allt.

**Route** Pinnacle Face, Grade 5, 700ft.
**Cliff** The cliffs of the North-East Corrie of Lochnagar.
**First Ascent** Summer: 1955; Winter: K. A. Grassick, J. Light and A. G. Nicol, January 1966.
**Map** See page 172.
**Guidebooks** See page 172.
**Nearest Road / Approach Time** See page 172.
**Route Summary / Conditions** A demanding route up grooves, ribs and slabs. Heavy snow and ice cover is essential, and these conditions are rare. The main difficulties are centred on the lower pitches, before the link with Route 1.
**Campsites and Bunkhouses** See page 172.
**Bibliography** Aberdeen University Lairg Club Journal 1967 *The Pinnacle Again* by Ken Grassick – an account of the first winter ascent

*Left: Ken Grassick, Jerry Light and Graeme Nicol tackling the crux pitch of Pinnacle Face during the first ascent in 1966. Photo: G. H. Leslie*

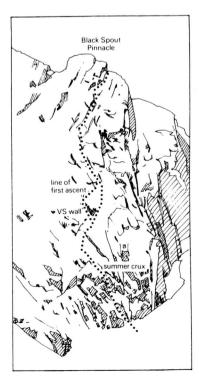

Black Spout Pinnacle

line of first ascent

VS wall

summer crux

*Above: The Black Spout Pinnacle of Lochnagar. Photo:*
*Rab Anderson*

*Top centre: The first pitch of Pinnacle Face. Climber:*
*Dougie Dinwoodie / Photo: Dave Stewart*

*Above: The final pitch of Eagle Ridge. Climber: Rob Milne /*
*Photo: Rab Anderson*

*Right: Eagle Ridge. Photo: Bert Jenkins*

# 42  Eagle Ridge

by Nick Banks

Lochnagar is a royal crag in two senses. It sits high up in the eastern Cairngorms above Balmoral Castle, on the Royal Estates; and by dictionary definition it is – noble, majestic, very fine. And Eagle Ridge Direct is the centrepiece of a wild and rugged crown. I climbed the route in the freezing February of 1979, in perfect weather sandwiched between two screaming Scottish storms.

Glen Muick stretched broad and desolate, its stands of pine and lavish hunting lodges battered by wind and wreathed in streaming cloud. The black loch was laced with white spray, while herds of deer wisely sheltered in the forest.

Approaching from the east there is no hint of a rugged crag, but it is there; unseen until you leave the bulldozed estate road and climb the boulder-strewn heather slope beside the Meikle Pap. Through the small col the cliff slowly grew from a white corniced rim to a snow-plastered wall. The storm has done its work well. Eagle Ridge stood out from the cliff, scalloped gold with a hint of morning sun.

Most Scottish routes have lost something to the vicious peck of the drooped axe, but not Eagle Ridge. First climbed in the winter of 1953, this is a true Tom Patey buttress route. There are no tumbling ice-sweeps here, just a thin plastering of ice and a good dollop of powder-snow over a respectable summer rock-climb.

The ridge is gained by a 60ft. cleft and a chimney a short way up the Douglas-Gibson Gully where monstrous summit cornices encourage rapid progress onto the ridge. Thereafter the climbing is perfect, following a series of grooves and corners. Your axes, never really solid, act mainly as balance points, with your feet doing all the work, often scraping and scratching on bare rock. Occasionally the sun touches on the ridge, a real treat on a Scottish winter route. The terrain and the interesting climbing keep the growing sense of exposure at bay until the bottom of the tower is reached. Then the ridge narrows and steepens, forcing you onto the jagged crest. It is here that you notice where you are, perched on a single, snowless granite block abutting a tower which the guidebook says is the crux. The drop into Douglas-Gibson Gully is impressive and direct and above, the infamous cornice leers menacingly.

*Left: Embarking on the Tower pitch of Eagle Ridge. The sentry-box is the obvious cleft on the skyline. Climber: Nick Banks / Photo: Dave Alcock*

I was in the lead. The tower was obviously steep, for I could see the sentry-box at the top, getting into which, is the crux. I noticed an old Stubai ice-peg pounded halfway into a crack. It looked very much of first ascent vintage. For some reason this made me feel better and I set off. The climbing was excellent, a bit of ice here and there, some snowy ledges, cracks for camming Terrordactyl picks – and always the exposure. I passed the old ice-peg and tied it off; the floor of the sentry-box was now at eye level. My companions were taking photographs from below. We had plenty of time, no need to rush, a rare luxury in Scotland. Bits of mist drifting across the cliff were being chased by the sun. The weather was still perfect.

Both walls of the sentry-box were bare, but the floor was covered with powder. Beneath it was a nice layer of ice. My axes seemed to be firmly placed in the floor so I started walking my feet up and hung back on my slings. Eventually my feet were level with the axe-shafts, and with a little whimper I collapsed into the niche. Very precariously I eased up into a standing position, lifting the points of the axes from the ice at my feet. For the first time on the climb I felt that I may have cheated in Patey's eyes. The guidebook says that the tower is 50ft. Somehow it seems higher than that. The ridge levels a little at its top and provides a splendid viewpoint for the rest of the cliff. Two stalwarts were patiently tunnelling through the Douglas-Gibson cornice as I brought the others up.

There seemed to have been a lot of climbing but we were only a little above halfway. From the top of the tower the ridge gallops off towards the summit plateau in a series of bumps, hollows, steps and arêtes. Hidden somewhere in here is the summer crux. Each feature has its own problems and this section is surprisingly sustained and satisfying until a last little bulge is solved and you are faced by a plateau instead of a ridge.

We wandered across the Black Spout and climbed down to the frozen loch. There was the ridge again from another angle, still with a hint of sun. It looked so good we felt like doing it again. The wind was starting to increase, blowing thin streamers of powder off the plateau, and the sky was turning grey as we crossed the col into a different world — no more ice and snow, but instead heather, grouse, and rushing streams. By the time we arrived back at Allt-na-giubhsaich the next storm was on its way.

**Route** Eagle Ridge, Grade 5, 650ft.
**Cliff** The cliffs of the North-East Corrie of Lochnagar.
**First Ascent** Summer: 1941; Winter: T. Patey, J. M. Taylor and W. D. Brooker, January 1953.
**Map** See page 172.
**Guidebooks** See page 172.
**Nearest Road / Approach Time** See page 172.
**Route Summary / Conditions** Steep, exciting and technically interesting with the main difficulties high on the ridge in exposed positions. Although the route is often in a climbable condition its difficulty varies greatly with the amount of consolidated snow and ice cover – the more the better.
**Campsites and Bunkhouses** See page 172.
**Bibliography** S.M.C.J. 1969 *Eagle Ridge of Lochnagar in Winter* by Douglas Lang gives a gripping account of an eventful early ascent.

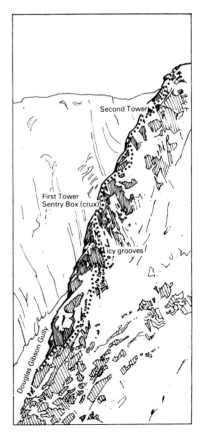

*Left: The difficult final chimney pitch of Parallel Gully B (see page 183). Climber: Bill March / Photo: Dave Alcock*

# 43  Labyrinth Direct

Andrew Nisbet

**Route** Labyrinth Direct, Grade 5, 800ft.
**Cliff** Creag an Dubh Loch.
**First Ascent** Winter: A. J. Boulton and
P. Arnold. March 1972.
**Map** O.S. 1:5,000 Sheet 44 (235825).
**Guidebooks** S.M.C. *Cairngorms Area, Vol. 4/5*
by G. S. Strange and D. S. Dinwoodie; *Scottish
Winter Climbs* by Hamish MacInnes
(Constable).
**Nearest Road / Approach Time** A car park at
Spittal of Glen Muick (310851) at the end of a
minor road, 9 miles south of Ballater. 6 miles/
1,600ft. Allow 3 hours. It is also possible to
approach the cliff by a slightly longer route from
Glen Clova.
**Route Summary / Conditions** A serous and
difficult climb that is rarely in condition (the
article gives specific advice).
**Campsites and Bunkhouses** Discreet camping
is possible in Glen Muick. Aberdeen University
Hut at Allt-na-Guibhsaich (298858).
**Bibliography.**

Creag an Dubh Loch characterises the extremes of
Scottish winter climbing. In good conditions the
huge tiers of ice-smeared slabs are the ultimate
reward for years of patience, but they tease and
frustrate the hopefuls who abandon the surety of
Lochnagar for the chance of something special.
Their tales of woe are of massive, bare, grey walls,
or the whiteness of hoar-frost only superficially
hiding the same bare walls. Ice is the key, as
unpredictable as a clear day on the Ben. The only
solution is to keep your ear close to the ground, and
let nothing stop you when you hear the whisper.
Afterwards you may wish to retire, for a big route
on the Dubh Loch converts the rest of Scotland to
mediocrity.

The winter development of Creag an Dubh Loch
has happened in distinct steps, not just because
increases in climbing standards have occurred in
stages following technological improvement, but
because excellent conditions are so rare. After
sporadic development of the classics, such as the
fine North-West Gully, significant advance has
been limited to three separate months: February
1959, when the first routes in the Hanging Garden
and Central Slabs were climbed; March 1972, when
Labyrinth Direct, then a notorious last great
problem, succumbed; and January 1980, when ice-
climbing techniques caught up with the possibilities
offered, and the White Elephant, Goliath, and
Mousetrap fell in an eight-day blitz. Ideal
conditions on three occasions in 21 years hardly
make a winter paradise. In March 1972 the latter
four were all in condition, but only Jim Bolton and
Paul Arnold took up the challenge, and they
naturally chose the dominating and impressively
steep groove line of Labyrinth Direct. The ascent
was years ahead of its time, the crux pitch
unrecognised as the hardest in the country at that
time. Not only that, but Bolton led it with only a
nominal belay. It was no surprise to Aberdonians
when Bolton, climbing with Dave Robinson,
snatched the first British winter ascent of the North
Face of Les Droites from the big names.

The big routes are so fickle because the ice
doesn't form by freeze and thaw as on most cliffs.
During a thaw the snow slithers off the polished
slabs and the routes can be stripped in a matter of
hours. The White Elephant, Vertigo Wall,
Goliath, Mousetrap, and of course Labyrinth
Direct, five Grade 5 routes to rival anything in
Scotland, are all a product of the drainage which

*Right: Creag an Dubh Loch. Labyrinth takes
the central couloir on the left-hand section of
the cliff. Photo: Greg Strange*

*Above: The crux pitch of Labyrinth Direct —
a steep rock wall coated with a thin layer of
ice. Climber: John Anderson / Photo: Andrew
Nisbet*

*Right: Labyrinth Direct and the Central Slabs.
Photo: Andrew Nisbet*

wouldn't admit anything, they were unable to hide their keenness to return. But the weather forecast was warm and wet, so Norman and Hamish went drinking and dart-playing, while Brian Sprunt submitted to the Romantic Alternative, leaving only John Anderson and myself, optimists as ever, to set off into the rain-drenched night.

As so often in a Scottish winter, the persistent were rewarded. Saturday was thawing, but only a little, although the lower slabs of the White Elephant were bared. We made the best of it by climbing the upper groove after entering by Labyrinth Edge. As we trudged away over the frozen Dubh Loch, at peace with the world after our icy meandering, we looked back to this most spectacular and forbidding of winter cliffs, our eyes drawn compellingly to the huge cleft of Labyrinth Direct. The weather could have turned bad but I knew it wouldn't. We would be back tomorrow, walking in the other direction, and we would be going to the Labyrinth, to the fiercest ice pitch in Scotland, to the pitch with no belay and no protection, to the pitch with a description I knew I couldn't climb – '30ft. of overhanging ice'.

Sunday morning, 4 a.m. It's frosty of course, and John is up, so it's breakfast in bed for me and away by 5 a.m. The first hint of dawn glows in the east, and the snow is crunchy. What a change from the slush-pools of yesterday. John stomps off on the six-mile trudge; I follow in the slipstream. A huge avalanche has swept over the road, and the debris is floating in Loch Muick. Is it a portent? Now we are following ski-tracks. It must be Norman and Hamish, making their entry a day late. Our pace increases. They'll never be away this early. They'll still be sleeping at Glas Allt. Let's tiptoe past. Ever tiptoed in boots over deep crunchy snow in the calm silence of a Scottish dawn? Past the lodge: 'No! More tracks, they must be ahead! Yes, there they are, probably after the Labyrinth too!'

'Fancy burning them off?' John asked, and he was away before I could catch my breath to approve. John overtook them easily on the steep section after the waterfall, and stormed up the path, needing to press home the advantage before reaching the fast skiing over the Loch. It was ironic, racing for a route like Labyrinth; on April Fool's Day too. Norman reached the cliff first, but went to the White Elephant! So we won.

Just in case of last-minute manoeuvres, John started up. As I followed in the footsteps, he was

often frustrates the summer visitor. But the springs are small and the ice takes at least a month to form. During that month it must neither thaw nor be so cold that the feeding springs freeze solid.

Labyrinth Direct, however, gives you an extra change. Late on in the year, after a big winter, it can hold enough snow to survive a thaw or two and form just enough ice. This is what the five of us were hoping when, at the very end of March, we arranged to go to the Dubh Loch. Three of the party were sceptical so late in the season, but Norman Keir and Hamish Towler had skied past the crag the previous weekend, and though they

already disappearing over the initial ice pitch into the sweeping curve of the lower gully, where endless easy snow leads into the upper section. John was waiting, stance cut, rope uncoiled. 'Bombproof belay!' he said enthusiastically. A single small Leeper which I later pulled out with my fingers.

'Toss for the lead.' I held a peg behind my back, but telepathic suggestion failed, and I won the crux. I had won, but I knew he should lead it. But my ego wouldn't let me refuse. It was a chance to show I wasn't just a passenger. As I looked up I could see a thin dribble of ice sweeping down the vertical left wall of the cul-de-sac, and I realised I'd never climbed ice that steep even for half the height. I knew I should lead the first pitch and leave him the crux, at least that would be shared leads. But it was too late, John was already away. The first whoosh of powder filled my neck.

'Just looking for a runner.'

Spindrift swirled down the gully and, meeting a gentle updraught, floated slowly downwards out behind John. He was up the pitch, looking for the belay that doesn't exist. For half an hour snow and ice crashed around me. Then a shout: 'Found a bombproof belay.' I climbed up to where John lurked, tied on to three pegs and a nut, all round a gigantic expanding block. I added a knifeblade in a horizontal crack nearby, and decided it was worth a lead: at least I'd live.

The ice starts 10ft. back down from the belay, a four-foot wide, convex drool of white ice on a blank wall. I went down 10ft., stepped left onto the ice, climbed up 10ft., and jumped back onto the belay; 'Your turn, John.' So he led it.

There were no rests; there was no escape from the verticality. It was not just a guidebook writer's vertical, not just weight on your arms, but really vertical. You couldn't cut steps up it; it was too thin for screws; just inescapably, arm-achingly vertical. A miniature bulge took the front four points to give half a rest halfway up. The ice was perfect. With 10ft. to go my arms were dying and still it was vertical. The concentration, the agony as you hung on a bent arm to place an axe higher. My arms were level with the lip of the impasse, but I couldn't pull up. No strength left. Icicles dripped off the lip; I leant back and wedged a shoulder, but gently – they were so thin. It was my only chance – a last big effort; only five feet to go. Last pull-up; could I make it? My right foot swivelled outwards to bridge across to the top of the icicles. What a position, just in balance, arms screaming. An icicle broke off and touched nothing for 200ft. Unique!

That remains my best memory of climbing with John, a day when the big man was in charge and in his element. Sadly, not long after he was to die in an unlucky accident in the Antarctic.

# 44  Look C Gully

by Doug Lang

**Route** Look C Gully, Grade 3, 700ft. B Gully Chimney, Grade 3, 450ft.
**Cliff** Corrie Fee of Mayar, Glen Clova.
**First Ascent** Look C Gully – Winter: C. L. Donaldson and J. R. Marshall, February 1953. B Gully Chimney – Summer: 1948; Winter: D. Crabb and D. F. Lang, December 1962.
**Map** O.S. 1:50,000 Sheet 44 (249746).
**Guidebooks** See page 198.
**Nearest Road / Approach Time** A Forestry Commission car park 'Braes of Angus' at the head of Glen Clova (284761), 18 miles north-west of Kirriemuir. 3 miles/600ft. Allow 1½ hours.
**Route Summary / Conditions** Both routes involve several pitches of good ice climbing. Look C's difficulties are concentrated in the lower 450ft. and these can be lengthened by traversing across to finish up the chimney of B Gully. A week of sustained frost usually brings the gullies into condition.
**Campsites and Bunkhouses** Campsite at the car park. Glen Doll Hut.

The prospect of winter has always posed an inevitable question, would we conquer Smith's, or the North Post, Astral Highway or Pinnacle Face, Red Chimney or Mitre Ridge; or some big unclimbed epic? But climb what we may, it is certain we would re-visit the gems of Glen Clova, Look C Gully and B Gully Chimney.

'We' being Neil Quinn and myself, to whom experience has taught that these two routes have continually provided some of the most satisfying ice-climbing in Scotland. Prior to front-pointing, Look C Gully was a yardstick. If you could cut the C's big pitch in an hour, you were fit to tackle most of the recorded routes of the day. Both routes are watercourses, carving their way down from the summit slopes of Mayar (3,043ft.) to Corrie Fee, lying within the Caenlochan Nature Reserve at the head of Glen Clova.

Early winter can provide problems in that the high hills may be out of condition, or the gateway to the North, the A9 through Drummochter can be blocked by blizzards. Being Dundee-based, we find that after a week of hard frost the Clova routes are usually climbable. The drive to Clova on the first sortie of winter is always a constant babble – re-living previous climbs, conditions, epics etc.

Under a grey sky we departed from the car park and discussed the perennial problem about Look C Gully. Would the chimney be formed? The 'wifie' at the farm confirmed that winter had arrived:

'Gie cauld?'

'Aye, that's why we are here.'

'Mind and tak care, then.'

The approach to our climb passed through a forestry plantation, the growth of which bore testimony that we had been climbing together as a team for many years. Yet still the excitement heightened as we finally escaped the forest, and it was possible to view our objective.

The most obvious feature in Corrie Fee is the well-defined B Gully. Midway up on the left of B Gully, B Gully Chimney carves a tortuous path, hidden from view. Below and to the right of B Gully, Look C Gully pours down its ice-ringlets, while to its right is the aptly-named Hooker's Joy.

The clamber up to Look C reminded us that we should have been training. Gear donned, a tentative poke at the entry ice, and up we went to a good chock belay. From here a series of short, steep ice-pillars end at a narrow chimney. Bursting with enthusiasm, to my pleasure I was given the

sharp end. It was great to feel the picks sink solidly into the ice, with a sound that stimulates confidence.

At the base of the chimney section, an *in situ* peg provided a comforting runner. Would-be ascensionists should not be put off by a gaping hole, exposing water hurtling down the back of the ice, at this point. I managed to tread delicately into a straddle position, my pick giving minimal security for about 20ft. Then solid ice was regained, and I took a belay on the left wall, having run out 180ft. of rope.

Quinn is heavier than I am, and the chimney can cause problems for people of that ilk. However, he arrived at the belay smiling as ever, glad to be back at the fray. He continued up the line of the watercourse to enter a large amphitheatre into which a great cascade of ice poured down – the base of which was well over 100ft. wide. He took a belay on a spur of rock below an obvious weakness in this great ice wall. After discussion, I was allowed to continue to lead the pitch, to avoid the ropes tangling.

A high step allowed entry to a steep depression, which I climbed until halted abruptly by a near-vertical wall. The crux moves came next. An icicle runner provided moral support while constricted manoeuvres were made up and over into a higher groove line, where the severity relented. It was then I was aware of the exposure. No place to panic – so I concentrated and climbed steadily up ramps and over bulges to exit on the tapering cone of this magnificent 150ft. ice-curtain. Neil duly arrived, proclaiming his appreciation of the fine ice architecture.

The following 200ft. pitch then involved Quinn's weaving his way through a multitude of frozen cascades, which required some delicate moves in places because of the nature of ice on this early-winter ascent. Above this level the gully continues without difficulty to the plateau.

We had been thrilled with the climbing so far. Although the hours of daylight are short in December, it was decided to execute Plan B. This involved climbing an obvious offshoot up to the left of the watercourse, which brought us out on the ridge overlooking B Gully, from where we could see straight into B Gully Chimney.

Without delay, Quinn tackled the first pitch of the Chimney in great style. Initially bridging up, he then launched himself onto a high-angled iced slab, then continued out of sight to a peg belay on a pedestal 120ft. up. On my arrival at the belay, I was quickly directed up a weakness in a nasty column of steep ice guarding the way to an easy open gully, which continued through the mountain until a huge rock wall barred the way. However, I had belayed before this impasse at a point where the ice cascades down a chasm breaching the right wall. To my consternation, I discovered that the pick of an axe had broken off. Fortunately, I carry three tools for safety, and was able to continue.

Our climb began to get serious again, and Quinn made his way up the chasm to take a belay in a large cave decorated by huge icicles. The way ahead was uncompromising to say the least. The sanctuary of the cave had to be abandoned by a delicate rightwards traverse onto the ice drooling from the gully above. The situation was decidedly airy – nothing below and nothing to the right, only space and a panoramic view of the now dimly-lit corrie. The only way was back or up. They say to retreat is to die, and there was no time to lose. The application of mind to control fear brought progress; front-points were inched higher up the vertical ice on this, the crux, until at last solid ice and elbow-room allowed a final pull into a comforting stance. The place abounded in weird phallic shapes of ice, presumably formed with the help of wind turbulence. The angle having relented, I made my way through this jungle to a commodious belay.

It was then Quinn's turn to feel the adrenalin flowing, after which we gained the plateau in two easy pitches. Once we had removed our gear, coiled the ropes, and packed the sacks, we made a jubilant descent down the easy D gully in the twilight. Darkness overtook us and torches were required for the walk back to the car.

Once again, we marvelled at the quality of the climbing, over 1,000ft. of immaculate ice. On returning through Kirriemuir we passed by J. M. Barrie's 'Window of Thrums', reminding us of the ageless Peter Pan, exciting hope that we could return again and again to the ever-fresh delights of these perfect ice-climbs.

*Right: Look C Gully on the cliffs of Corrie Fee above Glen Clova. Photo: Derek Laird*

# 45 South of Glencoe

by Bill Skidmore and John Mackenzie

**Route** Various.
**Cliff** The North-East Face of Beinn an Dothaidh.
The cliffs of Coire Daimh, Beinn Udlaidh.
**First Ascent** Various dates since 1969.
**Map** O.S. 1:50,000 Sheet 50. Beinn an Dothaidh
(328418), Beinn Udlaidh (273331).
**Guidebook** S.M.C. guidebook *Arran, Arrochar
and the Southern Highlands* in preparation.
**Nearest Road / Approach Time** Beinn an
Dothaidh – at Achallader Farm near the A82
(332442). 2 miles/2,000ft. Allow 1½ hours. Beinn
Udlaidh – the B8074 Glen Orchy road at 264353.
1 mile/1,800ft. Allow 1¼ hours.
**Route Summary / Conditions** The Beinn an
Dothaidh cliffs hold snow well and are
frequently in condition. Beinn Udlaidh needs a
good low-level freeze to bring its climbs into
condition.
**Campsites and Bunkhouses** Camping by Loch
Tulla, at Bridge of Orchy and Glen Orchy.
Climbing huts in Glencoe. Hostel at
Crianlarich.

### ICE CLIMBING NEAR BRIDGE OF ORCHY
by Bill Skidmore

'Somewhere between Arrochar and Glencoe' is the usual rejoinder to questions regarding the whereabouts of Beinn an Dothaidh and Beinn Udlaidh. The names are difficult enough to say, let alone locate or describe, so perhaps a few basic facts are called for . . .

Think of the tired winter journey back south from Glencoe. As you drop down the Black Mount road from Rannoch Moor you will see, directly ahead, a large, attractive, snow-plastered Nevis-type hill called Beinn an Dothaidh (pronounced Doe). A little further on, if you study the range south of Bridge of Orchy you might notice, if the light is right, a strange wall-like feature running up one of the hills. This is the well-known quartzite dyke of Beinn Udlaidh (pronounced Oodlie). Both hills offer recently developed winter-climbing of considerable interest and can be recommended as an alternative to nearby Glencoe.

On Beinn an Dothaidh only two reasonable winter climbs (Taxus and Haar) had been done there before 1973. In that year we managed to tear

ourselves away from Glencoe and its lousy conditions one Sunday, and trotted up to have a look at this 'new' corrie. Our spirits soared as we charged into the icy slit of what we supposed to be Haar only to be stopped dead at the first real ice pitch. It looked a bit much for a Grade 3 – overhanging and hollow. We retreated, using a worrying icicle for the rope.

Later that winter (March 1974) three of us returned. Everything was in better shape, ourselves included. The poor belay, steep ice, and dizzy, hard-frozen approach slope with its hidden rock-step below, all added up to a fair degree of exposure as I pulled over the top of the ice pitch. My increasing doubts about this being Haar were reinforced by the discovery of an abseil sling below the next ice pitch. It looked hard, but at least we had a belay on the sling. Big John Gillespie calmly tackled the pitch, and found it was soon possible to stride right to a hidden ledge and more secure climbing. We had it cracked. The gully continued as a steep snow scoop with only minor ice pitches and a long, belay-searching run-out at the top. We felt pleased with ourselves.

*Above: The left-hand section of the Beinn Udlaidh cliffs: 1. Ice Crew (Grade 3/4); 2. Quartzvein Scoop (Grade 3/4); 3. Captain Hook (Grade 5); 4. Cut Throat (Grade 4/5); 6. Peter Pan (Grade 4); 6a. Peter Pan Direct (Grade 5); 7. The Cramp (Grade 3/4) 8. South Gully of Black Wall (Grade 4); 9. Green Eyes (Grade 3/4); 10. Ramshead Gully (Grade 3). Photomontage: Rhod Stewart*

*Right: The Beinn an Lochain cliffs. Photo: Bill Skidmore*

The route was solid Grade 4 and didn't even fit the Haar description, so a triumphant letter and diagram was sent to the Editor of the SMC Journal, at that time one Robin Campbell, who, we knew, knew everything. 'Haar,' he wrote firmly on my diagram, 'is here', with a bold black arrow pointing to the gully we had just climbed.

The following winter we were back. A promising parallel gully system left of our first route gave us a most enjoyable climb. The trouble was, it fitted the old Haar description! But the Campbell still refused to budge. Gently cursing the spread of dead-hand bureaucracy, we eventually concluded that we were in danger of boring even ourselves; so we simply decided to carry on exploring the mountain. So did others.

Four years, ten new routes and one editor later saw the 'great muddle' cleared up. Ken Crocket published information in the Journal which made it clear that things were exactly as we had thought in the first place. Our first gully wasn't Haar, and we *had* made the first ascent; meanwhile, some other team had repeated it and, thinking it new, had named it Cirrus, which name it retains.

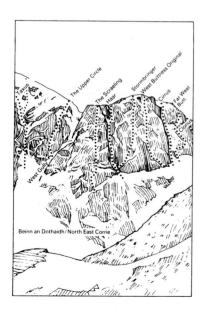

*Above: A section of the Beinn Udlaidh cliffs showing the ice walls taken by Captain Hook and Cut-Throat. Photo: Rhod Stewart*

Summing up, the best routes on Beinn an Dothaidh are as follows (from left to right): Taxus (Grade 3) – the original climb, then the easy but avalanche-prone, West Gully. The Scraeling gives a Grade 4 buttress climb. Then the genuine Haar – the left line of the parallel gully system, the right line being still unclimbed. West Buttress Original (Grade 3) takes the middle of the largest buttress on the cliff, and gives very enjoyable climbing. This is flanked by Cirrus, and, further right, beyond Far West Buttress, Clonus (Grade 4) takes a right-facing corner with some tricky slabs and a strange barrier at half-height.

As for Beinn Udlaidh, I knew of it, heard rumours and even climbed on it, yet somehow failed to appreciate the potential, not being tuned in to 'ice-crop' climbing. Coire Daimh of Beinn Udlaidh is a gloomy (the name means exactly that) low-level corrie with a rim of low, damp cliffs, lacking many positive features. It does have a certain atmosphere. A geologist could probably better explain the unusual layout of the crags. In

summer it is an awful place. A prolonged low-level winter freeze-up changes everything and the showpiece of the corrie – the Black Wall – becomes a veritable Niagara of ice-falls. This is pure ice climbing territory, ideally suited to the changing tastes and equipment of the seventies. Nearly 30 routes have been developed over a period of ten years. Most of this activity is credited to teams led by Geordie Skelton, Bob Duncan, Ian Duckworth and Dave Cuthbertson, in that chronological order. The 'ice-crop' nature of the climbs precludes a blow-by-blow account of any one route, but it should be noted that these short climbs are often very hard technically, and more sustained than other much longer routes elsewhere. The grades and lengths (average 3/4, 300ft.) might suggest otherwise. Routes that I would particularly recommend are Quartzvein Scoop, Captain Hook, Peter Pan Direct, South Gully of Black Wall, and Ramshead Gully all on the left-hand section of the cliff. On the right-hand side Doctor's Dilemma (Grade 4) and Organpipe Wall (Grade 4) are also worthwhile. The only line missing now in this high-development area would seem to be a grand girdle of the entire corrie, from left to right naturally. It could give a long day!

## MONOLITH GROOVES by John Mackenzie

'Arrochar as a winter climbing ground? Surely not?' That would almost certainly be the reaction of most climbers. But think again. The area has a number of things going for it. Its greatest advantage is that the hills hereabouts are formed from highly-foliated schists, and unlike many igneous areas, its steep cracks and fissures are often lined with turf. In fact, I know of nowhere that holds more, and as every true winter mountaineer knows, frozen turf is the real stuff of front-pointing. Ice is rarely vertical; turf-filled cracks often are. And while quantities of snow are just a hindrance, a good solid freeze, combined with a light cover, makes for good winter climbing here when other areas are out of condition.

The routes, though short, are full of variety with complex buttress lines far outnumbering the few boring old gullies. Buttress routes demand so much more from the mountaineer; not least in route-finding ability. Almost all the climbs of Grade 3 and above are worthwhile, and many offer very fine and unusual cruxes. Ben Ime boasts plenty of winter lines up to Grade 4, though the hardest route is on the Brack, where the summer VS route Great Central Groove gives a technical Grade 5. Like gritstone, 'short and hard' is the order of the day, and you may well take longer on an Arrochar 4 than on a classic Ben Nevis 5.

Beinn an Lochain is a neglected mountain, probably because it just fails to make the grade as a Munro. From the Rest and Be Thankful road on the way to Loch Fyne it throws out a fine ridge but the high north-eastern cliffs are safely tucked away out of sight. From close to, however, they are impressive; 500ft. of dramatically sculpted rock whose massive central plinth is topped by a crazily overhanging prow. The arête of 'Edge of Extinction' on the Brack, which some say is the hardest rock climb in Scotland, is repeated even more dramatically here. And in between all this bulging rock lies a cunning line with a straight-cut corner finish – Monolith Grooves, a vegetated summer V.Diff but a fine winter 4. It starts in a gully to the left of the lower plinth, though it is not always possible to enter directly. So alternatively a traverse across slabs leads in as far as the cave, which is not the *impasse* it seems and is escaped by a steep little arête on the right, which gives airy climbing to reach a huge platform, the Table. Steep ground above is avoided by sidling down and left to gain a thread of weakness, a hanging horizontal ramp. Not a good place to fall from, this leads to the heart of the mountain. Then a chimney which, following the schist's contortions, has a leftward lean. Awkward and pushing, it bulges at the top and is perhaps the crux. It is also the key to fine things and leads you into an enormous roofed cave called the Gallery. This is formed as a result of the cliff's freakish geology – a series of huge flakes resting more or less freely on one another.

The Gallery is open ended and would provide but a draughty shelter. Above it lies a splendidly steep corner which at first acquaintance looks improbable. Inspection, however, reveals a turf lining, and with excellent thread protection an overhang may be bridged to gain easier ground and a snowy finish, which brings you close to the summit. If you are lucky, the broad panorama of the Western Highlands awaits you.

On the way up the hill to the first ascent, a mild drama was played out. Barry Clarke and I left the car at the Rest and Be Thankful. A mile or so away at the foot of the North-East Ridge, Gerry Rooney and a friend were also heading up to the corrie. That two parties should be heading for a remote cliff at the same time was indeed an unlikely coincidence, but as Barry and I reached the summit, way down below and rounding the ridge's crest were two dot-like figures, moving strongly towards the base of our proposed line. Gone was our complacency, and instead a mad dash down a Grade 1 gully ensued, so fast that skis could hardly have bettered our progress. I remember cartwheeling at one point and arriving at the foot of the route in a flurry. With shame I remember yelling at Gerry, who was after all a friend, about the 'Spirit of the Hills' and 'non-competitive sport' and other such rubbish. I even had the nerve to invite them along with us. Being a gentleman he declined, saying it was a bit steep, and went off to do a new route of his own to our left. One nice memory is that they waited for us after completing their route to cheer us when we finished – a gesture worthy of the day, of Beinn an Lochain in general, and Monolith Grooves in particular.

**Route** Monolith Grooves, Grade 4, 520ft.
**Cliff** The North-East Face of Beinn an Lochain.
**First Ascent** B. Clarke and J. Mackenzie, January 1977.
**Map** O.S. 1:63,360 Tourist Map *Loch Lomond/ Trossachs* (208080).
**Guidebooks** S.M.T. District Guide *The Southern Highlands* by D. J. Bennet (route description on page 222).
**Nearest Road / Approach Time** The A83 Arrochar – Inveraray road at Butterbridge (233096) just beyond (north-west) the Rest and Be Thankful Pass. Follow the North-East Ridge of Beinn an Lochain until a traverse right leads to the cliffs. 1½ miles/2,000ft. Allow 1½ hours.
**Route Summary / Conditions** The climb comes into condition with moderate snowfall and a good frost.
**Campsites and Bunkhouses** Campsite by the Butterbridge car park.

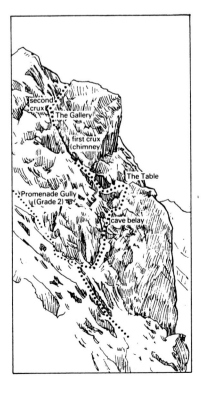

# 46  The Dreepie

by G. F. Dutton

**Route** The Dreepie, Grade 2/4, 500ft. (note: the difficulty depends on the quality of grass the previous summer.)
**Cliff** The north slope of Corse o'Whalloch, Moorfoot Range, Central Uplands.
**First Ascent** Unknown c.1905.
**Map** O.S. 1:10,000 Outdoor Leisure Map *The Western Moorfoots* (100001).
**Guidebook** Brief mention in S.M.T. District Guide *The Moorfoots and The Central Uplands*
**Nearest Road / Approach Time** The A70978 Threiphead – Bollyno road at Dreepiebridge (903671). 2 miles/1,000ft. Allow 45 minutes.
**Route Summary / Conditions** Technical ice climbing for the connoisseur. Two weeks of heavy rain followed by a sharp frost with intervening periods of humid drizzle and a south-east wind can usually be relied on to bring the climb into condition.
**Campsites and Bunkhouses** Infinitely preferable.
**Bibliography** Unaccountably ignored in S.M.C.J. Sealed correspondence and sundry archive material relating to the first ascent in the S.M.C. Library.

The forecast was frightful for the North. Gale winds, blizzards of powder snow. Gullies would be choked, faces wiped. All this after weeks of rain, and now in a final pipe-splitting frost. And the Apprentice had brand-new lobster-points to try out, cooked expensively to a gourmet's taste, and I a grinning Terrordactyl of advanced evolution, fierce from its creator; both of us fondled virgin ice-daggers fit for some sub-glacial Mafia. We had lightened our wallets for the new season, and this could have been the first run. We ached to prickle up some crisp verticality, glassy between admiring cliffs. We thought of Zero in two hours. We were bitter . . . .

So we fell for the Doctor's jovial invitation:

'I can fix you up!'

He would take us to some southern ice. Not the Lakes – weather just as bad there. Nor even the Grey Mare's Tail – that would fairly wag in this wind. But much nearer:

'Just outside Edinburgh – edge of the Moorfoots. Perfect just now – sheltered, private, fine for a practice.'

Our forebodings well-nourished on the past, gorged themselves as we trudged up the scabby grass of vast mounds ambling with sheep. But no: improbably, two of these heaps heaved back and exhibited, with considerable pride, an astonishingly high and apparently vertical earthen gully. On either side grazed well-belayed sheep; below lay more earth, and more sheep; but within, a sliver of ice launched dazzlingly upwards to a giddy bulge and then vanished backwards into blue sky.

The Doctor extended a long arm hospitably: 'This hill's the Corse o'Whalloch, and that's – Whalloch's Dreepie. It should fix you up all right.'

Apparently the Dreepie only dreeped after heavy rain, being fed from a bog above. Some geological quirk ensured its almost vertical incision in turfy earth.

We approached gingerly and prodded. The surface was yielding but sound; inside was hard. 'It's even better higher up,' announced our host complacently.

We demurred a little at the grass stems, rushes and bits of turf poking through here and there.

'Ah, they give it body. Make it tough, absolutely reliable. Can't come away. Never splits. Make it like fibreglass, reinforced concrete, bricks with straw; and all that.'

We cut short the Doctor's technical explanations of Griffith cracks and buckled on our new equipment. The Doctor was faithful to long axe, fishing hat, tweeds and tricounis. 'You can hold a long axe short, but not a short one long.' And tweeds stuck better than Terylene – but, he assured us, the Dreepie ice would be very adherent. It was.

He took to the proffered lead ('Might as well show the way') and bucketed up at a showering Charlet gallop. Earth and roots, as well as ice, fell around us. Unconvinced by the stems, we had agreed on a rope. We hoped only sheep were watching. Our leader hacked a platform, harrowed it, and summoned us.

The Apprentice went before me, taking the thin unbucketed edge, pointing elegantly. I followed, loops in hand. It was good stuff. A gentle kick and a stab: delicious admittance, firm grasp. Wonderfully safe. We mounted rapidly, calves thrilling. Marvellous to be back on ice – even if the Nordwand of a Corse o'Whalloch and ten feet wide, and even if sheep did munch mildly eye to eye with you as you passed. *Maa*. We were merry, and exchanged a word with each of them in turn. *Baa*.

The Doctor, having identified for us the local Traverse of the Gods and the White Spider (the latter carrying much grass in its web), began the final stretch below the bulge.

'Time me. See how much longer you are with spikes. No need for crampons in Scotland – take all the craft out of climbing. And as for daggers – too damned emotional.'

Multi-coloured débris rocketed past: the Apprentice drove in a peg to make sure, extracted his claws with difficulty and then slammed them well home; we would cut no steps. I did likewise, some 15ft. below and we settled to wait, muscles twanging. But it was good training for the Ben and Raven's and the rest.

The Doctor's toothy heels above us ceased to gnash: 'Come on up a bit. I'll need all the rope to get over that bulge.'

The Apprentice nodded, unclipped and heaved at his peg, cursed, bashed it, heaved and cursed again. Jammed fast.

'Ah, that's the Dreepie ice,' explained the Doctor. 'Particularly near the edge. It's the mud and stems. Plastic. Very binding. Leave it for now.'

The Apprentice cursed again, straightened up and tried to extract his left foot. Squirm.

His right foot. Squirm.

His dagger. Squirm.

He undulated on his points of attachment like a tent in a gale. But he did not take off. He was stuck.

Stuck.

Terrible oaths. Squirm.

Stuck . . . .

I informed our consultant.

'It'll be the grass again. Same as for the peg. Still, it does make it absolutely reliable . . . Pity you *had* to use those things. Rather spoilt a classic little climb. Shouldn't have kicked in so far; but then of course you mightn't have kicked in far enough . . . Need plenty of experience, crampons. Especially in Scotland.'

We decided to abandon the Apprentice meanwhile. I was to unclip the rope, reach the Doctor, and belay him. Then he could top the bulge, gain the bog, peg in, abseil down and prise our writhing companion from his flypaper.

'You just wait there,' the Doctor called down, 'you'll be fine, you can't fall; Dreepie ice is very firm . . . .'

It had begun to snow. I was fortunately below the really possessive stuff. I clawed up the steps. The Doctor then tackled the bulge.

The ice went *poop* under his axe. He explained how to carve such rubber. He feathered his slash ('like rowing Stroke in rough water'), then spooned each step backwards adze-wise ('like serving jelly; but firmer').

Much firmer. I found my prongs tight. I kicked back in alarm. But I must have offended some monocotyledon or other, for my left foot shot free and swung me backwards out of balance. I flung up both arms and my Terrordactyl took wing. I saw the Doctor silhouetted above, tongue out, reaching his axe over the bulge. With a fearful effort I lunged forward again on my right foot and drove the dagger well home before me; and clung. Relief. Sob.

But I had stabbed the rope and buried it through the dagger point well into the solid treacle. Irretrievable . . . .

And worse . . . Groans from above indicated that I had tautened the rope just as my leader had

fully extended himself and his tongue, arm over the bulge. He had been pulled down onto his tongue and his angular chin, his axe had been driven in hard somewhere up there and his grip plucked off it; so that his bony wrist now flapped weakly above, twisted firmly into the end of the axe-sling.

We were indeed in a fix; in a frozen frieze. Snow fell heavier, burying the Doctor's bitten and fragmentary oaths. The sheep were impressed. They crowded the top of The Dreepie, chewing knowledgeably. Then they scattered. They had been disturbed. We heard other voices:

'Aye, aye; ye'll be daein an ice-climb.'

'That'll be hit: they'll be daein an ice-climb!'

A miracle. Geordie and Wull. Two inveterate veteran hillbashers, cautious in all weathers. They masticated their jammy pieces above us, brushing snow off their balaclavas.

'Ye'll soon be there, lads. Hang on. There's naethin after this,' said Geordie.

'Aye, it ends here,' confirmed Wull. 'Stick tae it.' They consulted each other for a moment, crust to crust.

'A pity ye couldna' stop like yon for jist a bittie longer; for the ithers tae see ye,' suggested Geordie, through crumbs. 'If yer holds is good, mind.'

'Aye, they'd like fine tae see yese hack-hackin yir way up,' added Wull. 'Jist stay there, like, if ye can.'

It appeared that Geordie and Wull were but the van of a whole flutter of local sub-Munroists, the Pittemdoon Cairn Gatherers, who, like us, had been deterred from going north and had swooped on Corse o'Whalloch as suitable low-level carrion for their day.

We tried to explain, gurgles above and expletives beneath, our predicament, now truly horrendous. But Geordie and Wull were slow, and voices began to chirrup above us. O the shame, shame of it . . . I glimpsed orange

anoraks and peering eyes. I felt cameras being unpacked, lenses screwed on.

But Geordie was not that slow. He had his own camera in his hand, a huge mahogany box-like affair, and fixed his brassy tripod. Then he waved the others back, flourishing a jammy piece:

'Awa, awa. I'm takin a verra careful shot of thae lads, an I want a clear background. Awa, all o' ye, now!'

'Groogh.' agreed the Doctor through an ice-and-tongue sandwich under his immovable neck. 'We can't, oorgh, stay here, grrgh, like this all, urrgh, damned day.'

'Aye,' added Wull, catching on. 'These lads wants awa, they're no verra firm whaur they are. Hurry on doon tae yir bus, there's mair snaw comin in.' And he drove them off, breathing heavy experience.

Well, eventually they extricated us. It was a long job, for they were careful, gey careful, and every step they cut along the horizontal frozen bog (of course they had brought their axes) had to be brushed out and tested several times and their rope (of course they had brought their rope) had to be tied and untied several times and tugged and pondered over and discussed repeatedly; but by evening – and another couple of inches of snow – they had released the Doctor's axe, watched wonderingly our subsequent excruciating and arthritic manoeuvres, had rubbed us down and had helped us carry back the various blocks of mud and ice impounding our gear (we dared not chip too close). We thanked them with the bottle of Glen Reechie the Doctor had brought for our celebration, and watched them pack it away unopened in their van. As they left, Geordie promised to send us a print of the picture he had taken: 'It would be a better reproduction, like, than the one we would see in the *Journal*.'

'A fine climb. The Thweepie, in itthway,' concluded the Doctor over his mutilated tongue as we drove stiffly off. 'Hardly the Bwenva, or even Minuth One or Pawallel B, but gwand for exerthithe; and for teaching you thomethin about Thcottith Ithe.'

Behind the back seat, the glaciers – and their accompanying moraines – retreated silently from our 39 points into his – fortunately – open rucksack.

# 47   The Grey Mare's Tail

by Dave Kay

It was winter 1979 and the entire country had ground to a halt in the icy grip of the hardest January since Adam was a lad. Several long hauls to the Ben were followed by successive weekends of enforced idleness, trapped by heavy snow and drifted roads. This was too much for adventurous spirits, and the talk in the pub was of alternatives to slipping and sliding up the A74.

'Dove Crag Gully?'

'Did it Wednesday.'

'Trip up to Great End?'

'What, not again.'

More ale, then inspiration: 'The Grey Mare's Tail!'

'What the hell's that?' I asked. Apparently it is a frozen waterfall near Moffat where the outflow from Loch Skeen drops into the main valley. It's over 200ft. high — almost 400ft. if you count the easy stuff at the top. And it's only 200yds from the road! I was convinced, and we laid plans for the next weekend.

At Moffat the morning was still and our breath smoked in the icy air. Five minutes later we were off, dog and all, and after a short walk along the broad track up the right bank of Tail Burn we turned a corner and saw the fall itself. It was a spectacular sight. There in front of us were the waters from Loch Skeen, frozen into two icy pillars, stilled in their 200ft. plunge to Moffat Water. As we scrambled down into the bowl at the foot of the fall the burn's small unfrozen central flow filled the air with a freezing mist. The main cascade provided two obvious steep routes up its left and right-hand sides. In addition there was a much less intimidating route up a subsidiary stream on the right. All less than ten minutes from the road.

Steve had climbed the right-hand route earlier in the week. It had provided enjoyable climbing at the lower end of Grade 4, first up an ice-slab to a huge ice-pillar, then out left on a much steeper section to the top.

Our choice thus limited, we quickly roped up, and Steve led off up the steeper and harder left-hand route. A pitch of 80ft. of good water ice sculpted into rounded bollards and miniature ice-pillars gave fine climbing. Steve hammered up this fast and in great style. Nevertheless, I was deep in contemplation of my own discomfort, standing in the cold, damp atmosphere of the bowl, when he shouted that he was about to thread a large icicle as a runner. Two taps with the hammer and CRASH.

The bloody thing disintegrated, nearly dislodging him in the process and showering me with blocks of ice the size of footballs. My avoiding dance would have done credit to Fred Astaire. I jumped and skidded around from one foot to the other as the débris cannoned off the ice above me and ricocheted around the bowl.

This was high amusement for the dog, who assumed that the blocks were being thrown around for him to chase until a fist-sized lump of ice caught him squarely on the snout. This ended the game and sent him packing on the path out of the firing line. I let go the rope and scuttled up beside him, more concerned for my own safety than my leader's predicament. After all, what good is a dead second? Steve, however, suspended from one axe, had a different perspective. Quickly placing a nut runner in the hole where the icicle had been, he adjusted his stance, looked down, and quietly asked for the slack to be taken in. Not quite the tirade I deserved. Unashamed of my cowardice and wary of more falling blocks, I stayed on my perch, hopeful that my ice-ballet was over. I had no intention of moving until assured that the danger was passed.

Moving right from the runner, Steve stormed up the last 50ft. of the pitch without incident, despite the fact that the 20ft. vertical section above the late-departed icicle had now become the crux of the climb. A place for a peg was found in the left wall, and it was my turn.

The ice was superb and the short vertical sections were interspersed with good resting places. I quickly arrived at the icicle's old home. Its departure had left a neat cave and the best resting place of all. I sat down: 'Come on Dave, I'm freezing.' Thus encouraged I sped upwards. The runner came out easily enough, and a move right took me close to the unfrozen central stream and onto the crux. I pulled up. The stream was near enough to soak as I tap-tapped my way to the stance.

After a moment's rest for aching calves I led through, and found that the angle eased after 30ft. Another 20ft. and the problem was over. I belayed on the bank and when Steve came up we unroped and romped up the remaining 200ft. of easy climbing around little icy pools and over short ice steps. Then a glissade down the snowy slopes of White Coomb, and a five-minute walk to the car.

**Route** The Grey Mare's Tail, Grade 4, 350ft.
**Cliff** Tail Burn, White Coomb, Moffat Hills.
**First Ascent** G. Anderson, W. Anderson, D. Bathgate and I. MacEacheran. February, 1969.
**Map** O.S. 1:50,000 Sheet 79 (182150).
**Guidebooks** S.M.C.J. 1970 contains a note on the first ascent.
**Nearest Road / Approach Time** A layby on the A708 Moffat-Selkirk road, 10 miles north-east of Moffat. ¼ mile/200ft. Allow 15 minutes.
**Route Summary / Conditions** A frozen waterfall characterised by bulges, icicles and ledges. The main problems are concentrated in the bottom section of the fall. A prolonged low-level frost is necessary to bring the climb into condition.
**Campsites and Bunkhouses** Possible camping by the layby, hotels in Moffat.

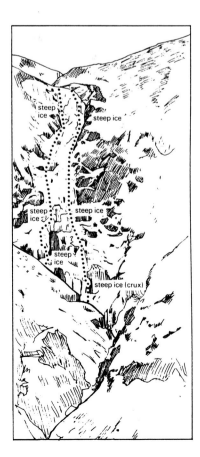

*Right: The Grey Mare's Tail below
Loch Skeen in the Moffat Hills.
Photo: Dave Alcock*

*Left: On the right-hand route of the
Grey Mare's Tail. Climber:
Robin Andrews / Photo: Steve Howe*

# 48  Moss Ghyll and Steep Ghyll

by Bob Bennett and Paul Nunn

**Route** Moss Ghyll, Grade 4, 400ft. Steep Ghyll, Grade 4/5, 650ft.

**Cliff** Scafell Crag.

**First Ascent** Moss Ghyll – 1892; Winter: O. G. Jones 1893. Steep Ghyll – Summer: 1894; Winter: S. H. Cross, Alice Nelson, A. T. Hargreaves and Ruth Hargreaves. c.1938/9 winter.

**Map** O.S. 1:63,360 Tourist Map *Lake District* (205069).

**Guidebooks** *Winter Climbs in the Lake District* by R. Bennett, W. Birkett and A. Hyslop (Cicerone).

**Nearest Road / Approach Time** A minor road along Wasdale at the Wasdale Head campsite (181076). 2 miles/2,200ft. Allow 2 hours.

**Route Summary / Conditions** The difficulties on both climbs involve iced rock. A good build-up of snow and ice, plus some freeze and thaw, is essential to bring them into condition. The problems on Moss Ghyll are grouped in the middle pitches whereas Steep Ghyll saves its most difficult section for the end. Steep Ghyll is serious because protection is sparse and belays are difficult to find.

**Campsites and Bunkhouses** National Trust campsite at Wasdale Head. Brackenclose (184073) is the nearest climbing hut (F.R.C.C.). Bunkhouse at the Wastwater Hotel (Tel. Wasdale 229).

**Bibliography** *Rock Climbing in the English Lake District* by Owen Glynne Jones (E. J. Morten); *Lakes in Winter – Moss Ghyll* by Bob Bennett (Mountain 70).

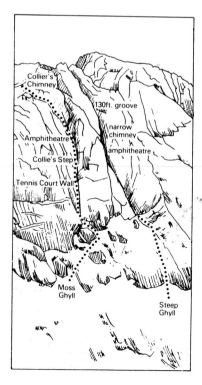

## MOSS GHYLL by Bob Bennett

Scafell Crag and its outlying Shamrock sport climbs of contrasting grades of difficulty. Right of Shamrock proper is a large area of broken ground frequently in good winter condition. This section presents a mixture of easy snow slopes and ice pitches of varying steepness which may be strung together to taste. Above and left of Lords Rake the main crag rises, broken by the obvious lines of Deep Ghyll, Steep Ghyll and Moss Ghyll. Little else seems a practical proposition on here, with one exception. The weep draining from the chimney above Botterill's Slab could give a magnificent winter climb if given the unlikely combination of good conditions and a strong party.

The three major gullies give climbs of great character and variation; Deep Ghyll with its two cave pitches, occasionally banked-out into one continuous slope; Steep Ghyll, probably the hardest of the traditional Lake District climbs; and Moss Ghyll. The last fits nicely between the other two, offering a high degree of technical interest coupled with large comfortable stances and good belays. Starting with a series of enclosed chimneys, it opens up in its middle section to give traditional gully pitches, before cleaving deeply back into the mountain in the form of a funnel-shaped amphitheatre. Escape from here brings another abrupt change in the character of the climb, with open, slabby pitches and increasing exposure towards the finish.

History was made here in the fine, dry winter of 1892 when Messrs. Collie, Hastings and Robinson made the first ascent of the Moss Ghyll. The gully had been attempted before but the jammed boulders blocking access to the upper amphitheatre had beaten parties back. Collie circumvented this problem by cutting his well-known step in the rock, earning himself a place in climbing posterity. Hard on their heels Owen Glynne Jones made what was certainly the first ascent of the gully under snow. Despite taking a fall off the 'Step', he managed to cross the slab at the second attempt, at which time he confessed to a feeling of 'lively apprehension'. Little more is known of the history of the Ghyll, although in 1961 Robin Smith and Dougal Haston attempted an ascent wearing one crampon each. They were obliged to retreat as darkness fell.

One unforgettable day in 1979 six of us arrived at the start in dismal weather, spurred on against our better judgement by Bill Birkett. We were joined by 'Tut' Braithwaite and partner, also intent on climbing the Ghyll, who were taken aback at finding such a large party with the same intention. Following true British climbing etiquette, all eight of us made a made dash for the start.

The snow in the gully was not well consolidated and the normally-easy lower pitches proved awkward, with loose snow covering thinly-iced rocks. Birkett made short work of Tennis Court Wall, and set about bringing the rest of the party up to the ledge above. With a cursory nod of the head he indicated that I should tackle the traverse back to the gully-bed. Well aware of the absence of protection on this pitch, I gingerly negotiated a 'step-through' move on sloping footholds, axes dangling and hands splayed. Carefully shifting balance in this precarious situation I was able to place an axe-pick across the gully and pull up into a secure bridging position to gain the snowslope above.

It was some time before all six of us were safely ensconced below the Collie Step pitch, the encroaching gloom brightened by sparks from the crampons of the party ahead as they attempted to cross the step. Conditions were far from ideal. The small slab that makes up the step was verglassed and the only good ice present was at full stretch. With moral support from a thread high up in the cave, Birkett hooked his left axe precariously in the ice and, after a very delicate two-step traverse across the slab, hauled himself onto thicker ice above. I appreciated his difficulties when my turn came and was thankful for the security of the backrope. Much later, we all gathered in the amphitheatre in the fading light of a winter's afternoon. As the one person who knew the gully I was elected to lead the way up the final slabs, so often the most enjoyable part of the climb. I was lucky to find the snow-covered rib and crack which are the key to the exit. At the start of the traverse below the overlap, an acute awareness of lack of protection had me groping for a runner. A promising crack turned out to be blind, and a half-placed piton bounded off down the crag, prompting gentle shouts of encouragement from the blackness below. I inched leftwards, feeling for yielding snow with both crampons and axes. The traverse seemed to go on for ever but I finally reached the exit chimney, a mixture of fear and exhaustion taxing my concentration to the point of indifference. At least I was now on safe ground. The other five

Above: The North Face of Scafell. Photo: Bert Jenkins

swarmed up the rope in darkness; but that wasn't the end of it. Bill and Ken went for a midnight bathe in Burnmoor Tarn followed by close encounters of a different kind in a well-known Eskdale Inn.

## STEEP GHYLL by Paul Nunn

There is a twisting slot between the upright tower of Scafell Pinnacle and the grey plaque of slabs where Central Buttress ends. In winter a tiny tongue of névé snow betrays the presence of something above, but bulging rocks from both sides come close to meeting in the lower reaches, where the Ghyll has more of the appearance of a chimney than a gully. Above, as the Pinnacle bellows out to the right, the Ghyll pods into a wide scoop-like depression before narrowing again in the upper section below the col of Jordan Gap.

It was rumoured that Robin Smith had done a winter ascent of the route in the late fifties. (It is a

215

*Above: Ice-glazed slabs that bar the way to the amphitheatre of Moss Ghyll. Climbers Bob Bennet and Martin Willey / Photo: Bert Jenkins*

*Right: On the Collie Step. Climber: Tom Proctor / Photo: Al Phizacklea*

lead. Jack Soper, Willis Ward, Oliver Woolcock and myself were in the team, and there may have been others. Strong as the party was, after a couple of pitches we stuck, with Les's frame out in front, sprawling and scraping for hours in the nasty, red, brittle scoop of the third pitch. Eventually, with darkness pending, the bored and cold back-markers abseiled off.

Steep Ghyll evidently needed more than a short, quick stab, so Clive and Steph Rowland and I returned some years later for a full Wasdale weekend. We had been convinced of the need for this a week or two earlier, in trying from Borrowdale. For hours we struggled up to our thighs round the Corridor. The hour became too late to climb and rather than plod back we hit the Wasdale Head for food and beer. As we were penniless the rope was put in hock and Clive even managed cigars for the re-crossing of Sty Head.

Brackenclose is the superior base. By 9 a.m. I was leading into the first scoop on a grey, steely day. The snow and ice was good with a smattering of worse stuff on top. Clive tackled the chimney by neat bridging, then spent an age getting a belay on the awkward ground of the scoop above. The slabs of the Pinnacle looked bare, but the steepening scoop was filled with a fragile névé which would just hold weight, the product of a recent north-westerly. Little rock showed.

It appeared likely that it would be one full run-out to Jordan Gap. In some sections the Gully was too flat-backed to allow a bridging technique. Straight ice-axes sculpted narrow and fragile hand holds which consolidated under mitten pressure, and the feet followed into these slots always wondering if the snow would hold. It was a delicate and balancy form of progress.

I've no idea how long it took; picking and chipping for little holds, teetering from one to another, holding some icy rock or ice-nubbin with one hand while poking around with the axe in the other. Front-points often broke through to the rock underneath, scraping and scratching. Once or twice dubious slings draped over even more dubious spikes created an illusion of protection. Clive shivered and juddered on his inhospitable shadowy shelf below, occasionally lighting up a fag. A black, close-fitting, woolly hat, like some leftover from Rebitsch and Vörg or the Death's Head Battalion, covered his ears. Cigarette smoke puffed upwards, alternating with a hacking cough.

route worthy of the man.) But then it was rarely attempted, so that on our first try we knew precious little about it. Climbing on Scafell from the Salving House in Borrowdale was common enough at the time. It was a long, straggling line that traversed the Corridor Path from Sty Head on the particular Alpha/Sheffield University Club campaign. Often it was useful to have a change of leaders on the walk, for in heavy snow it drifted in and was very time-consuming. But the first time to Steep Ghyll we were in luck, with hard, frozen conditions which boded well for the conditions on the mountain.

Mob-handed the team assailed the Gully, with the long, gaunt figure of Les Brown, not so long back from the first ascent of Nuptse (1960) in the

Spreading the weight on the snow-pockets became even more strenuous after 50ft. Spindrift from a wind sweeping across Scafell summit occasionally burst in a flurry down the scoop, filling face, anorak and holds. Progress got even slower but it looked harder still to go down. Legs and nerves tired at the endless chipping and balancing and hanging on with one mitten. A final steep section of ice at least promised an easing beyond. But with maximum rope-drag and no security beyond a good sense of balance it was the trickiest moment of all; that final move onto easier ground, the point of relaxation where so many leaders fall. There was really nothing to stop you for 100ft., which meant a fall of well over 200ft. The straight Charlet pick was carefully planted, and Grivel front-points placed safely out left before the other foot was recovered from below. Then it was a romp to the Jordan Gap.

Clive came quickly, very cold. It was never his way to hang about unnecessarily on ascent or descent. He was a concentration of mountain sense and agility and could be difficult to keep up with. On arrival he hardly paused. A savage wind blew through the Gap, flicking snow into nostrils and eyes. One glance from heavy-lidded eyes and 'Insecure, youth – good lead,' was comment enough as he scampered off on the final few feet.

Ten years later, with Terrordactyls, it was much less awe-inspiring. Pat Fearnehough had never used them and as a step-cutter without parallel he remained scornful. The mentor of my earliest winter climbs in Scotland, he was testy as he planted the tools high in the scoop pitch. He used them, but carefully and without bravado, his legs still in the balanced bridging positions of old. The instinct was 'agin it'. Yet I suspect that by the summit he was a grudging convert, seeing generations of technique and mountaineering practice of considerable sophistication go out the window, jettisoned like an old sock. Most convincing was the speed and the unjarred forearms. Broad Stand we descended with care, seeking the jug-handles and slippery little steps amid the snow-cover in a place we had romped so often on golden summer days. Later that night, as we sat in the pub, came as heavy a snowfall as you are likely to get in Britain. It was our last great climb together, February 1978, prior to the Latok Expedition on which Pat was killed in the Braldu Gorge, and the perfect conditions were obliterated.

# 49  Great Gully, Wasdale

by Ed Cleasby

The Wastwater Screes are an inspiring sight. As you emerge from the trees beyond Wasdale Hall they present themselves suddenly and forcefully, a great, sombre, north-facing hillside, looking rather lonely and haunted. For over two miles along Wastwater's far bank the great stone-chutes gather. Finely-textured towards their top, they become increasingly rugged as they slide steeply into the silent, dark waters of the lake. At their highest point, the screes stretch up for over 1,000ft., but towards the southern end of the lake they are half that, replaced by dark, brooding cliffs and gullies, starved of sun. The buttresses have always been avoided by climbers and retain, to this day, an aura of mystery. Not so the gullies.

Cleaving the great cliffs are two of the finest examples of their type to be found in the district – Great Gully, and the narrow, twisting C Gully. Over 1,000ft. long, Great Gully has no local peer. It is a great, deep scar cutting directly down from the ridge between Illgill Head and Whinrigg. It succumbed in 1891 to a determined assault by the experienced team of Collie, Hastings, and Robinson. Currently graded Severe, it is slightly easier than C Gully, which stopped several attempts before O. G. Jones met with success in 1897. Both gullies acquired a reputation for being dangerously unstable, especially C Gully, which prompted Jones to remark to his friends the Abrahams, 'Promise me you'll never climb C Gully on the screes, it's a deadly place.' A sentiment that could equally apply to Great Gully.

For much of the year Great Gully is a dank, chilling place, with water much in evidence, from a trickle to a torrent. Towards mid-height the rock walls open momentarily to expose a broad amphitheatre, collecting-point for several minor gullies and water slides. Closing again, the walls form a long, wet funnel which, after several hundred feet, lead to a dripping crux pitch guarding the exit to the summit slopes. This is Great Gully in its usual garb. But for a few winter weeks it freezes to become one of Lakeland's finest ice-climbs. Water-slides become ice-chutes, the rocks freeze into solidity, and the upper sections fill with snow. But this is not all – for standing slightly apart from the main line is the phenomenon which raises the stature of this fine route to classic level. Plunging into the side of the central basin is a broad 200ft. pillar of bulging ice. The Right-Hand Finish.

My first encounter with Great Gully was towards the end of January several years ago. An accidental and unprepared affair. Having wasted a day floundering in knee-deep snow on Scafell with hopes of Moss Ghyll, Mike Hillas and I, like many a disappointed pair before us, had retreated to the Wasdale Head to seek comfort from the bottle. Emerging a considerable time later with the best of the day gone we set off back down the valley. In deep morning shadow the Wastwater Screes had revealed little. They were like a black slumbering giant. Now, with the sun picking out a white-crested summit ridge, every detail stood out clear and sharp. Visible in the lower half of the gullies were the predictable water-ice pitches; but higher, piercing the top of Great Gully, a large smear of white ice was obvious. Moving down the valley our view improved and as the pillar of ice grew so did our amazement. In our ignorance we believed it to be unclimbed and despite the lateness of the day we could not resist the temptation at least to climb to the foot for a closer look.

Great Gully rose from a dent in the scree to a great chasm, squeezed between two cliffs. With crampons all-too-often grating on rock rather than ice, we soloed up the short initial ice-steps. 200ft. higher, great black walls drew in, sucking the light from the gully. A large frozen waterslide blocked the way, making the rope necessary. I tiptoed, easily at first, up the bubbly, fragile water-ice. The angle increased considerably 30ft. higher, but protected by a stout icicle runner, strenuous moves

**Route** Great Gully/Right-Hand Finish, Grade 4/5, 1,000ft.
**Cliff** The cliffs of the Wastwater Screes.
**First Ascent** Great Gully – Winter: N Collie, G. Hastings and J. W. Robinson, 1891. Details of the first ascent of the Right-Hand Finish are unknown.
**Map** O.S. 1:63,360 Tourist Map *Lake District* (150037).
**Guidebooks** See page 214.
**Nearest Road / Approach Time** The Wasdale road near Wasdale Hall (144045) 1 mile/800ft. Allow 45 minutes.
**Route Summary / Conditions** A low altitude climb which therefore needs a long cold spell to bring it into condition. The difficulties involve climbing frozen watercourses. The Right-Hand Finish is the hardest section consisting of 200ft. of steep ice.
**Campsites and Bunkhouses** See page 214.
**Bibliography** *Vergil Knew* by E. Banner Mendus (F.R.C.C.J. 1945) describes a gripping ascent of the gully in semi-winter conditions.

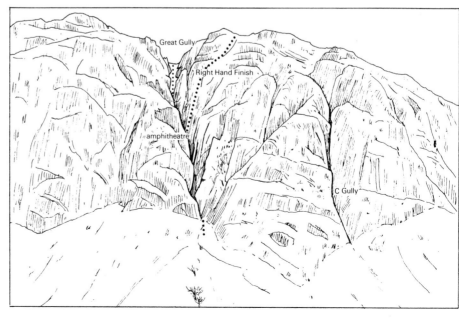

led to easier ground. We continued with increasing momentum, spurred on by the fast-fading light. Easy stretches separated by short water-ice pitches maintained the interest.

After 500ft. it dawned on us that we had underestimated the size of this giant. In failing light we contemplated retreat, but calculated that one more pitch would see us to the central amphitheatre. After three, we looked upon a great ice-spectacular. Across a firm snow slope at the head of a short, narrow gully rose a great obelisk of superb white ice. Between 200ft. and 300ft. high and 20ft. wide, it was sandwiched between a sheet black wall on the right and rocky outcrops on the left. At its base, a slim pillar of ice provided a possible entry through sentinel icicles. Still a rope-length short, and with the light almost gone, we realised it would have to wait for another day. We moved back into the main gully line and raced for the top.

A week later, this time accompanied by Nigel Bulmer, a young Sunderland climber, I again stood at the foot of that great ice-fall. No longer was the

*Top right: One of several water-ice pitches leading up to the amphitheatre. Climber: Brian McKinley / Photo: Pete Fleming*

*Bottom right: A view down the Right-Hand Finish to the amphitheatre. Climber: John Hool / Photo: Pete Fleming*

gully a haven of peace and solitude. At least a dozen climbers battled for grid positions. The lower sections resembled a racetrack. Foul play enabled Nigel and me to gain second place in the queue that was forming beneath the ice-pillar.

While some patiently waited their turn, others saw the hopelessness of the situation and retreated to the sanity of C Gully. The leader of Team A began to claw his way up the first pitch, emphasising his sole position by bombarding the idle mob below with ice. After 40ft. his initial impetus had slowed to a crawl. Drained and aware that another 100ft. of increasingly exposed, and no-less-steep ice loomed, he scurried left to the sanctuary of a belay.

Thinking this to be a rather weak effort I determined to go for a full run-out. For 20ft. a cone of ice could be followed pleasantly, but on stepping across to the main pillar the angle became distressingly steep. A further 20ft., and I willingly accepted the offer of half a belay ledge.

As others started, a fresh leader was weaving his way up the next pitch. Overhead a series of steep ice-bulges, each with a fragile ice-beard, cascaded down. Most of the steeper sections could be avoided by short deviations back and forth across the front of the pillar, but there was no avoiding one ice wall. Whilst the rest of us sheltered behind camera lenses, the leader betrayed his anxiety by nervously increasing his swing-rate as he sought to position his hammers more securely. Bolstered by a cluster of ice-screws, he stabbed and hacked his way up before a yell announced success. By the time Nigel and I found ourselves hanging from an ice-screw belay above pitch two, the afternoon had arrived. The next pitch would see us to the top of the icefall, and whilst the angle had only eased slightly the ice was good, solid snow stuff rather than the water variety. Nigel offered to lead this section, and with obvious relish tiptoped steadily up the next 70ft. till the pillar tapered and all that was left was a final snow-filled gully.

Ice-climbs are temporary things, subject to change. Perhaps this is their attraction. The Right-Hand Finish to Great Gully usually forms to some degree each year but it doesn't always become a colossus. When it does, however, you may share the opinion of a stranger whose guidebook I chanced to borrow. Next to Great Gully he had penned the date and details of his ascent, and as a postscript had added, 'fantastic route.'

# 50  Inaccessible Gully

by Steve Howe

It had been rumoured for some time that there was a hard winter route on Dove Crag. The guide book revealed its summer identity; 'Inaccessible Gully'. But, Mild VS and with a piton for aid? It seemed unlikely. Most probably it was done as a rock-climb; cold, snowy, maybe a little ice, but still basically a rock-climb, albeit out of condition. Or it might even be rumour unfounded. After all, nobody seemed to know who'd done the first ascent, or even anybody who'd actually done it. We decided that our time would be better spent on some established classic so we returned to the Great End or Helvellyn yet again.

This train of thought was typical of many local climbers in the seventies. High standards had been achieved years ago in Scotland, and now Lakeland climbers were repeating routes like Point Five and Orion Face as a matter of course; yet the Lakes remained largely a backwater. Granted, there had been exceptions like Steep Ghyll, but the difficulties there were on steep, snow-covered rock, verglas perhaps, but not much in the way of water-ice. By the late seventies the rumours had frozen to fact, and so it was that one February day in 1979 Dave Kay and myself, emboldened by our recent successes in Scotland, decided to take ourselves to the Eastern Fells.

The normally busy campsite at Brotherswater was quietly shrouded in fresh snow and our footsteps were the first that morning. The path led through the fields, then up through a ghostly wood until it reached the open fell. Dove Crag, visible ahead, was intimidating. Its impending central walls were still free of snow, though our route was out of sight, and would remain so until we were at its very foot. Nevertheless, the sustained period of cold weather over the last two weeks promised optimum conditions.

At last we were struggling up the soft slopes of South Gully, into which Inaccessible falls, and turning a last corner we saw the route a few hundred feet ahead. Nothing had prepared us for a sight quite like it. From a concealed rift a stupendous column of pale blue ice 10ft. wide dropped nearly 100ft. into the gully bed. From close-to it was even more impressive, and as we geared up on a ledge cut out in the snow we chatted nervously.

Some 40ft. up on the right of the pillar a sling hung from the promised piton, providing something reassuring to aim for. I set off, piton firmly in mind. The preliminary section consisted of a series of short, steep walls, separated by banked up

ledges, and proved decidedly exhilarating as the gully bed dropped away below. I moved up and right.

The haven of the runner was difficult to leave. Very steep moves led leftwards onto the front face of the pillar. The ice was rather brittle, adding to the tension. Some distance up, a natural ice-thread gave small comfort; and then the way led up left again into the bounding corner of ice and rock where a few frozen tufts provided some security. It was too steep to rest easily here, however, and I resolved to finish the pitch quickly. The ice thinned unpleasantly, which was surprising in view of the volume of ice that had formed below. A strip about six inches wide offered the best alternative and so, knees and elbows brushing awkwardly together, I moved up and pulled over onto an easier-angled runnel above. Some 30ft. up this I got a good peg in, above which a large chockstone was poised with depressing menace.

Dave followed with little apparent difficulty – it was definitely a leader's problem – the atmosphere exaggerating the actual difficulties, to the extent that I was already tired physically and mentally. A quick change of position, and minutes later I was hunched up on a boss of ice below the chockstone; it was indeed going to be hard.

There was no ice at all, just steep rock with powder snow masking every hold. A nut between the chockstone and the right wall gave me sufficient courage to embark on a series of wild laybacks up and away from the gully-bed. By a series of lunges I achieved a position that will be recognised by any gully climber; knees on the bottom lip of the chockstone and axes flailing uselessly in the snow above. A Terrordactyl pick lodged in some semi-frozen scree provided the solution at the eleventh hour, and then I was ploughing waist-deep up to and over another chockstone

Dave followed with wide bridging, more elegance, and an occasional spark, before leading up towards the final obstacle – a short, steep chimney. This went relatively easily, with flake holds on the left wall onto which crampons slotted in a satisfying manner. A wide amphitheatre was all that remained, with an easy descent to follow.

As an experience it hardly matches up to the Big Ben giants, but in Inaccessible Gully you will find enough for much more than just a good day. Fine, steep water-ice combine with an absorbing mixture of snow and rock. What more could you want?

**Route** Inaccessible Gully, Grade 4, 350ft.
**Cliff** Dove Crag, Dovedale.
**First Ascent** Summer: 1937; Winter: Unknown but before 1970.
**Map** O.S. 1:63,360 Tourist Map *Lake District* (375105).
**Guidebooks** See page 214.
**Nearest Road / Approach Time** The A592 Windermere-Patterdale road at the Brothers Water Inn (404119). 2½ miles/1,500ft. Allow 1½ hours.
**Route Summary / Conditions** Steep ice and chockstone obstacles constitute the main difficulties. Because it is predominently an ice climb a good freeze is needed to produce good conditions.
**Campsites and Bunkhouses** Campsite by the Brotherswater Inn. Beetham Cottage (F.R.C.C.) near Patterdale.
**Bibliography** *Lakes in Winter – Inaccessible Gully* by Andy Hyslop (Mountain 70).

*Left: A small spindrift avalanche pouring over a climber engrossed on the first pitch of Inaccessible Gully. Climber: Phil Rigby/ Photo: Kevin Howe*

# 51 Chock Gully

by Bill Birkett

**Route** Chock Gully, Grade 3/4, 370ft.
**Cliff** Falcon Crag, Dollywagon Pike, Helvellyn.
**First Ascent** Summer: 1910; Winter: Unknown.
**Map** O.S. 1:63,360 Tourist Map *Lake District* (352126).
**Guidebooks** See page 214.
**Nearest Road / Approach Time** The A591 Ambleside-Keswick road at Dunmail Raise (328116). 2 miles/1,300ft. Allow 1½ hours. Can also be approached by a slightly longer route from Glenridding.
**Route Summary / Conditions** Characterised by a large chockstone and ice bulges, interspersed with easy snow slopes. Good conditions are usually to be found whenever Helvellyn is snow-covered.
**Campsites and Bunkhouses** Youth Hostel and Hotel accommodation in Grasmere. Camping at Skelwith Bridge or Glenridding. Ruthwaite Lodge (Sheffield U.M.C.) in Grisedale. Rawhead (F.R.C.C.) and Robertson Lamb Hut (Wayfarers) in Langdale. Beetham Cottage (F.R.C.C.) at Patterdale.

It was on Chock Gully that I first wore crampons. The day was a typical Lakeland excuse for winter: a thin snow-covering giving a hint of white, drowning all other colour except crag black. We started from the summit of Dunmail Raise. It was very cold but there was precious little snow as we left the black burial mound of Dunmail, slipping and sliding on icy ground to a frozen Grisedale Tarn. Traversing the northern shore we broke out and up across the steep fell, while below the Grisedale Valley plunged away.

It was a mournful grey-cold day. The crag was black, ice-bound and discomfitingly snowless, a sizeable buttress touched only by paltry rations of early morning winter sun. Chock Gully cleaves the rock, at first staggered, merging in and out of the hillside, but soon gaining momentum, depth, impact. Today the line looked hard and unattractive; the water-ice looked brittle and unfriendly. Still, it had to be climbed – aesthetic considerations, conditions, enjoyment – these were of secondary importance.

Now, on with the crampons! Dave Mounsey sat in silence, immaculate in green gaiters, yellow anorak and purple balaclava, watching my embarrassing performance with the spikes. I cursed and sweated, crouched, sat, stood and fought to put them on. Time passed, Dave shivered, until Eureka! They were on! Or were they? Alas! It didn't take long before I realised that those funny pointed things on the front looked to be angled in the wrong direction! Off they came. More cursing and sweating. I resembled a fighting, hissing ferret tied up in a bundle of rags. At last they were on again, this time on the right feet!

Now Dave was a relatively experienced winter climber, having done some Scottish Grade 3s, while I didn't even know what Grade 3 meant, being used to a world of Diffs and Severes. It was therefore only right and proper that he should go first to demonstrate the use of the crampon and axe on steep ice. I suggested this; Dave wisely agreed.

'Give it hell, Dave,' I urged as he teetered up the shattering ice. He didn't and I was most unimpressed with those crampon-things. All they seemed to do was smash the ice down in alarmingly large chunks. Eventually Dave belayed, by which time I was cold and disillusioned. I started off next. It was awful, frightening, and I did not like it one little bit.

My instinct was to try and stand on something other than the front-points but this merely resulted in an even greater sense of insecurity. Putting the front-points in the ice was bad enough, actually standing on the things was an exercise in self-torture. I climbed – no, that's the wrong word – crawled up the pitch by a technique of first smashing holes in the ice with the crampons and then using the rock underneath. The ice-axe hung redundant from a cord around my wrist while my gloved hands plunged desperately into any available hole in the ice. The stance brought the meagre joy of being able to sit down and the great sadness of hot-aches. Hands and fingers felt like sausages under a grill.

At this time I didn't care much for winter climbing; in fact I hated it. Maybe, I thought, things will improve if I use my ice-axe. The gully constricted, deepened, reared up. We could have walked out to the right but things to come towered above us, a gaunt commitment to which we had to keep. Confined by the dank, streaked walls, overhung by the great wedged block, the challenge of the place was its fearful attraction. A terrible steepness loomed above and the next pitch looked formidable. It is generally reckoned now to be Grade 4, but the only thing I was aware of was that it was going to be harder than the first pitch. Dave suggested a retreat: 'After all, conditions are dire.'

'No way Dave, we're going to get up it!' I could hardly believe my own ears. Was that really me talking? Incredulous at my own words, I re-opened the campaign.

By bridging and thumping I arrived teetering, below a fearsome chockstone, which temporarily forbade progress. Dave informs me that I drove in a peg somewhere on the pitch but I have no recollection of having done so; perhaps the subconscious has removed this dreadful deed from my memory. Each move was a nightmare. First the ice-axe would bounce ineffectually off the ice, then the ice would be all hollow and simply fall away. I think I preferred the crampons on the rocky bits, at least it was a familiar feeling. My front-points flexed awfully in the ice and I just could not bring myself to trust them; the steeper the pitch became the closer I hugged it; but it showed no affection.

A runner, a long sling hung pathetically over a nubbin of rock, brought brief respite. But the feeling of well-being rapidly disappeared; I just could not get past the chock. A 70ft. pitch and only a few feet to go, but it wouldn't, so I retreated. The

*Above: Chock Gully. Photo: Bill Birkett*

sling fell away and I was relieved to get down, yet bitterly disappointed at my defeat. 'Go on, you do it Dave,' I urged, with as much enthusiasm as possible.

Dave started off, but it was late and cold and I had given in. We decided to retreat. I persuaded Dave to leave a sling and set off down. Once down, however, there was time for reflection. My trousers and socks hung in shreds, mute testimony to my crampon technique. Dave had lost some gear and we had both been beaten. Apart from that things were hunky-dory.

We had been ever so near to climbing Chock Gully, for above the chock lies easy-angled snow.

Indeed, although the route continues through impressive rock scenery and the bulk of its length lies above that chock, the going is straightforward with the exception of a small ice-step. The early pitches, usually climbed as one, can also be avoided by traversing in directly from the right to give immediate access to the crux pitch. By whichever way, Chock Gully is a splendid Lakeland winter climb, almost 400ft. long and sporting a magnificently vertical 70ft. pitch.

But failure is not nice; it gnaws at the mind, taunts the ego, frays the temper and finally leaves a sadness. It is, however, better than dying. And there is always another day . . . .

# 52  Dove Crag Gully, Grasmoor

by Chris Bonington

**Route** Dove Crag Gully, Grade 4, 300ft.
**Cliff** Dove Crag, Grasmoor.
**First Ascent** Unknown.
**Map** O.S. 1:63,360 Tourist Map *Lake District* (179204).
**Guidebooks** See page 214.
**Nearest Road / Approach Time** The B5289 Buttermere-Cockermouth road at Lanthwaite Green (159208). 1½ miles/1,500ft. Allow 1¼ hours.
**Route Summary / Conditions** The direct pitches are difficult and rarely in condition – a considerable ice build-up being required, particularly for the first pitch. Usually climbed by the easier variations which are more often in condition.
**Campsites and Bunkhouses** Youth Hostel, Birkness Cottage (F.R.C.C.) and campsites at Buttermere.

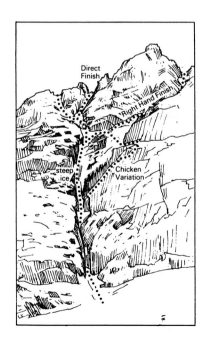

Most Lakeland ice-climbs are small gems lost in a large setting. They have none of the majesty of Scottish winter lines or the fierce steepness of those in Wales, and yet what they lack in scale, some make up for with a delicate, often surprising, quality. One such is Dove Crag Gully, tucked away at the side of a rocky buttress on the north-east flank of the northern combe of Grasmoor. From the road it is difficult to believe that there could be any climbing at all, for Grasmoor is a great rounded hump of a hill, in summer clad in scree and heather, so thick that even in winter they often protrude darkly from the white of the snow.

The best way to the crag lies up Gasgale Gill from Lanthwaite Green. There is a faint path that contours the northern slope but in heavy snow it is easily lost and it is best to follow the bed of the gill to where it bends round the northern end of Grasmoor, and then a long slog up the slope leads into the combe.

At first glance Dove Crag looks a dull lump. It is only on closer inspection that its hidden delights are revealed. In summer, it is an undistinguished, mossy and vegetated mess of rock, but in a good winter, its very dampness is an advantage and it bristles with icy moustaches. Dove Crag Gully nestles into its left-hand side, a pronounced gash bounded by a rambling buttress on one side and a steep rock wall on the other. One wall is sheer, the other gently impending, to give the effect of an inverted V. You walk into the gully, as if it was the nave of a church, till even the chockstone, partly blocking the top, is jutting above. The climb is up the vertical ice of the left-hand wall and at first the gully is too wide to get any help from the other side.

You need a good hard winter for sufficient ice, and the first time I went up to try it there was not enough. Instead, we teetered up the broken buttress to the left, crampons biting into the turf hidden by soft powder snow. This led across to the top of the bottleneck, where the gully opens out into a series of icy bulges. These were also too thin and fragile. But there was an alternative line to the right out across a slabby ramp barred by a trellis of icicles. The angle was not quite so steep, and the ice was sufficiently thick to pick our way across. It gave an airy pitch of some 80ft., ample compensation for the plod up Grasmoor and it is often in condition when the gully itself is still thinly shod in ice.

I returned to Grasmoor in the winter of '78 with Brian Hall and this time conditions were right. It

had been thawing and freezing for the past fortnight and even the slopes up to the combe were covered in firm hard snow. The gully itself was sheathed in a thick layer of water-ice, Brian had a hangover and I therefore got the first pitch. At the bottom, the gully is just too wide to bridge, but in a couple of moves you can step back onto the impending wall behind and take the weight off your

arms. Enclosed in the gully, with a level snowy floor, the feeling is that of an indoor climbing wall set in a deep freeze. As you gain height the wall behind crushes in, constricting movement, until a tenuous wriggle takes you out through the bottleneck into the widening of the gully.

Brian, his hangover squeezed out of him, led the next pitch. It is steep with a couple of bulging ice-steps of more conventional climbing. Above, there is the usual little scramble to the top of the buttress, which lies up near the top of Grasmoor itself. The climb is short, even by Lakeland standards, but no matter. Each pitch is delectable, the situation superb, and the view from the summit as fine as any in the Lake District. Even better, there is a good chance that you will see no-one else all day.

*Left: The Screen from the top of the Chicken Variation. The direct line takes the gully on the left. Climber: Simon Yearsley / Photo: Bert Jenkins*

*Above: Dove Crag Gully. When the first pitch is unclimbable, a traverse across the terraces on the left leads to the gully. Photo: Bert Jenkins*

## 53  The Climbs of Great End

by Bert Jenkins

**Route** South-East Gully, Grade 2/3, 650ft. Central Gully, Grade 3, 650ft.
**Cliff** Great End.
**First Ascent** Summer: 1882; Winter: O. G. Jones recorded winter ascents in the 1890's but they may have been climbed earlier.
**Map** O.S. 1:63,360 Tourist Map *Lake District* (228085).
**Guidebooks** See page 214.
**Nearest Road / Approach Time** A minor road at Seathwaite (236122) at the end of Borrowdale. 3 miles/2,000ft. Allow 2 hours. The crag can also be approached by slightly longer routes from Langdale and Wasdale.
**Route Summary / Conditions** The most popular Lakeland winter crag because of its reliability: after snowfall its gullies come into condition quickly and stay in condition longer. Difficult sections can usually be turned by easier variations if they are not well iced.
**Campsites and Bunkhouses** Campsites in Langdale, Borrowdale and Wasdale, Salving House (F.R.C.C.) in Rosthwaite. Other F.R.C.C. huts in Langdale and Wasdale.
**Bibliography** *Rock Climbing in the English Lake District* by Owen Glynne Jones (E. J. Morten) has detailed accounts of ascents of Central Gully and South-East Gully. *Great End* by H. Jenkins and another article by R. Andrews (Climber and Rambler, November 1979).

Great End is to Lakes ice what Shepherds' is to Lakes rock, and to the Lakes climber in winter what Shepherds' is in summer. Probably we have equal difficulty in taking either seriously. We're too close to both to see them new and fresh again; we've been there too much and too often when there was nowhere else to go; a wet but drying day in what passes for summer for the one; a weekend after new snow and cold for the other. But therein lies their value – the place would be the poorer without them.

Great End is usually the first Lakes crag in winter condition. In its broad outline, it has always been for everyone, and is accessible from three-quarters of the Lakes. By 'broad outline' I mean the two major gullies and Cust's. If that's all you've done, read on, for Great End has detail too, and it sports it all on ground perfectly angled for winter climbing at the easy to middle grades, with the odd harder bit. The steep ground takes drainage in strange places, a slow, steady seep down a crag facing the perfect direction for winter; steep pastures of summer studded with groove and crag, gathering and holding snow for a slow maturing; fine noble features of rock and snow, ridge and ice, either to climb or merely to frame the view.

The major lines, then? South-East Gully is not as interesting as Central Gully, having little scope for variation. Central has – how many finishes? Right-Hand, Middle Way, Left-Hand, (Grade 3 ice pitch, hard early in the season, but with a spike runner; easier later, but the runner gets buried), Far Left, and a chicken route for people failing on Far Left, up the buttress, left again. Right-Hand has a big and well-named avalanche slope leading to the plateau rim, and in a tower on its left is a very steep chimney, not often climbed, or in condition. You can leave the Central main line low down, (but it will take you a lot of visits before you find just where) and follow a ramp in the buttress on the left that will take you to the foot of Far Left. You can do the ice pitch of Left-Hand, and traverse left above it to climb the awkward rock step of Far Left. If there are crowds in the main line, or the snow is soft, you can solo up the ridge on the right of the lower half, drop down into the Amphitheatre at the parting of the ways, and scurry across to do Left-Hand, maybe not ahead of the crowds, but certainly out of the way of avalanches. You can . . . but you must have got the idea by now. This is only one line, the biggest gully on a face with more

*Right: The cliffs of Great End from near the head of Grains Gill. Photo: Bert Jenkins*

besides. Have you done Window Gully? Climbed the ice tower in its right, above the finish? What about the line of ice between Window and Central? Easy at first, but there's a steepening halfway up, and thereafter the freedom of a strange bit of crag is yours, a broad but narrowing triangle increasingly squeezed between Window on the right and the ridge of Central on the left, up little grooves and gullies invisible from Sprinkling Tarn.

But make no mistake. This is no Lochnagar of size and seriousness, no Orion Face of isolation, no Meagaidh of immensity. The smilingness of the place remains *nearly* always unchanged – there are still the doubts and memories, the cornice cracking on Central, the helicopter hovering, the slide to the screes, death and permanent injury. Yes, this is still a mountain crag, and sometimes you know it. But with a basic knowledge of the thermodynamics of

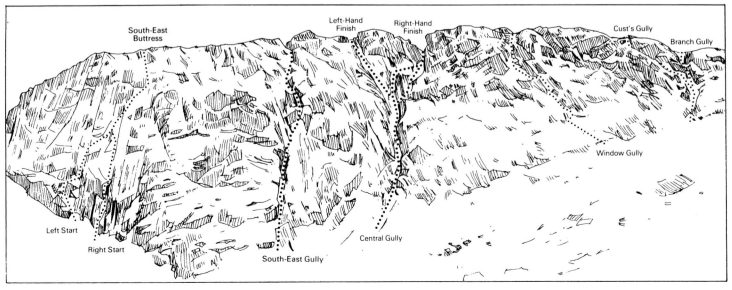

*Top left: Central Gully on Great End. There is a choice of four finishes from the amphitheatre halfway up the gully. Far Left, Left-Hand and Middle Way start from the left fork and Right-Hand takes a line from the snow bay in the right fork.*
*Bottom left: The first pitch of Central Gully.*
*Bottom right: The steep pitch, which sometimes banks-out, that starts the Middle Way.*
*Climbers: Pete Baines and Martin Willey / Photos: Bert Jenkins*

water, it shouldn't happen to you. Yes, people walk off the plateau down Eskdale rather than Wasdale. Well, that's life. It's not like walking the wrong way off Meagaidh or Lochnagar or the Ben or . . . .

But *no* seriousness . . .? Not quite. In 1978 and 1979, two big icefalls developed in the area of crag left of South-East Gully. These were exceptional winters of great ice build-up, and many climbers missed both of these routes because conditions were so good elsewhere that no-one thought to reconsider Great End. Descriptions of both routes exist, though oddly enough they are not in the Winter Guide, and if the message is that Great End is in condition every winter, then a rider should be added that these two icefalls may be no more than variably thick verglas. But when they do form, they are magnificent. The Left-Hand, the harder, forms 200ft. of steep ice and snowy grooves, Grade 4 on its main pitch, with good belays but no protection. The Right-Hand is slightly easier, and its equally unprotected grooves hold snow rather than ice, so good conditions are essential. Both land you on a central snowfield (if you've just done Left-Hand you'll have to look hard for a belay), and by various entry pitches gain a shallow gully devoid of difficulty but set on a crag cast in the same mould as the Little Brenva Face of Ben Nevis. This upper face is little-known, steeper than it appears from below, and much remains to be done. Fortunately, no history exists in the Lakes of claiming first winter ascents – perhaps due to the FRCC neglect in their guides – so, explorer, you are, as ever, your own first. The central snowfield can be gained from the foot of South-East Gully, should the icefalls be absent and the upper face look good.

If Great End, then, is so obviously for everyone, and it is equally obvious to the general mind that everyone goes there, then conceivably you may ask why any advertisement is needed. Well, I have my doubts about crowds. I haven't queued there for years. Come to that, it's a long time since I queued on a rock-climb, either. Sometimes I doubt whether there are as many of us as there were ten years ago. And now, with Lakes ice much better documented, we have every excuse for sanity, and little for following crowds. (Granted, we are still at the mercy of the bloody awful weather.) Great End has room for everybody. It can even accommodate those poor souls struggling up Moss Ghyll or Steep Ghyll in slush or verglas. They'll certainly enjoy it more.

# 54 Raven Crag Gully

by Bert Jenkins

By the middle of February 1979 it seemed that we were set for a good winter. Yes, the usual things on Great End and the Shamrock were in condition, and there were times enough in the past when we'd been grateful for them; but there were tales of icefalls on Black Crag Dovedale, the right-hand finish to Great Gully of the Screes had formed (pity you had to climb wet rock to reach it), Dove Crag, Grassmoor and the Great End icefalls left of South-East were building up nicely, and Raven Crag Gully, Comb Gill was being climbed. It was really a problem of how best to use one day a week; you could lose sleep over it. Some people were hitting it right and climbing good stuff every time. By contrast, I boasted a mere 35ft. of ice-climbing that winter and most of that done in the course of failing on Great Gully. It was starting to hurt.

Then one weekend it started to work out right and we climbed Sergeant Crag Gully. Dove next, we thought, for the tales of Raven did not omit mention of queues stretching back to Keswick. Raven was also traditionally graded 4, which was worrying in view of the few successes that winter so far. A climb with a reputation may indeed inspire the top-class climber to an appropriate effort, while ordinary mortals merely bite their lips and worry. We changed our minds, however, on the day.

There were three of us. Martin Willey and I had climbed together for many years and were well-versed in the arts of abseiling off in both summer and winter. It was all new for Sandra Corbett, whom we had enticed into the field with promises of infinities and vast horizons (or spindrift and verglas anyhow) and who wasn't yet sure to what extent her difficulties on ice were inherent in her own technique, or were due to bendy boots, flexible crampons, and my spare axe and hammer. We kept quiet for her benefit, and hoped the big pitches weren't too vertical.

Raven Crag lies in the valley of Comb Gill at the southern end of Borrowdale. It faces north-east and the Gully takes a lot of drainage (as a summer rock-climb it is frequently a waterfall). The crag itself is contained within the 1,500 and 2,000ft. contours. Only in the coldest winters will it be at its best, and ideally, ascents should follow extensive snowfall and prolonged maturing. It has been in good condition several times since the hard winter of 1976. Access is easy and the approach scenery superb; Lakeland fell-country at its finest. On the day of our ascent snow lay to low level, but the

going was good.

We ran easily up a preliminary pitch to the foot of the first icefall. It lay back at an accommodating angle; watery ice running ramp-wise over a small chockstone in the gully narrows at the top, and then there is a waterslide between broadening walls, falling in part over a cave easily passed by the continuation of the waterslide. Rock walls, free of snow, substantially dry and full of cracks for nuts like a summer rock-climb, confined the ice rigidly to its bed. The ice had formed into small cups and concavities, rarely running for more than a few unbroken feet, with the result that you had footholds for every step and warm, supple ice for axes conceding jugs for every move. There was a belay at the top, at about 70ft. Above, the next pitch rose in steps. Up first into a recess with an ancient peg at the back; now face left to two more steps in the gully wall. A big effort on steepness for the first; then the second, the ice thinning now to reveal bare rock scarred with crampon wounds, and a landing on an easing in the gully angle. There were belays on nuts, a big stance for a party, and above there was a cave.

It must be about here that the escape lines run off left, should you suddenly find need of them. Two pitches have taken you into the sheep-traverse area of the crag, and the cave ahead is an accident in the geography of the gully, avoidable on the left. Two fast parties came up and we let them through. We had our own pace and didn't mind.

Where was the cold, where was the wind, where was the spindrift and the mist? Why were there belays, why was there protection, why was it so safe, why weren't we on edge all the time; why were we enjoying it? Everyone knows you're not supposed to enjoy winter climbing. You could take a climb like this to court for infringing the Trade Descriptions Act. Escape lines? Why, the only reason you'd need to escape is if the top pitch were 100ft. and vertical . . . .

Dachsteins back on and get to it. This route must have got its grade from somewhere. Steepening snow and some ice led into the cave and protection. Its right wall, of rock, bore big holds; Dachsteins off and axes away for a few scratchy moves on these, then Dachsteins back on axes out again as the ice returns. And now only a plain snow slope up to the final pitch.

This pitch is surely one of the most beautiful ever to form in the Lakes. Only the big curtain of Dove

**Route** Raven Crag Gully, Grade 3, 500ft.
**Cliff** Raven Crag, Comb Gill.
**First Ascent** Summer: 1893; Winter: Unknown.
**Map** O.S. 1:63,360 Tourist Map *Lake District* (248114).
**Guidebooks** See page 214.
**Nearest Road / Approach Time** The B5289 Buttermere-Keswick road at Seatoller (245138) where there is a car park. 1 mile/1,000ft. Allow 1 hour.
**Route Summary / Conditions** A natural watercourse that gives good ice climbing after a sustained freeze at low altitude. Stances and belays are good.
**Campsites and Bunkhouses** Salving House (F.R.C.C.) in Rosthwaite. Hostels at Borrowdale and Keswick. Camping at Stonethwaite and Grange.
**Bibliography** *Lakes in Winter – Raven Crag Gully* by Bill Birkett (Mountain 70).

*Left: The top pitch of Raven Crag Gully. Climber: Malcolm Pearson / Photo: Bert Jenkins*

move was as gentle as the overall angle of the pitch implied. At each bulge, then, you reached above and measured yourself against its steepness, and moved only when confident of your adequacy. In such a manner you gained, after some 30ft., the peg. It was a well-used crack and on a rock-climb would have served a small nut; but now, in winter, a peg. A stretch of slab-angle ice trending away from the comfort of the big wall led to a steepening beneath two possible exits. That on the left, close against the gully-wall, had gathered beneath it a sweep of smooth ice in the gully-corner, down which the eye travelled too fast for comfort, and which swept past the bottom of the pitch. Equally, the gully wall promised no security. The right-hand exit, although more open, led over the snowy crystalline material that capped all the bulges, and traded off its openness against a more friendly type of air beneath your feet. A ledge with an outward curl, undercut beneath, led to a relatively straight-forward move over the top.

The back of the ledge had been much quarried by previous aspirants and for the first time on the whole route the incipient verticality, dubious material and distance from the peg combined to induce a mood of mantra-like concentration. Thus distracted from the frailties of the flesh, the air provided steps the ice lacked, and where the ice lacked solidity so too the body lacked weight, and you possessed first the ledge and secondly the ice beyond it. Then a simple move over the top, and a tree rooted in the snow with its branches delicate against the grey winter of the sky.

Under the conditions of our ascent the climb presented difficulties of no more than Grade 3, and was well-protected with good belays, big stances, and no great sense of exposure. Raven Crag Gully in good condition has about it an air of light-heartedness; it is easy to remember good thing about it. It seems to be attempted most winters, usually with success, but with varying recourse to rock-climbing and deviousness, particularly on the last pitch. It seems that on the last few feet of the climb ice builds up very slowly, and they are sometimes only verglassed. Its reputation and grade perhaps derive from such conditions. We climbed it some weeks after a very big snowfall that provided plenty of cover and ice-making material. Lacking such, you are dependent solely on freezing water and you may only have verglas. It might then be a very different proposition.

Crag Gully comes remotely near it. Great hanging walls confined the ice on its left. From the top a snick of light spilled down the ice and lit the curve of each bulge and convexity, a pattern of lights and greynesses and occasional rock.

At length the party in front tiptoed out of the ice into the barely-differentiated grey of the sky above. A different kind of aesthetics now. A few feet in the icy gully bed led to a nut runner and a rightward traverse beneath the first bulge; then beyond, up and left to the safety of the gully wall, a peg runner, and a change in detail. No move was steep to the point of putting undue strain on the arms, but no

# 55  Great Gully, Craig yr Ysfa

by Wil Hurford

1979 was one of the great winters in Wales. The snow arrived early and stayed. By February there was so much that a uniform easy-angled slope formed through the Devil's Kitchen and skiing from the very summit of Tryfan provided a quick way home. Huge patches lingered in the gullies as late as May, allowing after-work evening climbing on snow and ice! Word of the excellent conditions spread quickly. It was no surprise therefore when Nigel Cooper rang me, asking if I'd be willing to lead him up Great Gully the following weekend.

I had better explain that Nigel is no newcomer to mountaineering: indeed he is old enough to be my father and was climbing before I was born. But he's now at the stage in life where family and professional responsibilities have reduced his appetite for risk, hence 'The Guide'. We agreed to meet at Ogwen Cottage the following Saturday.

It snowed on Friday night — hard. Approaching from Anglesey I couldn't get past Bethesda until the plough had cleared the road. Meanwhile at Betws-y-coed Nigel had managed to wrap his vehicle round another coming in the opposite direction. We eventually set off, in none-too-good humour, at about 10 a.m.

The approach to Great Gully from the A5 normally takes about one and a half hours. That morning, sinking in soft snow up to our knees, it took three. From the col above Ffynnon Llugwy, we dropped down to contour under the huge rambling buttresses of Craig yr Ysfa. We crossed the base of the Amphitheatre, its huge walls black and clear of snow, and skirted round below Great Buttress to gain the slopes below the gully. The line was obvious, towering above us for some 800ft. hemmed in on the left by icy buttresses and walls. At the foot of the gully we stopped for a bite to eat and held a council of war. Time was not on our side; only four hours of daylight remained. The route was long, with the crux at the top. Furthermore, there was an unexpected addition to the party, for Nigel had brought along his son Adrian, making us a rope of three. On the other hand, the route was obviously well snowed up; the descent would be easy and moonlit, and the weather was good. We all had head-torches and spare batteries. The decision was to press on.

At first it seemed that our luck was in. The lower section of the gully was a uniform snow slope and in good condition. We moved quickly for several hundred feet to the point where, in summer, it is usual to climb a steep groove on the right wall in order to avoid a cave formed by an enormous boulder known as the 'Door Jamb' which completely blocks the gully. On this particular day however, ice hung down the wall on the left of the boulder, allowing direct progress and the avoidance of the usual time-consuming detour to the right. This was good news and, after one more pitch up an ice-filled groove with a swing round a huge icicle to regain the gully bed, we were at the foot of the notorious chimney pitch.

The difficulty here in summer is well-known: the walls are usually wet and uncomfortably far apart for backing up. But crampons solve the problem by increasing the length of one's legs. And to quote from an obscure source, 'Crampons grip grot when vibrams do not.' In no time we were up the chimney and tackling a little corner, which I recalled being easy in summer. But covered in powder snow it was one of the hardest pitches of the climb.

It was 4 p.m. and time for decisions. We discussed the alternatives: 1. Abseil off immediately to reach the foot of the climb by nightfall and then ascend nearly 1,000ft. in darkness to the col; 2. Continue up the gully a few hundred feet, climb the Great Cave Pitch by torch, and thence downhill all the way to Ogwen.

The first would be safe, long and boring; the latter a gamble. If it paid off we would not only complete the route but we might even be back home earlier! We gambled – and lost.

Bulges and ice-grooves loomed ahead, shadowy and mysterious. They reminded me of a pre-dawn bergschrund crossing, but here neither séracs nor alpinists flew over our head.

By 6 p.m. we were gathered in the Great Cave. I wasted a little time trying to climb the right wall, an exit I had once used in summer to avoid the awkward chockstone pitch, but it was too difficult in the dark. The chockstone it had to be. After fixing a high runner in the back of the cave I launched out towards the famous jammed boulder. 'Using the arm as a pivot, perform a pirouette to the south,' were Archer Thomson's instructions. He obviously didn't try that at night, in winter, wearing crampons and Dachstein mitts! It doesn't work. I landed slightly shaken on the floor of the cave. The second time I used a no-nonsense lunge-and-jump technique, which would no doubt have solved the problem had not my right crampon decided to jam itself firmly in the crack beside the

**Route** Great Gully, Grade 3/4, 900ft.
**Cliff** Craig yr Ysfa.
**First Ascent** Summer: 1900; Winter: (earliest known ascent) J. L. Longland and A. Bridge, 1928.
**Map** O.S. 1:50,000 Sheet 115 (693637).
**Guidebook** *Winter Climbs in North Wales* by Rick Newcombe (Cicerone).
**Nearest Road / Approach Time** The A5 Capel Curig – Bangor road at 687603. Follow a straight road (locked gate) to Ffynnon Llugwy and thence over a col to the cliff. 2 miles/1,750ft. Allow 1¾ hours.
**Route Summary / Conditions** A classic gully climb set amidst interesting mountain architecture. The pitches are varied and the crux, usually the Great Cave Pitch, is high on the route. A heavy build-up of snow gives the best conditions. The cliff faces south-east and therefore tends to lose its snow quicker than other winter cliffs (e.g. Lliwedd or the Black Ladders).
**Campsites / Bunkhouses** M.A.M., C.C., L.U.M.C. and Leicester M.C. Huts in Ogwen Valley and Cwm Eigiau. Camping at Gwern y Gof Isaf.

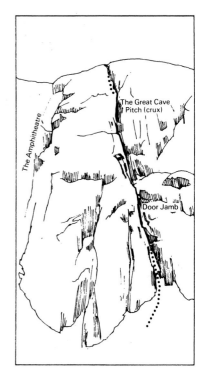

*Left: A view down the converging walls of the Great Cave Pitch of Great Gully. Climber: Tony Ashton / Photo: Steve Ashton*

chockstone. A desperate struggle succeeded only in detaching my head-torch wires from their battery. I lay helpless on the chockstone, unable to go up or down. The 'clients' gallantly formed a human pyramid and attempted to raise the stricken Guide's foot from the crevice in which it was firmly lodged. This plan was abandoned after Adrian's crampons had bored holes in his father's shoulders and the pyramid had collapsed several times severely testing the belays. The hapless Guide, tiring, trapped, and blind, was getting desperate. He urged them to try again. Then Adrian had a bright idea. He would tension off the runner and, held in place by his father's outstretched arms, would undo the Guide's crampon straps. Escape at last! The exhausted Guide was now able to quit his crampon and fall off without leaving his leg behind. He was skilfully fielded by his clients. At this juncture Nigel vetoed any further attempts on the chockstone, pointing out that I was likely to maim myself before I succeeded in overcoming the obstacle. I might then have difficulty leading the party up the rest of the route. This was a valid argument (the customer is always right anyway) – except that if we bivouacked where we stood, there was a good chance that we'd all freeze to death before dawn. Nigel however, had no intention of letting his leader die and denying me my only honourable exit, he insisted that I sit between himself and Adrian in the bivouac tent, enveloped in mountains of down. Hot coffee unexpectedly appeared from his sack. It might have been a very comfortable night, except that one of the party was excessively flatulent. At 2 a.m. democratic opinion set against him and he was sent out into the spindrift to do something about it.

After 15 long, dark hours, daybreak finally arrived, and with renewed vigour I set about the problem above. I had had enough of that monstrous, foot-grabbing boulder. Two pegs and a nut later I was up the right wall and perched on the smaller, outer chock. Nigel and Adrian followed easily enough, sacrificing the nut to protect the last man. One more easy pitch saw all three of us sitting at the top of the crag thawing out in the welcoming sun, just 24 hours after leaving the road.

Surprisingly perhaps, Nigel still asks me to accompany him on the hills. One wet day nine months later we returned together to recover the nut. It was still there. The approach took one and a half hours. So did the climb.

# 56   The Black Ladders / Western Gully

by Jim Perrin and Paul Nunn

In summer, Ysgolion Duon ('the Black Ladders') is not the most immediately attractive of cliffs. It is vast, lurks in a high cwm far from any road, and there is something reptilian, sinister even, about the peculiar set of its strata and drip of its moss-grown clefts. Vegetation and water, the staples of the iceman's craft, abound, and thus winter brings it into its own. For a cliff outside Scotland, the scale is startling. At its lower, left-hand end it is about 600ft. high, but to the right of Western Gully it towers up to more than 1,000ft. Well up near the summit of one of the highest Welsh hills, it stretches a long way round the head of a desolate cwm. It is one of the classic seasonal cliffs, a Welsh counterpart to Meagaidh, and there has been much activity here on the part of the connoisseurs over the last ten years, with more surely yet to come. Probably no other cliff south of the Border has the same scope for hard mixed climbing.

Apart from its one outstanding classic, there are a dozen other fine lines and a host of possibilities as yet unrealised. The gullies hold snow late into the spring, and the height and aspect ensure that the cliff is frequently in condition when others are not. The layout is slightly confusing until you grasp the basic fact that Western Gully lies more or less at the cliff's centre, with the higher bastions to its immediate right. Most of the development and nearly all the summer lines, however, lie to the left. On the extreme left, the bounding feature is

Eastern Gully, a pleasant Grade 2, better if the steeper right-hand finish is taken. Starting just right of the foot of Eastern Gully and cutting sharply back right is the well-concealed Pyramid Gully which, when climbed direct, gives an excellent ice-pitch at Grade 4. This was first climbed by Boysen and Estcourt in 1967. When approached from slightly higher in Eastern Gully, avoiding the ice pitch, it is much easier, but still very good. It defines one side of a pyramidal buttress, the other side of which falls into the deeply-incised Central Gully, the crag's other classic Grade 2, although in sparse snow conditions it can quite easily be harder than that grade. This triangular buttress, in hard winters, shows two icefalls in its lower section, the left-hand one following the summer route of Jacob's Ladder and the other one flowing down further to the right. These have both been climbed at Grade 4, one by Fowler, the other by Boysen and Brown. Above the preliminary sections they lie back a little, but are nonetheless substantial 600ft. buttress climbs.

Next comes the real meat of the crag. Between Central and Western Gullies sprawls the immense Central Buttress. Its western bounding rib is climbed by the esoteric but worthwhile summer route of Flanders (HVS), Alcock, Lowe, Crew, and Brown's route of 1969, which set the theme of Great War nomenclature for later routes on the crag. It is a sort of hard man's Amphitheatre

**Route** Western Gully, Grade 4, 1,000ft.
**Cliff** Ysgolion Duon (Black Ladders).
**First Ascent** Summer: 1901; Winter: (earliest known ascent) J. Brown and R. Moseley, c. 1952.
**Map** O.S. 1:50,000 Sheet 115 (670632).
**Guidebook** See page 235.
**Nearest Road / Approach Time** A minor road south of Gerlan above Bethesda (638659). Walk through marshy fields into Cwm Llafar where a good path leads directly to the cliff. 2¼ miles/ 1,500ft. Allow 1½ hours. The cliff can also be approached from the Ogwen Valley by a route up the south side of Craig Llugwy.
**Route Summary / Conditions** A long and sustained gully that stays in climbable condition after snow for longer than other Welsh climbs. The crucial pitches involve verglassed rock and the difficulty varies considerably according to the exact thickness of the ice. Belays are good.
**Campsites / Bunkhouses** Campsites below the cliff or in the Ogwen Valley. Huts and a Hostel in the Ogwen Valley.

Buttress. In a hard winter, it might provide a super-Eagle Ridge – if it could be climbed at all. The position in the upper reaches, on a knife-edged serrated arête above the plunging walls of the gully, is frighteningly exposed.

Western Gully is the best of the traditional winter climbs in Wales, and a route which can hold its own in any company. Joe Brown, of notoriously fickle memory, has a distant recollection of having

climbed the route in the early fifties – probably the first winter ascent. Putting aside the question of history, where nothing is certain, the quality of the route is beyond doubt. It has architecture as well as interesting climbing. Below the terrace at a third height, there are a couple of intricate pitches up grooves which can become very heavily iced and are often as difficult as anything above. They can be, and quite frequently are, avoided by following

the summer route, which traverses in to the foot of the main gully-line along the terrace from the right. The middle section of the climb, up to the great chockstone which the crux slab circumvents, has more of a massive open groove configuration than the traditional gully form, with little chockstone pitches and easier sections between. After the crux it slices back far into the mountain, great walls soaring out to the upper reaches of Flanders,

before giving out into a névé basin under the summit ridge. At one time it saw as many failures as ascents, and there were tales of all-star teams fighting their way out in the dark after long hours of epic striving. It retained for many years a high reputation for difficulty, probably due to the smooth, high-angle rock walls which have to be climbed in its middle reaches.

The Central Buttress itself gives two superb

*Above: The central section of the Black Ladders with Central Gully on the left and Western Gully on the right. Photomontage: Ken Wilson*

Above: The Black Ladders from the summit
of Carnedd Dafydd. Photo: Ken Wilson

Right: The lower section of Western Gully.
Climber: Dave Walsh / Photo: John Barry

mixed climbs. Gallipoli takes a very direct line from
the foot of Central Gully, steep, mixed ground all
the way and sustained at Grade 4. Passchendaele is
completely different in character. It traverses a
long way left from Western Gully along the snow
ramp (a direct start would surely be in order),
climbs a short, difficult slab which may well be
Grade 5, and which is said to be harder than the
crux of Western Gully, then subsides back into
easier grooves and shallow gullies veering up to the
right. Both routes were climbed on consecutive
days in the winter of 1972 by Dave Alcock and
Martin Boysen.

To the right of Western Gully the cliff attains its
maximum height, and has so far yielded up three
major routes. Ypres (previously known as Gofrit),
Alcock and Mo Anthoine's route of 1968, climbs
the lower icefalls of Western Gully, traverses to the
end of a terrace leading out right, then ascends a
difficult 80ft. groove (Grade 4) over a bulge into the
obvious and easier gully above. Right again are two
mammoth undertakings – The Somme and Icefall
Gully, both routes of 1,000ft. or more. The Somme
saw some degree of competition for its first ascent
in 1979. Rick Newcombe first tried it early in the
season, before its main ice pitch was fully formed,
and was forced to retreat. A few weeks later,
Boysen and Alcock succeeded, with Newcombe
swooping in to snatch the second ascent shortly

afterwards. It takes a faint series of icy grooves and
slabby runnels which delineate the left-hand side of
a black, overhanging mass, Mid-West Buttress,
and it gives difficult, sustained climbing in its
middle third. The highlight of the route is a
magnificent pitch, a full 150ft. long, of 70° ice, but its
grade of 5 is probably based more on length and
seriousness than on any especial technical
difficulty. People who have done it claim it to be
one of the more important winter routes in Wales.
Icefall Gully, the right-bounding line of the main
cliff, was climbed by Jack Street and Paul Nunn in
1968. The substance of the route in a good year lies
in three or four consecutive medium-length pitches
of ice with rock belays in between. The ice tends to
be watery, as it forms from a persistent spring, and
even in bitter weather a hefty swing of the pick can
be rewarded by a squirt in the eye and soaking
hands which subsequently freeze. It is quite stiffly
graded at 4, and both routes are major undertakings. This is more or less the state of play –
a traditional cliff transformed by a series of open
and serious buttress and face climbs which,
however technology develops, will always remain
important and difficult winter routes, for the style
of climbing offered here is on snowed-up rock
rather than the straightforward ice or snow which
lend themselves most willingly to the new
implements.

Above: The crux of Western Gully, an ice-coated slab which is climbed to avoid a large chockstone. Climber: Dick Renshaw / Photo: Renshaw collection

**AN ASCENT OF WESTERN GULLY by Paul Nunn**

One of my most rewarding climbs on the Ladders was when Bob Toogood and myself snatched an ascent of Western Gully one March day in 1970. It was perhaps something of an effrontery on our part to start at 4 p.m. in early March. We had just enjoyed a pleasant sprint up Central Gully, its only difficult pitch banked out by snow. As we passed the bottom of Western Gully, some hapless party lost a full bandolier of gear, and the prospect of booty was not to be missed. If we were quick, we might grab the gully and the gear.

Toogood fired off into the first ice-pitches, and we moved up together for a couple of rope-lengths. There were awkward bits and delicate shufflings, but we gained a lot of height quickly. Above the

terrace we were forced out of the bed as it disappeared into a steep section of icicled overhangs. We were glad that the weather was clear and still as we ground to a halt at a shelf beneath snowy walls. A few old slings and pitons were mute testimony to past efforts and retreats.

Above us, grey rock showed here and there, with only thin streaks of ice. Time for gloves off and a bit of the bare-knuckle stuff, groping for rock holds in the powder and under verglas. It was painfully slow, with the agony of hot-aches to be endured, and it was an hour before I could traverse round a little corner back to where the gully re-asserted itself. Here there was a cave of sorts and a bulging section beyond, where a chockstone barred the way. We had arrived at the famous crux pitch. A crack over on the right seemed to offer the best hope. One crampon scraped its way up this whilst the other scratched at the slab on its left and a mittened hand fumbled for rock-holds. Sometimes a mittened handjam worked best, at other times a quick lob of the pick into a dribble of ice or a frozen sod. It was a style of climbing typical of the cliff's harder routes.

The approach of night brought with it a sense of urgency, and after some trouble I was relieved to get a belay and bring up Toogood. Things looked very black above, the sombre walls of huge buttresses curving round to crowd in a gleam of snow. Bob went at it very rapidly, sparks flying from his crampons in the gloom. Fortunately it was easier, and when he lit his head-torch and it glinted round the confining walls, things became easier still. At last the rope ran out and I followed. Seconding, I found it much simpler than it had looked from below. There was more mixed climbing above, but it gradually eased until eventually we emerged onto good late-winter névé in the final basin.

On the summit ridge clouds were blowing up and there was an occasional flash of moonlight which helped us as we searched out the top of Central Gully, and followed our tracks leading from here to the descent. We scuttled down the slopes to the east and loped off along the interminable valley to Bethesda. It seemed like midnight, but this was not Scotland – the pubs were open and it was nothing like so late. There was still time to bend people's ears in the Padarn, and tomorrow we could look forward to a day on Holyhead's sun-warmed rock. Which all made up for not having found the gear.

# 57  Devil's Appendix

by John Barry

## TO THE UNKNOWN CLIMBER

There was a queue. It was, I suppose, to be expected for so seldom does the Devil bare his Appendix. And Boysen was impatient. He nearly always is. We were fourth or fifth in line, which wasn't anything like good enough for him. Wasn't it sufficient frustration that the first ascent should have been snatched by two unknown upstarts without so much as a credential between them whilst he, doyen and co-creator of the Black Cleft and a dozen other Welsh winter horrors, hungered impotently in Altrincham?

The year before, Joe Brown had stood second in the queue while those upstarts stole the route from under his nose. Joe's partner was Davey Jones of Ogwen Cottage – and though the Appendix grew like Jack's beanstalk out of his backyard, yet still they were beaten to it. It was a terrible thing. Mind you, as the upstarts would doubtless be the first to point out, folk, including Small Brown, had been sniffing at it for 15 years, dogs round the Devil's Lamp-post. And for 15 years the 'out of condition' ploy had given best to the physical and psychological barrier of 300ft. of very steep ice. How strange, then, that the route has been in 'nick' for three or four years since that first ascent. A new ice-age, or new ice-tools . . .? Full marks to the upstarts.

After its 15 years of growing into climbers' consciousness, the Appendix aged rapidly. First climbed by two unknown Englishmen; second ascent three minutes later by an indigenous instructor and an ageing rock-star. Shortly afterwards a Scot declared that his country had nothing like it, which is as close as those north of the border will come to admitting that they found a climb south of it hard. In 1981 an Irishman soloed it for Christmas. Come on, ladies – make it an easy day.

Martin stomped about, all sulphurous vim and vigour, for two minutes or so before exhausting what passed in him for patience and charging off to find another route. I followed reluctantly in his wake. After all, it was a grand day, and a couple of hours of Appendix-watching suited me fine. I lived just down the road and could nip up in a minute on any of the next two or three times this century that the Devil obliged us with his route. But Martin, fraught from the teaching of biology to 15-year-old recalcitrants, needed his climb and needed it quick.

He selected an improbable line and shot up it to snatch the first winter ascent of the Devil's Pipes. Ten minutes later we were back at the foot of the Appendix where the queue was scarcely diminished, though a man-and-wife team were abseiling off the climb. While wifey froze at her belay, hubby had struggled manfully to the top of the first pitch, at which point, extended beyond the call of marital duty and his own ability, he abseiled off muttering that it was 'too hard for the wife'. Surely the most unchivalrous 'climbing down gracefully' ploy of all time.

Martin set about the rest of the queue with the same galvanic energy with which he had cleared out the 'Pipes'. I could but wonder at his nerve. Aspirants five and six were despatched to a 'much better route' around the corner. Lamely they departed, only, as I later discovered, to fail on this improvement. Numbers three and four were plainly told that the route was far too hard for them and, relieved of their burden, they wandered happily away in search of easier ground. One and two, made of sterner stuff, held their ground and **prepared to launch themselves at the first pitch with Martin, outraged at this intrusion into the Master's design, castigating their temerity.** I marvelled at the *hauteur* of the great.

And even as I marvelled a second energy registered somewhere in the subconscious. The atmosphere was suddenly gravid with matters of great moment. As though drawn by some psychic power (or on reflection it might have been those awful animal grunts) our heads were turned as one, our gaze rivetted by an unforgettable display.

Just across the 'Kitchen' an 'instructor' front-pointed with fastidious precision to the upper rim of an ice cliff, where he paused, *Piolet Gibbon*, in order to demonstrate some *arcanum* to assembled and awestruck tiros. Extracting his dues in gasps of admiration he disappeared from his charges' view and pounded up the ensuing 40° snow slope in search of a belay. He was 150ft. from the ground but still 10ft short of his target when the first victim, assuming a tight rope signalled his turn, set off with prodigal energy.

The pupil flailed upward for 15ft or so, *Piolet Attila*, discovering in those luminous seconds that ice-climbing was more biceps than brains. Meanwhile, the instructor sedulously embraced a boulder with a textbook belay, consuming the rope, as chance would have it, at precisely the same

**Route** The Devil's Appendix, Grade 5, 300ft.
**Cliff** Clogwyn y Geifr, Cwm Idwal.
**First Ascent** Summer: 1937; Winter: M. Poynton and P. Kershaw, January 1978.
**Map** O.S. 1:50,000 Sheet 115 (638589).
**Guidebook** See page 235.
**Nearest Road / Approach Time** The A5 Capel Curig – Bangor road at Ogwen Cottage (650603). 1 mile/600ft. Allow 45 minutes.
**Route Summary / Conditions** A continuous drainage line (near waterfall in heavy rain) that builds up a spectacular ice cascade in a hard winter. The climb involves three pitches. The hard section of Pitch 1 is well protected but thereafter the climb is progressively more difficult to protect. The first belay is good, the second poor. It is possible to traverse in or off between the first and second pitchs.
**Campsites / Bunkhouses** C.C., M.A.M. and L.U.M.C. Huts in the Ogwen Valley. Idwal Cottage Youth Hostel. Camping in the Ogwen Valley or by Llyn Idwal.
**Bibliography** *Crags 17* has a photo and useful notes.

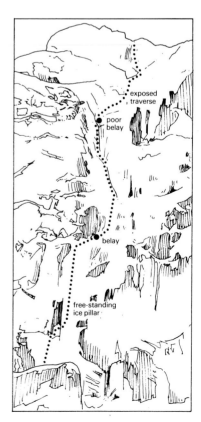

*Far left and top left: Two views of the first pitch of Devil's
Appendix. Photos: Greg Strange and Dick Renshaw*

*Lower left and right: The second and third pitches of the
Appendix — an enclosed groove and an exposed wall — set
amidst wild and beautiful ice scenery.
Climber: David Howard Jones / Photos: Dave Alcock*

speed as the victim climbed. Awesome though the
latter's energy was, it was also human, and at 30ft.
his quadrupedal threshings wilted fast until
crampons and axes, lacking power or accuracy,
ricocheted to nowhere. Weaker still he grew. A
search in the engine room of his soul found a final
calorie which fired some terrible grunts and a last
convulsion; and then that calorie was thrown, with
his axe, to the wind. With no more to give, not even
the energy to fuel a yell, he sank into his harness,
slumped into the rope, hung free and limp and
dangled, as if from a yardarm, 30ft. from the ground
– utterly spent. Boysen, numbers one, two, and I
stood in mute admiration, too stunned to salute.
Had I been alone I think I might have wept.

A split second later this stunned silence was
shattered. The instructor, having double-checked
his belay, squared his gear, fixed feet firmly,
checked it all again and found no fault, sat smugly
and called with the measured, practised sonority
which is the hallmark of those who ply that trade:
'Come-up-when-you-are-ready.' The command,
for such it was, reverberated about the cwm and
one by one, separated only by the speed of sound, a
dozen spectating teams collapsed in mass hysteria.

Martin pitched forward, face into the snow,
clutching at his throat and convulsed in apoplectic
laughter. The other Appendix team did much the
same while hoots and howls floated up from all
around. The whole Kitchen was aboil with laughter.

At last numbers one and two tumbled off, no
longer capable of mustering the necessary
aggression for an appendectomy; which left Martin
and me. One of the departing climbers offered me a
shot with a pair of Hummingbird axes: 'Perfect for
steep water-ice,' he said. I had never seen them
before but thought to give them a try and left my
own axes on the floor. Looking up, the flesh of the
Appendix was plain to see. A trunk of water-ice
rose 120ft. to a ledge and belay. At mid-height
there was a painful-looking swelling, then a comparatively benign groove led up and left for a
second 120ft. or so. The belay was not obvious. On
Pitch 3 a horizontal traverse sneaked rightwards to
an angry, vertical chunk festooned with malignant
icicles, each a huge anti-climber missile as
long as a lance. The full breadth of the upper face
was hung with these, often grotesquely contorted
like the grasping fingers of Hokusai's waves. Some
Appendix! I briefly pictured myself picking a way
through such a canvas, but here at base imagery

escaped me and levity ruled.

I giggled my way up 10ft. of steepish ice, where I attempted to lodge a Hummingbird in a vee formed by two converging icicles. They would have accommodated my own axes happily, but for some reason rejected this new-fangled tool. As I fiddled, an enormous tug on the rope plucked at me, and glancing quickly down I saw my second pulling on the rope with truly satanic fury. With a levity-shattering splat I landed at his feet, where the Hummingbirds were snatched from my wrists. Martin was angry again, cursed my time-wasting:

'Balls to those bloody parrots – use your own gear – and get a move on!'

I did as I was commanded, fearing Martin more than the Devil – they seemed to be sharing the same pair of horns. Ten minutes later I belayed above 100ft. of steep ice. I recall nothing of that first pitch. Martin sprinted up the next and spent all of 20 seconds engineering the worst belay imagin-able – an axe loosely jammed across a groove of rotten ice. Faith and his left hand held it in position while he managed the rope with the right.

'Quickly!' he snapped, as I eyed it.

Quickly I went. To the traverse, exposed, exhilarating and 300 near-vertical feet above the floor. And then the final bulge, as exciting as any chunk of ice I can remember.

Not so much to tell about a great ice-climb, you will say. Not much indeed for, though it is a great climb, I still remember the laugh we had better. Anyway what can you say about steep water-ice? If the axes stay, so do you. And they did; biceps not brains, see? On the way down the lines of a song occurred to me: 'Now I ain't saying we beat the devil,' but we laughed at his joke for nothing – and then we climbed his climb.

*Left: The Devil's Appendix with a party on the second pitch. Photo: Dave Alcock*

## 58  Central Gully and Slanting Gully

by Martin Boysen and Colin Goodey

### CENTRAL GULLY by Martin Boysen

It is easy to understand the awe and fascination which Lliwedd held for early climbers. Rock-climbing was still being excused as practise for the Alps and where better to practise than on the 1,000ft. face sweeping from the lake to the twin summits of Lliwedd? This was a serious crag – a place for the skilled cragsman to demonstrate the skills of mountain craft, and many of the early ascents were done in semi-winter conditions with late-lying snow providing an Alpine ambience.

Times have changed. The tweed-dressed gentlemen became rock-climbers, who in turn have become sun-worshipping rock-athletes. Now Lliwedd in summer is splendidly neglected and has a mournful grandeur. But in winter it recaptures its old glory, for draped in snow and ice it is still one of the great crags – an exciting and satisfyingly beautiful place to climb.

The winter routes are not easy and the climbers' eye is drawn to the gully weaknesses in search of a build-up of climbable ice. The gullies are poor affairs though, mere dents in the surrounding acres of slabs and grooves. Nevertheless three such gullies are obvious; one each on the East and West Peak, whilst neatly bisecting the mountain lies the complex of Central Gully. It is a large feature which breaks down into a clutch of steep cracks, grooves, and interconnecting ledges. In summer various possibilities lead through this area of rock but in winter ice dictates a narrower choice.

I first set out to climb the gully in the Arctic winter of 1963. I was with Baz Ingle. We were ice-climbing novices. After wading up to the crag in thick mist and even thicker snow we beat a retreat as an avalanche thundered invisibly down. My next attempt came in March 1968. I had just returned from Patagonia and Nick Estcourt was driving me down to Wales. I wondered if the Welsh hills might seem disappointingly tame, but I need not have worried, for the sight of icy Snowdon from Llynnau Mymbyr was as thrilling as ever I remembered it and my appetite for climbing was as keen as ever.

We followed a line of footsteps to Lliwedd and discovered they belonged to Dave Alcock and 'Fred' Fuller, who were at that moment engaged on the first pitch of Central Gully. We exchanged cheerful abuse and after Fred had completed a spectacular pendulum manoeuvre, which he claimed to have planned, we followed, branching leftwards up Shallow Gully.

Years later I returned, this time with Dave
Alcock, and we went to look at the Direct Start to
Central Gully. Conditions were far from ideal, with
masses of powder snow and little ice. It hardly
looked worth the effort, so we moved left and
tackled the ordinary start. I was elected to lead the
hard pitches, Dave having already done them. The
first pitch which had merely been difficult before,
was now desperate. Dribbles of frozen teardrop
ice provided the only hope for upward progress.
Crampon points scraped, and only the most
tenderly placed axe was of any use. After a while
the ice petered out altogether and the only way
ahead was sideways left. As always on Lliwedd
there was a total lack of runners, which was now
making itself felt. I scratched around hopefully,
poking and prodding, no doubt as some form of
distraction, not wanting to admit to myself that I
was very scared. There was only one course of
action and tired legs forced me into a tricky couple
of moves, until my axe sank into a tuft of grass. I
had reached the Bowling Green.

Things eased off for a while and Dave led an
honest bit of snow-thrashing which warmed the
system up splendidly. A fine snow-balcony led
rightwards, rising through steep rock, to end
suddenly above the continuation of the gully.
Getting into this was the next problem, and judging
by the enigmatic smile on Dave's face, it was
unlikely to be easy. He belayed with extra
thoroughness and, noticing my puzzlement, he
suggested a tension-traverse as a solution. I did not
take kindly to this and after a few miserable
attempts I stormed directly above him up a steep
rock rib, hoping to traverse right at a higher level.
A couple of grass tufts unexpectedly gave
anchorage and led me on. Before I had time to
regret it I was fully committed and once more in
desperate straits with disintegrating heather and no
holds. My ice-axe held a hold so small I dared not
examine it. Gently I felt round the corner, groping
with my ice-hammer. Miraculously it stuck and
without thinking I clattered round and gratefully
buried myself into deep embracing snow.

Dave informed me that the rest was easy.
Somehow it didn't turn out that way. Perhaps we
were lost, for a mist had descended, adding an air of
mystery. We reached the top, pleasantly tired, and
scrambled to the summit, where Dave produced a
flask of coffee. Then we luxuriated in the warmth
of hot coffee and a marvellous day.

## SLANTING GULLY by Colin Goodey

The climbs on Lliwedd are long and serious. In winter the cliff takes on an Alpine aura as snow clings and gathers on its many sloping terraces. There is little drainage from the ridge above, but in a long, hard winter, with the cycle of snow, thaw, freeze running its course, climbing on Lliwedd becomes a major proposition.

This is a cliff with a history, a focus for the pioneering efforts of past generations. All the grandly-remembered notables of the turn of the century played their parts here: Archer Thomson, Mallory, Winthrop Young, the brothers Abraham. But Slanting Gully has a longer history. Did the King Arthur of myth retreat to its cave after his last battle on Bwlch y Saethau? Do his knights rest therein, on their shields, awaiting the call for their return? A group of Welsh miners from Nantgwynant must have thought so, for in the eighteen-sixties they climbed halfway up this majestic gash in search of Arthur's gold. All they found was that it was more daunting to descend than to press on, and by doing so they made one of the most extraordinary first ascents in the history of our sport. Being working men, they only recorded it by word of mouth. It was left to the Abraham brothers to sign their names to this splendid route some 30 years later, in 1897. The first winter ascent was made by Joe Brown and Ally Cowburn in 1964. There was plenty of snow for them in the gully, but the ice was very thin and the crux slab covered with a thin layer of snow on a verglas base. Brown climbed the iced-up crack direct, finding it desperate. Nowadays, provided the ice is reasonably thick, it is more usual, and easier, to climb the slab for 45ft. before rejoining the crack.

Lliwedd has always fascinated me. As a young mountain fanatic of little more than 12 years of age, I gazed up at its huge buttresses and wondered how any cragsman could find a route through its maze of grooves, chimneys, slabs and heather. The gullies separating these buttresses seemed even more mysterious, particularly Slanting Gully, and I longed to enter its oblique depths, for I knew much of its interesting history. After several years of walking and scrambling, I found my way onto steeper things and this eventually led to a meeting with Bill Trench, a Colwyn Bay chimney sweep and *aficionado* of Lliwedd climbs. Bill belonged to the old school, of pipe-smoking climbers with a love of mountains and a great spirit of adventure. He

usually found his own ways up the cliff, and over the years had climbed all the popular routes and learnt to identify the neglected ones. I was fascinated to hear him talk of such routes as The Clam and Elliptical Central West Rib, and became his willing apprentice. After climbing several routes together, we embarked upon Slanting Gully in June 1952, and I can remember leading the famous slab pitch, which was very wet, and marvelling how well my Scarpetti gripped the rock. The slab is really quite thin and I think my confidence stemmed more from the presence of Bill behind me, puffing quietly at his pipe, than from any special technique or footgear of mine.

Although I climbed often on Lliwedd in the interim, it was to be 27 years before I returned to Slanting Gully, with an equally colourful character but from a different generation and indeed a different country. I had met Nick Banks, a New Zealander, a year before in Scotland and we had quickly formed a firm friendship. He had recently climbed Everest with a German Expedition and was very fit. I, on the other hand, was older, and had not climbed regularly, owing to a recurrent dislocating shoulder, for several years. As we walked up to Lliwedd on a cold, misty February morning in 1979, many doubts assailed my mind and I wondered whether my shoulder would hold out.

The scene was now very different to my previous visit. The gully was full of snow and ice and the temperature well below freezing. We followed a line of bucket steps up the first 200ft. and as a

*Above: The crux pitch of Slanting Gully where the route emerges from the bed of the gully on to poorly protected slabs. Climber: David Howard Jones / Photo: Howard Jones collection*

249

**Route** Central Gully, Grade 4, 850ft. Slanting Gully, Grade 4, 700ft.

**Cliff** The North Face of Lliwedd.

**First Ascent** Central Gully – Summer: 1906; Winter: (via Bowling Green entry) D. Alcock and B. A. Fuller, 1968; Direct Start (earliest known ascent) A. Kellas and party, 1975. Slanting Gully – Summer: 1897; Winter: J. Brown and A. Cowburn, 1965.

**Map** O.S. 1:50,000 Sheet 115 (623534).

**Guidebook** See page 235.

**Nearest Road / Approach Time** The A4086 Capel Curig – Llanberis road at Pen y Pass (647556). 2 miles/1,100ft. Allow 1¼ hours.

**Route Summary / Conditions** Although particularly greasy and unpleasant in wet weather Lliwedd is not a basically wet cliff. It has few large areas of water-holding vegetation and its gullies lack rivulets and springs. Good winter conditions, therefore, depend on heavy snow followed by periods of freeze and thaw. The climbs are also difficult to protect as the rock form lacks cracks and spikes. On Central Gully the slabs and traverse of the first 200ft. provide the main difficulties. The Direct Start only comes into condition in the hardest winters. Slanting Gully, also comparatively arid, involves climbing on thinly iced slabs.

**Campsites / Bunkhouses** C.C. and R.C. Huts in Llanberis Pass. Youth Hostel at Pen y Pass. Camping and bivouac boulders in Llanberis Pass or by Llyn Teryn by the approach path.

**Bibliography** *Lliwedd* by Harold Drasdo (C.C.) has a lengthy note about winter climbing on the cliff. *Crags 17* has useful notes on winter climbing on Lliwedd.

freezing mist enveloped the crag, the place took on a sinister appearance. The first real climbing pitch occurs after this 200ft. section where the gully rears up steeply in the form of two narrow chimneys, forming pitches of some 100ft. The snow now steepened as it rose up to meet the two ice chimneys. We had soloed very quickly up the lower gully bed and on arriving at this first ice pitch, discovered another party roped, belayed and in the process of starting up the left-hand ice chimney. I was in a hot sweat after practically sprinting behind Nick up the easy section, and felt relief on seeing the other party. Now I could regain my breath and cool down a little. But Nick can count, and had noticed that the party ahead of us consisted of four climbers. For fear of being held up for some time, he decided to press on quickly past them before they got too high in the chimney:

'You happy on this terrain, Colin? Don't need the rope yet do you?'

The ice was quite good and my axes worked well. I reluctantly nodded. As I climbed past the leader of the other party, I asked if he minded us shooting through. He grunted his disapproval and requested us not to smash all the ice out of the chimney. By this time, Nick was up the pitch and waiting 150ft. above. I suddenly felt alone. The mist swirled about me, and the other party gazed up at what they must have considered a pair of smart-arse climbers.

I felt confident as I moved up inside the chimney

on good ice, to where it became too steep to continue. At this point, the best route lies on the left retaining wall, which on this occasion was well-covered with ice. The move out to the left needed one axe well-placed in the narrow chimney-crack, enabling the other to be placed out to the left. I did this, and after moving my left front points on to the slab, attempted to recover my right-hand axe. Both axes were now well-embedded out to either side, but in the effort of pulling the pick out, my right shoulder dislocated and my useless arm, with axe attached, fell down across my chest. Terror rushed through me when I realised the seriousness of my position. Glancing down I saw faces peering up through the mist totally unaware of my predicament and probably thinking me an idiot who had bitten off more than he could chew:

'Drop me a rope for Christ's sake, Nick! My right arm has fallen off!'

In a flash he had uncoiled, tied a figure-of-eight, attached a karabiner, and lowered the rope to me. By this time I was in considerable pain and almost shaking off my points of contact. I'll never know how I clipped the krab to my belt, but the fear of crashing down the gully inspired some form of reflex action. From that moment, as the gravity was switched off, I knew I was safer and it would be a relatively simple matter to relocate the offending shoulder, for it had happened many times before. The move left out of the crack is a good one and the hardest on this pitch, for the left wall falls steeply over the lower part of the gully. I climbed the remaining part of the pitch with a tight rope and one axe to the easy gully bed above, where I was able to rejoin Nick. The shoulder refused to go back into joint and Nick went pale when I told him that he would have to help. He was reluctant at first, but faced with the prospect of retreat, his attitude was, 'No problem, mate – just tell me what to do'. With a howl and a sickening crunch, it popped back and I was ready to climb again.

We were now both standing in the famous cave of Slanting Gully, and it would be difficult to find a more impressive place on a Welsh winter route. In summer, you wonder how an escape can be effected from here, since the deep, high cave blocks all upward progress. In winter, the feelings of being a prisoner are accentuated when icicles hang from the cave roof and festoon the enclosing walls. Such were my thoughts as I belayed Nick from a super-safe nut wedged deeply in the cave wall. The

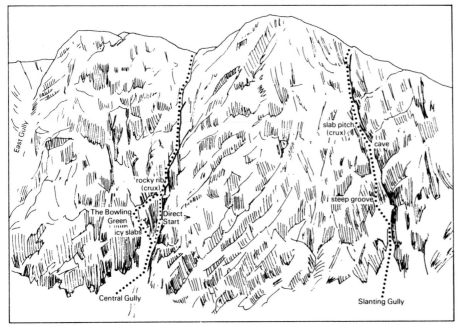

*Above: The East and West Buttress of the North Face of Lliwedd. Photo: Colin Beechey*

obvious way out is the steep slab to the left of the cave, which, in a good winter, ices up due to meltwater from the grassy ledges above. Nick examined the ice carefully:

'Bit thin, Col.'

He moved upwards quickly and confidently until the angle eased and he was able to enter the crack on the right, which rises directly from the cave roof. He fixed a runner on some doubtful-looking flakes which protruded from the icy crack, and soon afterwards was calling for me to follow.

The position was superb. I moved up slowly on my front-points, with the axes delicately placed in the thin ice. In spite of an aching shoulder, I savoured every inch of the pitch. I rested at the runner, and appreciated the outstanding view over Cwm Dyli as the mists lifted. I recalled my boyhood memory of standing out on the slab to the left. 'Great pitch, mate! How's the shoulder?' Nick asked, as I arrived at the belay. I knew from previous experience that the gully held no more serious barriers, and the remaining deep chimneys and steep snow channels were now sheer joy, particularly as they led almost to the summit of the mountain. The last rope-length up a snow-bed finished suddenly on the ridge. Nick coiled the ropes and fitted a sling for my arm. In five minutes, we were standing on the summit of Lliwedd.

## 59   The Black Cleft

by Martin Boysen

The pace and direction of climbing developments is dictated as much as anything by the availability of transport to the climbing grounds. This observation occurred to me in the early sixties as my climbing companions and rivals rushed here and there snapping up routes whilst I was still hitching and catching buses. In the Autumn of 1962 Maggie, my girlfriend, acquired a sky-blue and maroon Ford van. At last we were mobile and ready to take advantage of a memorable winter in Wales.

My experience of ice-climbing was minimal – an abortive alpine season. But a cold snap at New Year in the Lake District introduced me to the exhilarating delights, and my appetite was well whetted. I was lucky enough to team up with Baz Ingle who, equipped with a shortened axe and twelve-point Grivel crampons, proved to be a polished ice-climber. I, though far less accomplished, made do with ten-point crampons and an overlong axe. Baz was in the middle of one of his periodic cooling-off phases with Pete Crew, his normal climbing partner. This suited me as it coincided with the great freeze which started in January 1963. Baz, who lived nearby, was happy to team up and accept weekend lifts.

In February the snow and frost continued; Stanage was completely drifted over, roads remained blocked, and a change seemed unlikely. Every Friday evening Maggie would drive us bumping and sliding over empty rutted roads to Snowdonia. Wales was almost deserted, blanketed in drifting powder and sparkling in the sun whilst a nose-tingling north-east wind gently blew.

We started modestly on small gullies and frozen streams, extended ourselves on Western Gully on Black Ladders, and slowly realised the enormous potential for new routes. The most obvious features of the Llanberis Pass were the tremendous icefalls on Craig y Rhaeadr. We went up timorously to have a look, were encouraged by what we saw, and climbed the classic line of Waterfall Climb. We were well pleased when we returned to Ynys Ettws and were delighted to find it full of fellow Alpha Club Members, including Paul Nunn and Pete Crew. That night, as we sat around a huge fire enthusing over our climb, our thoughts turned to our next ambition.

'Cloggy', the greatest Welsh crag and held in awe at that time, is not a natural winter cliff. Even so, in this exceptional winter we were confident that the great drain of the Black Cleft would be frozen. To

bag the winter ascent of a hard summer route would crown our campaign.

The four of us made a leisurely departure the next morning, more to examine the Black Cleft's feasibility than to climb it. The walk through deep powder direct to Clogwyn station was slow and arduous but, when at last we emerged onto the ridge in sunshine, we were able to study the ghostly sweeps of the crag rising white and cold from an ice-crazed lake. We remained spellbound for a few moments, and then cast our misgivings aside as we tumbled down to the foot of the cliff. Passing round Middle Rock we were faced with a giant ice-pyramid which spewed out from the spring halfway up Black Cleft. It looked horribly steep and far too hard – and yet we felt compelled to give it a try. The jockeying for positions began. Paul and Pete were as keen as we were but it was obvious that there was only room for two. Pete, ever impetuous, made a sprint up the approaches, but Baz and I, with our newly-acquired expertise, overtook him as he came to a halt at the first bulge. Thus we established our claim. Pete and Paul backed off, a trifle deflated, and we were left to do battle alone.

I set off up the first pitch, traversing across steep ice, by laboriously chopping steps, until I was able to climb iced rock to an icy groove. I belayed in a tiny grotto and felt glad that the next pitch was Baz's. To our left was a huge pillar of ice to which Baz traversed. From this point he had to cut up it vertically for a long way till the angle eased a little. This was extremely strenuous and unprotected, for lacking curved axes and ice-screws, we had to hang on with one hand while cutting with the other. It may sound easy enough, but a great deal of technique went into cutting holds in the right shape and position quickly enough to avoid the collapse of both ice and body. Whilst Baz patiently carved his way upwards I cowered in my den, smoked fags and tried, despite showers of spindrift and ice-chips, to remain cheerful by whistling an irritating pop song which defeated my attempts to forget it. Baz advanced slowly and, after a couple of hours, the sound of a rock-peg signalled some sort of progress. He was by now completely exhausted. The ice continued unrelenting above and as daylight was running out we retreated.

We were weary by the time we arrived back, but although it was Sunday night we had no intention of returning home. Perhaps our tiredness accounted for the late start next day; or perhaps it was the

**Route** The Black Cleft, Grade 5, 490ft.
**Cliff** Clogwyn du'r Arddu.
**First Ascent** Summer: 1952; Winter: M. Boysen and B. Ingle, 1963.
**Map** O.S. 1:50,000 Sheet 115 (600555).
**Guidebook** See page 235.
**Nearest Road / Approach Time** A minor road at Hadodty Newydd 2 miles south of Llanberis (586580). 2 miles/1,500ft. Allow 1½ hours. (Note: A section of this road is very steep and usually impassable in black ice.)
**Route Summary / Conditions** A difficult mixed climb consisting of a big ice pitch followed by two rock/ice pitches, each with an overhang. Technically difficult and serious, particularly on the final pitch where protection is sparse. Comes into condition after a prolonged, snowy cold spell. The route is sometimes completely ice-plastered in which condition it will probably by technically easier.
**Campsites / Bunkhouses** Accommodation in Llanberis. Various club huts, barns and campsites in Nant Peris and Llanberis Pass.
**Bibliography** *The Black Cliff* by Pete Crew, Jack Soper and Ken Wilson (Kaye and Ward).

*Left: The Black Cleft with its prominent ice column squeezed between the Boulder and the West Buttress on Clogwyn du'r Arddu. Photo: Dave Alcock*

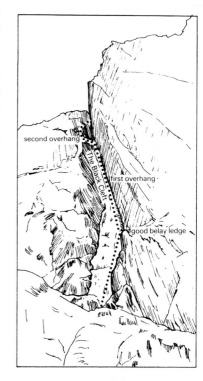

thought of the long flog back up. In any event it was already very late when we reached Cloggy and skimmed up the rope we had left in place. It was my turn to lead and I enjoyed tripping up the steps to our high point. However, I was not as enthusiastic when I surveyed the work to be done. Still, once embarked, I became fully absorbed in making steps and moving upwards. Oblivious to the passing of time, I delicately chiselled handholds and not so delicately hewed out substantial footholds large enough to accommodate my inadequate ten-point crampons. Just as my arms were about to give up I discovered a crack between ice and rock and I thankfully hand-jammed up for a few feet. But then I felt even more precarious as I had to chop a foot-hold left-handed. The last few feet of ice were thin, and with ebbing strength I scuttled into a tiny niche below a roof where I could just sit down, feet projecting outwards into space. As I arranged a belay Baz informed me it was pointless going on because we would only have to bivvy. Once again we slunk off back to the valley annoyed with ourselves for this second retreat. Next day we would not be beaten.

We arose early and set off, grimly husbanding our strength. We had packed bivvy gear. Once more I climbed up to my tiny niche. Baz quickly followed and attacked the overhang above. Above this the problem was a blank verglassed slab, made even more difficult by a covering of powder snow. Baz teetered and scraped, sweeping snow away with his arms while maintaining an ominous silence. I crept to the back of my cave expecting the worst and was heartily relieved when a triumphal shout, our first that day, indicated the end of the horror. I ascended with tight rope.

A last difficulty remained; another overhang with an iced-up layback leading through. Placing a piton, I swung round into deep powder and a heathery embrace. A final stomp up wind-fluted snow, a joyous whoop, and we were delivered from the Black Cleft's clutches. We stood on the open, sunlit slopes, breathed deeply, and gazed with delight at the glittering, silent landscape. We were utterly alone and enraptured by the deserted scene. We had given our all and won through, unseen, unheard, in the most magnificent of arenas.

Since 1963 'Black Cleft Winters' have been few, but with modern gear it is done in a day. I have been tempted to return to it but have refrained, afraid of disturbing a fragile memory.

# 60   The Snowdon Summit Gullies

by Rob Collister

**Route** Various.
**Cliff** Clogwyn y Garnedd, Snowdon.
**First Ascent** Winter: Ladies Gully and Cave Gully were first climbed in 1898 by J. M. Archer Thomson. The first ascents of the other routes are unknown but mostly before 1920.
**Map** O.S. 1:50,000 Sheet 115 (615544).
**Guidebook** See page 235.
**Nearest Road / Approach Time** See page 250. 2½ miles/2,000ft. Allow 2 hours.
**Route Summary / Conditions** Set between the 3,000 and 3,500ft. contours this cliff holds snow for longer than most Welsh cliffs. The climbs come into condition nearly every winter except Snowdrop which requires hard conditions. The upper part of Snowdon is often in cloud and the routes are prone to spindrift flurries created by the summit winds.
**Campsites / Bunkhouses** See page 250.
**Bibliography** *Lets Go Climbing* by C. F. Kirkus (Nelson) contains an account of an ascent of Central Trinity Gully. *On Climbing* by Charles Evans (Museum Press) has an informative chapter about winter climbing on Snowdon.

*Right: The Clogwyn y Garnedd cliffs of Snowdon. Photo: John Allen*

Not only is Snowdon the highest peak in England and Wales, but it is also the finest. Ice-honed arêtes radiate in all directions, embracing high-backed cwms and deep glacial lakes. From north and east in particular the summit is defined by crags directly beneath it, sweeping in a 200° arc from the Bwlch Main ridge to the railway line. From the Pyg track or across the cwm from Crib-y-ddysgl, tiny silhouetted figures around the summit cairn appear poised dramatically above a huge drop. This area of steep ground can be divided into three sections. On the left, from the Watkin path to the ill-defined south-east ridge, the terrain in winter is entertaining, not difficult for the climber but a notorious accident spot for the walker. North of the ridge the cliffs of Clogwyn y Garnedd extend almost to the top of the zig-zags on the Miners' Track. In summer they appeal more to the botanist than the climber but like many other damp, vegetated crags they afford excellent winter climbing. The east facet of the cliffs is steep and forbidding and has been little touched as yet, but there is undoubtedly scope for the the future. The northern facet, bounded on its left by Great Gully, which is so named for its relative length rather than any intrinsic merit, lies back at a more amenable angle and is seamed by numerous gullies. Here at over 3000ft. snow can be found most of the winter from November to April, even when it has long vanished from the nether regions. It is probably the most reliable winter climbing south of the Border. And here countless climbers have been initiated into the mysteries of step-kicking and step-cutting,

cramponing and ice-axe belaying. On a fine day it is no place for lovers of solitude. From above come shouts and the occasional beer can. Below, a myriad of brightly-coloured dots wind their way up from Glaslyn. And in the snow bay beneath the Trinity gullies, on stances the size of cricket pitches, cheerful clusters of aspirant ice men are to be found at most times of day and even night. Nevertheless, it is steep ground, dropping some 300ft. to the tiny and sometimes frozen lake among the mine workings, and it is not to be treated too lightly. Moreover, as with all winter climbs, difficulty varies wildly according to conditions. With a big build-up, you could probably ski down Central Trinity. Yet one April, when from the road barely a snowpatch was to be seen in the mountains, it gave four run-outs of perfect cramponing, including nearly 100ft. of technical climbing on a ribbon of hard ice.

First impressions last longest, however, and my introduction to the face, on a route mid-way between Great Gully and the Trinities, was on a day when we saw not a soul. The essence of Welsh winter climbing is glinting frozen water against a backdrop of blue sky, axes wobbling in improbable pockets on booming icicles, whilst Scottish climbing is still characterised by blowing spindrift, matted Dachsteins and flailing assaults on crumbling cornices. This day seemed more Scottish than Welsh. It was mid-week, one November. There was plenty of snow about but it was drizzling at Pen y Pass and cloud had settled on Glaslyn. Wind was rushing about noisily among the crags. As we walked up the Miners' Track, the refrain from one of Yeats' poems echoed insistently through my mind – surely we must be 'Mad as the mist and snow'. More by luck than judgement, we groped our way through the mines to the big snow slope of the Trinities, located a shelf slanting leftwards and found ourselves at the foot of a corner with a slabby right wall blotched with snow. This was Snowdrop, described by the guide, with justice, as containing 'one of the finest steep snow pitches in Wales', albeit overgraded. The slab demanded delicate cramponing, axe and feet carefully placed where the ice was thickest, until at 50ft. the corner was capped by a small roof. A lot of digging unearthed a chockstone runner from which to bridge up with confidence beneath the overhang. Reaching tentatively over the top, picks bit deeply into firm snow, all things became possible, and with

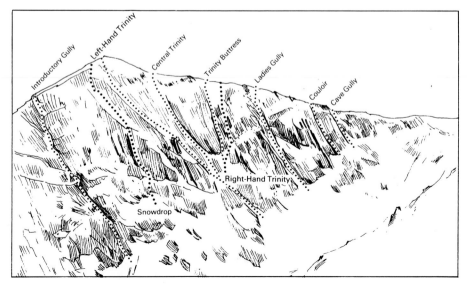

*Above and left: Two views of Right-Hand Trinity Gully.*
*Climber: John Daniells / Photos: Colin Beechey*

a heave the crux was behind. Ian led through up a shallow gully, something of an anti-climax as it wove its way through easier, hoar-encrusted rocks to open snow slopes and an angry wind which sought to hurl us back down the way we had come. A few feet further and, huge and unexpected through the mist, the deserted cairn was before us.

Right of Snowdrop there is an area of steep ground up which Little Gully finds its way, before the Trinity Face itself. The Trinity Gullies, in good conditions and on clear, sunny days, will not cause many problems, which is perhaps as well since belays on this face are notably scarce. In poor weather conditions, however, the vague and featureless terrain onto which they all give out in their upper reaches can be quite dangerous. Right of the Trinity Face are the parallel, shorter lines of Ladies' Gully and Cave Gully, both Grade 3. Cave Gully in particular can be distinctly difficult in sparse snow. All these routes lead to the summit ridge, high and far from home, and a place whose familiarity should never breed contempt.

# 61   Some Climbs in Cwm Idwal

by David Howard Jones and Rick Newcombe

At one time, blue-grey ice, tottering séracs, and dark, menacing crevasses blocked progress into the remoter regions of the valley. The migrant elk had to climb high across the precipitous slopes of Pen yr Oleu Wen to gain the Nant y Benglog. But each year its passage grew easier. The glacier was shrinking. Food grew more abundantly on the slopes. Grey slabs and dark gullies emerged from under the festooning snows, which now came seasonally, or not at all.

The Welsh winter – two, at best three, weeks of it, and perhaps twice a year between December and late March. A flurry of snow, cold east winds down the lake, the reeds spear-like and brown blades of grass sheathed in ice. On one such occasion in March 1895, two local men, Archer Thomson and Harold Hughes, walked across the frozen lake of Idwal to the Devil's Kitchen armed with a domestic wood-chopping axe from that early centre of Welsh climbing, Ogwen Cottage. The axe was a more practical implement than the long alpine axes of the day in the Kitchen's icy confines. Twll Du was banked high with snow; steps were cut to aid their climb to the rim. It was the first bold step towards the development of Cwm Idwal as a popular winter climbing area.

Few climbers refer to Cwm Idwal by name during the winter months, simply calling it the 'Kitchen'. The Kitchen itself seldom freezes, but the route first climbed by O. G. Jones and the Abrahams in 1899, on the thinly-verglassed rock wall to the left of the waterfall, can give fine sport when the snow is good. My most recent ascent of this was in December 1981 – a particularly memorable

occasion. A bad back precluded climbing, but Joe Brown lured me into Cwm Idwal on the pretext that we would 'just check on the conditions'. The inevitable happened. I found myself belaying as Joe led up the first pitch, crampons scratching at the icy surface. The rope went tight and I started to climb, grunting with back-pain. The stance brought some relief, and I looked around. Beneath our feet the Kitchen, dark and gloomy, opened out onto Cwm Idwal. The route led out right over dripping icicles and snow-covered ledges onto the rim of the cliffs. Water splashed down continually onto the rocky floor of the chasm:

'What am I doing here in my condition?' I asked, in disbelief.

'Convalescing,' was the reply, as Brown moved off towards the wan daylight of a 4 p.m. December sky.

The chief constituent of a good winter climb is individual preference. For example, I like the Devil's Staircase, which others dismiss as merely an out-of-condition rock-climb. The first pitch is by far the hardest, but the upper reaches have some spectacular situations. Joe stood contemplating a move to the right. A dubious runner by him, he was leaning out on an icicle:

'Is that runner a good one?' I shouted up. Just at that precise moment there was a crack, sparks, whirling limbs, the clanking of gear.

'Yes,' came the reply, amidst peals of laughter. 'And this harness is very comfortable to fall off on,' he added, as he scrambled back up, muttering about friends in high places.

Many think the Devil's Appendix is the epitome

**Route** Devil's Staircase, Grade 4, 300ft. South Gully, Grade 3/4, 300ft. Central Gully, Grade 3, 700ft. Clogwyn Du Gully (Left-Hand Branch), Grade 4, 300ft.
**Cliffs** Clogwyn y Geifr, Upper Cliff of Glyder Fawr and Clogwyn du Ymhen y Glyder.
**First Ascents** Devil's Staircase – Summer: 1892; Winter: (earliest known ascent A. J. J. Moulam and party, 1948. South Gully Summer: 1933; Winter: (earliest known ascent) J. Brown and R. Moseley, 1952. Central Gully – Summer (November): 1894; Winter: O. G. Jones, G. and A. Abraham, 1899. Clogwyn Du Gully – Summer: 1895; Winter: O. G. Jones and party climbed the Right-Hand Branch in 1899 but the first ascent of the Left-Hand Branch is unknown.
**Map** O.S. 1:50,000 Sheet 115 (645582).
**Guidebooks** See page 235.
**Nearest Road / Approach Time** See page 243. Approach times – Clogwyn y Geifr: 1¼ miles/ 600ft. Allow 45 minutes. Glyder Fawr: 1¼ miles/ 1,500ft. Allow 1¼ hours. Clogwyn Du: 1½ miles/ 2,000ft. Allow 1¾ hours.
**Route Summary / Conditions** Devil's Staircase usually gives a stiff exercise in verglassed rock-climbing. Heavy snow improves the climb but may block the upper chimney.
South Gully, essentially a water-ice climb, can usually be climbed whenever the Kitchen cliffs are in condition.
Central Gully is difficult in lean conditions but improves and is easier with more snow.
Clogwyn Du Gully and the neighbouring Pillar Chimney come into condition quickly and usually stay in condition longer than any other Welsh gullies. This is because of the height and exposed position of the cliff and the aspect of the climbs.
**Campsites / Bunkhouses** See page 235.
**Bibliography** *Crags 17* has extensive notes on winter climbing in Cwm Idwal.

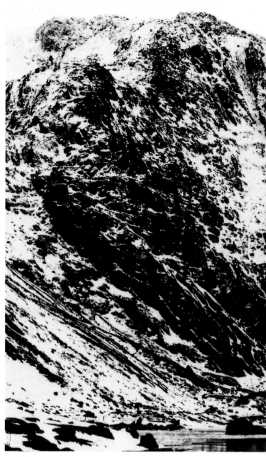

of a good winter route – steep ice throughout, and exciting positions. Since its first ascent in 1978, the Appendix has been in condition for three of our winters, remaining intact for as long as two weeks at a time. Immediately right of its impressive icefall is Hanging Garden Gully, similar in character to the Staircase. A steep ice-runnel gives access to a large ledge-system, from which the rim is gained by strenuous mixed climbing up a vegetated corner. Right again is the Devil's Cellar, a fine introduction to the harder ice-climbs in the area.

To the left of Twll Du, the cliff is not so impressive and lacks the serious air of the other Kitchen routes, though the 'Dump' and 'Dive' lines can offer a challenge of sorts. The lower buttress, below the main synclinal fold, has several popular routes of various grades. South Gully bounds its left side. Central Climb, Chicane, and The Ramp are excellent introductions to ice-climbing skills. The Devil's Pipes can give an intimidating, though unfortunately avoidable route, when its ice-tear cries for attention. All in all, the Kitchen cliffs must appeal to the British climber's temperament. Leave the tea-shack at 10 or 11 a.m. and there is still time for a couple of classic routes – a sort of ice-climbing Tremadog.

Enough of generalities! Now for a day out. Three idle climbers moved over the snow-covered moraine at the edge of Llyn Idwal as the wintry sun reached its zenith:

Above: *The cliffs of Cwm Idwal.*
*Photomontage: Ken Wilson*

Left: *The big ice pitch of South Gully on the*
*Devil's Kitchen cliffs. Climber:*
*Colin Beechey / Photo: Beechey collection*

'What shall we do?' I queried, anxious for organisation.

'It's up to you,' said Joe.

'South Gully it is, then,' came a lazy, mumbled drawl from Martin Boysen, third member of the party.

We roped up at its foot. All three of us had done this classic Grade 4 previously, but today it was not in good condition. The main pitch would obviously have to be climbed out rightwards from under the overhang. I extricated myself from a skein of gear and ropes and reduced my 'Hummingbirds' to distorted relics in the space of the first pitch. Martin and Joe joined me and Martin led off up the crux pitch. A curving sheet of thin, rippled ice led out and across from the cave where we were belayed, to merge with the icefall over to the right. Martin scuttled out and then up, unconcerned about runners or any such fripperies, to belay after 80ft. on Botany Bay Climb. At the top we turned our attention to the upper cliffs of Glyder Fawr. We traversed the steep névé to reach the base of Central Gully.

'These gullies offer the steepest snow-climbs in Wales' I opined, mimicking one of Joe's weighty pronouncements. Joe said nothing. He was gazing up at these fine lines set at an impressively uniform angle. On we went up the gully. At the top of the second pitch Martin and I got into an argument over the adequacy of a nut, carefully balanced across a corner, which he had placed as main belay. Nevertheless, a leader emerged to forge ahead up the near-perfect névé, and moving together we reached the top.

'Three o'clock. Still time for another route.' Joe was off, leaving me to coil the ropes. Within 30 minutes we were at the top of the first pitch of Y Gully, Left-Hand Branch, on Clogwyn Du, which, as so often, was in excellent condition with good ice throughout. We climbed out and round and slid down the headwall of the Nameless Cwm and soon were walking back down towards Ogwen Cottage for another session of brews, after a memorable day of good banter, fine climbing, and friendly company.

From the foot of the Kitchen cliffs to the summit of Glyder Fawr by the sort of itinerary we took on this day, gives some of the best winter terrain in Wales. There is a whole spectrum of routes, from the easiest grades to the most demanding. Variety, accessibility, and reliable conditions further underwrite the value of this enduringly popular area.

## CLOGWYN DU GULLY by Rick Newcombe

Most winters the highest routes come into condition first and amongst these the icefalls of Clogwyn Du at the head of Cwm Cneifion are probably the best. The crag is just on the 3,000ft. contour and is backed by the Glyder plateau, from

Top left: South Gully with a climber on the main ice pitch.
Photo: Ken Wilson

Bottom left: The main Devil's Kitchen gullies — Devil's Staircase
(left), Devil's Appendix (centre) and Hanging Garden Gully
(right). Photo: John Barry

Right: Clogwyn Du from Cwm Cneifion. Photo: Wil Hurford

which a few small streams flow, giving the earliest
ice of the season. There are three main winter
routes: Easy Route, Pillar Chimney, and Clogwyn
Du Gully with its two branches.

To the left of the cliff a short icy gully leads to a
superb ledge-traverse just below the top. A
diagonal fault from bottom left to centre is the line
of Pillar Chimney which finishes directly up the big
ice-flow at the top of the crag; this same ice drains
to the right in its lower part to produce the best of
the climbs – the very steep left-hand branch of
Clogwyn Du Gully.

Saturday, 7 January, 1977 had been preceded by
two days of heavy snow, so much so that the A5 at
Ogwen was banked with fresh powder. Visibility
was zero; a typical 'good' Welsh winter day. With
the motor safely parked in a snowdrift, we donned
sacks Dave Blyth and I and headed up a track to
Idwal gate. Here we set out into a virgin winter
world; and that day we saw not a soul. Climbing the
steep hillside we entered the cloud and moved in a
sphere of vagueness barely 20 yards across, muted,
almost silent.

Thick, new snow is a menace, hiding ice,
boulder-traps, and unexpected drifts. We stumbled
on; two up, one down. At the head of Cwm
Cneifion the snow was especially deep, we spared a
thought for avalanches – and pressed on. The
first section of the gully was only 30ft. but real
armpit stuff which threatened to engulf us. Now
would we see if the great grind was to be
worthwhile. The snow thinned and out of it rose a
glassy wall, smooth with tints of blue and black.
Clogwyn Du had kept its promise.

On the first section of the route the climber
bridges the gully, one foot on the ice the other on
rock. At 30ft. the gully divides. Here you commit
yourself by traversing left onto the icefall to gain a
slight weakness leading up through its bulging
armour. I placed two ice-pitons, my last protection,
and reaching left slammed in the pick and pulled. I
was on my way. It was steep, strenuous, hard; but
with axes and crampons biting well came control,
the essence of winter climbing. It was too early in
the season for the ice to be thick, but it had quality
and that's what counts.

At 90ft. the pitch eases into a gully and the
problems of finding a belay begin. Scrape away the
powder – frozen grass underneath; clear ice from
promising spikes – too rounded; hammer at cracks
– blind. Eventually a fourth-class compromise is

accepted; a large hex between two rock projections, a short angle in a shorter crack, and a thumb-sized spike.

Dave climbed slowly at first, thawing frozen joints, then with gusto, flowing up the steep ice with a slow rhythm. The centre section is easy, a snow slope interspersed with rock-steps. Dave starts and I lapse into the belayer's reverie. The rope runs out.

Suddenly, the silence is shattered, crampons rasp on rock, a shout, the soft thud and gasp of a falling body. Dave is passing me and accelerating into the grey void below. He disappears down the steep ice and the rope tightens with a jerk. The belay! I'm braced and the rope whips through my mitts and slows to a stop. I can think again. Assurances are exchanged. Dave (head down) rights himself and establishes himself on the ice again while I glance thoughtfully at the belay.

We take stock. Dave has fallen from about 20ft. above me and, making a conscious effort to miss me with his axes and crampons, has zoomed down 50ft. of runnerless ice. The wrench has stripped the gear-

carrier from my harness and Dave has lost the slings from round his neck into the whiteness beneath. He climbed back. Dave is a good climber. It was a chance slip on snow-covered rock and it was unlikely to happen again.

The last pitch, from a poor final belay, comprised a short chimney of ice-studded rock with a bulge at the top. By bridging and back-and-footing I gained that bulge. Here spindrift from the upper slopes and updraught from the Cwm below combined in a vortex of dancing ice crystals. Eddies clogged my eyes and froze my breath – familiar stuff to the winter climber. I reached as far over the bulge as I could, drove an axe into firm, old snow and pulled over.

Now there are only eight hours of daylight in early January, and we had used them all. The descent was going to need care. We belayed down the steep, wind-blown powder, kicking to release potential avalanches. There was no chance of retrieving the gear we had dropped in the grey gloom, so we plodded on down our own, now faint, tracks.

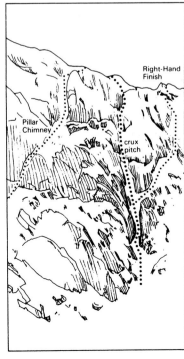

# 62 Trojan

by John Sumner

**Route** Trojan, Grade 5, 300ft.
**Cliff** The North Face of Cyfrwy, Cader Idris.
**First Ascent** Summer: 1974. Winter: J. Codling, J. A. Summer and G. Kirkham, January, 1979.
**Map** O.S. 1:50 000 Sheet 124 (698136).
**Guidebook** See page 235.
**Nearest Road / Approach Time** A minor road from Dollgellau to Arthog at a National Trust car-park (698152) ½ mile west of Gwernan Lake Hotel. Follow the Rhiw Gwredydd path and branch left to the crag. 1¼ miles/1,500ft. Allow 1¼ hours
**Route Summary / Conditions** A frozen watercourse down a steep cliff. A sustained cold spell is needed for the ice to develop.
**Campsites / Bunkhouses** Camping at Owen Tyddyn Farm near the car-park. Kings Youth Hostel 1 mile from the car-park. Mountain Club (Stafford) Hut in Cwm Cywarch (10 miles)..

'What were you doing in the winter of '79?'

There were the best winter conditions for a decade, and the mountains of Mid-Wales gave up some of their closest-guarded wintry secrets. Sloose, Joe Brown's dripping central corner line on Gist Ddu, was climbed, and so were the Falls of Maesglasau — magnificent undertakings which needed these unique conditions. A pioneering spirit prevailed in this cold and splendid isolation, and there was no racing to be first unlike the Spaghetti Junction climbing scene which ran riot in Central Snowdonia.

Cader Idris, standing majestically alone and close to the sea, offered up some superb new winter routes on its east-facing Craig Cau. On the same crag Owen Glynne Jones's 1895 classic, Great Gully, was in particular demand, its icy depths giving fine views out over Llyn Cau to the summit of the mountain. But the best ice-route in Mid-Wales remained to be done, over the other side of the mountain on the unfrequented north-facing cliffs of Cyfrwy, overlooking the Mawddach Estuary.

Trojan is a slabby 300ft. corner rising from the back of a small amphitheatre. Its streak of near-perpendicular ice beckons siren-like and sinuous, calling to every ice-man worthy of the name to come and climb. It is quite clearly visible from the car-park half a mile past the Gwernan Lake Hotel, but not until you breast the foothill ridge does the triangular overhang at 200ft. come into view. The ice seems to take the same line every year, flowing down the left-hand side of the overhang before curving perfectly back round into the corner. It runs out halfway down this, at the Narrows, but continues again for the final 80ft. to the ground. Given good, hard frosts pure ice seems to form each winter, and it needs not a flake of snow to render it climbable. We had looked at it, probed at it, and retreated from it on several occasions, but it still remained unclimbed.

In January 1979 three of us approached the route on a day of evil sleet. Glen Kirkham, known as 'Clem', and I were getting on a bit, whilst John Codling was young, powerfully-built, and bursting with enthusiasm. Before Clem and I had geared up, John was 20ft. up the first pitch. The youngster showing us old chaps the way, or did the old 'uns know something? After a few hours of thin ice, insecurity, and inadequate protection, John gave up, retreating from a peg at 80ft. in the Narrows. It was a dice all the way, and he looked knackered.

One week later the conditions were fantastic. We were beneath the route at 8 a.m. Ice was plastered everywhere; even the Narrows were full of it. John soon reached his high point to find just the tip of his abseil sling showing through the ice. The next section seemed to ease a little, but where to belay? The overhang could not be reached in a rope's length and the groove below was without belay or stance. John made a mind-blowing pendulum from a tied-off blade to a bay on the right. It was little better than the groove as far as belays were concerned, but at least it was out of the line of fire.

Now it was my turn. I made a complete balls-up of seconding the first pitch, and was then faced with leading the sensational slab of blue ice up to the triangular overhang. I traversed back high from the belay into the corner, and crossed thin ice on the slab to reach thicker stuff on its left edge. As I moved up to a small ledge level with the overhang, the ice was dinner-plating in the most hair-raising fashion. But once there, the superb position, allied to a bombproof belay-peg gave me time to reflect. The purity of line, continuous ice, and exposure made it feel better than the Curtain or Hadrian's Wall on the Ben. It had something of the feel of Zero Gully about it, except that it was harder.

Meanwhile, Clem had been hit by a large lump of falling ice. He suspected a broken arm, but the competent manner in which he seconded the first pitch did not go far to confirm this. John suggested that to save time I should lead the final pitch. An ominous bulge 30ft. above made me think that there might be an element of cunning in this, but I set off and to my delight found that the ice was in perfect condition. It continued thus for a full run-out to a spike belay at the top of the corner.

The moon was up by the time we had regrouped and coiled our ropes on the broad ridge of the mountain. Happy as sandboys, we romped off down the pony-track and made our way to the pub, to relive the action of the day.

*Right: Two views of Trojan in lean conditions. Even in the absence of snow there is always sufficient water flowing down the groove to produce climbable ice, given a sustained cold spell. Photos: Gareth Lambe*

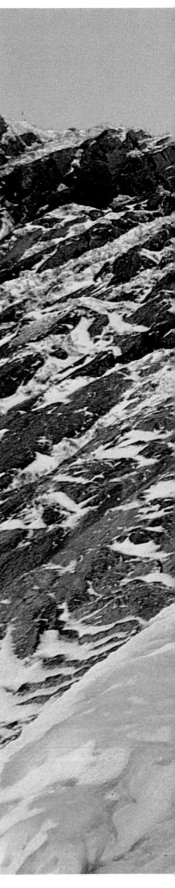

*Three views of Trojan in normal winter conditions – 'the purity of line, continuous ice, and exposure make it feel superior to the Curtain or Hadrian's Wall on the Ben.'*
*Climbers: John Sumner and John Codling /*
*Photos: Sumner collection*

# 63  Cascade and Central Icefall Direct

by Mick Fowler

**Route** Cascade, Grade 5, 330ft. Central Icefall Direct, Grade 5, 330ft.
**Cliff** Craig y Rhaeadr.
**First Ascent** Cascade – M. Fowler and P. Thomas, 1978. Central Icefall – M. Fowler with P. Thomas and C. Griffiths, 1979.
**Map** O.S. 1:50,000 Sheet 115 (621561).
**Guidebook** See page 235.
**Nearest Road / Approach Time** The A4086 Capel Curig – Llanberis road (623570). 1 mile/1,000ft. Allow 40 minutes.
**Route Summary / Conditions** Both climbs come into condition after a prolonged cold spell. The build-up of ice can be seen from the road but a closer inspection is required to judge its quality. The crucial icicle on Central Icefall Direct takes longer to develop than the main ice sheets. In certain conditions the climbs become unstable and dangerous.
**Campsite / Bunkhouses** Campsite at the farm, and Ynys Ettws (C.C. Hut) by the road below the cliff. Bivouac boulders at Pont y Gromlech and below Dinas Mot.
**Bibliography** Useful notes in *Crags 17.*

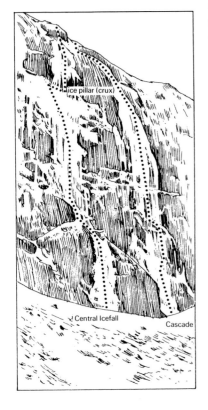

Back in the dim and distant past of 1978 the realisation of the winter potential of North Wales first hit me. The Black Cleft was *the* route in those days although, despite its magnificent quality, little attention seemed to have been paid to it since the first ascent in 1963. Having been duly impressed by its delights and horrors Phill Thomas persuaded me to visit Craig y Rhaeadr for the other route of the area, the classic Waterfall Climb, which appeared to have suffered a similar fate – notoriety after the first ascent (1963 again) and obscurity ever since. It is too easy to blame conditions for this neglect but, as the numerous ascents since the 1979 season have indicated, the truth appears to be that front-pointing had not then made a real impact on the North Wales ice scene.

On arriving at the crag we were somewhat confused and not just a little excited by the presence of three superb frozen waterfalls, none of which was apparently ascended by the inappropriately named Waterfall Climb, which seemed to follow a devious line crossing both falls without actually going up either.

The 300ft. Central Icefall, with a free-standing column over a six-foot overhang at the top of the crag, presented the obvious plum but lack of experience and natural cowardice forced us to struggle on the right-hand alternative, which we climbed (not without difficulty!) to produce 'Cascade'. Much as we were proud of our achievement and longed to return, conditions were very variable that year and the ice soon collapsed. However, we vowed to return the following winter and the vision of the Central Icefall survived through the hot summer.

Conditions were kind and by mid-January 1979 the falls were all in position once more. Phill sent out an alert to London and come Saturday morning we were prepared at the foot of the crag. Unbelievably, it seemed that nobody had tried the Central Fall, although a local team was already well engrossed on Cascade. The free-standing column was looking particularly thin, but we could not give up now and, fearful of other parties stepping in front of us, we grovelled up the first pitch of Waterfall Climb, to avoid another ascent of the first pitch of the Waterfall itself.

Above us the ice soared up for a disturbingly long way to be capped by overhangs boasting the free-standing column. Somewhat dubious that our 150ft. ropes would be sufficient (they would have been)

we opted to shorten the big pitch by stepping right to the stance of Waterfall Climb after 30ft. This pitch is in fact the crux of Waterfall Climb, and gave excellent 65° ice-climbing followed by a comfortingly reliable belay. It was imediately obvious that the ice was in far better condition than the previous year. Rather than shattering uncontrollably it allowed solid first-time security, greatly easing the difficulty and boosting our much needed confidence for the pitches above.

From the stance, the next pitch appeared phenomenal. Almost vertical ice for 30ft. led to a slight easing of angle, then a further 80ft. of 75° ice up to the overhangs. No welcome stance beckoned, but we convinced ourselves that the rocky underside of the overhang (being the only visible expanse of rock) would provide solid belays. Launching out onto the near-vertical wall, the extreme angle immediately made itself known to my arms. But the axes sank straight in, twanging with security, saving the day and allowing swift, secure progress. Arms pumping hard, the long-awaited rest came at 30ft. where the angle eased; a teetering rest poised on front points maybe, but relief nonetheless – and a necessity for my arms prior to the giant icicle looming above. The strenuous nature of the previous 30ft. was clearly about to be replaced by the mental strain of precarious, unprotected climbing leading up for 80ft. to the roof. Admittedly, the ice was thick and good, but somehow a feeling of security was lacking. My one subsequent ice-screw runnner refused to bite deeply and I left it tied off, a useless memento to my efforts. A sense of urgency and the strain on my calf muscles was to prevent any further hanging about placing runners.

After what seemed a particularly long time the pitch came to a somewhat abrupt end, although whether or not it had really ended was open to dispute. No comforting ledge or belay welcomed me, merely an icy niche 10ft. below the overhangs providing a stance of some sort. the belays were tied-off ice-screws, which did not exactly inspire confidence. Above, the roof displayed discouragingly little in the way of peg cracks or belays of any kind. But there was no better position, and after many contortions a belay of sorts was arranged. Phill quickly seconded, full of praise for this most remarkable pitch.

The crag had become popular by now, with queues forming on Waterfall Climb and the shouts

*Above: Craig Rhaeadr above Llanberis Pass.*
*Photo: John Allen*

of climbers at play inducing a flippant, non-serious atmosphere. It was difficult to recall the isolation we felt the previous year, when we were the only people on the crag, and we could only consider ourselves amazingly lucky to be able to grab such a sensational route.

From our stance the icicle was about 20ft. to the right. It appeared to be dubious from below, but from close quarters it became apparent that the glorious column of the previous year did not now even join the ice beneath the overhang. A flimsy series of long organ-pipe icicles merely decorated the iip, but having come this far we could hardly give up now – not without a fight anyway!

The ice below the icicle was uncomfortably steep and manoeuvring into a take-off position presented a tricky problem. An approach from behind the icicle. However, the heavy-handed action was

269

clearly not appreciated and with a resounding crash 50% of the icicle descended the crag, bouncing uncomfortably off my knee in the process and scattering people on the Waterfall Climb below.

The remains offered no hope of success and we slunk off up to the top pitch of Chequered Wall, moaning quietly to ourselves. Another week's frost was clearly called for, but how could we guarantee that the locals would not get there before us? Not being prepared to rush up for the day from London, it was left that either of us should go for it at the earliest opportunity.

Returning three weeks later with Chris Griffiths, it seemed that my luck had held, and that despite the increased dimensions of the icicle no-one had made an attempt.

Approaching via hard, mixed climbing on the lower section of Chequered Wall we regained the stance after the big ice pitch of the Central Fall. Conditions were much better this time, with the column *in situ*, albeit rather wetly! A problem had arisen in the absence of a front-point on my crampons (which had parted company on the first pitch of the Chequered Wall) but I was not in the mood to fail a second time.

Hopping out to the icicle with liberal encouragement from Chris I again adopted my cold, wet position squelched between ice and rock; ice-screw inserted, axe placed high. I had been dreading a repetition of my previous effort but the ice seemed much more solid this time. A wild swing out onto the front face and into the open; a quick perusal of my pick protruding through the icicle, and, after a couple of steep moves I was at a resting-place and the top. The icicle section had actually proved much shorter than expected but the magnificent position on the front of the icicle induced great feelings of elation that more than compensated for the brevity.

Dancing down to the car we vowed to scour the country for similar features . . . and do our best to climb all over them! I've yet to find one quite the same though . . . .

Left and above: Mick Fowler shows the strain of sustained high-standard ice-climbing during his first attempt to climb the Central Icefall in January 1979. The crucial icicle is in the background fringed with weird ice fangs. On this attempt the icicle was too fragile and half of it collapsed at the first blow. Three weeks later the icicle was more substantial and allowed Fowler to complete his bold first ascent (above). Photos: Phill Thomas and Chris Griffiths

Right: The magnificent ice sheets of Cascade and Central Icefall with a leader powering up the latter — a photo that does justice to the architectural grandeur of the cliff under ice. Climbers: Stevie Haston and Pete Minks / Photo: Malcolm Griffith

# 64 Maria

by Nigel Shepherd

'It's almost always wet', the oracle says. A glance confirms this observation and you would do well to avoid this slimy slit in all but the driest of summers or the iciest of winters. Gallt yr Ogof is a two-tiered rambling crag overlooking the Nant y Benglog. At the centre of its upper tier is an evil, dark recess, shadowy and cavernous, like a slightly smaller version of Ossian's Cave. As a summer line it looks curiously and uniquely repellent.

First climbed as a rock route by Joe Brown and Trevor Jones in 1959, it was generally neglected until it was climbed in the winter of 1978, 'The year of the Appendix', by Martin Boysen and David Howard Jones. Shortly afterwards, much to the chagrin of a host of hopefuls, the ice evaporated and the climb returned to its normal condition. Then, to everyone's surprise, the water turned solid state again the following year. This time ice-hungry axes were at the ready.

Max Halliday and I strode purposefully towards the cliff, heads down against the wind, happy in the knowledge that the route was in condition and hopeful that we might find an icy haven within the hillside. A lull in the driving snow allowed a fleeting glimpse of Damoclean icicles and a smooth blue-green slab perched high above the entrance of the cave.

The first pitch looks steep; a wax-like coated wall

of knobbles and rivolets of ice. It looks thin too, but Max sets off at a steady rate announcing that the ice is good. Certainly it succumbs with little resistance to his brutal blows. Amid a barrage of shrapnel Max weaves a way between blue bulges to the cave.

I await my summons, anxious to get to grips, and nervously stabbing my Terrordactyl into the ice like a boxer's warming hooks. Then the happy ring of a peg being driven home, and it's time.

It's steep! It didn't look it but my arms are weakening by the time I arrive at the stance. 'Good old Max', I'm glad I didn't have to lead that first thing. But I envy him in his rocky womb hemmed about by icicles. He has sorted out the gear and thrusts it upon me.

I address myself to the problem, to which the solution is immediately obvious. Be bold of heart and brutal with the axe. A swing out leftwards, feet dangling over the abyss and a wild scrabble, first with knees, then crampons, and I am established on the slab hoping that it all didn't look as bad as it felt.

A good nut in a crack on the right gives me confidence to continue. A narrowing slab of thinning ice leads to a series of small bulges and a tree way out on the right. It looks as if it's all over. Trying to rest my calves I look around. There's a storm raging and no view; just driving snow and the rope curling down out of sight into the gloom.

Back to battle, and it's not as simple as it first appeared — it never is. The corner steepens and I bridge across it, ice for one foot, rock and heather for the other. A few moves delicately upwards brings me within spitting distance of that sturdy rowan, and looking up at that pillar of security I wish myself there now, for the last few tentative moves had shown the ice to be brittle and thin. With 20ft. to my last runner I begin to feel afraid.

But I am going to have to go somewhere so best if it is up. The axes hold only tenuously, but they are the best I've had for a while. Go now! Maybe one move. Tap . . . and the ice springs from the rock and crashes down to the swirling void below. The fear is upon me. Wild gyrations, then incredibly my Terrordactyls lodge firmly into the frozen turf and the tree only inches away. Seconds later it is caressed by a strong blue sling and smothered in gratitude.

'OK?' shouts Max. I look down. Could he have seen me? No, thank goodness. My fear is safe; only I know.

**Route** Maria, Grade 4, 200ft.
**Cliff** Gallt yr Ogof (Upper Tier).
**First Ascent** Summer: 1959; Winter: M. Boysen and D. Howard Jones, 1979.
**Map** G.S. 1:50 000 Sheet 115 (596691).
**Guidebook** See page 235.
**Nearest Road / Approach Time** The A5 Capel Curig - Bangor road at Gwern y Gof Isaf (685602). Mile/500ft. Allow 20 minutes.
**Route Summary / Conditions** A steep two-pitch ice climb at relatively low altitude and therefore needing a sustained cold spell is needed to produce good conditions.
**Campsites / Bunkhouses** Bunkhouse, Campsite and L.U.M.C. Hut at Gwern y Gof Isaf. Helyg (C.C. Hut) by the road directly below the cliff.

*Far left: The first pitch of Maria — the route follows the full length of the icicle to gain a cave stance. Climber: John Barry / Photo: Rob Collister*

*Near left: The second pitch — a left-facing slabby corner, difficult to start but easing as height is gained. Climber: Malcolm Creasey / Photo: Dave Alcock*

# 65  Samples of Irish Ice

by Dawson Stelfox and Joss Lynam

**Route** Black Stairs, Grade 2/3.
**Cliff** Thomas Mount (Mournes).
**Map** O.S. 1:25,000 Sheet Mourne Country (365294).

**Route** Rock 'n' Roll Gully, Grade 2/3.
**Cliff** Eagle Mount (Mournes).
**Map** As above (247225).

**Route** Blue Lough River Gully, Grade 3.
**Cliff** East Side, Ben Crom.
**Map** As above (316265).

**Route** Blue Lough Buttress Downfall, Grade 4.
**Cliff** Blue Louth (Slieve Binnian).
**Map** As above (326246).

**Route** The Mane, Grade 3. Fall Out, Grade 2/3.
The Veil, Grade 4/5.
**Cliff** The North side of Glenariff. County Antrim.
**Map** O.S. 1:50,000 Sheet 9 (2223).

## ULSTER AND DONEGAL by Dawson Stelfox

Irish ice does not readily spring to the minds of white tigers sharpening their claws for winter – a migrational scavenge being the normal means of satisfying the hunger amongst native beasts. Otherwise they tend to become nearly as frustrated, as Englishmen searching for the rumoured huge Irish crags that everyone knows exist, and yet somehow never get reported in the guides.

In contrast with the other white stuff which makes an occasional seasonal appearance, the likelihood of ice is eagerly anticipated – speculation beginning with the first sign of gritting lorries. More time and energy are probably expended poring over weather charts, watching the birds and the hedgerows, and listening to old wives' tales, than is ever spent climbing.

Even in the rare good year possibilities are few, and the ice is often demolished by a *blitzkrieg* of hungry predators before the inevitable and usually rapid thaw. Good snow-ice is so rare as to be discounted, but Ireland, the land of rain, is also the land of waterfalls, and these form the backbone of Irish ice-climbing.

By one of those curious natural laws designed to continually frustrate climbers, the best ice appears fleetingly mid-week. By Friday night, it has dissolved into dreams as the unemployed relate stories of blue skies and perfect conditions, which seem another world from the grey mists and collapsing icicles the listeners know, deep down, will be theirs on the morrow. Consequently, most of my best native routes have been completed mid-week and the impossible schedules, long walks, and descents in the dark, seem an integral part of the experience.

To the enthusiasts, any waterfall is a potential route, and every team has its secret fall hidden in the back of some secluded glen, waiting for the fabled freeze. Although three falls in Antrim, and one in Donegal have been climbed in exceptional winters, the Mourne Mountains remain the most reliable and prolific area, with half-a-dozen good-quality routes. The Black Stairs, on the slopes of Slieve Donard above Newcastle, climbed by Phil Gribbon and John White in 1962, was the first recorded ice-route in the Mournes. Giving an entertaining two-pitch route, it is generally around Grade 3, the main difficulties being concentrated on the overhanging lip at the top of the second pitch. Further up the same valley, on the slopes of

Slieve Commedagh a number of shallow gullies give easier, but enjoyable climbing.

Eagle Mountain, in the western Mournes, has so far proved to be the most reliable spot to head for after a cold spell. To the right of the main crag is a system of gullies, starting with Great Gully. This gives a couple of good short pitches in tremendously grand rock scenery, but is overshadowed by its nextdoor neighbour, Rock 'n' Roll Gully, for sustained interest. The good winter of 1978/9 combined with an upsurge in experience and equipment to ensure keen competition for the available plums. Allister McQuoid and Norman Smith narrowly beat the field, but within a few days at least six parties (including Billy Ireland, solo) climbed its three excellent pitches. The crux is usually the short, steep wall on the top pitch. Like all winter routes the difficulties vary tremendously but it is usually around Grade 3. Further right again, much ice-bouldering can be found on short steps and slabs.

The prize for the longest waterfall in the Mournes goes to that on Ben Crom, flowing into the reservoir of the same name. In a 500ft drop it contains about eight falls, from 20ft to 80ft in height, with convenient pools between. In one of the less-frequented valleys, and all but concealed by a deep and narrow gorge, it was first climbed almost by accident. After an unsuccessful attempt on the reservoir overflow in 1979, Billy Ireland and myself wandered across and found this superb piece of climbing. Once committed, escape out over the steep flanks is rarely possible, although most pitches have a number of alternatives. The volume of water here means it rarely freezes entirely, and in 1979 the top pitch was avoided by escaping up an icicle on the left. In 1982, however, enough ice was present for Willie Brown-Kerr and myself to complete the route.

The latest addition to this selection appeared in January 1982, when a seepage line over Blue Lough Buttress on Slieve Binnian froze to give a 300ft climb on iced-up slabs and short walls. Alan Currans and Andy Barden got in first this time, finding the two short ice-steps at the top worthy of Grade 4. Not far away, the waterfall from Binnian Lough gave a longer but more relaxed route.

A chance find by a Queen's University Mountaineering Club party in the Bingorm area of Donegal, in February 1979, led to one of the most spectacular Irish ice-routes being completed by

*Right: Three views of Rock 'n' Roll Gully, the classic Grade 3 route on Eagle Mountain in the Mournes: Pitch 1 (top left), Pitch 2 (far right), Pitch 3 (bottom left). Climbers: Norman Smith and Terry Mooney / Photos: Allister McQuoid and Norman Smith*

eight climbers with only three sets of gear between them. After a couple of hundred feet of straightforward soloing, one long, steep ramp pitch led through the main difficulties onto easier ground above. The constant interchange of the available gear led to quite a few comic situations, with, at one stage, half the group stranded at a belay without as much as a crampon. The locals were so amazed by both the waterfall and the ensuing performance that a set of photographs is now displayed in the nearby bar. Ice climbing may be commonplace, and even expected, in the Scottish Highlands but is a rather incongruous sight in rural Donegal, with its warm, wet climate.

The exceptional cold spell of 1981/2 saw the first ascents of some of the long-talked-about waterfalls in Glenariff, County Antrim but the possibilities were by no means exhausted. The routes are on the North side of the glen. The finest fall, the Mare's Tail didn't fully freeze, but three others, to its right, did. The Mane (Grade 3) lies about 200 yards down the glen, whilst a quarter of a mile further towards Waterfoot is a deep river bed containing Fall Out (200ft. Grade 2/3), near its base and The Veil (300ft. Grade 4), higher up. All routes fell to Martin Manson and Eddie Cooper, and seem to have been in a climbable condition for about three days.

Future possibilities are endless, with Donegal in particular having vast potential. However, national pride notwithstanding, it must be said that Irish ice is a very poor substitute for Scotland, Wales, or even (shame) the Lakes. This probably directly accounts for the relative scarcity of major Alpine ice-routes climbed by the Irish – who feel much more at home on Chamonix granite. Nevertheless, it does serve to keep the rust off the gear between raiding forays abroad.

**KERRY AND WICKLOW by Joss Lynam**
In general, the Irish hills are disappointing for winter climbing. The Gulf Stream runs close to the West Coast so the Connemara, Mayo, and Donegal Hills (which are mostly in the 2,000–2,500ft. height bracket) hardly ever hold snow long enough for it to give good climbing.

Around Carrauntoohill (3,414ft.) in Kerry, the extra 1,000ft. provides better conditions, and I have had some good days on hard snow in north-facing gullies. The most likely place to get good climbing is the cirque above the Devil's Looking Glass

(803848). This lake (not named on the map) is overlooked by broken crags sweeping from Carrauntoohill right around to Beenkeragh. There are three or four gullies at Grade 1 or 2 and about 700ft. long on the south-west side of the coum. You may also find some interesting pitches below the lake. The approach is through the Hag's Glen from the secondary road from Dunloe to Glencar. The next most likely choice is the head of Coumloughra (7984), under Caher and the ridge to Carrauntoohill. The obvious gullies (500–800ft.) have been climbed and again are Grade 1 or 2. The approach is from Lough Acoose on the Killorglin to Glencar road.

The east coast has a colder climate, and the Wicklow Hills are often snow-covered. Most winters, good climbing can be had on the highest of these hills, Lugnaquilla (3,039ft.). The North Prison (0392) is the best area. Behind the small lake (not marked on the map) an obvious gully runs up to the summit plateau. A little left of the gully, a waterfall pitch is often to be found. The gully (about 500ft.) long) gives a straightforward climb, which is generally topped by a fair-sized cornice. It is possible to climb all over the broken face to the right of this gully where the standard varies from Grade 1 to 3. The easiest approach is from the Glen of Imaal up the track over Camara Hill. (This passes through an Army firing area, and even when it is not being used, the Army may try and dissuade you from entering it; however generations of climbers and walkers have passed this way without blowing themselves up, and provided you do not pick up metal objects, the danger is minimal.)

In a hard winter the South Prison (0391) will also give 500ft. of climbing. Grades 1–3. There are two obvious gullies, and many variations are possible. The South Prison can be approached from Camara Hill over the saddle between Lugnaquilla and Slieve Maan, and then by contouring below the 2,500ft. level. It can also be reached by following forest tracks up the Ow valley from Aghavanagh.

*Left: The waterfall on Ben Crom in the Mournes. During exceptionally cold spells this can provide 500ft. of ice-climbing usually involving eight steps of between 20ft. and 80ft. in length. Photo: Dawson Stelfox*

*Right: The Black Stairs (Grade 3), the first recorded ice climb in the Mournes. Climber: Alister McQuoid / Photo: Norman Smith*

# Index

# Cold Climbs
## 2001 Supplement

(previous page) The crux traverse of Orion Face Direct on Ben Nevis, in a heavily iced condition (compare with photo on p.54 of Cold Climbs). Climber: Stephen Prior / Photo: Gary Baum
(below) On Parallel Buttress (p.179), Lochnagar, where the turfy grooves lead diagonally left to the Tower. Climber: John Ashbridge / Photo: Simon Richardson

# Historical Notes

Lake District winter-climbing history is being reassessed following a commentary on early ascents in Colin Wells's carefully researched article "Accidental Heroes" (*FRCC Journal* 1998)*. This established a more illustrious record of achievement than had been previously noted. As Wasdale was a cosmopolitan focal point of active British climbing in years 1880–1914 a high level of winter activity is hardly surprising, but the apparent difficulty of some of the ascents is remarkable. Several recently claimed winter routes, graded IV and V, were found to have been climbed nearly 100 years earlier. The highlights (including subsequent discoveries) are recorded below. The grades are those given in the 1997 Cicerone guide.

* With acknowledgements to Al Phizacklea, George Watkins, Alan Hankinson, Mike Cocker, Bill Birkett and others. *Note:* The term Ghyll is now spelt Gill according to Lakeland authorities.

| | | |
|---|---|---|
| 1870 | I | **Bowfell Buttress, South Gully** G.H. Woolaston, A.R. and J. Stogden. |
| 1880 | I | **Cust's Gully** *Great End* A.Cust and twenty AC members but probably climbed earlier by Cust. |
| 1887 | V(?) | **Pinnacle Face** *Scafell* C. Hopkinson and party. A near successful bid on a hard face route though the exact line is unclear. |
| 1890 | III | **Central Gully** *Great End* Ascent in full winter garb (possibly climbed earlier) J.W. Robinson and party. |
| | III | **South East Gully** *Great End* First known proper winter ascent by 'A.G.' and party (possibly H.A. Gwynne). |
| 1891 | V/4 | **Steep Ghyll** *Scafell* N.Collie, G. Hastings and J.W. Robinson. A major ascent … probably the hardest British winter climb for some time. |
| 1892 | IV/5 | **Oblique Chimney** *Pillar Rock* O.G. Jones, L.S. Amery and Kershaw |
| 1899 | V/5 | **Slingsby's Chimney** *Scafell Pinnacle* G. and C. Barton, Cowley and Davey |
| 1907 | V/4 | **Engineers Chimney** *Gable Crag* J.D. Gemmell, C. Worthington, C. Ormiston-Chant |
| | V/4 | **Walker's Gully** *Pillar Rock* S. Herford, G.S. Sansom and C.F. Holland. "… encased in thick ice … a truly homeric struggle." Climbed in thaw conditions in c. 1899. |
| 1914 | III | **Easter Gully, Black Chimney, Blizzard Chimney, South Chimney** *Dow Crag*. Climbed variously by C. Worthington, S. Herford, G.S. Sansom, A.R. Thomson and W.R. Gouden – probable true winter ascents with six inches of snow cover. |

**Cold Climbs 2001 Supplement** © Bâton Wicks, 2001, is added to newly bound editions of *Cold Climbs*. It is also available (at £5.99 by mail-order or through certain equipment stores, while stocks last) to those who already have the book (designed to be affixed to the final endpaper). The Supplement contains new historical and technical information and new photographs illustrating climbs not fully covered in the original edition. The authors are indebted to Simon Richardson, Richard Turnbull, Dave Cuthbertson, Greg Strange, Gary Baum, John Allen, Alastair Matthewson, Martin Wragg, Rab Anderson, Iain Peter, Roger Payne, Alan Shand, Brian Findlay, Malcolm Creasey, Ian Dillon, Nigel Shepherd, Jonathan Williams and Rhona Prescott for photographs and sundry advice and assistance. We are also indebted to Colin Wells for his valuable Lakeland historical work (see adjoining item). All editorial and mail order enquiries: Bâton Wicks, Clough House, Cockhall Lane, Langley, Macclesfield SK11 0DE. Email: kwilson@batonwicks.demon.co.uk Trade enquiries: Cordee, 3a DeMontfort Street, Leicester LE1 7HD

# Developments

*Cold Climbs* depicts the winter climbing scene up to 1982. Since then equipment, clothing and technique have seen a steady development and these, in turn, have led to a general rise in standards and more confident activity in a pursuit that still remains fundamentally hazardous and precarious.

Frozen ice-sheet climbing, first developed fully in Canada in the 1970s, had its British examples in climbs like The Chancer (1970), Labyrinth Direct (1972), Devil's Appendix (1978) and Creag Rhaeadr (1979). This type of problem has seen a rapid development. Sub-alpine areas in Europe and America, with months of low temperatures and easily reached on roads kept open to ski resorts, have produced many climbs of this type. With a corresponding increase in popularity and ability, the market for equipment has grown leading to greater innovation and enabling climbers to become ever bolder in the vertical environment.

Indirect influences such as these, plus the greater athleticism brought about by rock-climbing trends, have contributed to a rise in standards in Britain. The more accessible "ice-sheets" had already been identified and climbed during infrequent and short lower altitude "cold snaps" but the higher and more remote cliffs still offered a range of unclimbed possibilities. On Ben Nevis Mega Route X (now a popular classic) and Gemini were the best new ice sheet climbs. Liathach, Beinn Eighe, Fuar Tholl and the Applecross cliffs also contributed fine climbs to the repertoire.

Iced up rock climbs have been another new area of activity with their more reliable protection possibilities and susceptibility to ice-axe torqueing techniques (particularly with banana-shaped picks). These have brought the smaller cliffs back into fashion (e.g. Northern Corries, The Cobbler, Bidean nam Bian).

Gully climbing has seen little advance, yet routes like Point Five and Smith's Gullies, while easier to climb with better axes, remain as serious and challenging as ever, often hard to protect, their technical difficulty frequently bolstered by spindrift avalanches and variable snow and ice quality.

The "Cold Climbs" that maintain their difficulty (indeed some have been upgraded) are the mixed climbs, especially those with scant vegetation and poor protection. Observatory Buttress, the Minus Face routes, Galactic Hitchhiker, Parallel Buttress, Sticil Face, Eagle Ridge, Pinnacle Face and Der Riesenwand, for example, remain enterprises that demand an all-round ability. These climbs can vary in seriousness according to rock type – e.g. the granite Cairngorm cliffs being easier to protect than the more open sections of Ben Nevis. Cliffs with vegetated ledges, often those of mica-schist that have little summer climbing, have provided interesting new climbs with good security.

**Grading** In 1992 the SMC instituted a new grading system to differentiate between "seriousness" and "technical difficulty". This used a two figure system – Roman and Arabic. Thus a climb graded IV, 5 would have Grade 5 technical difficulties in a not overserious situation (soft landings, good belays and runners etc) whereas a climb graded V, 4 (e.g. Zero Gully), would have not too great difficulties but in far more serious positions (poor belays or protection, etc). In practice most of the easier "Cold Climbs" have (in ideal conditions) matched difficulties, the differences only becoming marked in the higher grades.

**Ice Axes** Banana picks have steadily replaced the inclined terrordactyl and hummingbird designs and curved picks as more suitable for steep ice – easier to place securely and allowing a longer swing. Curved shafts added a further sophistication to prevent bruised knuckles. Choosing the correct tool for the climb has become an ever more specialised skill. Though conventional straight shaft/curved pick axes remain relevant for alpinism and general winter activity and are superior for braking sudden slips, the banana pick designs are increasingly preferred.

**Crampons** The choice between rigid or hinged crampons depends on the type of climb. Crampon designs with single front points (monopoints) have been developed for iced-up rock climbs and the most recent models allow for interchangeable front points (double or single). Crampon straps have also improved, clip in types now being very reliable.

**Ice Screws** The old small-circumference tubular screws which had lost popularity to drive-in/screw-out pitons (snargs and warthogs), have seen a renaissance following Russian and American influences. With larger circumferences, better metals (titanium and stainless steel), slicker threads and hinged handles, these now offer quick-to-place, secure protection – particularly suitable for steep ice. Modern ice hooks also have an increasing role on steep ice and mixed ground. Long, old-fashioned ice pitons remain very useful where frozen turf is to be found.

**Boots** The greater stress on mixed climbing has led to a decline in popularity for the cumbersome plastic double-boot in favour of bonded, better lasted, lighter and more precisely designed leather boots (the first and most influential being La Sportiva's Nepal Top c.1996).

**Clothing** Lighter, warmer, inner clothes combined with breathable salopettes and jackets have also made a contribution to effectiveness. The main improvement in outer garments is better tailoring thus allowing more fluent movement, but in typical British humid conditions condensation problems remain, though they have been somewhat reduced.

**Protection equipment** Conventional nuts (Stoppers and Hexes) are as useful as ever, but camming devices work poorly in iced lined cracks. Piton selection and placement remains an essential skill for establishing secure belays. With pitons now rarely used in conventional summer rock-climbing their effective use on winter climbs may require practice. The use of deadmen and stakes is also declining though in suitable locations (e.g. upper gully snow bays and below cornices) they can be important as a recent, near disaster on Parallel Gully B re-emphasised. Skilful placement is essential however, and here again practice is advised.

**Conventional techniques** Cramponing, ice-axe braking, belaying and ropework skills remain critically important as accidents still occur in the most mundane places. If new to the sport, or even when experienced (particularly after a long lay-off), advance practice is recommended. Avalanche dangers should be carefully noted and the Scottish Avalanche Information Service (Tel. 0800 0960 007) is in this respect very useful.

**Books** Jeff Lowe's *Ice World* (The Mountaineers), Martin Moran's *Scotland's Winter Mountains* (David and Charles), and *The Handbook of Climbing* by Allen Fyffe and Iain Peter (Michael Joseph) are important sources of technical wisdom and general advice. *Scottish Winter Climbs* by Andy Nisbet and Rab Anderson (SMC, 1996) is a guidebook, containing a selection of the finest routes with good advice and useful information. More information is to be found in the definitive SMC winter/summer guidebooks. Cicerone's *Winter Climbs in the Lake District* by Bob Bennett, Bill Birkett and Brian Davidson and *Welsh Winter Climbs* by Malcolm Campbell and Andy Newton deal with England and Wales.

*Above: Abseiling into the Thearlaich-Dubh Gap. Photo: Alastair Matthewson*

**The Cuillin Ridge** *(p32)*
*Above: Looking north to Sgurr MhicCoinnich from Sgurr Thearlaich. Sgurr Dearg and the Inaccessible Pinnacle are on the left. Collie's Ledge is the obvious diagonal snow terrace on Sgurr MhicCoinnich with King's Chimney above its right end – the re-entrant below the first sunlit snowstep right of the summit. Photo: John Allen*

*Left: Sgurr MhicCoinnich, Sgurr and Sgurr Alasdair seen from below An Stac. Photomontage: Martin Wragg*

*Right: Alan Willoner and Jamie Fisher on Collie's Ledge, here in dangerous windslab condition and very serious. Photo Alastair Matthewson.*

**Beinn Eighe**
*The Triple Buttresses seen from below West Central Gully with*
*Fuselage Gully on the right. The initial left-slanting line of Central*
*Buttress (p.24) is discernible on the lower tier. Photo Rab Anderson.*

*Right insets: Central Buttress (p.24) – on the middle tier and starting*
*the final corner pitch on the upper tier, soon quit by a traverse to the*
*right. The climb is now graded VI, 7! Climbers: Libby Peter and*
*Grahame Nicoll / Photographers: Iain Peter and Rab Anderson*

**Beinn Eighe** *(continued)    Above: The slanting corner below the Bottleneck Chimney on the upper tier of Central Buttress. Climbers: Grahame Nicoll and Jim Fotheringham.    Below left: The upper tier's steepness is evident in this view from below East Central Gully. East Central Wall (V,4) and Pelican (VI,6) take lines on the headwall to the left of Central Buttress. Photos: Rab Anderson, whose article in Climber, February 1998, is a useful reference source for the Beinn Eighe climbs.*

**Bheinn Bhan**    *Near right: The icefall of Mad Hatter's Gully (p.26). Photo: Roger Payne*

**Creag Meaghaidh**    *Opposite page: Bish Macara on the steep initial ice wall of Ritchie's Gully (IV,4) – a shorter and easier alternative to Smith's Gully (p.126). Photo: Alan Shand*

**Creag Meaghaidh** (continued)
*Above left: Raeburn's Gully (left), Pinnacle Buttress, the Post Face, the Inner Corrie and the Window (extreme right) seen from the approach path. Photomontage: Roger Payne*

*Left: Two views of North Post Direct – one of the longest and most sustained routes on the Post Face (p.131). With the direct finish included, Godefroy Perroux (the French Guide and Scottish winter aficionado) hailed it as one of the "most interesting" Scottish gullies. From the top of the main gully the conventional route takes a vertical chimney on the left. The direct way takes an ice pillar (far left photo) to reach a stance on the Post Horn Gallop traverse (near left). The climb continues up an ice-sheeted headwall (above) which provides an exciting finale set in a impressive position overlooking the lower part of the gully. Climbers: Brian Findlay (far left) and Greg Strange / Photos: Strange and Findlay*

**Ben Nevis**

*Far left: Brian Shackleton climbs up to the Basin on Orion Face Direct (p.52) seen from Zero Gully. Photo: Brian Findlay*

*Top centre: Teams on the initial pitches of Point Five Gully (p.65). Photo: Roger Payne.*

*Above: Bob Ross on the ice pitch to enter Comb Gully (p.87). This is often banked out in heavy snow. Photo: Brian Findlay*

*Left: Sandy Gibson leads up one of the icy corner/groove pitches of Minus Two Gully (p.43). Photo: Malcolm Creasey*

**Carn Etchachan**
Left: Shaun Roberts on the final 'sting in the tail' corner pitch of Scorpion (p.165). Photo: Ian Dillon

**Braeriach**
Right: One of the remotest Scottish winter classics is White Nile (p.156) which provides 400ft of superb Grade 4 ice climbing leading to the lonely summit plateau of Scotland's third highest peak. Alastair Matthewson is seen tackling the first pitch. Photo: Alec Keith (Matthewson collection).

**Beinn Udlaidh**
Far left: Tim Whitaker engrossed on the icy Quartzvein Scoop (Grade III/IV) one of the best climbs on this very accessible cliff (p.204). Photo: Alan Shand

**Corrie Fee**
Near left: Bob Ross on the crux of Look C Gully (p.202) on Mayar. After a sustained cold spell this offers an easily accessible line of frozen waterfalls. If combined with the adjacent B Gully Chimney a sustained 700ft., Grade IV climb can be enjoyed. Photo: Brian Findlay

**Creag an Dubh-loch**
*Above: Crossing the frozen Dubh-loch on a direct approach to the cliff. Labyrinth Direct (p.198) takes the obvious snaking snow couloir in the left-hand buttress.
Photo: Brian Findlay.*

*Left: The often insecure approach pitch to Labyrinth Direct's crucial ice wall. The wall gives 30ft of vertical, poorly-protected climbing (as the ice is invariably too thin for screws) in a very exposed position (graded VII/6).
Climber: Greg Strange / Photo: Brian Findlay*